Little Sparrow

LITTLE
SPARROW:
A Portrait of
SOPHIA
KOVALEVSKY

by
Don H. Kennedy

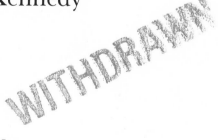

OHIO UNIVERSITY PRESS
ATHENS, OHIO   LONDON

Library of Congress Cataloging in Publication Data

Kennedy, Don H.
    Little sparrow.

    Bibliography: p.
    1. Kovalevskaía, S. V. (Sof'ía Vasil'evna),
1850-1891.   2. Women mathematicians—Soviet Union
—Biography.   I. Title.
QA29.K67K46   1983   510'.92'4 [B]   82-12405
ISBN 0-8214-0692-2
ISBN 0-8214-0703-1 pbk.

Contents

Pictures appear on pages 162 through 174.

Foreword

THIS BOOK is lovingly dedicated to my wife, Nina, who laboriously translated hundreds of Russian pages from books and old periodicals to make available to me material on Sophia Kovalevsky.

As a schoolgirl struggling with arithmetic, for which she had no liking, Nina was bedeviled by parental efforts to inspire her by frequent references to her collateral relation whose mathematical genius had startled the academics of Europe; and not surprisingly, Nina grew up with a distinct aversion to that distant Sophia, that paragon for imitation. Nina's mother had learned her first arithmetic under the dedicated man who had been Sophia's first tutor.

Not until she received a copy of Sophia's *Recollections of Childhood* did my wife at last develop some interest in the adventurous woman whose unconventional life had been passionately devoted to pure and applied mathematics—and to a much lesser degree to furthering the education and liberation of Russian girls—and who as an anonymous young woman in competition with the foremost mathematical-physicists, solved a problem that had vexed them all, winning thereby instant scientific fame.

This biography has drawn chiefly on works cited in the bibliography but also has benefited from recollections handed down to several individuals in the Tchirikoff, Uraneff, and Hmelov families connected by marriage with the Korvin-Krukovsky family into which Sophia was born.

The foregoing names are spelled in the manner adopted by family members in the West. This suggests the problems in transliterating Russian, involving different systems and individual preferences. In general the Library of Congress system has been used but without ligatures and without most diacritical signs. Nevertheless, many person and place names are spelled in ways long familiar in English. Thus, Sophia Kovalevsky is used instead of Sofia Kovalevskii or the feminine form of the surname, Kovalevskaia. For other Russian women mentioned, however, the feminine surname form ending in "a" is used, this being a convenience to indicate gender. For consistency, the terminal "sky" is used also for other surnames in addition to Kovalevsky and Korvin-Krukovsky.

The patronymic in Russian may seem confusing, but it offers a most convenient means of identification. In masculine or feminine form it serves as a middle name and indicates the father's first name, which in Sophia's case was Vasily. Thus Sophia was originally Sofia Vasilevna Korvin-Krukovskaia, and later she became not Mrs. Vladimir Onufrievich Kovalevsky but Sofia Vasilevna Kovalevskaia or simply S. V. Kovalevskaia. In her later years Sophia used "Sonja Kovalevsky" on her visiting cards. As for first names, if a familiar equivalent exists in English, this has been used. Only within the immediate family, incidentally, or by the most intimate friends, would a first name have been used without the patronymic, which was even politely added in addressing a governess, although not with lower servants.

The terms "noble" and "nobility" in old Russia applied to a much larger class than would be so in other countries. Nobility was not limited to titled persons but embraced also what in English usage might be termed "gentry."

All dates, which in Sophia's Russia lagged Gregorian dates by twelve days (thirteen later on), have been converted to Gregorian usage. Sophia sent many letters undated. Some approximate dates were incorrectly assigned in source material, and such have had to be more accurately fixed by internal evidence.

Sophia's own recollections provide the primary source for details of her early life, as do her letters and diary for her adult life. She wrote hundreds of letters, and over the years the contents of these, some from the U.S.S.R. archives, have gradually appeared, in whole or in part, in books and periodicals printed in four languages, although no substantial collection exists in print. While friends saved many of Sophia's letters—since obviously she was destined to be remembered—she kept very few that she received. A fortunate exception were the 80-odd letters from her mathematical master, especially fortuitous since he destroyed a like number received from her. To close friends Sophia poured out her affection, but wrote little feminine gossip; she could be amusing, ironical, and discursive, but usually wrote logically to the point.

To supplement her letters, recourse wherever possible has been to autobiographical material in her published work, her mother's published diary excerpts, and published recollections by her tutor, her cousin, her brother, her daughter, and by persons who knew her intimately. This material has been supplemented from other old and new Russian sources, including the helpful notes of Soviet annotators. No adequate biography has appeared, however, in Russian or any other language.

Although Sophia is a heroine of science in the U.S.S.R., writers there have shown little or no interest whatever in the highly gifted families that not only shaped her development but supplied the genes of her inheritance. The impression is created that she attained worldwide eminence only by rejecting family and class. This is only true to the extent that she did enter a sham marriage in order to escape the parental roof and find abroad the higher education denied her as a woman in Russia.

Soviet works, understandably biased against the old aristocracy, tend to present an unbalanced picture by ignoring or minimizing or distorting things not furthering ideological doctrine and by overstressing Sophia's commitment to social change, although she always was very liberal. Pre-revolutionary writers, on the other hand, almost entirely ignored her liberal views regarding society, and they saw no need to place her against her family and class background in a manner understandable today, for they belonged to her class and assumed familiarity with it. An effort has been made to correct these deficiencies by showing that Sophia stood perhaps midway between the old and the new Russia, but in the forefront of the struggle for women's equality, especially in education.

The biography is not about a mathematician, as such, but about an unusual woman who happens to have a secure place in the history of science as she does in Russian literature. Only superficially is her scientific work examined. For the curious specialist in higher mathematics, reference may be had to the analysis of her mathematics by P. Y. Polubarinova-Kochina, as translated into English and appended to Beatrice Stillman's version of *A Russian Childhood*. Mathematical letters to Sophia from Weierstrass may be found in the 1923 issue of *Acta Mathematica*, volume 39.

Thanks for special assistance must go to Miss Hilja Kukk, of the Hoover Institution on War, Revolution, and Peace; to Professor Olga Taussky Todd, of the California Institute of Technology, whose interest in Sophia as a person spans many years; to Professor Fritz John, of the Courant Institute, New York University; and to Dr. Hildegarde Borner; but these generous individuals bear no responsibility whatever for any shortcomings.

CHAPTER 1

The General's Daughter

i

IN LATER years Sophia Vasilevna Kovalevsky (*née* Korvin-Krukovsky) could not recall with certainty that significant moment when, for the very first time, she had a distinct conception of her own personality, her own ego. She only knew that an experience with her bondswoman nurse was the earliest she could remember.

That experience involved attending in Moscow a Russian divine liturgy, or mass, when she was two or three years old. Holding the hand of Praskovia, the nurse, she then noticed the flickering of many candles, the odor of liturgical incense, the crush of standing worshippers, and the sound of bells. When leaving the church she was introduced to the chanter, a layman, who handed her a bit of unconsecrated altar bread, which was sometimes given to somebody as an honor, and who asked her name. She remained shyly mute until the nurse prompted her.

"Tell him, my dear, 'My name is Sónetchka and my father is General Krukovsky.' "

That her father was not only "papa" and Vasily Vasilevich but also General Krukovsky was a new fact to her. On the way home, as she skipped ahead while the nurse accompanied by the chanter followed, she kept trying to repeat the new name. When they reached the gate to her house the chanter said, "You see, little miss, there is a hook hanging on the gate. So when you forget your papa's name, all you have to do is to think, 'a hook [*kriuk*] hangs on Krukovsky's gate.' "

This chanter's pun, she later recalled, "imprinted itself on my memory. . . . from it I date my chronology, the first invasion upon me of a distinct idea of who I was, and what was my position in the world."

Sónetchka, the name used by her nurse, was a diminutive for Sonya, which in turn was a nickname for Sophia. The little girl had been named for her grandmother and great-grandmothers on the maternal side. In childhood Sophia was called by various pet names, especially by the nurse that loved her, such names as Little Sparrow (*Vorobyshek*) because she was small and lively, and later, affectionately but respectfully, Dear Little Mother (*Matotchka*). Her father usually called her Sofa (Little Sophia). When she was older her intimate friends usually addressed her as Sonya or sometimes referred to her as the Little Sparrow.

ii

ON THE eve of Sophia's birth in Moscow on 15 January 1850 her father gambled at cards for high stakes and lost so heavily that he had to pawn his wife's jewels to square accounts. Vasily Vasilevich Korvin-Krukovsky was by then fifty-one years of age; his wife, Elizabeth Fedrovna, whom he usually called Lisa or Lizochka, was about thirty. As owner of two large estates yielding income to supplement his military pay, Vasily lived the free-spending, pleasure-seeking life of a Russian nobleman, without neglecting his army duties.

The Korvin-Krukovskys had waited impatiently for over six years for a son and heir. Thus, when Sophia arrived as a second daughter, it was a great disappointment, a fact that was greatly to affect her life. So certain had Elizabeth been of a son that she had prepared lace caps with blue ribbons.

When Elizabeth first beheld the girl baby, tiny and brown as a nut, she wept and turned away. She did not even record the birth in the diary she kept sporadically for the first twenty-five years of her marriage. The birth occurred at home, then located in the second quarter of the Stretenskii section of the first capital area of Moscow, at Number 1 Kolobovskii Lane 14. Two days later at the nearby Church of the Apparition, the first entry for the new year of the old Russian calendar was the one for Sophia, her father being noted down as then a colonel of artillery. The godparents were the colonel's younger brother, Sublieutenant Simon Vasilevich, and their then maiden sister, Anna Vasilevna.

Sophia became the charge of Praskovia, the serf nurse who already cared for six-year-old Anna. The latter, by family and friends, apparently was called Aniuta throughout her life. The nurse had seen the mother's rejection of Sophia at birth, an attitude that never fundamentally changed. So much fuss had been made by the parents over Aniuta as the first born that the nurse never felt Aniuta had really been her own to love. Consequently Sophia became her particular favorite. This favoritism continued even after Fedor, the male heir, was born five years after Sophia. Fedor received even more parental attention than Aniuta. The parents might send to the nursery for Aniuta and Fedor to show them off to friends in the drawing room, but if the nurse sent back word that Sophia was dressed presentably, too, instructions would come back that "Sónetchka was not wanted." The nurse did not hide her displeasure from Sophia but lavished upon the little outcast all her own affection.

At seven Aniuta had already become the queen of children's parties, and as she grew older her father might remark jokingly, "Our Aniuta when she grows up can be taken right to court; she'll drive any tsarevich out of his mind." Both sisters took such statements seriously. If occasionally Sophia was brought into the presence of visitors, she would grasp her nurse's hand and remain obstinately silent, so that her mother would soon remark, "Well, nurse, take away your savage; one is shamed by her in front of guests."

Doubtless this situation, however, contributed significantly to Sophia's future success. Feeling unloved, she tried to draw attention to herself by being outstanding in nearly everything she did. Eventually she became her father's favorite, but his natural manner was so reserved that she never realised this until almost the day of his death. As for Aniuta, willful and spoiled beyond redemption, she was to waste her considerable literary talent; and as for Fedor, whose mathematical potential may have been as great as Sophia's, he was to take his degree in mathematics—a degree denied in Russia to Sophia because she was a woman—but never expanded or employed his knowledge in any useful way. Except for their relation to Sophia, Aniuta would be remembered only as an episode in Dostoevsky's life, and Fedor would be altogether forgotten.

Sophia on the other hand was to become the world's first great woman mathematician, the fiftieth anniversary of whose birth would be observed in Imperial Russia (although some of her literary work was banned there), and the hundredth anniversary of whose birth would be marked in the Soviet Union (although a few passages in her work not in accord with ideology are missing from Soviet books).

iii

BORN IN 1799, the son of a wealthy landowner, Sophia's father had gone through all the steps of a military education from the cadet corps to the general staff school. In 1828 he served in three campaigns to the Balkans and participated in the taking of Adrianople. For his daring

[3]

and zeal he received successively the medals of Stanislaus, Vladimir, and then Anna second degree with diamond decoration and title of Chevalier. The award he valued highest, however, was the Cross of St. George for bravery, which on special occasions in later years he might pin on his civilian suit. Unlike the other decorations, it was one a common soldier could earn, comparable to the U.S. Medal of Honor.

When in 1843 he inherited Palibino from his father, he realized it was time at last to settle down, abandoning some of the passing pleasures of life to which he had given himself wholeheartedly, and to produce an heir.

Probably a widower without children, Vasily was tall and lean and dark with challenging eyes under what was called a Mongolian fold of the eyelids. His forehead was high and his nose rather sharp and prominent. Very likely he had a mustache, but probably not a beard as in later life. As an artilleryman versed in mathematics Vasily certainly knew General Fedor Fedorovich Shubert, the eminent mathematician and astronomer. He had also met the general's lively daughter, Elizabeth, among the marriageable young women frequenting the balls and other social events of St. Petersburg.

Elizabeth was pretty and friendly, with a merry disposition that contrasted with Vasily's dignified demeanor. Her father had given her an education much beyond that of most young women of her day. She knew four European languages (Russian, German, French, and English), was well read in classical and modern literature, enjoyed the theatre, danced gracefully, painted like a talented amateur, and had unusual musical ability. She had, moreover, the gift of gladdening others. This Vasily found especially attractive. She on her part, her mother being dead, had grown weary of her father's learned friends and especially of the guardianship by several old maid aunts. Therefore at age twenty, after only brief hesitation, she had been willing to marry the rather elegant officer, even though he was twenty-one years her senior. The Russian Orthodox wedding ceremony took place 17 January 1843. Although Elizabeth was nominally a Lutheran she did not remain so after marriage, Russian religious observances being followed not too strictly by the family.

iv

TWO "INSERTS" intended for but apparently not used in a foreign edition of Sophia's *Recollections of Childhood* have been preserved, in her own handwriting. The first insert states that Elizabeth's mother had died young and that thereafter the daughter had been supervised by maiden aunts, with the result that Elizabeth never learned the practical side of managing a household but had merely "the role of a fresh, fragrant flower, gracefully delineated against the grey background of academic wisdom surrounding her." The second insert indicates that Vasily was a childless widower whose established household was efficiently staffed by bond servants who were not about to surrender their power to an inexperienced girl. In the beginning Elizabeth tried to throw off their yoke, but any independent order of hers, while respectfully received, somehow was carried out in a way to cause deplorable confusion. She therefore soon surrendered to the servants' tyranny, became a guest in her own house, never learned to manage a household, and—as Sophia stated in print—often was treated by her husband more like a daughter than a wife. He was satisfied to have his man Ilia run the household competently.

The result was that Elizabeth often complained to her diary, originally in French and later in Russian, of being lonely. All was not brightness for the young wife whose nature had been compared with dancing rays of sunshine. Vasily was a Russian gentleman; as such he had in the years prior to marriage led a full life. Among the gentry of the day, moreover, it was not unusual for husband and wife, if their preferences differed, to lead partially separate social lives. Doubtless Vasily's friends included some he considered unsuitable for his wife to know. It could be said he had been one of the "life-burners," a term applied to those enjoying the gambling at Baden-Baden, the night life of Paris, and the frivolities of Petersburg. Nevertheless, with marriage he had settled down, but still played cards at his club and sometimes accompanied old friends for an evening of gypsy entertainment. A month after her marriage Elizabeth confided to her diary that she was "tormented by the devil of jealousy" upon learning of Amelia, who probably was an entertainer but may have been a former mistress. After three years of marriage her diary states: "Our anniversary. My husband is at the club, where gypsies sing."

Although Elizabeth lamented being denied the delights of society, it appears she was insatiable in desiring such pleasures. She longed to penetrate the highest society but remained on the fringe: There were two reasons for this. First, in reaction to what had prevailed under several earlier Germanophile rulers, Russians of German ancestry did not really enjoy wide social favor, (although many occupied positions of power). Second, the General moved largely in his own military social circle.

Nevertheless, in her diary Elizabeth referred to Vasily as charming, dear, generous to all, and gentle toward her. Fears that marriage to an older man would end enjoyments really proved groundless. On the

[5]

contrary, the couple led a fairly active social life, first in Petersburg and later in Moscow where Vasily as a major-general had charge of Moscow artillery garrison and arsenal. Diary entries gradually changed from accounts of masquerade balls and flirtations to comments about concerts, plays, horseback rides, carriage outings, walks with friends, and pleasures with Vasily. She loved for Vasily to read new novels aloud to her, or to play with her four-handed Beethoven, Liszt, or Schubert. She enjoyed singing to his accompaniment or just sitting quietly together before a window to watch the rising moon.

They had as guests, or were entertained by, such individuals among many others as the writer-historian, E. P. Karnovich; the painter, F. A. Möller; the artillery school instructor and future socialist leader Colonel P. L. Lavrov; the brilliant surgeon, N. I. Pirogov; and Sophia's uncle by marriage, O. I. Senkovsky, professor of Eastern languages at the University of St. Petersburg. On occasion, however, Vasily remained at his club when certain guests were expected.

V

ANIUTA HAD been born late during the couple's first year of marriage, to be followed a full six years later by Sophia. On the January day of Sophia's own birth, world rulers included Nicholas I of Russia, Victoria of Great Britain, Louis Napoleon of France, and Zachary Taylor of the United States. Bismarck, at age thirty-five, had not yet begun to unify the German states under William IV of Prussia. Of the many famous individuals Sophia was to know in later life, Darwin at age forty-one was formulating his theory of evolution, Dostoevsky at twenty-four was an exile in Siberia, and Grieg at seven had his entire musical life ahead of him. Two other persons, whose political ideas were to influence Sophia, then were alive; they were Marx and Engels, who had written their Communist Manifesto two years earlier.

At the age of three Sophia was blissfully unaware of what the future would bring, but she already had a well-developed will of her own, and on one occasion she showed her determination in a way the family long remembered. Although she and her sister were entrusted to an illiterate nurse, their father nevertheless paid particular attention himself to their health. At that time some medical authority had proclaimed that soup was indispensable for a healthy child. Therefore, although the girls found soup highly disagreeable, orders were that they were each to take at least twenty spoonfuls at dinner. When Sophia wept about this, her father declared that, should she behave so the next day, she would have to spend the dinner hour standing in the corner. Next day when the family sat down to dinner Sophia was missing. Such laxity not being permitted, the General glowered darkly until he spotted her in a corner partly concealed by a heavy piece of furniture. To his sharp query as to what she was doing there, she looked him in the eye and replied, "Rather than have that nasty soup I stood myself in the corner." The outcome of that confrontation was not recorded. One supposes the little girl remained in the corner that day, but that soup soon disappeared from the daily menu.

This incident would be unexceptional except that it illustrates a trait of Sophia's character. Throughout life she preferred to meet situations head-on rather than to wait in doubt or trepidation for their slow development. Time and again this happened.

About that time, 1855, Fedor was born. This took place on Grandfather Shubert's estate near Pavlovsk, on the River Don, about 400 miles SSE of Moscow. Sophia announced the birth to her cousin, Sophia Adelung, in Stuttgart, Germany. With adult help she penciled a note in Russian but with Gothic German letters: "Tell me about your little brother. My little brother is very handsome and cries little. I sent you a blanket for your doll. Aniuta says hello. Kiss your mother, your father, and Aunt Minna for me. Kiss your brother and say hello to Nana. I am happy in Pavlovsk, and it is a pity that you are not here. Goodby, dear Sonya."

The two Sophias were of an age and often played together at their grandfather's place in Petersburg. In later years the German Sophia remembered that she and her cousin wore white party dresses with red polka dots; that in children's games Sophia was dominant and wanted her way; and that if words failed she used her fists.

It was at her grandfather's house that Sophia first experienced love, if such can be termed the emotion she experienced when a student visited there. In later years she would recall loving him with a strong, silent love that she confided only to a stone lion in grandfather's garden.

vi

THE YEAR of Fedor's birth saw the General transferred to Kaluga, located about a hundred miles south of Moscow. The family traveled there in a large public coach, enveloped in a cloud of dust; and during each change of horses they reclined to rest in the post stations on the hard divans or upon two chairs placed together.

It appears that at one point during this tiresome journey, or on a similar one, Sophia in a fit of petulance threw Aniuta's doll out of the coach window. Doubtless when retrieved it was broken. As recorded by Fedor in his recollections of his famous sister, this may have been be-

[7]

cause of Sophia's antipathy toward dolls, a superstitious fear that eventually she felt also in the presence of cats. Concerning dolls, Sophia herself wrote that "the sight of a broken doll inspired me with terror; when I chanced to drop my doll, nurse had to pick her up and tell me whether or not her head was broken; if it was, she had to take her away without showing me. I still remember how, one day, Aniuta caught me alone, without nurse, and wishing to tease me, began forcibly to thrust before my eyes a wax doll from whose head dangled a black eye that had been torn out, and thereby threw me into convulsions."

Sophia's remembrance of early nursery days probably dated from the period in Kaluga, where Praskovia kept the windows tightly closed for fear the children would catch cold. The memory always evoked the peculiar odor of the nursery, an odor compounded of childish body odors mixed with incense, balsam, olive oil burnt in the vigil light before the ikon, and candle smoke. Each morning, while the children were still abed, the French governess would appear to awaken her pupil, Aniuta. Holding a handkerchief over her nose the governess would direct the nurse in broken Russian to open the window. This the nurse customarily ignored. During winter, in fact, windows probably could not be opened at all, because in Russia it was customary to install sealed storm windows on the inside, with a layer of sand or other material on the sill between panes to absorb moisture.

As soon as the governess departed, the nurse permitted the children to loll about in bed, have pillow fights, jump from a chair onto her own mountainous feather bed, or to doze off again while the nurse breakfasted on coffee and rolls. Back would come the governess for Aniuta, who had not even begun dressing. Then poured forth a torrent of angry words in mixed French and Russian and sometimes dire threats to complain to the master, but the nurse ignored any threats, because she knew enough about the French governess to cause trouble, too. Nevertheless, Aniuta would hurriedly be made ready and sent off, while the younger children remained to be casually washed, dressed, combed, and fed, and then frequently permitted, because of their earlier exhausting play, to doze off to sleep again until perhaps 11 o'clock.

This relaxed atmosphere did not last long, however, when a proper English governess came into the family.

vii

"WHEN I recall my mother during this first period of my childhood," wrote Sophia in her *Recollections*, "she always presents herself to me as a very young, very pretty woman. I see her always very merry and handsomely dressed. I recall her most frequently as in a ball gown with low-cut bodice and bare arms, with a multitude of bracelets and rings. She is going somewhere to an evening party and has come to take leave of us. As soon as she showed herself at the door of the nursery Aniuta would run to her, begin to kiss her arms and neck, and to inspect and handle all her golden trinkets.

" 'I am going to be such a beauty as mama when I grow up!' she says, fastening one of mama's ornaments on herself, and standing on tiptoe to get a look at herself in the little mirror on the wall. This greatly amuses mama.

"Sometimes I feel an inclination to caress mama, to climb upon her knees; but, somehow or other, these attempts always end by my hurting mama through my awkwardness, or tearing her gown, and then I run away and hide myself in the corner with shame. For this reason I began to develop a sort of shyness toward mama, and this shyness was further augmented by the fact that I often heard my nurse say that Aniuta and Fedya were mama's favorites, and that mama disliked me. I do not know whether this was true or not, but nurse always said it quite regardless of my presence."

Doubtless it was true, for the mother's attitude that began at birth apparently continued through life. The impression is also inescapable that Sophia as a child must have been heavy-handed with delicate things. Her nurse did not call her Little Sparrow without reason. She was lively and energetic and seldom in repose. Being compact of build, she lacked the suppleness and grace of her sister and was always somewhat careless in dress.

Sophia's large and bright eyes seem to have been her most noticeable feature and by different individuals were variously described as gray or green or brown. Her friend and first biographer said that under varying conditions the eyes appeared to change from one to another of those colors. The child Sophia sometimes created a feeling of unease, however, when she fixed her penetrating gaze upon some visitor, as though analyzing or even passing judgment upon the individual. This characteristic she had in common with her father, together with his dark complexion. From her earliest years she had a keen sense of justice and resisted any compromise.

By contrast, sister Aniuta was blond, slender, rather tall, usually considered charming and beautiful, and consequently was in every way more to her mother's liking. The mother, despite her good education, had rather frivolous values. She always dressed well and was quite aware of her own good looks. Thus, apart from her initial disappointment over Sophia's sex, Sophia's traits and manner did not appeal to

[9]

her, and probably she never considered Sophia attractive or socially presentable.

Certainly little Sophia developed the conviction that she was little liked, and this was reflected in her character. She grew more shy and self-contained. From strange children she held aloof and was happiest when alone with her nurse, who would cuddle her and relate fairy tales, some of them about dragons and other frightening creatures. Some of these tales created in the child oppressive fears.

"About this time in my life," she wrote, "something strange began to take place in me: a feeling of involuntary distress, of anguish, began to come over me. I have a vivid recollection of this feeling. All at once I would look and see behind me a sharp, black strip of shadow, creeping out from under the bed, or from a corner. A sensation would seize upon me as if some strange presence had crept into the room; and this new unfamiliar presence would suddenly clutch at my heart so painfully that I flew headlong in search of my nurse, whose proximity usually had the power to soothe me."

She went on to explain that many nervous children experience something similar, usually attributed to fear of the dark, but that actually it was more anguish than fear and more occasioned by oncoming darkness than by darkness itself. She sometimes experienced the same feeling when seeing a half-built house with solid walls but only empty openings instead of windows and doors, or when lying on her back and gazing into a cloudless sky.

"Other symptoms of great nervousness," she wrote, "also began to make their appearance in me: disgust, which approached fear in its intensity, for all sorts of physical monstrosities. If a two-headed chicken or three-legged calf was mentioned in my presence, I began to tremble all over, and then, at night, I inevitably saw the monster in my dreams, and woke nurse with a piercing scream. Even now I remember the three-legged man who persecuted me in my dreams during the whole of my childhood. . . . On the whole, I was on the highway to turn out a nervous, sickly child; but soon all my surroundings changed, and there was an end to all that had gone before."

The change was a move to the country. In 1858, having some time before been promoted to lieutenant-general, Vasily Vasilevich resigned his commission in order to put his estate at Palibino in order. The family with governess and servants moved there permanently that same year.

Before proceeding with life at Palibino, however, more should be said about Sophia's position in Russian society, her ancestry on both sides, and the nature of serfdom. Otherwise the forces and traditions with which she struggled, the boldness of her reactions as an emerging young woman, and her subsequent role in social justice will not be appreciated, nor will the source of the inherited genes that permitted development of her mathematical genius be made clear. While IQ hereditability remains a matter of dispute, if the conclusions of the hereditarians be true, as much as eighty percent of an individual's capacity for abstract thought might be attributed to genetics.

CHAPTER 2

The Noble Class

A BRIEF look at the nature of Russian nobility will help to understand the position of Sophia's families and their friends. To anybody familiar with western feudalism and the slow development of democracy, the term "nobility" suggests an actual hierarchy of many grades—dukes and barons and all the rest—in which individual nobles were occasionally as powerful as kings. In Russia, from the time the princes of Moscow threw off the Tartar overlords and unified the princedoms to become tsars, the situation was quite different. There, only late in time did nobles get a Magna Carta. There all nobles came to be on one level, officially if not actually, even if some had titles. From about 1480 all new land grants carried the requirement for lifelong obligatory service to the tsar, and within less than a hundred years the old nobles who had held estates in fee simple lost their right to ownership without similar service. Thus, until the second half of the eighteenth century, property did not pass automatically to designated heirs; rather, if the tsar approved, it went to family members capable of rendering military or civil service, whether to son, brother, uncle, or daughter whose husband could serve.

During a long period, moreover, passports were required, not only for approved travel within the country but even between the family estate and the capital. Such close control over property and travel prevented the rise of powerful nobles as a constant threat to the throne. Thus, for much of Russian history the noble class is perhaps more properly understood as having been one of closely supervised gentry.

The title of "prince" derived from the old princedoms, and since all males in princely families were princes and all females princesses, the title often was more a matter of polite address than anything else. To be sure, a prince might occupy one of the highest posts in the land, but it was his temporary post and not his title that delegated power. A prince might also be a mere private in the guards or a minor functionary in some ministry. In later days princes, like counts and barons, were occasionally created by letters patent; also some titled foreign nobles emigrated to Russia and were officially accepted.

Sophia's grandfather was the first in the family to escape obligatory service. Nobles of his generation were permitted to flock to their estates. Then the charter of 1785, exacted from the aging Catherine the Great, protected Sophia's grandfather and other nobles from being deprived of honor, life, or property without trial by their peers (whereas formerly they could be exiled or killed at the mere pleasure of the tsar), prohibited beating by the knout or other corporal punishment, and gave rights to be free from the billet, to travel within Russia or abroad, to inherit property and serfs, to own industrial enterprises, and to exploit the mineral and forest resources of their estates.

They could also participate in local government. Provincial and district marshals of nobility were elected for three-year terms to act as leaders of hereditary nobles; marshals also performed such functions as administering the estates of widows and orphans and keeping up-to-date the registers of nobles. Sophia's father first served as Nevel district marshal and later as provincial marshal.

Although supposedly no official ranking existed among nobles, human nature being what it is, there were nevertheless definite social and other distinctions based not only on birth but also upon title and wealth and influence. The primary distinction—perhaps after wealth—was between family nobility that dated before, and that dating after, the reign of Peter the Great. This was because Peter, needing officers for his new navy, had to ennoble many common seamen; and, needing educated foreigners for his modernization program, had to ennoble many non-Russians. The Korvin-Krukovskys just qualified as nobles dating from before Peter's time. Somewhat higher in prestige were nobles whose ancestors' names appeared in the Velvet Book kept by the Heraldry Office and last copied in 1682. Although Sophia's family missed this by two years, some of her relatives married into families whose records for each generation extended back to the mid-thirteenth century.

Peter established a Table of Ranks under which promotion to the higher grades conferred nobility. This table underwent only slight revision over the years. Persons in all fourteen civil ranks as well as those in the like number of military ranks wore uniforms, dress and undress. The top eight civil and military grades were limited to nobles. The

[13]

military rank of lieutenant-general held by Sophia's father was second to that of marshal at the top. All individuals in the highest four military and civilian grades were called generals, wore appropriate stars, and were addressed as "Your Excellency" even in retirement. Having any title, whether prince or general, did actually signify.

Two institutions prepared boys for Table of Rank positions. One was the Corp of Pages in which influential nobles obtained preferment for sons and nephews. Both Sophia's father and maternal grandfather began as pages. The other avenue for advancement was through the Cadet Corps. Further training usually followed at a university or special military school or in one of the elite guards regiments limited to nobles in which officers automatically received the pay and prestige of officers one or two steps higher in the regular army.

Thus the nobility, for better and for worse, formed a highly favored class that controlled the civil government, the military, and through marriage and prestige was self-perpetuating. Some nobles were very poor, some uneducated; a few families had lost nobility through an ancestor's marriage to a commoner; a great many very rich or well-educated individuals were non-nobles. Not wealth or property but only birth or the occasional pleasure of a tsar were determinants.

As a noble Sophia's brother could look forward to all the advantages of his class, including a higher education. But what of Sophia? As a girl she could expect her participation in Russian life to be only through a husband or male relation. The few gymnasiums (approximately equivalent to fourth through twelfth grades) for girls were inferior, while universities would be closed to her. Although this situation was typical at that time for Europe, it was one she would attempt to change. Normally her future would be to learn French more correctly than Russian, to have a smattering of literature, to paint like a talented amateur, to play the piano, and to converse politely so that she could shine in society and attract a suitable mate. That Sophia's parents were enlightened and that she had unusual ability and vigorous will power permitted her atypical development.

CHAPTER 3

The Korvin-Krukovskys

i

SOPHIA'S EARLY education under governess and tutor will be covered later in some detail. Education is not, however, all blackboards and school books. What most teachers lack is the ability to inspire. This inspiration Sophia found in her father's older brother, grandfatherly Peter Vasilevich Korvin-Krukovsky. He provided the affection that her parents seemed to deny and the intellectual stimulation that her governess entirely and her tutor partly failed to supply. Her tutor was miffed when she wrote in her *Recollections* that she attributed her success largely to the interest and encouragement of her Uncle Peter.

Because Peter's parents recognized during his adolescence that his weak and amiable character made him unfit for the military career that would be traditional in his family, they permitted him to remain at home and gave him only a secondary education. During a period of war he did spend a brief time in army service, but in 1826 he retired as a mere sub-lieutenant. A handsome young man but an impractical dreamer, he caught the eye of an outstanding beauty who was the richest heiress of the entire province. Dominant in character, she brought Peter to his knees before he quite realized what was happening. Having captured him, and although greatly loving him, she often, with her ungovernable temper, made his married life miserable. On more than one occasion she repeatedly struck him on the face with her slipper or threw his books and papers into the fire. Usually her rage originated in her failure to control lazy or impertinent servants. Therefore, she beat the serfs herself. Mistreatment of serfs was condemned by society. Her mistreatment created a real scandal, exposing her violent nature when a half dozen serfs, led by her own personal maid, smothered her in bed while she was otherwise alone in the house.

Years later, secretly informed by an aunt of this horrible incident, Sophia felt haunted to the point that she sometimes imagined being smothered by her own maid Dunyasha, who customarily undressed her. "When bedtime approached, this tale pursued me, and would not let me sleep," she wrote. One evening while alone in the library with her uncle, she stopped bouncing her ball around the room to stand and observe him speculatively. He looked up from his book to ask what she was thinking. Unable to restrain herself, she blurted out, "Uncle, were you very unhappy with your wife?"

"I shall never forget how this unexpected question acted on my poor uncle," she recalled. "His calm, stern face suddenly became furrowed with fine wrinkles, as if from physical pain. He even stretched out his hand in front of him, as if he were warding off a blow. . . . " Crimson with shame, Sophia asked his forgiveness, hugging him and hiding her face in his coat. And then "my kind uncle had to comfort me for my indiscretion."

Not long after his wife's death Peter Vasilevich had relinquished his large estate at Ryzhakov, about twenty versts (fourteen miles) from Palibino, in return for a small monthly allowance. He lived the rest of his life as he wished, visiting friends, going to Petersburg, or staying for long periods with his relatives. "We always regarded his arrival as a festival," wrote Sophia. She described him as "an extremely pictur-esque old man, of lofty stature, with a massive head framed in thick white curls. His face, with regular, severe profile, with thick, bushy eyebrows, and with a deep vertical furrow cutting through his high forehead . . . might have seemed stern, almost harsh, in effect, had it not been lighted up by such kind, ingenuous eyes, such as belong only to Newfoundland dogs and to small children." She added that he had, in fact, the soul of a child always hovering in the realm of fantasy.

At the time of Sophia's embarrassing question, this uncle was over sixty-five years of age, so that he was more like a grandfather, one who for Sophia "existed in the world especially for our pleasure." She was his favorite niece. Their relationship thus was the close one that some-times exists between a doting grandfather having time always available and a child who feels neglected, a middle child envious of the privi-leges enjoyed by her older sister and sometimes jealous of the attention given her small brother, the only son and heir.

The library in the tower at Palibino was her uncle's favorite nook. She remembered: "He was excessively lazy where any sort of physical exertion was concerned and would sit motionless for days together on a large leather-covered divan, with one leg tucked up under him, with his left eye, which was weaker than the right, screwed up, and wholly absorbed in the perusal of the *Revue des Deux Mondes*, his favorite periodical." He also read with equal enthusiasm romances, travels, history, and especially world politics. In family arguments he became explosive in condemning Bismarck in Germany and the British in India.

He always took time to play chess with Sophia, to make her paper boats, to tell her stories, or to discuss some scientific or other subject with her as though she were an adult, meanwhile providing the attention and the demonstrated affection she did not get from her father, who seemed always to be busy in his study with the business of his estate or the affairs of the district. Uncle Peter, sometimes carried away by his thoughts, would reveal to Sophia "the secrets of different economical and social projects with which he dreamed of heaping benefits upon mankind." Doubtless this influenced Sophia in her later political idealism.

More than anything else, however, her uncle awakened in Sophia an intellectual curiosity about mathematics. "Although he had never studied mathematics," she wrote, "he cherished the most profound respect for that science. He had gathered a certain amount of mathematical knowledge from various books, and loved to philosophize about them, on which occasions he often thought aloud in my presence. I heard from him for the first time, for example, about the quadrature of the circle, about the asymptotes which the curve always approaches without ever attaining them, and about many other things of the same sort—the sense of which I could of course not understand as yet, but which acted on my mind, imbuing me with a reverence for mathematics, as for a very lofty and mysterious science, which opened out to those who consecrated themselves to it a new and wonderful world not attained by simple mortals."

Almost the last we hear of Uncle Peter is that in 1867 he wrote to Sophia, addressing her as "Beloved of my heart" and exclaiming, "How happy I would be if only I could look at you now." He died three years later when Sophia was twenty.

ii

IT WAS Peter's father, Sophia's grandfather, who changed the family name from plain Krukovsky to the hyphenated Korvin-Krukovsky. He wanted to connect the family with its Hungarian origins and before that its Roman origins. This change came about because in 1797 each noble family in Russia was ordered by Tsar Paul to submit its coat-of-arms and an account of family origins, supported by historical documents and by attestations by three other noblemen as to the accuracy of the material.

The family's history supposedly went back to Roman times. It was believed that the name originated with Marcus Valerius Messalius, a Roman general, as the result of a curious incident in battle. The general one day was losing a military skirmish when a nearly blind crow, perhaps somebody's lost pet, settled upon his helmet. At every attempt of the enemy to close for a kill, the crow threatened with its beak and wings, and thanks to the impression created by this symbol of ill-omen, the enemy was routed. To keep alive the memory of this incident the general adopted the name Corvinus, derived from the Latin for crow, which eventually became Corvin or Korvin.

One of the general's descendants, John Corvinus, settled on land granted him in Rumania. His son became king and led Hungary to its pinnacle of power. The king was Matthias Corvinus (1443-90), who ascended the throne in 1458 and was crowned by Emperor Frederick II with the holy crown of St. Stephen. It was this crown and associated regalia that the United States withheld so long from the Communist regime after World War II because throughout the centuries the crown had become a powerful symbol giving its holder implied rights to rule. Supposedly the Krukovskys in Russia descended from a daughter of Matthias Corvinus. She married a Krukovsky from greater Poland, where the family had been established since 1233, when a knight-ancestor had received land from Duke Conrad of Masovia as a reward for help in the defeat of the Borussians.

iii

THE FIRST documented ancestor in Russia to bear the family name was Michael Mikhailovich Krukovsky, who in 1654 received an estate with serfs, together with the village of Juravlinz, in the Poldolsk command area. His son, Ivan, in 1726 commanded an old Cossack regiment guarding the border provinces. Ivan's son, Vasily, fathered Sophia's great-grandfather, Simon, who sold the Juravlinz estate in 1787. Thereafter the Krukovskys held property only in the area of Pskov and Vitebsk.

Sophia told a girlfriend that both her paternal grandfather and great-great-grandfather had married gypsies. This may have been true for the earlier ancestor, but could hardly have been so for her grandfather because in his time the children of such a union would have lost their nobility. The grandmother could, however, have been a noblewoman with some mixture of gypsy blood. The entire gypsy relationship may have been merely a romantic fiction to explain Sophia's dark complexion. As a child she sometimes pretended to be a gypsy herself.

At any rate, Sophia's grandfather, Vasily Semenovich, had three sons and two daughters. The oldest, Sophia's beloved Uncle Peter, has already been mentioned. Sophia's father came next, born 1799. Simon was the third. The daughters were Anna and Marfa; the former had an estate apparently from a deceased husband, located not far from Palibino, while the later apparently lived with one sibling or another. Uncle Peter's estate of 9,800 acres with 252 serfs in Velikiye Luki had been turned over to his son Andre and his grandson Peter. Apparently it was the latter, Peter Andreevich Korvin-Krukovsky, who wrote plays in French about Russian life and who in 1878 presented one in Paris called *Aniuta* (probably about Sophia's sister).

The hyphenation of the family name by Sophia's grandfather caused some confusion because the old name continued to be official, pending action by the attorney-general. Several times Sophia's father petitioned for approval of the change, but the bureaucracy was not to be hurried in its slow procedure of verifying the genealogy and arms of all the nobles. Thus a half-century elapsed before "Korvin-Krukovsky" received official approval, by which time Sophia was seven years of age. She was twenty-four when they received confirmation of the family coat-of-arms. The arms displayed on a cross a blind crow holding a man's ring in its beak. Behind the shield and helmet rose three ostrich plumes, the right to display which the Empress Anna (1730-40) had granted to certain men prominent during her reign.

CHAPTER 4

Palibino

i

FROM THE age of eight to eighteen Sophia lived at Palibino. When they moved there from Petersburg, her father was fifty-seven and her mother thirty-six years of age. During the first several years of their stay the estate for Sophia consisted only of what she could view in all directions from the tower windows of the stone house, which was situated on high ground, a house she once described as being large enough for several families to occupy without encountering one another. In a chapter left out of her published *Recollections* (perhaps for one reason because she wanted to use much of the material in her novel) Sophia went into considerable detail about Palibino. This information is confirmed and amplified by factual descriptions from other sources.

On one side of the house lay the forest, crowding close to the farm structures, a forest thinned out for a short distance to resemble a park but gradually thickening into an almost impenetrable stand of pine and spruce. A linden tree alley led to the yards of the peasants, their huts of pine logs roofed with boards.

On the opposite side of the house Sophia could see open land, except for several clumps of oak and maple, land somewhat rolling, dotted at intervals with great rocks deposited in glacial times, rocks most peasants thought had been left by ancient giants.

On the back side of the house, below the raised terrace, lay the household gardens of flowers in heart-shaped or urn-shaped plots, with graveled pathways, many berry bushes, and rows of peach, apricot, and cherry trees. The garden sloped all the way down to an artificial lake that had long ago been dug by serfs. Beyond the lake stretched fields and meadows, through which meandered a stream that varied with the season from a trickle to a rushing stream.

PALIBINO

From the front window of the tower Sophia could look down a verst-long birch alley to the road leading to the estate village of Palibino three versts (two miles) away. The road could be viewed for a considerable distance in either direction, but was little traveled. Usually it was rutted, often muddy from rain, or in late autumn frozen hard and joltingly rough. But in winter, buried in snow, the road afforded a smooth passageway for an occasional peasant's sledge pulled by lean horses or for a fast troika pulled by three horses abreast, harness bells jingling as they passed.

Except for infrequent travelers along the main road, Sophia remembered the winter view in all directions from the tower windows as that of an unpeopled land, an expanse of white drifts extending to the forest edge. It seemed to her as though everything and everybody had died. Only comforting wisps of smoke from the peasant dwellings hinted at real life within. Disregarding occasional extremes, typically the January temperature at Palibino varied from fourteen degrees above to four below zero Fahrenheit. The climate in that part of Byelorussia might roughly be compared with that of the Dakotas. The thick-walled house, however, was well heated by typical tall Russian stoves entirely faced with glazed tile, which occupied a corner in each of a number of principal rooms.

In the spring the outdoor greenhouses provided blooms for inside the house, and in the summer the terrace was edged with roses, lilacs, and jasmine. Summers were long and cool, with July temperatures hovering between fifty and seventy degrees Fahrenheit. Year-round precipitation totaled from twenty to forty inches, a large percentage in the form of snow.

The original two-story portion of the house probably dated from about 1820. Wings had been added later. A three-story tower rose at one corner of the original house and was the favorite daytime refuge of Sophia's sister and Sophia's beloved uncle. On sultry summer evenings a pleasant breeze could sometimes be enjoyed in the tower.

Sophia recalled one rather idyllic summer evening in the tower with the family when she was about thirteen. While sitting in silence near the end of the day, they heard the housekeeper scolding the servants for arriving late to eat. Then little by little the medley of voices became quiet, and from a copse of trees beyond the gardens could be heard a harmonica played by one of the gardeners. After sunset a ground fog arose over the meadows. Light lingered in the sky, but inside the tower room it grew dark. Only the glow from the General's pipe, as at intervals he sucked upon the stem, illuminated his swarthy face. Somewhat thin and stooped at age sixty-three, he wore a gray robe with general's stripes on the sleeves. Some of the family members were lost in thought, others half asleep. A single mosquito droned about. Then the greyhound, Griz, slumbering in a corner, jumped up as Ilia entered to light candles and inquire if the family was ready for supper. Ilia was the General's valet and trusted factotum. Instructed to have the meal served there, he departed silently, but the spell had been broken and general conversation ensued.

In her novel, *The Nihilist*, Sophia further described the house, supposedly that of a Count and Countess Vorontsov (for whom her parents were obvious models), as being located on an elevated site, and as having stone walls three feet thick, to which wings and balconies had been attached. She characterized it as of "bond-serf style," by which she meant that while the materials were very good, the finish was in places somewhat crude, the house having been designed in simple style and built by serfs. Tiles had been fired on the property. Parquetry flooring from oak cut nearby was in places somewhat imperfectly laid. Windowsills were of marble.

Sophia the novelist wrote: "Above, dwelt the family; on the first floor the children; and in the basement the kitchen and servants' quarters were found. The Countess entered the basement only once a year, on Easter Day, when she went down to give the customary kiss of peace to each servant."

Apart from living quarters for the immediate family and for visitors, the house had ample room for a fair-sized ballroom with a curtained stage for musicians or family theatricals at one end, as well as rooms for special purposes, such as library and sewing and storage. At the foot of the tower, with inside and outside entrances, the master had his retreat which was also the estate office. A photograph shows that the house was not "fantastic" as Sophia declared, whatever its lack of architectural style.

If in winter the view from the windows of Palibino looked bleak, inside it was warm and pleasant when the family gathered around the samovar for evening tea. "In the large salon the crystal chandeliers were lit in rows," wrote Sophia in the chapter deleted from *Recollections* "and the flames of the candles were merrily reflected in numerous mirrors on the walls. Along the walls stood silk-upholstered furniture. In front of the windows the spreading fronds of the palms and other greenery from the hot house were wonderfully displayed. On the table were thrown about books and foreign magazines." When tea was finished the children usually remained for a time with their parents, while the General, smoking his pipe, played solitaire, and the mother at the pianoforte "played a Beethoven sonata or a romance of

Schumann." Aniuta, pacing back and forth, was "lost somewhere far, far away in her imagination," seeing herself perhaps as "a queen at a brilliant social ball," while Sophia and her brother read or played quiet games.

ii

SOPHIA CONTINUED the evening scene in the salon: "Suddenly Ilia appears at the door. He stands silently, shifting his weight from foot to foot, his constant habit when he prepares himself to announce something unusual.

" 'What do you want, Ilia,' finally calls the General.

" 'Nothing, Your Excellency,' answers Ilia with a strange smile. 'I only came to report that many wolves have gathered on our lake. Would your lordships be interested in hearing them?'

"At this news the children naturally become indescribably excited and implore their parents for permission to walk out on the terrace." Receiving permission, they are wrapped in down-filled scarves and venture out with Ilia.

"A wonderful winter night. The frost is so strong that one dare not breathe deeply. Although there is no moon, it is still very light because of the snow reflecting the myriads of stars appearing as though huge nails driven into the entire sky. . . ."

Snow is so drifted that the steps of the terrace are covered, and even the terrace itself seems on a level with the rest of the garden. There is no sound. The stillness is almost oppressive. No howl of wolves is heard.

" 'Wait a little,' Ilia suggests. 'Maybe they'll start again.'

"And indeed, suddenly comes a drawn out wail with roulades, immediately answered by several other voices from the other side of the lake." The sound becomes a mournful antiphonal chorus that causes the heart to contract.

" 'There they are, darlings,' Ilia triumphantly exclaims, 'singing their songs. But why have they taken a fancy to our lake? At nightfall they come onto the lake in packs.' "

Ilia says to the large water spaniel that followed the children onto the porch, "Friend, Polkan, don't you want to go to them?" But the bold bitch, ordinarily ready for a fight, presses close to the children, tail lowered, and like them is oppressed by the elemental chorus and is quite ready to reenter the warm house.

iii

BY THE end of April, however, the wolves had retreated deep into the forests, even beyond Palibino holdings and into the crown lands that stretched farther on by many leagues. Ice on the lake had broken up and the snow melted, although the cold continued at night, so that spring developed slowly, two steps forward and one step back. "But suddenly," Sophia wrote in her novel, "one night a mild, warm rain began to fall, and from that moment all went as if by magic. It was as if a secret power of effervescence lay hidden in the fine, fragrant rain. Everything bestirred itself, everything throbbed with the desire to live. . . . In one night there had been such a change that one could no longer recognize garden or field or grove. Yesterday everything had been dark and naked, and now it looked as if a thin light-green veil had been thrown over all. Neither was the air the same as yesterday. The odor was quite different, and it was easy to breathe!

"All nature was smitten with a real spring fever. The birches had already clothed themselves in a fine, transparent network of leaves, light and delicate as lace. From the swelling buds of the poplars fell scales that filled the air with strong perfume. The yellow fragrant pollen from the tassels of the alders and hazelnuts floated over everything, along with stray petals from the wild cherrytree blossoms. The spruce shot out long pale green cones, straight as candles, that showed strangely against the remaining brown ones of last year. Only the oak stood naked and surly . . . .

"Every day new guests came flying from the south. A week had already passed since the first dark triangle of cranes had been seen against the sky; the woodpecker was hammering on a hollow beech; swallows circled under the verandah roof, seeking their old nests, carrying on a bitter warfare with the sparrows that had usurped their lawful dwellings. . . . One almost felt the mysterious work going on in the bosom of the earth."

iv

NAMED FOR its village, Palibino was one of two estates inherited by the General. It was situated in the area called Byelorussia or White Russia, not far from Nevel, in the Vitebsk district of Pskov province, roughly 280 miles south of St. Petersburg (Leningrad) and fifty miles or so east of what is today Latvia's border. Palibino estate consisted of 2,200 desiatina (5,940 acres). The other nearby property, Moshino, comprised 1,400 desiatina (3,780 acres), so that together they totaled 9,720 acres, equivalent to about fifteen square miles. This compared with an average landholding at that time of 1,655 acres and a median holding of much less.

The General's nephew, Andre (Peter's son), and the General's younger brother, Simon, also had Korvin-Krukovsky estates in the area. The one called Piatnitskoë, where Simon resided, lay about twenty-five miles from the city of Toropetz. Since Peter was the older brother and had married a very wealthy woman, his son's property probably comprised larger acreage than that of the others. Therefore the family held title, more or less, to perhaps fifty square miles in all, not counting property the widowed sister, Anna, held for her children from her late husband. Other families allied by marriage to the Korvin-Krukovskys—such as the Uraneffs (with Peschivitz about twenty-five miles from Toropetz) and the Tchirikoffs—likewise held large tracts. Thus the combined influence of these interlinked families in the district was considerable, perhaps especially that of the Tchirikoffs who had long been dapifers or courtiers close to the tsar and military men. Palibino and Moshino pastured many sheep and thoroughbred cattle and had large areas allotted for rye, wheat, buckwheat, and hay, with smaller areas for vegetables and fruits. A distillery converted much of the rye into vodka for estate use and for sale. A dairy farm produced milk and cheese. Other outbuildings included a smoke house, an ice house, a bath house, a stable and coach house, a small clinic for treating peasants, a workshop, and storage structures. Lakes scattered about the two properties produced fish that were sold in Vitebsk and Dvinsk. The forest yielded salable resin, firewood, and charcoal. In the forests roamed not only hundred-pound timber wolves but also bears, lynx, elk, deer, fox, and many smaller animals.

V

A FURTHER description of Palibino, its environs, and its residents—combining memories of visits nearly thirty years apart—appeared in the magazine *Russkaia starina (Russian Antiquity)* from the pen of its editor, M. I. Semevsky, a former neighbor, who had sought the hand in marriage of Sophia's sister. By the time of Semevsky's second visit in 1890, landowners had cleared much forest land to sell for firewood. En route from Velikiye Luki toward Palibino he had seen new growth among the stumps and also observed through the newly opened vistas numerous glittering lakes once hidden by pines. Nearing Palibino, six miles from the Senkova post station, the writer observed "on a hillock in a shady grove" the stone chapel "where repose the remains of the lieutenant-general" and his wife. The one-time suitor's recollection of rejection by the General doubtless colored his description of the "cold" and "proud" nobleman "who went to his grave as though avoiding the ordinary dead" of a common cemetery.

Harking back to when the General was still very much alive, however, and still the father of "two remarkable young women," Semevsky recalled the winter of 1862-63 when he visited the family on several occasions. "We drive up to the nobleman's house, built according to the taste of about the 1830's . . . having wings that seem to take the courtyard gates into its embrace. We walk inside—numerous servants, the house is full of everything as in a bowl. Father, mother, a bold handsome boy, the tutor, an English governess, a very pretty girl of eleven or twelve [nearly thirteen]—that is Sofochka, a tomboy who in time became a master of arts, doctor of philosophy, and professor of higher mathematics—her older sister, at that time seventeen or eighteen [nearly nineteen] years old, a graceful, beautiful blond with blue eyes, at times as if green, and a wonderful braid of wavy hair. The mother of these young women is plump, a most friendly little lady, who can't forget that she herself was once pretty—this is the mistress-generalsha—and finally the dry, affected general—you can just see him playing cards face to face with the tutor.

"Hardly a day has passed before the lively literary conversation of the older young woman delights us; one is astonished how in a country house, so remotely located, during the course of several years of a confined life, could grow such a marvelous young girl: she is full of the highest ideals for life; what has she not reread in three or four languages, what a close acquaintance with history—and all this comes forth in such simple, charming forms that one is not rebuked by all this knowledge and meditation on what has been read and learned.

"And here at the same time rings out the resonant laughter of Sofochka: a tomboy, a pretty girl whose luxurious auburn curls shake as she bounces a ball, then pauses to embrace and kiss her sister, and again flies through the rooms. Delightful, charming days!"

When Semevsky revisited Palibino in 1890 to recapture the bitter-sweet memory of an episode in his life—when he had loved and had found at least temporary favor in the eyes of the beautiful Aniuta—he now found only disappointment. He kept the coachman waiting only twenty minutes while he wandered through the neglected gardens and walked through some of the rooms of the house, which he said was at this time under different ownership. One wing had been torn down, and everywhere he sensed disorder and desolation, a lack of pride in ownership and of the culture and hospitality of the old nobility. For him Palibino had become a ghost of the past, although this view apparently was partly one of literary license to contrast with his cherished memory of the past. Within several years of Semevsky's last visit, a Uraneff girl, whose grandmother had been a Korvin-Krukovsky, visited the estate with her uncle, Nicholas Semenovich Korvin-Krukovsky, and remembered it as "a lovely place with a large garden where there were plenty of berries and fruit." Sophia's brother, having inherited Palibino, had sold it to his cousin, Nicholas, who lived on his own estate about twenty-five miles away. The sturdy house itself apparently survived until the German invasion of World War II.

vi

REGARDLESS, MANY years were to elapse and many events to occur between Semevsky's two visits. Twice he had referred to Sophia as a tomboy. Actually he was mistaken. For years she could not leave the house except under the strict supervision of her governess or occasionally in the sedate company of a family member. So she had developed the habit of combining exercise and relaxation with her study of geography by bouncing a ball about the house. This both worked off her pent-up energy and gave her the imaginary pleasure of traveling from country to country—as from Russia to Finland to Sweden, or to contiguous countries elsewhere in the world—as she bounced the ball from room to room. Sometimes she mentally recited poetry or composed verses, the bouncing of the ball coinciding with the poetic accents. Sophia never rode horses, as did her sister, never ice-skated, and never could play with the yard children she watched frolicking in the sunshine. Years were to pass before she actually visited in person portions of the estate she could see from the house.

It was not until the strict English governess was replaced by a Swiss one that Sophia's wanderings could be extended. To be sure, at no time did proper young ladies venture forth without being accompanied by relatives or maids. Actually there were real dangers, and not only human ones, for any woman alone. For example, the English governess, having ignored warnings, once ventured by herself into the edge of the forest, where she was badly frightened by a she-bear with two cubs. In fact, not even peasants entered the woods unless accompanied by an armed escort, for there were instances of men being clawed; bears occasionally emerged into open pastures to kill a cow or a horse. Peasants also believed that there were robber dens and army deserters in the forest depths, and some claimed to have seen werewolves and even water nymphs. If a peasant woman missed her child in the evening, she immediately assumed he had wandered into the forest, and she began wailing as though for one dead.

vii

THE EXCURSION into the forest that Sophia described (in another chapter she deleted from her *Recollections*) had been well planned for days in advance. In view of her restricted life this was indeed to be a great event. The excursion was really a holiday, with the excuse of gathering strawberries and more especially birch and aspen mushrooms. Strawberries in the woods ripened later than those in the fields but were more juicy and fragrant. Deep blue bilberries ripened later, followed by wild stone-fruit, then raspberries, red bilberries, and finally nuts and the late types of mushrooms. Crowds of peasants with woven or bark baskets would spend whole days gathering the largess of the forest, while men with old matchlock guns would hunt rabbits, woodcocks, and partridge that abounded.

Those from the Palibino household, however, were to go deeper into the forest than the peasants usually ventured; in fact, they went beyond Palibino boundaries into the crown forest. In the early light of summer, about 3:00 A.M., carts arrived by the porch to be loaded by bustling maids carrying the samovar, provisions for tea, cheese cakes, little *piroshki*, tableware for about two dozen persons, and many empty baskets. Children and dogs ran about excitedly, getting in everybody's way. With preparations finally completed, everybody found places in the carts; Sophia enumerated the governess, the tutor, Aniuta, Fedor, Sophia herself, ten maids, a gardener, two or three men servants, and about five yard children, besides the coachman driving one cart and volunteer drivers for the others.

"At the last minute, just as the carts moved," wrote Sophia, "suddenly five-year-old Aksiutka, the dishwasher's daughter, howled so for her departing mother that it was necessary to stop and take her along."

The road through the forest was so rough in places that when one cart hit a root, not only was there the sound of breaking glassware among the supplies, but the little girl was thrown into the air and only saved from falling beneath the wheels by a maid who caught her by her dress collar as one might grasp a puppy.

Jokes and laughter dispelled some of the gloom in the tall pines, not yet penetrated by the sun. Scrubby hazel, elder, alder, and birch edged the road. After traveling about five miles the party entered crown lands, marked by a sentry hut having only one small window because of the rigors of winter. A white-bearded forester, about seventy years of age, lived there in complete isolation with his wife. They grew in a clearing most of what they consumed, such as cabbages, other vegetables, apples, and sunflowers for seeds. Together they bowed low from the waist and invited the visitors to enter for tea. The clay floor of the hut was covered with fir branches. Benches ran along the walls. A tame jackdaw hopped about, unafraid of a black tomcat. The children, gentry and peasant alike, all called the forester Uncle Jacob, knowing him from his occasional visits to Palibino when he brought unusual gifts, such as on one occasion a young elk that never became completely tame. He assiduously entertained his Orthodox guests but would not eat with them, as he belonged to some heretical sect having an oratory hidden somewhere in the woods. It was known that he paid off petty officials to be left alone.

By now it was six o'clock. So the party proceeded farther into the forest, scattering members afoot in pairs or threes along the way, each person intent upon finding the most and finest mushrooms, but occasionally calling to one another so as not to get lost. "Dear Lord, send me many mushrooms," Sophia prayed. Glimpsing the red cup of an aspen mushroom or the black cup of a birch variety, she raced to get them before anybody else; but how many disappointments she had, mistaking a curled dry leaf for a mushroom, or a worthless variety for an edible one, only to have sharp-eyed Feklusha find a treasure that had escaped her. Soon Feklusha's basket was nearly full of choice specimens, small and clean and perfect, whereas Sophia's basket was only half-full of mostly large and flabby mushrooms too shameful to show.

Meanwhile the carts had slowly moved on ahead to an open meadow where the horses could be unharnessed to graze and a fire started. By three in the afternoon the pickers had all assembled there. Cloths were spread and set with dishes, the samovar filled from a stream, the luncheon unpacked. At first the gentry and servants sat in separate groups but soon intermingled, displaying their mushrooms, telling of the badger or snake encountered.

After eating and resting the pickers dispersed again, but by now their former enthusiasm had diminished, and at sunset all gathered again for the homeward journey. They laughed at one another, for there were sunburnt faces, hairpins had been lost, braids had come loose, clothing had been torn, and several maids had even lost their shoes. Some younger maids had decorated their heads with ferns or other growth. Sophia wore a crown twined from a branch of hop flowers, the yellowish-green pods of which mingled with her disarranged auburn hair. She fancied herself a bacchante, but her brother exclaimed, "Long live her highness, Queen of the Gypsys!" How she wished she could turn into a real gypsy and could realize the nomadic longings aroused by a day in the woods.

At first everybody was quiet during the return home in the long summer twilight that lasted until 10:00 or 11:00 P.M. But soon the young maids began a quiet and doleful song, seeming to express their sadness at the end of an exciting day. Sophia, too, felt oppressed by a feeling of unreasonable grief, and that night in bed, despite eighteen hours of activity, she tossed sleeplessly as she reviewed in detail the events of the day, until finally near dawn she fell into a leaden slumber.

CHAPTER 5

Serfdom and Emancipation

i

FURTHER TO understand Sophia's position in Russian society, and to comprehend the profound changes and economic disruption caused by the Emancipation, a quick look at serfdom may be useful.

If a wealthy and free-spending family holding several hundred serfs lost them all on a particular day, the effects, even if partially offset in advance, had to be calamitous in the long run. This was one reason for Sophia's severe financial troubles in later life. On the two estates the General probably had about 300 serfs. The family had twenty-five to thirty household servants, all being serfs except the tutor, the governess, the seamstress, the estates' steward, and the special chef from Petersburg. The General had Ilia, his valet-butler and general household factotum; his wife and daughters their personal maids; Fedor his nurse; also there were Daria the housekeeper, Yakov the coachman, the dishwasher, the footmen, about ten general maids, the carpenter, the gardeners, the stable hands, and the night watchman.

After the Emancipation the number of servants remained about the same, but the former serfs had to be compensated, some in cash, some in extra land or allotments to their relatives. Meanwhile, urban standards of luxury were maintained, liveries for the inside servants, carpets over floors usually left bare in the country, fine liqueurs, new coaches, good horses. Relatives and friends enjoyed open-handed hospitality for weeks and months.

Serfdom in Russia had a long and complex history, having begun as a form of feudalism when numerous princes ruled different parts of the country. In those troubled times more and more peasants put themselves under the protection of individual nobles in return for service, until this became the normal condition. At first the peasants could move about from noble to noble or from one principality to another;

but as the Princes of Moscow gradually annexed the other principalities and became overlords and then absolute tsars, all peasants, whether bound or free, became fixed to the land because otherwise some areas would be left with no workers and other areas with too many.

The tsars also imposed obligatory service upon all nobles, even those of the oldest families that had owned land in fee simple. Consequently, the nobles argued successfully that if they were to spend a lifetime in military or civil service, then to preserve their estates and families they had to have greater control over the peasants. And so the noose tightened gradually on the serfs, until their service was not owed to the land but directly to their landowner, who eventually could give, sell, mortgage, or bequeath them.

The situation was such that through much of Russian history the nobles were serfs of the tsars, who could on a whim beat, exile, or kill them. In turn, most peasants were serfs of the nobles, who could chain or beat them or send them to Siberia, and punish for every crime except armed robbery and murder. When, however, the nobles were freed from obligatory service to the tsar and won civil rights, the same freedom was not extended to the serfs. This was perceived by many as an inequality to be corrected. It is true that a serf could terminate his status by joining the church or the army. But few felt called to the church and army life was a fate worse than serfdom. If called up, a serf, often with money from his master, might purchase another serf to go instead. A few serfs also owned other serfs, and some even acquired land, town houses, even factories, all under the dummy ownership of nobles. But serfs were not free.

The status of agricultural serfs was effectively that of tenant farmers. Under one system the serf family owed the landowner an annual rental in cash, or produce, or service, or some combination thereof. Alternately, the system they preferred was to work a portion of the land for themselves and a portion for the master. By whichever method, yield to the landowner was usually far less than would be considered an adequate yield on capital today.

ii

IN HER *Recollections* Sophia did not describe the Emancipation. Her novel *The Nihilist* in its earlier parts was essentially autobiographical, however, and in it she left a vivid description of that fateful day for landowners on 19 February 1861 when she was 11 years old. Quotations are from the English translation of the novel published in 1895 as *Vera Vorontsoff*. Vera was the supposed daughter of a count who, like Sophia's father, continued to live an opulent country life.

At Palibino, as outlined in the novel, household serfs first learned of the Tsar's forthcoming manifesto by eavesdropping on the animated discussion in the drawing room. Word quickly spread from the house to outbuildings to village. What did it all mean? Were they really to be free at last? Soon the official word did go out that on the appointed day everybody was to meet at the village church. There, following the liturgy, the priest was to read the manifesto.

The novel continues: "Already, at nine o'clock in the morning, everyone in the house is dressed and ready. Everything is done today with feverish haste and at the same time with a certain ceremoniousness, almost the same as when one is going to a funeral—one and all afraid to speak a word too much. Even the children have an instinctive feeling for the great importance and significance of the day; they keep silent and dare not ask questions.

"Before the main entrance two calashes are standing; the carriages have been carefully polished, the horses are in their best harnesses, and the coachmen have new caftans. The count, also, is in full dress uniform with orders on his breast; the countess has a new velvet mantilla, and the children are dressed like dolls." In the first carriage rides the family, in the second the governess, housekeeper, and steward. Others from the estate follow on foot, two miles to the church. "During the drive the countess carries her perfumed handkerchief to her eyes from time to time. The count maintains a bitter silence.

"The open space before the church is black with people. Two or three thousand peasants, with their women, have assembled from the neighboring villages. At a distance, it looks like a firm mass of gray overcoats, among which the showy headress of a peasant wife shows, here and there."

The countess begins an exclamation hysterically in French, to which the count replies in French, "For God's sake be quiet, my dear."

"Even today, as on all other holy days, the sexton, up in the tower, watches for the approach of the calash from the count's estate, and when it becomes visible at a turn of the road, the bell begins to ring.

"The church is packed full of people, as full as it will hold; but from an old deeply-rooted custom, this impenetrable mass steps aside to let their Graces pass, so that they can go forward to their usual place in the right choir.

" 'Let us in peace pray to the Lord,' announces the priest, who, in full vestments, advances from behind the altar. 'And to the Holy Ghost,' replies the choir." The service continues, the congregation praying devoutly, signing the cross, falling to its knees, awaiting the moment when the imperial seal on the manifesto will be broken to disclose its rumored contents.

"The unusual mass of people and the many lighted candles have, in spite of the open doors and windows, made it unenduringly suffocating in the narrow little church. The unpleasant odor of sweaty garments and greased shoes blends itself with the smoke from the wax candles and the fumes of incense. The wreaths from the censers struggle up in blue spirals. It is impossible to get air· the breast rises and falls pantingly, and the physical discomfort of not being able to draw a deep breath becomes, together with the universal mental strain, most intolerable suffering and deepest, unspeakable anxiety.

" 'Will it ever end!' whispers the countess hysterically, pressing her husband's hand spasmodically.

"The priest bears the cross forward. It is a good half hour before all those present have kissed it. Finally, the ceremony of kissing is ended. The priest disappears for an instant into the sacristy and then advances to the altar; in his hand he bears a paper roll from which hangs the great seal of state.

"A long deep sigh passes through the church, as if the whole people sighed at once, as if out of one breast. But at this moment occurs an unexpected interruption. Persons thronging outside, unable to find a place in the church, waited while the service was in progress, but now their patience is ended. Through the wide-open door they make a concerted and unexpected forward movement, which produces an indescribable confusion. Those who were standing forward fall headlong on the steps of the altar. Shrieks, oaths, groans, and crying children's voices are heard."

In French the countess exclaims, "My God! My God! Have pity on us," although she and the terrified children, sitting in the protected choir, have nothing to fear.

"After a while, order is again restored in the church. Again a strained, soundless, devout pause. All listen greedily, with bated breath; only now and then a smothered rattling is heard forcing itself from the breast of some asthmatic old man, or a babe in arms begins to cry, but the mother hastens to soothe it . . .

"The priest reads slowly, with a chanting tone, drawling out the syllables, as when he reads Scriptures. The manifesto is couched in heavy, crooked, judicial language. The peasants listen, without daring to draw a breath; but no matter how they exert their brains, they understand, of this document, which is to solve for them the question, 'to be or not to be,' only disconnected words. The meaning of the whole remains obscure to them. As the reading draws to a close, the fierce tension of their faces relaxes by degrees, and is succeeded by an expression of dull, terrified irresolution.

"The priest has finished the reading. The peasants do not know yet, of a surety, if they are free or not, and, what is of most importance—the burning question, the question of their lives—whose is the land now?

"Silently, with bowed heads, the crowd begins to disperse. The calash from the mansion presses forward, step by step, in the crush. The peasants step aside for it, and take off their caps, but do not make the accustomed deep bows, and maintain an unusual, foreboding silence."

Such was the uncertainty produced on the peasants by the half-understood legalistic prose of the manifesto. The family returns home, fearful for its own economic future and also of what might happen if vodka inflames the peasants. One old servant brings tea, but in the downstairs quarters a noisy party is in progress. Although always forbidden to go there, Vera [Sophia] goes down to the basement floor. She smells cabbage soup, alcoholic fumes of "schnapps," and through a cloud of tobacco smoke sees flushed cheeks and watery eyes of the celebrants as they sway to accordion music and out-shriek one another.

The coachman sees her holding back at the doorway and calls out, "Miss, little miss, come in! Don't be afraid. Are their Highnesses up there crying? Are they sad because they cannot trample on us longer?"

Vera defends her parents, says that the peasants are ungrateful. They cannot deny that they have been well-treated by her parents. But how about her grandfather? And they cite old wrongs still remembered! How about her father when he was a bachelor and was after the girls? At that moment the governess, who had just entered in search of her missing charge, berates the servants as being godless corrupters of an innocent child, and in the moment of silence that ensues she marches the girl back to the upstairs precincts.

Although having come to understand that they are free but that as yet they are to receive no land, the servants resume their interrupted celebration. A few clearer heads among them wonder if freedom without land is any better than serfdom.

Did events happen exactly so for the Korvin-Krukovskys? Although doubtless the novelist molded the material slightly for dramatic effect, there are so many touches that only an eyewitness could have supplied that the account must be accepted as substantially correct.

iii

AGRARIAN REFORM actually was a gradual process. The Emancipation Act only granted freedom. A law of 1863 then specified that male agricultural serfs could buy their homestead acreage without the owner's consent. Further, it provided down-payment loans (which entangled peasants in a commune bureaucracy from which many never escaped) with which male serfs could buy an allotment of about eighty-eight acres of arable land with the owners' consent. Not until 1881 were owners required to sell eighty-eight acre allotments. Within about twenty years of the Emancipation about eighty percent of noble land-owners, by economic necessity or otherwise, had sold all or most of their land to peasants or merchant speculators. Although the various Korvin-Krukovskys encountered financial difficulties, some managed to retain much of their holdings until the Russian revolution because they were richer than most and better managers.

As the years passed for Sophia's immediate family, only the General was fully aware of the burdens with which he wrestled in his study. Old debts, some dating from his military years, came due. Little by little he drew upon his capital, sold or mortgaged forest wood, conveyed parcels of land to former serfs. Peasants were slow in paying. Those on a rental basis appropriated more than their share of produce. According to an old Russian proverb, "A peasant will get the better of God himself." Estate stewards were known for dishonesty. With freedom some of the best servants left, to be replaced by inferior ones unafraid of discipline as in the old days. Some stole household supplies. The General's wife was incapable, even had that been his wish, of running an economical household. About all she could do was to use womanly wiles to keep the General from visiting other landowners, where he might gamble and lose.

CHAPTER 6

The German Connection

i

DOUBTLESS MUCH of Sophia's capacity for abstract thought and her consequent ability in higher mathematics came as an inheritance from her mother's family, the Shuberts.

More than that, however—although Sophia credited her interest in mathematics to inspiration by her father's brother, Peter V. Korvin-Krukovsky—it is evident that the scientific accomplishments of her Shubert forebears were also a conscious spur to achievement. This is shown by a letter written in Stockholm in the spring of 1886 to her intimate friend Anna Charlotte Leffler, sister of the Swedish mathematician who advanced Sophia's career. Indulging in a flight of fancy, Sophia wrote Anna Charlotte: "This morning I awakened with a great desire to enjoy myself today when suddenly there appeared before me my grandfather on my mother's side, a fat pedant (that is, astronomer), who pointed sternly at all the scholarly treatises that I had intended to study during the Easter vacation and who rebuked me in the most serious manner because I was wasting my precious time in such an unworthy manner. His stern words caused my poor gypsy grandmother (from my father's side) to run away. Now I am sitting at my writing desk in bathrobe and slippers, deeply absorbed in mathematical thoughts, without the slightest desire to take part in your excursion. There are so many of you that undoubtedly it will be gay for you without me. Consequently I hope that you will graciously forgive me in my refusal."

ii

THE FIRST Shubert in Russia was Sophia's great-grandfather, Fedor Ivanovich Shubert (1758-1825), German-born at Helmstdadt as the son of a prominent Lutheran theologian and raised in Pomerania near the

[36]

Baltic. At age twenty-one he became tutor in the Swedish household of an ardent amateur astronomer and there became interested in astronomy and mathematics. Four years later he emigrated to Russia, beginning a career that soon found him as a geographer and mathematician at the St. Petersburg Imperial Academy of Sciences, where at the age of thirty-one he became a full academician, an honor sought by his great-granddaughter about a century later.

At that time most of Russia lay unsurveyed, and what maps existed were inaccurate. Shubert spent the rest of his life in one aspect or another of producing accurate land maps, coastal charts, and celestial navigational data. His text in German on theoretical astronomy was translated into French. He took charge of all Russian observatories in 1804 and for many years was the army staff officer in charge of instruction in geodetic science. He also edited the *St. Petersburg Academical Journal* in German and belonged to scientific societies in Germany, France, Sweden, Denmark, Italy, and the United States. His miscellaneous articles on astronomy, physics, mathematics, and philosophy appear in the three-volume *Vermischte Schriften*.

Among the great-aunts Sophia knew were his two daughters, Wilhelmina (1792-1877) and Frederika (1794-1865). He died a Russian noble, by letters patent, who had always remained a German scientist in his love for truth, his indefatigable energy, and his international viewpoint.

•••
iii

IT WAS his son, Fedor Fedorovich Shubert, to whom Sophia referred as her fat grandfather in the letter previously quoted. That passing reference seems almost to be Sophia's only mention of her mother's father. Because he lived until she reached the age of fifteen, they must have seen one another many times, but there is no indication anywhere of an affectionate relationship and no evidence that he had any personal part in directing her scientific interests. Certainly she was aware of his theoretical as well as his practical work, and after his death, as she advanced in knowledge, this must have been of considerable interest to her. One of the treatises she prepared as a student was a mathematical study of the rings around Saturn, something her grandfather might have attempted without success. One supposes that the old man, who had taken over direction of all Russian observatories from his father, must at some time have allowed his granddaughter to peer through a telescope at Saturn. Perhaps in Petersburg she even peered through one of the world's two largest telescopes, which he had obtained for Russia and which was duplicated at Harvard University.

Grandfather Fedor Fedorovich (1789-1865) was born in Petersburg and at age fourteen became a page in the retinue of Tsar Alexander I. At age seventeen he became a general staff sub-lieutenant and his father's assistant but in the wars that followed saw much active service. At the bloody battle in 1807 at Preussisch Eylau in East Prussia against Napoleon's forces he suffered a chest wound. Following recovery he fought in Finland and Moldavia; against the Turks he sustained another wound and received a golden sword for bravery. When Napoleon invaded Russia he served in the rear guard during the disastrous Russian retreat and in the advanced guard during the final rout of the French. As a full colonel, having also become a Chevalier in the Order of Anna, he participated in the siege of Paris and was honored by Prussia and Sweden. Obviously during this period he was quite unlike the "fat pedant" Sophia remembered.

Although he remained in military service all his life, eventually becoming a lieutenant-general, his fighting days were soon over, and he continued the life work of his father. He founded the Corps of Military Topographers and directed surveys of the Gulf of Finland and the Baltic Sea as well as of land areas. He found time also to serve on numerous commissions and to head various bureaus involved with military affairs, standardization of weights and measures, and evaluation of projects and inventions.

When in 1858 Sophia was just beginning to study higher mathematics, he published his major work in French. This publication was an explanation of the astronomical and geodetic work accomplished in Russia to the year 1855. It included a catalog of 14,500 points in Russia that had precisely been defined under his and his father's supervision. The book long served as the basis for Russian mapmaking.

Today the most interesting aspect of the work of Sophia's grandfather would be his speculations about the true shape of the earth. Postulating that the earth might have three axes, he determined the dimensions of a triaxial earth ellipsoid in an effort to explain significant discrepancies in geodetic and angle measurements. However, this hypothesis was not the solution, from which he concluded that the earth has an irregular shape, a shape that later physicists called a geoid. The problem of the earth's shape and errors in triangulation became acute when men became capable of delivering missiles to hit a target within a circle of small diameter, if only the exact distance between two points on different continents thousands of miles apart could be precisely determined. The electronic computer and earth satellites finally provided solutions that eluded Shubert and others for so long.

iv

GENERAL SHUBERT married Sophia Alexandrovna Rall (1801-1833), a daughter of Baron Alexander A. Rall, banker to the imperial court. They became parents of a son, named confusingly the same as his father, Fedor Fedorovich Shubert (1831-1877), and of two daughters, one being Sophia's mother, Elizabeth Fedorovna Shubert, born about 1820. Elizabeth's sister, Sophie, married Fedor P. Adelung, tutor to Nicholas and Michael, the sons of Tsar Nicholas I. Adelung later headed the classical section of Eastern languages at St. Petersburg University. Their daughter, just Sophia's age and her friend in childhood, later lived in Stüttgart.

In Sophia's day, and for a long time before, the Shubert family occupied what had come to be called the House of Shubert, a large structure located on Line One of Vasilevsky Island, across the Neva, not far from the university and the Academy of Fine Arts. Various aunts and female relations lived there in Sophia's youth. They probably included the sisters of Sophia's maternal grandmother, *née* Rall; one had married O. I. Senkovsky, professor of Arabian, Persian, and Turkish languages but better known for his stories published under the pen name of Baron Brambeus; the other sister married A. P. Briullov, architect for many public buildings and a painter of portraits including one of Sir Walter Scott.

It was at this House of Shubert that Aniuta with her mother, and later also Sophia, would stay while enjoying annual periods of city life away from the rural Palibino atmosphere. Obviously the Germanic Shuberts and their in-laws were rather dull and stodgy, but also intellectual and in an old-fashioned way rather liberal.

V

SOPHIA'S MOTHER was greatly attached to her brother, Fedor Fedorovich, about ten years her junior, who held a civilian post in the War Ministry. Sophia in her autobiography wrote of her own fascination for this uncle; at first it was a child's infatuation for a handsome university graduate, aged twenty-eight, who paid her special attention, a fascination with an embarrassing termination, and later it was only the warm affection that may exist among family members.

In her *Recollections* Sophia wrote: "This uncle, the only son of my deceased grandfather . . . lived permanently in Petersburg, and, in his quality of sole male representative of the Shubert family, he enjoyed the unbounded adoration of all his sisters, and of numerous aunts and cousins, all unmarried spinsters.

"His arrival to visit us in the country was regarded as a real event. I was nine years old when he came to us for the first time. Uncle's coming had been talked about for many weeks in advance. The best room in the house was assigned to him, and mama herself saw to it that the most comfortable furniture was placed in it. The carriage was sent to meet him at the capital of the government, one hundred and fifty versts distant; and in the carriage were placed a fur coat, a fur lap-robe, and a plaid, that uncle might not take cold, as it was late in the autumn.

"All of a sudden, on the eve of the day when uncle was expected, we looked out, and behold, driving up to the porch, came a simple peasant cart, harnessed to three post-horses, regular old nags, and out of it leaped a young man in a light city overcoat, with a leather traveling-bag slung over his shoulder.

" 'Good heavens! Why, it's brother Fedya!' cried mama, as she looked out of the window.

" 'Uncle, uncle has come!' resounded through the whole house, and we all ran out into the ante-chamber to welcome the guest.

" 'Fedya, my poor dear! how could you come with relay horses? Didn't you meet the carriage we sent for you? You must be jolted to pieces,' said mama, in a voice of compassion, as she embraced her brother.

"It appeared that uncle had set out from Petersburg twenty-four hours earlier than he had intended.

" 'Christ be with thee, Liza!' he said, laughing and wiping the drops of ice from his mustache before he kissed his sister. 'I had no idea that you would make such a turmoil over my coming! Why should you send for me? Am I an old woman that I cannot travel one hundred and fifty versts in a post-cart?'

"Uncle spoke in a deep, agreeable, tenor voice, with a rather peculiar lisp. . . . His closely cut chestnut hair framed his head in a thick, velvety mass, like beaver fur; his red cheeks were shining with cold, his brown eyes were warm and merry in their gaze, and a set of large, white teeth peeped out every moment from between his full, brilliantly red lips, surrounded by handsome whiskers.

" 'What a fine, dashing fellow uncle is! He's a dear!' I said to myself, as I gazed rapturously at him."

When introduced to her uncle, who at first confused her with her older sister, he laughingly kissed her. "I felt an involuntary shame and blushed all over at his kiss," she recalled.

She noticed that even her father treated Uncle Fedya with much respect. The more she saw of Uncle Fedya the better she liked him. She noticed the good English material of his short coat, his large well-cared-for hands, with nails like large pink almonds. She never took her eyes from him during the entire dinner, during which he often broke out into merry laughter, and was so absorbed in him, she later confessed, that she even forgot to eat.

He it was who first compared her eyes to gooseberries. It happened that dessert was garnished with a jam containing whole gooseberries. He looked at the berries and then, as she sat intently watching him, he gazed into Sophia's eyes. "You know, Lisa," he said laughingly to his sister, "I was wondering what Sonya's eyes resemble. Now I know. They look as large and as green and as sweet as gooseberries." This embarrassed Sophia, and so he added, "Very beautiful and very green!"

"After dinner," Sophia remembered, "uncle seated himself on the little corner divan in the drawing room and took me on his knee.

" 'Come let's get acquainted, mademoiselle, my niece!,' said he. Uncle began to question me as to what I was studying, what I was reading. Children know themselves, generally, much better than grown people imagine; they know their own strong points and their weak points. Thus, for example, I knew perfectly that I learned my lessons well, and that every one considered me very 'advanced' in my studies for my age. Consequently I was greatly pleased when my uncle took it into his head to question me about it, and I answered all his queries willingly and freely, 'Here's a clever girl! She knows all that already!' he kept repeating every moment.

" 'Uncle, tell me something new!' I entreated him, in my turn.

" 'Well, here goes; only one can't tell fairy tales to such a clever young lady as you,' he said, jestingly.

" 'One must talk to you only of serious things.' So he began to tell me about infusoria, about marine algae, about the formation of coral reefs. Uncle had not been out of the university very long, so that all this information was still fresh in his memory. He narrated very well, and it pleased him that I listened with so much attention, with eyes opened very wide and fixed firmly upon him."

Similar conversations on all kinds of subjects came to be repeated each day during the time after dinner when the parents went off to nap for half an hour. The uncle proposed that the other children listen, too; but Aniuta, freed from the schoolroom, considered herself too grown up for childish "scientific lectures," while brother Fedor, having listened once, preferred to play horse elsewhere. Thus it was that Sophia had Uncle Fedya all to herself for a precious half-hour, the highlight of her day. "I actually adored him; to speak frankly, I will not swear that there was not mingled with this feeling a certain childish falling in love, of which little girls are much more capable than their elders suspect. I felt a certain confusion every time that I had to utter uncle's name, even if only to inquire, 'Is uncle at home?' If any one, observing at dinner that I never took my eyes from him, asked me, 'Evidently you are very fond of your uncle, Sofa?' I blushed up to my ears and made no reply.

"I hardly saw anything of him all day long, as my life was almost entirely separated from the life of the grown-up members of the family. But during the whole time of my lessons, the whole time of my recreation, my constant thought was, 'Won't evening come soon? Shall not I soon be with my uncle?' "

Then one day a snake entered this paradise. Neighboring landowners came early to visit, bringing their daughter, Olga, just Sophia's age, who infrequently spent a day or two at Palibino. Although there was no genuine friendship between them, since their characters and interests were dissimilar, nevertheless Sophia usually rejoiced at her arrival because it meant a holiday from lessons. On this occasion, however, Sophia foresaw that she needed somehow to prevent Olga from being present at the "lecture." So she exacted a promise from Olga, agreeing to do whatever the visitor wished all during the day, if in return Olga would not intrude after dinner. Sophia fulfilled her part of the bargain, taking the secondary role in all kinds of imaginative games.

"After dinner," wrote Sophia, "I kissed papa's and mama's hands as usual, and then pressed close to uncle, and waited to hear what he would say.

" 'Well, little girl, are we to have our chat to-day?' asked uncle, pinching my chin affectionately. I fairly leaped for joy, and, merrily grasping his hand, was preparing to set off with him for our wonted place. But all at once I perceived that faithless Olga was following us.

" 'May I go with you?' she asked, in a voice of entreaty, raising her lovely blue eyes to my uncle.

" 'Of course you can, my dear,' replied my uncle, and looked at her very graciously, evidently admiring her pretty, rosy face.

"I cast a glance of wrathful disapproval on Olga, but it did not confuse her in the least.

" 'But Olga certainly knows nothing about these things. She will not understand anything anyway,' I ventured to remark in an angry voice. But this effort to rid myself of my intrusive friend had no result.

" 'Well, then to-day we will talk of matters in a more simple way, so that they may be interesting to Olga,' said uncle good-naturedly; and taking us both by the hand, he set out with us for the little divan.

"I walked along in sullen silence. This conversation of three, in which uncle was going to talk for Olga, taking into consideration her tastes and her understanding, was not in the least what I wished. It seemed to me that something had been taken from me which belonged to me by right, which was inviolable and precious.

" 'Come, Sofa, climb up on my knee,' said uncle, evidently quite unconscious of my evil frame of mind.

"But I felt so hurt that this proposal did not soften me in the least.

" 'I won't!' I answered angrily, and going off to a corner I sulked.

"Uncle stared at me with astonished, laughing eyes. I do not know whether he understood what a feeling of jealousy was stirring in my soul, and whether he wished to tease me; but he suddenly turned to Olga and said to her, 'Well, if Sonya doesn't wish it, do you wish to sit on my knee?'

"Olga did not force him to repeat this invitation, and before I had recovered myself, before I had succeeded in realizing what was happening, she had taken my place on my uncle's knee. I had not in the least expected this. It had never entered my head that matters would take that dreadful turn. It seemed to me, literally, as if the earth were giving way under my feet.

"I was too astounded to give voice to any protest; all I could do was to stare, with widely opened eyes, at my happy friend; and she, a little confused, but much pleased nevertheless, settled herself on my uncle's knee as if there were nothing the matter. . . .

"I stared and stared at her, and suddenly—I swear that even now I do not know how it happened—something terrible took place. It was exactly as if some one were urging me on. Without stopping to think what I was doing, I suddenly, quite unexpectedly to myself, fastened my teeth in her bare, plump little arm, somewhat above the elbow, and bit her until I drew blood.

"My attack was so sudden, so unforeseen, that for a moment all three of us remained stupefied, and merely stared at each other in silence. Then all at once Olga gave a piercing shriek, and her scream brought us all to ourselves.

"Shame, wild, bitter shame, took possession of me. I fled headlong from the room. 'Hateful, wicked little girl!' my uncle's angry voice called after me.

Sophia fled sobbing to the room of her former nurse, who comforted her and let her remain the rest of the day. Since the governess that day had been free to visit another estate, no punishment resulted. In fact, inasmuch as neither Olga nor the uncle mentioned the incident, no other adults learned of it.

Those after-dinner conversations were never renewed, however. Sophia no longer "adored" her Shubert uncle, who died childless at age forty-six when Sophia was twenty-seven years old.

CHAPTER 7

Early Education

i

SOPHIA'S BROTHER Fedor, in his written recollections, declared that his sister at a very early age pestered her parents with requests to be taught reading because she saw her older sister immersed in books. They kept putting her off, saying she was too young for lessons. Therefore, displaying already that trait of perseverance and determination that guided her through life, she began teaching herself.

At every opportunity Sophia would take the *Moscow Gazette* newspaper and attempt to decipher first the title and then the headlines, asking one person or another what a particular letter was called and then firmly imprinting it in her mind by seeking out similar letters through the text. In this way, little by little, she learned the alphabet and then syllables and individual words until one day she interrupted her father in the reading of his newspaper to say, "Papa, I know what is written there."

"Well, now, Sofa," he exclaimed, "somebody told you because you cannot read."

To his amazement, however, she read syllable by syllable every word he pointed out to her. This accomplishment was remembered in the family as the first indication of her independent mental ability. Not for several more years did her formal education begin.

ii

SOPHIA'S FORMAL education did not in fact begin until she was nearly six. Before that she had only the nurse while the governess had charge only of her sister. That governess was a Frenchwoman, lax in her duties but presumably attractive. The children never learned exactly what happened, but the entire household had been in an uproar

[44]

of rage and tears for days until the woman left. She was replaced by an English woman who accompanied the family into the country.

Once settled at Palibino, the General, having more time at home to observe his children more closely, soon realized that Aniuta was dreadfully spoiled and at the age of twelve also ignorant; and seeing that Sophia was following in her path, he transferred Sophia's nurse to the laundry and put Sophia completely under the governess. He also resolved to get the best tutor available. In an ordinary household of that period the relative ignorance of the daughters might not have been of much concern, for many noblewomen, while accomplished in painting and embroidery and music and well-trained in French, were deficient in written Russian and especially in general knowledge. This would not do, however, for a family with the wide intellectual interests of the Korvin-Krukovskys.

It was just about this time that Dr. Nicholas Pirogov, rector of Kiev University, initiated the long Russian debate over education for women. The General several years earlier had known Pirogov as a military surgeon during the Crimean War, when the Tsar's sister-in-law had asked the surgeon to organize a unit of nuns and laywomen for frontline service. Florence Nightingale served the wounded on the opposite side. From this experience Pirogov perceived the need for better education so that women could fulfill a role corresponding to their human value. He published an article denigrating education that "turned upperclass girls into dolls, dressed up and put on display" for society and marriage. Girls should be "challenged academically as intelligent beings." They should develop independent ideas in order to share men's struggle and thus become better wives and mothers. This argument to strengthen the family provoked reaction from some feminist women but was approved by the Tsar and influenced many Russian parents. The Korvin-Krukovskys would in any event have favored good basic education for their daughters, but what must have swayed the General with respect to Sophia's future was Pirogov's further belief that girls should receive some scientific training. Otherwise perhaps Sophia would not have received the same instruction as a boy under the Polish nobleman who entered into the life at Palibino as a house tutor.

First, however, the role of the strict English governess, Margarita Frantsevna Smith, cannot be overlooked. At age thirty-two she had no beauty whatever but was most capable. Although raised in Russia, she was to the core firmly Anglo-Saxon, steadfast and straightforward in manner, characteristics that permitted her to acquire unusual influence in a household where careless traits were everywhere. Fortunately she was forbidden to inflict corporal punishment. Therefore her usual punishment took two forms. For a minor transgression the child was humiliated before parents and servants by having to go to dinner with a yellow ticket spelling out her misdeed in large letters pinned to her shoulder. For example, the ticket might read: "LAZY." The governess also disapproved of Sophia writing verses, and if she found such, she pinned the paper to Sophia's shoulder and read them aloud mockingly. For something more serious, such as reading in the library from a book that had not previously been approved by the governess, Sophia was sent to her father's study. This room not even her mother entered without permission. In reality the father was not severe; when the children were ill only he could soothe them so gently; but as a military man he believed in backing up the discipline imposed by subordinates, and so he adopted a stern visage for a miscreant Sophia, directing her to stand in a corner. Sometimes, as he went on about his work while wreathed in clouds of pipe smoke, he forgot her presence altogether, or so it seemed to Sophia.

Margarita Frantsevna converted one of the first floor rooms into a proper nursery and set about instilling in the disorderly and careless Russian girls some of the qualities of an English miss. At least she tried. She partially succeeded with Sophia, who nonetheless always remained somewhat careless in dress. With Aniuta she never succeeded at all, really, and at age fifteen Aniuta escaped from the nursery authority altogether by ordering her bed removed to a second floor adult chamber adjoining her mother's. She firmly declared to the family that she would never again accept reprimands from anybody whomsoever. If she thought this included the General she was mistaken.

After announcing to the General that she washed her hands of Aniuta's future conduct, the governess was thereafter free to concentrate all her vigor upon Sophia, entirely isolating the lively girl from her old nurse and other servants of the household and yards and attempting to guard her from the influence of Aniuta.

Sophia's day began at 7:00 A.M., which in winter meant rising by candlelight, with a maid giving her a quick wash in cold water and braiding her hair. Breakfast with the grumpy governess followed in the dining room. Then for an hour and one-half came piano practice in the large upstairs salon, during which the governess beat time on the piano with a stick, sometimes with such maddening persistence that Sophia's shrieks resounded through the rooms. Quite possibly this ordeal accounts for the fact that in later years Sophia, unlike so many mathematicians who turn to music for relaxation, had little taste for music. Although her brother said she lacked an ear for music, she did love to hear her mother play. Following the music lesson it was a relief for Sophia to go downstairs again for her morning session with the tutor until the hour set for lunch with the governess. After a short rest came the only outdoor exercise Sophia received, a sedate walk with the governess through the linden alley or elsewhere, lasting about an hour in winter or somewhat longer in other seasons. Then back to lessons with the tutor or governess until it was time for early dinner. A maid would dress her, if a change was needed, and the braids would be combed out for this meal. When released Sophia might rush upstairs joyously to see her mother, only to find her arrival entirely unnoticed as her mother sat on a divan with one arm about Fedor while chatting gaily with Aniuta. "They are happy without me," Sophia would think, as she made herself inconspicuous. After dinner came a period of freedom and then more studies, followed by evening tea shortly before bedtime. Ordinarily the family saw one another only at dinnertime and teatime. That was the routine of Sophia's normal day.

The governess instructed Sophia in French and English and, being herself Russian Orthodox, also taught religion. She likewise supervised Sophia's diet. During her limited free time Sophia's occupation, if not with a book, usually consisted of simply bouncing a ball from room to room. Obviously Sophia's strict regimen had the approval, or at least not the disapproval, of the General, but he permitted Aniuta, who of course was much older, to exercise outside as she wished and to make pets of young farm animals, including piglets that she carried about in her arms. As part of her nature studies, however, Sophia kept a collection of live butterflies, beetles, and other creepers and crawlers that she had collected on her walks. She also delighted in picking various plants and flowers to identify in botany.

In later years, when her tutor submitted to Sophia his verbose memoirs of her early education under him, giving her permission to delete anything she wished, she eliminated all mention of those hated piano lessons. She also suppressed the tutor's view, although agreeing he was not entirely wrong, that much of the influence of the governess had been harmful. At that time the governess was still alive; upon leaving Palibino she went to stay with the Shuberts in Petersburg, and in her old age, apparently until her death in 1914, she lived in a house owned by the Tsarina and assisted in the latter's charitable work.

On more than one occasion, when Sophia resisted her authority, or when she did not get her way in the household, Margarita Frantsevna threatened to leave, only to be persuaded otherwise. Finally came the day, however, when she threatened once too often. She was not requested to remain.

Sophia was then twelve and described the emotional departure scene. Jacob held the reins of three restive horses hitched to an old coach he considered adequate for a governess the servants disliked, a coach loaded down with a large collection of trunks, boxes, bags, and baskets, all awaiting the journey to the railway station. The entire household assembled in the dining room. "In accordance with the customary ceremony," wrote Sophia, "papa invites all to seat themselves before the journey is begun. The gentry occupy the first row, and the whole of the house servants are collected in a dense group a short distance away, sitting respectfully on the edges of their chairs. Several minutes pass in reverent silence, during which time the sensation of nervous anguish inevitably evoked by every departure and parting involuntarily takes possession of the soul. But now father gives the signal to rise, crosses himself before the ikon, and the others follow his example, and then begin the tears and embraces."

To Sophia the governess seemed suddenly to have grown old; her eyes, which never failed to see a misdeed, now were red and swollen. "For the first time in my life I think that she is to be pitied. She embraces me long and convulsively, with such vehement affection as I never expected from her." Sobbing, Sophia promised to write and already felt an irreparable loss. "I am ashamed, even to the verge of pain, when I remember that during all these last days, even as late as this very morning, a secret joy has seized upon me at the thought of her departure and my impending freedom."

Sophia ran weeping to an upstairs window to watch the coach disappear down the long tree-lined driveway to the road. When her brother mimicked her sobs, he was reprimanded by an old aunt whom neither liked. Sophia rushed off to her own room, only to be comforted by the thought that now nobody could hinder her from being with Aniuta as much as she wished. She ran to find Aniuta, only to discover that now Aniuta looked upon her as a mere child. However, during ensuing days Sophia persisted so lovingly that Aniuta, having no other confidant, began sharing her innermost thoughts and secret dreams with her little sister.

iii

I T W A S clear to Sophia's parents that their rural miss still needed further training to become a proper young lady. Perhaps a governess of different nationality would be successful. Soon a well-recommended Swiss governess came to Palibino. Sophia remembered her as a "sentimental, peace-loving, good-natured old maid," which was fortunate, because, having rid herself, however painfully, of one strict monitor,

Sophia was not about to accept another. At first she displayed the will to rebel, but as soon as the governess gave up trying to have any real influence, they reached a compromise. "Her only demand," Sophia later wrote, "was that I study French with her for two hours every day, memorize long monologues from Racine and Corneille, and in the evening read her two or three pages from the Bible, and besides this to listen to her stories of the prince and princesses that had been her charges before coming to us. In everything else she allowed me almost complete freedom."

iv

DURING THE last three years of her five-year reign in the Korvin-Krukovsky household, the English governess had shared pedagogical responsibility with Joseph Ignatevich Malevich, accredited by Vilensk University as a house tutor, who was diplomatic enough after nearly 20 years of experience to avoid clashing headlong with any governess but who probably had at least a secondary role in her departure. The governess for her part recognized her superior, and although she usually took the opposite side of any household discussion, she realized that Malevich, as the General's card partner, was on a basis of daily intimacy that she did not enjoy. He himself was to spend the rest of his life, except for one brief interruption, under a Korvin-Krukovsky roof.

The tutor was born in 1813 in a small town in the Vitebsk district, the son of a minor Polish noble. At the age of 45 he arrived at Palibino with excellent references, having just spent five years at the Piatnitskoë estate of the General's brother, Simon. There he had prepared the sons for higher education, together with several Tchirikoff children related to Simon's wife. Before that Malevich had tutored the six sons of Simon's neighbor, Ivan Igorovich Semevsky, one of whom became a doctor of Russian history. He had also prepared the son of a famous general to enter the Corps of Pages.

Although Malevich's prior experience had been almost exclusively in preparing boys for military, civil, or scholarly careers, he apparently did not substantially alter his methodology for his new feminine pupils, and in fact he brought to them the mature benefits of his past experience. Since Fedor was then only three and did not begin his studies for several years, and since Aniuta soon became a young lady too dignified and willful for the schoolroom, the tutor's principal efforts were with Sophia from the age of eight to seventeen.

He described her as he first met her in October of 1858 as a girl "of rather solid build, sweet and attractive in appearance, whose eyes showed a receptive intellect and a kind heart." He continued, "In the very first lessons she displayed unusual attention, a quick assimilation . . . a precise completion of assignment, and always a sound knowledge of her lessons."

Once during dinner soon after lessons began, her father asked, "Well, now, Sofa, have you fallen in love with arithmetic?"

"No, papochka," she replied.

"Well, then," interposed Malevich, interpreting the General's interest, "do fall in love with it; learn to love it more than your other studies."

Four months later the General again asked Sophia the same question, to which she dutifully replied, "Yes, papochka, I like to study arithmetic; it gives me great pleasure."

This pleased the General, which may have been the intent of the girl's answer, because it was not for a number of years that Malevich noticed in her any special mathematical ability.

There is no photograph of Malevich at this early period but one taken in later life shows him with the full beard and mustache of the time, both already turned white, his dark hair streaked with gray, a large head, large ears, intelligent-looking face, and with small metal-rimmed glasses supported low on his bold nose. He had especially long and tapering fingers. He was full-shouldered and well-built, with only the suggestion of a paunch, across which looped a heavy gold watch chain.

Malevich used the texts of the best Russian and French pedagogs of the age but adapted their methods to suit his own experience. He distinguished two aspects of education—first and foremost, the development of the pupil's abilities, including the habit of logical thought and the formation of a moral-religious character, and second the teaching of the facts and theories of the various subjects comprising the educational curriculum. He looked upon his pupils as foster children, attempting to maintain with them during free time a relaxed and friendly relationship.

In the classroom he attempted to avoid boring routine without deserting a coherent program stressing application, concentration, analysis, the ability to make comparisons and to proceed from the known to the unknown, to take opposite views, but always to reach reasonable conclusions clearly and simply. However much or little credit Sophia later accorded to Malevich, his approach must have been of inestimable value in her life.

Under him she learned Russian grammar, spelling, penmanship, writing from dictation, writing original compositions, oral declamation, etymology, ancient and modern history, mathematics, and a general knowledge of botany, zoology, mineralogy, and the more important phenomena of nature. Of course these subjects were covered at appropriate times in her development, some together, others with exclusive concentration. Malevich used proverbs, anecdotes, stories, and supplemented texts with current periodicals or by serious discussion among members of the family in which Sophia was encouraged to participate. Usually the General just listened, his expression sometimes amused, sometimes sardonic, sometimes obviously approving, as others became heated in espousing their views. To these almost daily discussions must be ascribed Sophia's unusual ability in later life to converse nimbly or argue convincingly on almost any subject.

In the schoolroom Malevich had a different approach for each subject. Perhaps easiest to summarize as an example would be that for geography. He started with the known and proceeded to the unknown, first the family estate and its village—their nature, extent, and function as an economic unit—and then progressed in ever-widening circles to nearby estates, to the district, the cities, the province, eventually to all of Russia, and then to each country and finally each continent. Study went from streams to oceans, from Palibino's garden and fields to the soils and products of ever larger areas, and by increments from local peoples and customs to those throughout the world. All this was accompanied by the drawing and correcting of many maps on paper and blackboard. Both pupil and teacher took imaginary journeys to the capitals of Europe, observing scenes along the way, and on arrival visiting museums, libraries, and public buildings.

Literature was not begun until Sophia was eleven. Once begun, however, instruction proceeded without interruption from simple fables and tales through psalms, poems, essays, novels, and classical literature. Not only was the material read but also analyzed, evaluated, and appreciated; biographical information about authors complemented the reading. Malevich found in Sophia a definite preference for literature and therefore considered it essential that no interruptions occur to delay her progress. It is no wonder that Sophia later became an accomplished writer and at one time almost abandoned mathematics for the pen. It was in literature, in fact, that Malevich envisioned her future, for in that field, as Jane Austen and George Sand had shown, a woman could become eminent.

Of Sophia's studies in general, Malevich wrote that "the correctness and strength of presented proofs, their order and judgment, and her understanding amazed me, convincing me that my labors had been such that it would have been impossible to expect anything better. It would be necessary to see the 15-year-old girl's sparkling eyes, in which the mind was shining through, gazing into distant space, as if foreseeing there all that could strengthen her understanding of the questions posed by me."

After one classroom session Malevich returned to his room and "thought for a long time about the unusual accomplishments of my talented pupil" and her possible future. What if fate permitted her to get a higher education, "which unfortunately is inaccessible to women in our universities," and then fate deprived her of financial means, so that she had the spur of having to write for a living? "Then, oh, then, I was positive that my talented pupil would occupy the highest place in the literary world."

It should not be overlooked that Malevich was writing in old age, after Sophia had already achieved her initial mathematical success, did have financial problems, and had just turned to literature as a way out; that he was then a beneficiary of the Korvin-Krukovskys; and that her occasional gazing into space during adolescence might have been an escape from boredom into daydreaming.

It may even be that during those dreamy times Sophia was thinking of "Michel," doubtless a pseudonym for a distant Korvin-Krukovsky relation she called her cousin, then staying at Palibino with his widowed mother. Several years older than Sophia, Michel was the first young man with whom she had close contact and as such seems to have had a considerable influence on the development of her immature ideas of love that she carried into young adulthood.

Having been a governess, the youth's mother had been rejected by her aristocratic mother-in-law. Then, when the youth's father, having failed in long and costly efforts to make vodka from wood shavings, died young, the mother spurned the mother-in-law in turn, raising and spoiling the child entirely herself. Despite efforts by successive tutors, Michel had not applied himself in mathematics and could not qualify for university. The widow appealed to the General for advice, with the result that she was invited to spend many months at Palibino and place her son under Malevich. At first the tutor had no success with the spoiled youth until he conceived the successful idea of pitting him against the much younger Sophia so that he would be shamed into accomplishment. Thus, during the last part of Michel's stay, the two young people studied algebra and geometry together.

More importantly, they took long walks and spent much time together outside the classroom. Michel's upbringing had been such that he never had a confidant except his mother; at least he told Sophia that she was his first friend. As he had a good mind and a smattering of knowledge, she was flattered by his confidences and impressed by his intention to achieve fame for the good of the people, preferably in art or law. She was blind to the fact that he supposed he could accomplish this without any real personal effort. His ideas about life, a subject on which Sophia had speculated but had formed no opinions, she found particularly appealing. He was, as she later recalled, an especially shy and pure young man whose manner with her was strictly proper and considerably condescending. It was as though she listened to vaporous soliloquies by a disembodied spirit who described love, of which he was actually as ignorant as she, as some ideal state of blissful but almost suspended animation. He imbued her mind with an impossible idea of human love.

Had the young man been less of a mama's boy, Sophia might have advanced her own emotional maturity, but then such a youth probably would have been less interested in discussing love abstractly with an awkward girl in her early teens than in forming a more intimate acquaintance with one of the maids.

Michel did more than contribute an idealistic idea of interpersonal love. He seems also to have infused in Sophia the idea of voluntary suffering for the sake of the people, a theme that would appear in her later fiction. Actually, earlier during spring cleaning, she had found an old religious book covering the lives of men and women Christian martyrs. This had so captivated her that she wished she had been born in the early days of Christianity. Apparently Michel focused the impressions she gained from that book upon the society of her day.

If one may judge from a photograph, one taken very likely at Palibino by a traveling photographer, Sophia at that time had little of the feminine attractiveness shown in later pictures but rather had the somewhat amorphous features of a developing teenager. She is seen wearing a long-sleeved, round-collared shirtwaist beneath a dress with half-sleeves and a very full floor-length skirt. Over this there is a knee-length schoolgirl apron with shoulder straps. It would appear this was her typical everyday garb, at least until dinnertime when the apron would be removed and sometimes a different dress substituted.

V

TO RETURN to the schoolroom, it may seem strange that Malevich did not detect Sophia's growing interest in mathematics, in which she became the first woman in the world to achieve so high a degree of knowledge. Apparently Malevich was limited in that field himself. Perhaps Sophia's own interest, under the influence of her grandfatherly uncle, had developed somewhat late. Simple arithmetic, on which Malevich had spent two and one-half years, often is uninspiring for the mathematical mind. Fortunately he had stressed logical deduction instead of mere mechanical calculation. With regard to Sophia's further study of mathematics and the attitude of her father on the subject, considerable confusion exists between accounts left by Sophia and by her tutor.

Consider first the tutor's recollections, which he prepared at about the age of seventy-five at the urging of his former pupil, M. I. Semevsky, in whose *Russkaia starina (Russian Antiquity)* they appeared in December of 1890. Malevich wrote that he proceeded from arithmetic to algebra, using the two-volume text of Bourdon, and then introduced Sophia first to plane and then solid geometry. During this period he first perceived her attraction to mathematics and felt, since she was a girl, that he might have progressed too far in this subject to the detriment of other material. Therefore he consulted the General.

As reconstructed by Malevich, the General's reaction was spoken with feeling: "I thank you, thank you from my soul for your efforts with my beloved daughter. I am not concerned but happy that Sophia has grown to love mathematics so much, because I wanted her to love it as much as I. Judging by the success of my nephew, whom I presented to the Naval Corps, I was confident that you would achieve even more with my Sophia. I want you to continue these studies."

About this time, too, it happened that during one lesson in geometry the tutor explained the relationship of the circle to its diameter, and in the following lesson asked her to demonstrate this relationship in a problem. Her solution produced the correct relationship by a different path. While admitting the correctness of her answer, the tutor chided her for seeking a solution in so roundabout a way and asked her to follow his method. This hurt her pride, so that she turned red and began to weep. The tutor cheered her with kind words and put off study for the rest of the day. "Those were the first and last tears of my pupil during lessons in the entire time of my nine-year instruction," he recalled.

When the General heard of his daughter's inventiveness, he exclaimed with pleasure, "Clever, Sofa!"

According to Sophia, however, the General's overall reaction to her study of mathematics was rather different. She claimed that he had decided that as a girl she had progressed far enough in mathematics; therefore, at one period she studied advanced algebra secretly at night by the dim night light, while her governess slept soundly in the same room behind a screen. It was, she related, their nearest neighbor who changed the General's attitude. This neighbor was Nicholas N.

Tyrtov, professor of physics at the Naval Academy, who spent summers on his estate. He one day brought her father a copy of his new physics text. This Sophia attempted to study but in the section on optics encountered trigonometric formulas and references to sines, cosines, and tangents. For a solution to these riddles she turned to Malevich, but as trigonometry didn't enter into his program, he answered that he didn't know what a sine was. "Then," she recalled, "considering the formulas in the book, I attempted to solve them myself, and through a strange coincidence I went by the same path as used historically; that is, in place of the sine I took the chord of an arc. For small angles these quantities almost coincide with one another, and since Tyrtov had used only acute angles, then by my method the answers coincided very well.

"After some time had passed I conversed with the professor about his book. He at first doubted that I could understand it, and to my assertion that I had read it with great interest, said, 'Well, now you are boasting.' But when I explained to him by what manner I had arrived at a solution of a trigonometric formula, then he entirely changed his tone. He went immediately to my father to convince him of the necessity of teaching me in a serious way. Moreover, he compared me with Pascal. So after a certain period of indecision, my father agreed to hire Strannoliubsky as my teacher."

It is possible, in order to spare Malevich's feelings, that he was not informed of Sophia's first lessons under Strannoliubsky during a visit to Petersburg early in 1866, because upon her return to the country her studies under Malevich apparently continued at a lower mathematical level. For all practical purposes his time as tutor to Sophia ended in September 1867 when (as the aftermath of the Dostoevsky affair, to be discussed later) the dispirited condition of Aniuta caused the mother to take both daughters to spend the winter at Montreux on Lake Leman in Switzerland.

En route they paused in Stuttgart to visit Adelung relatives. There Sophia was presented to Queen Olga von Wurttemberg, daughter of Tsar Nicholas. The rural miss kissed the queen on the lips instead of the hand and was afterward teased for this blunder. The incident doubtless convinced the mother that she had been wrong in exposing only Aniuta to the social life of Petersburg. Sophia's cousin with the same first name observed that Sophia was somewhat uncomfortable in a fashionable dress with a train.

From Switzerland in December Sophia wrote asking her father to join them for Christmas and to bring along Malevich with his mathematical books. It was not, however, until late February of 1867 that the father and son and tutor joined the others. Because of the delay in Malevich's arrival, Sophia had bought herself a microscope to look at blood corpuscles and other things as part of her self-study of natural science. She also had made considerable progress under a native tutor in improving her German. She had also made several friends. So she had little time for mathematics when Malevich did arrive.

One of Sophia's future friends, Elizabeth Fedorovna Litvinova, who would first meet the family six years later in Zurich, wrote a short paperback biography about Sophia. In it she described Sophia's parents in words appropriate here. After describing the parents in character and physical detail, much as others saw them, she added an interesting metaphorical comparison: "In one word, the wife gave the impression of a birch grove, lightened by the sun; the husband of a sleepy forest into which it was frightening to look." Yet she also added that the General joined with wit and laughter into conversations with her and Sophia. She felt that Sophia was really quite close to her father, despite her later statements, and also that she was rather like him in concentration of thought, depth of feeling, and strength of passion, but like her mother in her sweet face and "pleasant soft attitude toward everyone."

Early in 1867 Sophia wrote her Stuttgart cousin a letter that the latter showed to a graphologist. He noted a talent for mathematics and a misleading character; one's first impression on meeting her would be of a warm and open and spontaneous nature, but on further acquaintance she would turn into a sphinx whom nobody could understand. Obviously Sophia von Adelung agreed with this analysis, which was not without some measure of truth.

Young Fedor soon found life in Switzerland boring, and the General agreed, and so in the middle of March the family moved on to the waters and the gambling of Baden-Baden in the Black Forest, and then on to visit briefly again the Adelungs in Stuttgart.

Sophia Adelung, Sophia's cousin, observed the latter's body movements at this time, and for the rest of her life, to be rapid; her talk so spontaneous among persons she knew that she often talked like a waterfall, sometimes so fast that she stumbled over words, and that although always shy in the presence of strangers, once she felt at ease she usually took over the conversation. Adelung noted further, in an article written much later, that her cousin had an "unbelievably versatile nature and grasped at everything that appealed to her fantasy, her emotions, or her intelligence—all three aspects being developed equally, enthusiastically, and passionately." At the same time, both Sophia and her sister were very self-centered. For ideals or humanity Sophia would go through fire, but to everyday life with its obligations of love for others she was indifferent. She knew how to appear childlike and charming and modest, so that few persons penetrated to the person beneath. "During the visit," Adelung further recalled, "she showed a strong will and a desire for her own way even in little things. She seldom wanted what others wanted." When Adelung proposed a walk, Sophia stayed at home; when the cousin proposed some indoor activity, Sophia wanted to go out. "Her winning and flexible personality could change into inflexible willfulness."

After a few days in Stuttgart the Korvin-Krukovsky family, with real homesickness, headed back for Russia and Palibino.

Upon returning to the country the tutor recommended that Fedor, then about fourteen and somewhat feckless, should be enrolled in the fourth level (seventh grade) of a good gymnasium school in Petersburg. In his view Fedor was too much under the feminine influence of his mother, his sisters, and the Swiss governess and needed masculine supervision. Not willing to part with the boy, the General at first refused but soon came around to the wisdom of the suggestion. Therefore at the beginning of 1868 Fedor was enrolled in Petersburg, looking toward his degree in mathematics ten years later.

What Sophia studied under Malevich from April to the end of 1867 is uncertain. Apparently she had already progressed as far in mathematics as she was to go under him. At any rate, it was opportune for her to go to Petersburg when the entire family transferred there to enroll Fedor. It was explained to Malevich that it was time to introduce Sophia to Petersburg society. He therefore went to live for several years with Evreinov, at that time the Nevel district marshal of nobility. When in 1871 Malevich retired as a house tutor from the Ministry of Public Instruction, the General invited him to live again at Palibino, where he remained until the General's death in 1875. Thereafter he lived in retirement at the Piatnitskoë estate of the General's brother, Simon. He did not remain entirely inactive, however, but for a time at about the age of eighty had as pupils the landowner's grandson, Constantine, and young niece, Alexandra.

It was at Piatnitskoë that Malevich wrote his previously mentioned recollections covering the years Sophia spent under him. Upon completing the first draft he would write to Sophia in Stockholm, and she would reply that she felt reluctant to be the subject of such a work. Malevich nevertheless persisted and sent her his manuscript, with permission to change or delete as she wished. After long delay she returned it, seemingly without comment, having made several deletions of a personal nature involving others.

Malevich was deeply hurt by the reference later in Sophia's *Recol-*

lections to his teaching, which she said was "so long ago that now I do not recall his lessons at all; they remain with me as a dark memory." The old tutor commented in a letter to Semevsky, "This strange sally for a boast casts a strange shadow on the bright personality, up to this time, of an unusual mathematician." Later Sophia made substantially the same statement in a talk before Petersburg students, except that she added: "Without question, however, his lessons influenced me greatly and had an important part in my development."

Sophia's minimizing of Malevich's teaching is inexplicable unless understood not as a "sally" or a "boast" but as clearly a snub. To that date in 1890, first as tutor and then for nineteen years in comfortable retirement, Malevich had been living in one Korvin-Krukovsky house or another for thirty-five years. It was unbecoming of him, especially in view of Sophia's expressed preference to the contrary, to discuss in print the family on whose bounty he lived. Moreover, his self-congratulatory claims to a portion of her fame were presented in a verbose, ill-organized, and pedantic manner that must have annoyed her considerably.

One final word about Malevich. Certainly he was a dedicated teacher and quite naturally proud of the progress of all his pupils. He used the best texts and methodology of his day. Nevertheless, between the theoretical and the actual always falls the shadow, so that while doubtless a superior house tutor, he surely was not quite the paragon he seems in old age to have imagined himself to have been.

CHAPTER 8

Two Sisters

i

BECAUSE SOPHIA'S education, almost to the time of her marriage, formed the solid basis of her later progress, this early period has been covered with little interruption. During those same years other important events were of course occurring in her life at Palibino and Petersburg, events involving Sophia alone as she encountered new ideas and happenings, as she experienced the stirrings of sex; and also events involving Aniuta and which, because of Sophia's renewed intimacy with Aniuta, drew the younger sister into participation in many of Aniuta's views and actions. Insofar as possible this period will be considered chronologically, although of course some situations overlapped or coincided. Sophia herself in later years was vague and sometimes contradictory about events when she was young, because she sought to obscure the date of her birth and the sequence of datable events in her life in order to appear younger by three or four years.

The years between 1860 and 1870 were years in Russia of conflict, not only between classes but between generations. This period, during which occurred the prolonged Polish uprising initiated by students and its violent suppression, in some ways compares with the student unrest and divisiveness in the United States during the Vietnam War. In the educated nobility many children quarreled with parents over abstract questions—such as the existence of the soul and Darwin's evolutionary views—to the point where some young people left the parental roof, while others were disowned and forced to leave.

Rumors circulated of daughters running off to Europe or to join the nihilists in Petersburg. In the Palibino area it was widely believed that a large community of runaways had been established in the capital where both sexes lived together. One had only to get there to be accepted and cared for communally. That was an exaggeration, but a commune of both sexes did actually exist for several years on Znamen-skaya Street. Most nihilist activity, however, centered in various groups, mostly male university students or graduates. The groups, which were fragmented according to many varying views on scientific and political topics, met together to discuss questions of the day. Insofar as possible they published their views in various organs or spread them through underground leaflets or periodicals.

ii

CERTAIN OF these new views Aniuta learned from Alexie, son of Father Philip, the Palibino village priest. This happened about 1860 or 1861 when she was about seventeen and Sophia about eleven years of age. As a mildly progressive family the Korvin-Krukovskys subscribed to *Revue des Deux Mondes* of France, the *Athenaeum* of England, *Russkii vestnik* (*The Russian Messenger*), and even Dostoevsky's short-lived *Epokha* (*The Epoch*). But Alexie, home from the university on his first vacation, provided Aniuta with books she could not otherwise have obtained, as well as access to issues of *Sovremennik* (*The Contemporary*) and *Russkoe slovo* (*The Russian Word*), the first being the organ of the revolutionary democrats, the second that of the liberal intelligentsia and nihilists of several types. He even had a copy of Alexander Ivanovich Herzen's proscribed *Kolokol* (*The Bell*), an accusatory biweekly published in London and smuggled into Russia despite all attempts to stop it.

The ideas of Herzen soon would have an important influence, at second hand, upon Sophia, especially since Herzen supported the Polish rebellion that she so ardently favored. Born in 1812, the illegitimate son of a Russian nobleman, Herzen was Russia's first important socialist. He came to believe that mid-century reforms and revolutionary movements only proved the moral decline of European society. The avarice of landowners was no worse than the envy of those wishing to take over. If society were overturned the new masters would soon become as arrogant as those they supplanted. He believed in a federalist system for a primarily agrarian Russia with regional self-government and many cooperative landowners. Peasant communes would be abolished, except for a few as charitable centers for peasants who could not otherwise fit into society. For the first half of its ten-year life from 1857 to 1867, *The Bell* was the most influential publication in Russia and helped prepare the ruling class for the emancipation of serfs.

Such were some of the ideas introduced to Palibino by the priest's son. Aniuta took long walks with the young man, accepting some of the ideas he propounded, such as the injustice of the social system, and rejecting others, such as that men were descended from monkeys and had no souls. Of course Alexie had quarreled with his own father, who on one occasion considered him possessed by the devil and sprinkled him with holy water. Not surprisingly when the priest's son called upon the General as though upon an equal, he was turned away by Ilia.

That rejection raised Aniuta's wrath. Thereafter she took every occasion to be with the young man, who with his own eyes had seen such idols of Russian youth as the liberal philosopher, Nicholas Chernyshevsky, and the critic-poet, Nicholas Dobroliubov, one of whose poems Aniuta kept on her desk for inspiration. The association with Alexie ended, however, when he had to return to university. Actually, that lank and awkward and uncouth individual was not the shining knight of whom she had been dreaming in her Palibino tower, where she had cleaned out a little room to be her inviolate retreat. Nevertheless, his ideas had created in her a determination to go to a medical-surgical school in Petersburg, an objective supplanting her earlier plan to become an actress. She argued with her father that just because he was obliged to live in the country was no reason she should be denied the pleasures of city life. Quite simply, she wanted freedom to be involved with young people in the student ferment of the day.

From this desire an angry exchange with her father soon developed, until finally he shouted at her words to this effect: "If you don't understand that it is the duty of every respectable girl to live with her parents until she marries, then I won't argue further with such a stupid girl."

For a long time afterward open discord reigned in the household. Family life became divisive and soon affected Sophia, whose English governess used every stratagem and punishment to keep Sophia away from her sister except at the principal meals, which were often eaten in hostile silence. Sophia's quarrels with the governess soon began occurring almost daily and, as mentioned earlier, eventually led to the departure of the governess. After that the sisters became inseparable.

Meanwhile, even the servants and peasants had been scandalized by Aniuta's open association with the priest's son and her subsequent behavior. Partly this was because, in the normal course of events, Father Philip's son would have married into an ecclesiastical family, been ordained, and then succeeded his father as their Palibino priest. Among the peasants, and even by fringe members of her own family, it was suspected that Aniuta might run away to marry Alexie. That thought can hardly even have crossed her mind. Nevertheless, servant gossip had spread.

Aniuta, inspired by her new ideas, for the first time became interested in learning. She used her allowance to send for boxes of books instead of the latest fashions in dress. To economize and to express her new seriousness, she wore drab dresses with plain white collars; and instead of dressing her blond hair becomingly, she merely gathered it straight back into a net or let it hang in two heavy waist-long braids.

While visiting Palibino in June of 1862, Elizabeth's sister, Sophia Fedorovna von Adelung, wrote to her daughter, the other young Sophia: "I need not speak of the pleasure of visiting here with Lisa and her charming children—that you can imagine; even Aniuta whose faults I have previously mentioned, faults in my mind quite substantial, doesn't interrupt the peace and harmony. Aniuta appears only at table. The remaining time she spends in her room where she studies Aristotle and Leibnitz and fills whole pages with excerpts and discourses. She never joins anyone with her handiwork, never takes part in walks, and only in the evening, when the others are at the card table, does she at times, absorbed in her philosophical reflections, walk through the drawing room with hurried steps.

"In my view it is inexcusable that Lisa has allowed her daughter to choose such a false and dangerous course and unforgivable that she does not even now take measures to guide her on a different path."

The writer went on to mention Aniuta's egotism, her lack of feeling for others, and her great indifference. However, she added, "With all this, she is polite, wise, extremely well-informed, and lively; I understand that the neighbors, people considerably beneath her, are blind to her deficiencies and consider her an outstanding personality."

Then Sophia Fedorovna went on about 12-year-old Sophia: "As to my favorite Sofinka, she has a completely opposite character. Possessing a very warm heart and being very sensitive, she attaches great importance to love and success . . . she is very generous with those attentions and kindnesses that Aniuta called 'Chinese ceremonies.' One observes in her a clearly defined inclination toward pride and ambition; but with good guidance these undoubtedly serious defects can become even attractive. With her warmth and gentleness she has completely conquered my heart.

"Despite the fact that outwardly she has changed greatly, there has remained with her that deep gaze that always surprised me; her beautiful, moist, and at times brilliant eyes are expressive and eloquent to such an extent that the eyes alone would be enough to distinguish her as beautiful, even if all her facial features were insignificant. At the present time she is in a most unfavorable transitory period: her face has become long, her nose very large. But this does not prevent her from being charming, with intelligent, lively features, dark complexion, and dimple in her chin. Sofa gives promise of becoming a young woman beautiful enough to arouse general attention in society, if only Lisa will take her out."

Soon after her aunt's departure Aniuta grew weary of her self-imposed isolation. She no longer rode her horse Frida, accompanied by the coachman. She didn't enjoy rowing on the lake, or walking, or gathering mushrooms. So she found an outlet, under the spur of her new ideas, by teaching in the school for peasant children that had been established on the estate by her mother. Not only had the mother built the school but also a dormitory, so that children from distant villages could attend class during severe winter weather. Since there were few children's books available in Russian, the mother translated some from German and also taught at the school herself. Later Sophia would help at the school and doubtless from this experience derived her keen interest in education for girls. Aniuta, besides teaching, also talked to peasant women about their problems and dispensed advice and medicine from the little clinic the family maintained. By her attentions Aniuta regained the respect of the peasants.

iii

AT THIS point the tutor, Malevich, conceived the idea of a double advantage possibly resulting from his introduction into the household of a young man, a former pupil, mildly liberal, who needed a wife from a well-to-do family and who could counteract the nihilist influences from the priest's son. With the approval of the family he invited Michael Ivanovich Semevsky to stay at Palibino. He was one of six sons of a nearby landowner. Late in 1862 Semevsky spent some days at Palibino, probably over the Christmas holidays, and obviously wished to marry Aniuta. His lyrical description of her and of Palibino, published years later when he became editor-publisher of *Russian Antiquity*, has already been cited.

Seven years older than Aniuta, Semevsky had left the army to enter journalism, a calling not considered by the General to be suitable for a nobleman. Something about that army resignation also alerted the General. As one of many sons, moreover, Semevsky had no money and no estate. This did not endear him to the General, who always considered Aniuta worthy of a brilliant marriage. It appears that Aniuta's parents realized that she, while not in love, felt inclined to accept Semevsky's proposal merely to escape. Just before the new year

Semevsky went home with neither the General's permission to marry nor Aniuta's clear refusal.

The first week in January of 1863 the family, according to Elizabeth's diary, from which most events in connection with Semevsky are taken, went to Toropets, probably to the house of the General's widowed sister, Marfa Vasilevna, and her children Alexander, Sergei, and Anna. In Toropets Aniuta danced with Semevsky at several balls, at one of which he became involved in some unpleasantness with older nobles present for which he refused to apologize. Apparently this was rather insignificant but mitigated against him socially. He also called several times on Aniuta. In view of the General's opposition to the match, all this produced recriminations that only caused headstrong Aniuta to defy her father. However, she herself had actually been doubtful and had made inquiry about Semevsky from a friend, L. Miliutina, daughter of the war minister, Baron D. A. Miliutin. Back again at Palibino, Elizabeth on January 21 recorded that Aniuta had received a reply "with very unfavorable news about her hero." Elizabeth also had a letter from her brother "with details about Semevsky not good at all." Still, Aniuta kept her suitor dangling.

The General conveyed the news from the inquiries to Malevich, requesting him to do what Aniuta herself refused to do—namely, to send his candidate a definite refusal. This the tutor refused to do, and following an argument that lasted far into the night, he resigned his position. Two days later, however, without agreeing to write, he withdrew his resignation.

Aniuta and Semevsky met again at a wedding. But later, one day in late February, she was in her room and entirely unaware of his arrival at Palibino. He called to see the General and was informed of the unfavorable reports, although not of their sources. Several days later Semevsky departed the country for Petersburg, Malevich having gone to bid goodby to his "foster child," as Elizabeth characterized Semevsky. Aniuta's cousin Alexander had refused to be a secret go-between in Semevsky's quest for Aniuta's hand, and so the romance ended.

As regards Semevsky's future, apart from considerations of character, Malevich had a better assessment of his capabilities than Aniuta's parents, for Semevsky became financially successful in journalism, married about nine years later, and advanced to the civilian rank of privy councilor, which in the Table of Ranks was only one grade below the military rank attained by the General.

iv

RUSSIAN SOCIETY at about this time was split over persecution of the Poles, and Sophia became emotionally involved. The Polish situation, festering since students in 1861 reacted against Russian oppression, erupted in a general uprising in January of 1863. Earlier the unrest had spread also to Lithuania, which had once been connected with Poland and earlier had ruled over parts of western Russia, including the area in which lay Palibino. Guerrillas therefore were led by sons of nobles living not only in Poland and Lithuania proper but even from the Russian area of Vitebsk where many landowners were sympathetic and some were of Polish or Lithuanian origin.

In January of 1863 nobles of Polish persuasion in Vitebsk had, by their absence, prevented the election of a new provincial Marshal of Nobility. To fill this post, it would appear from Elizabeth's diary, the new Vitebsk governor appointed General Korvin-Krukovsky to be leader of the nobles. It is unclear whether he had any special duties in addition to those ordinarily assumed by the Marshal of Nobility. In any event, it put him, as Elizabeth recorded, in an extremely difficult position.

The insurrection was harshly put down. Many Polish and Lithuanian nobles lost their lands, which were distributed to peasants, or were awarded to military leaders of the worst type (worst, because many other Russian officers had resigned their commissions rather than fight against Poles). Other lands were auctioned off to rich speculators of the merchant class. Young nobles who survived the hostilities emigrated or were sent into exile. On those Lithuanian estates not confiscated a ten percent fine was levied. In Poland the Russian language supplanted Polish as the language of instruction, Roman Catholic churches were seized, press censorship became rigid, and by 1885 the Polish government had been entirely reorganized along Russian lines. A niece of the General had married into the Uraneffs, one of whose members, appointed to the highest Polish court, helped revise Poland's entire legal system.

For some years the Polish problem affected the Korvin-Krukovskys —the General socially and politically, his daughters by eliminating eligible suitors. As marshal, the General was in a very exposed position. Servants or former serfs with a grudge might have reported to authorities any evidence of Polish sympathy. Additionally the family had come originally from Dvinsk, in that part of Lithuania later called Latvia. The tutor definitely was Polish and partisan; often, in the privacy of the library, he apparently told Sophia stories about "our deeply beloved mother," as he called Poland. The General secretly favored the oppressed people but, being a trained military man, considered their cause hopeless from the first. For several years this Polish uprising was the subject of heated but discreet conversation in the household.

Sophia later wrote "Recollections of the Polish Uprising," a sketch that had to be left out when the foreign-printed book was eventually allowed to be reprinted in imperial Russia. Very likely the material of the sketch had originally been intended as a chapter in her *Recollections* but had not been used, being obviously compromising, and had been altered to a Lithuanian setting and enhanced dramatically. In the sketch she mixed fact and probably fiction involving her family. Certainly all of her fiction and sketches have a strong autobiographical content, and this sketch refers to all the members of her family as well as to the tutor and the governess. Party guests, the boorish Russian military commander, and the young Polish noblemen are drawn as actual people. Only the strings of the narrative are too neatly tied together to be entirely straight reporting. Certainly Sophia's sympathy was always strong for the insurrectionists; later in Paris she had Polish exiles as close friends.

Supposedly, during the insurrection period, in the closed library after regular study hours, Sophia learned Polish from Malevich. Possibly this is true. As she was adept in languages, it would not have been difficult to master a language having similarities with Russian. Obviously, if she learned Polish, Malevich would not have mentioned so prejudicial a fact in his account of her education.

In the sketch Sophia relates the visits of a young Polish nobleman from Lithuania, supposedly an ex-suitor of Aniuta's, who soon became caught up in the Polish situation. Sophia, as a trusted confidant who understood Polish, supposedly was the only other person allowed to be present during the young man's discourses with Malevich. For her he was a romantic hero, who trusted her with his very life, and who eventually joined the guerrillas and was never heard from again.

To understand how problems in Lithuania could affect social intercourse at Palibino, it is necessary to understand that, in a land of vast distances and large estates, the term "neighbor" had an extended meaning. As Sophia explained in her sketch: "If you leave home in the morning in a good troika and by zealously prodding the horses reach another landlord before that day's twilight, then both consider themselves neighbors and as such obligated to congratulate one another, wishing happiness and good fortune, on all names' days and other festive family occasions. On such days invitations are not sent out; friends and neighbors must themselves remember. Only the closest neighbors would return home the same day, while the greater number would spend the night or even two nights."

Since the family never knew how many guests to expect, sleeping arrangements were very informal. With the exception of the large living and dining rooms, all the many other rooms became bedrooms.

The host family squeezed into two rooms, vacating their usual places so that the oldest and most honored visitors could have beds. For other adults temporary beds were erected. Young girls pressed into one large room to giggle until dawn while reclining on divans and chairs. Young men slept on straw mattresses on the floor, wherever there was room. Such inconveniences were expected by guests. As many as twenty noblemen with their families, except for young children who remained at home, might be accommodated in this way.

Obviously such get-togethers, at which plays or "living-pictures" might be staged or fireworks displayed, and at which dancing in the ballroom always continued long into the morning hours, afforded young men and women the occasion to form friendships, fall in love, sometimes to have their engagements announced. Since many Korvin-Krukovsky neighbors lived in the area where young men either were away fighting or had left the area entirely, this, over a critical period of years for Aniuta, and later for Sophia, severely reduced the number of possible suitors.

In June of 1864, having partly in mind the Polish troubles, Elizabeth confided in her diary: "What a hard year has passed; how much misfortune threatened us, how many disappointments, how many unfulfilled desires for me. Now we live, it seems, peacefully and happily. The life of a wealthy landlord on a good estate surrounded by dear children—what else, it would seem, is needed for earthly happiness? But in the soul of everyone is its own bitter thought poisoning this material happiness. Aniuta is weary, wants the unknown, those to her obscure delights of life. Looking at her, although I do not approve of her views on life, I still understand the dreams and desires of youth that cost me so much!"

CHAPTER 9

The Dostoevsky Affair

i

To occupy her days in her tower room and to provide an outlet for her ideas, Aniuta turned secretly to writing. Finally one day in early 1864 she called Sophia into her room to disclose her great secret. From a bureau drawer she withdrew an envelope with a red seal bearing the name *The Epoch* and addressed to the housekeeper, who was devoted to her. Inside was a second envelope directed to Aniuta, from which she extracted a letter reading as follows:

"My dear Madam Anna Vasilevna!

"Your letter full of such kind and sincere confidence in me interested me so much that I immediately began reading the story you sent me.

"I must confess that I began reading not without a secret fear, for to editors of journals often falls the sad duty of disillusioning beginning writers who send us their first literary efforts for evaluation. But as I read, my fear was dissipated, and I more and more came under the enchantment of that youthful immediacy, that sincerity and warmth of feeling, with which your story is penetrated.

"And these are the qualities that work as a bribe for you (for your composition) so that I'm afraid that I'm perhaps under their influence; therefore I dare not answer categorically and impartially the question you put to me: 'Will I with time become a great writer?'

"One thing I can say to you: your story will be printed by me (and with great pleasure) in the future No. 25 of my journal; as to your question, I advise you: write and work; time will show the rest. [Actually the story appeared in the next issue for August 1864.]

"I won't conceal from you—there is much in your story that is unfinished, much that is naive; there are (occasions) even, forgive my frankness, of sins against Russian grammar. But all these are defects which with effort you can overcome; the general impression is most favorable.

"Therefore, I repeat, write and write. I shall be happy sincerely if you find an opportunity to write me more about yourself; tell me your age and what are the circumstances of your life. Knowing this is important for a correct evaluation of your talent.

"Devoted to you, F.D."

The initials were those of Fedor Dostoevsky. Thus began a lifelong relationship between the two sisters and the great novelist.

Although at the age of fourteen Sophia had read nothing by Dostoevsky, she gratified Aniuta by being suitably impressed. She had heard disputes between Aniuta and her father about the merits of the author's work. Of course the acceptance of her story overjoyed Aniuta, who was positively enraptured some weeks later when *The Epoch* arrived with its table of contents listing " 'The Dream,' a novel by Yu.O------v." Aniuta had chosen Yury Obryelov as her pseudonym. Predictably the story concerned a heroine very much like Aniuta, who one day meets a young student, acts like a proper lady, loses him, has a dream that impels her to run away and seek him out, only to find him dead; she returns home to sorrow over her wasted youth and dies a lingering death.

Aniuta wasted no time in writing and submitting another story. It concerned a young man reared by his uncle, a monk in a monastery. This character, Michael, had some resemblance to the later Alyosha in *The Brothers Karamazov* (1880), as Dostoevsky years later admitted to Aniuta to be true, while disclaiming any direct influence unless unconsciously on his part. Relatives of Sophia always believed that in *The Idiot* (1869) Dostoevsky based the character of Alexandra on Sophia, that of Aglia on Aniuta, and that of Prince Mishkin on himself. That Aniuta and Dostoevsky were character prototypes would appear to be correct, but Alexandra could have been any strong-willed young woman.

When the letter of acceptance for Aniuta's second story arrived at Palibino, the postbag reached the General's desk before undergoing a preliminary examination. Seeing a letter from *The Epoch* addressed to the housekeeper, the General was alerted and sent for her to open it in his presence. Then for certain the fat was on the fire. Worst of all, the letter contained about 300 roubles in payment for the two stories. That his daughter had not only engaged in secret correspondence with a stranger—a disgraced nobleman once sentenced to be shot for political activity but exiled instead to Siberia for five years and then required to serve in the ranks as a common soldier for four more years—but actually had received money from him, struck the General as so disgraceful that he became ill. To compound the situation, as a sufferer from heart trouble he had been warned to avoid all emotional situations.

It happened that the letter arrived on September 5 (old style), 1864, St. Elizabeth's Day on the liturgical calendar and therefore his wife's name's day. Such a day always was observed in Russia and particularly Elizabeth's in the Korvin-Krukovsky family. Therefore the house was full of guests. The festival dinner having taken place three hours earlier, the upstairs ballroom was ablaze with candles; and the guests, having rested, were dressed for the occasion. The colonel and officers of a regiment stationed nearby had also come to honor the General's wife and had brought along the regimental band. Aniuta and other young women in tarletan and crinoline preened before mirrors; young men drew on their white gloves; musicians in an adjoining room awaited their signal for the opening quadrille. Only the General's appearance was awaited for festivities to begin.

Word came to Elizabeth, however, "His Excellency is ill and begs you to come to his study."

Half an hour elapsed before Elizabeth returned to explain to guests that her husband was ill but that the dancing should proceed. She informed Aniuta of the trouble and the need to avoid gossip. Acting therefore as though nothing had happened, mother and daughter danced with the others until nearly dawn. Sophia was too young for dancing and in fact did not for some years learn to dance.

Not until nearly noon the next day, when the last guests had departed, did the explosive confrontation between father and daughter take place. The valet listened to everything, impatient to spread the latest scandal among the servants. Very soon a distorted version spread through the countryside, reducing Aniuta's reputation to a new low. Although she was not without at least some concern for her father's health, efforts within the household to smooth out the situation were only partly successful, because Aniuta refused to give up her great career as an author.

Women writers, it should be understood, were in the General's view, of the demimonde. Had he not as a young officer sought the favor of a beautiful Russian poet, Evdokia Petrovna Sushkova, whose life when he later saw her in Paris had become a scandal, and was not George Sand leading a notorious life? This explains the General's terminating remark to Aniuta during their confrontation, "Now you're selling your stories; who knows if the time will come when you sell yourself."

Then occurred a process that Sophia called a re-education of the elders, first of the mother and then partly through her of the father.

[70]

After about a week the General consented to hear Aniuta read her story aloud, listened in complete silence, and then left the room without a word. But that evening when Aniuta appeared at the dinner table, he treated her with tender kindness. Thus father and daughter were reconciled. The housekeeper, who had been dismissed because of her complicity, returned again to her position. The General even agreed that Aniuta could correspond with Dostoevsky, on condition that she show him the letters, and he promised to meet the author when next he visited Petersburg.

In former years Aniuta and her mother had sometimes gone to Petersburg during the winter for six-week visits with the Shuberts, visits not very satisfactory to Aniuta because they terminated just as she got into the swing of things. Her mother no longer had a large circle of urban friends, and the Shuberts only moved in tiresome academic circles. Thus the only high points for Aniuta were several visits to theatres, a small evening party in her honor, and perhaps a ball at the Club of the Nobility. During such short visits no suitable opportunities for marriage had time to develop.

The pending visit, however, Aniuta awaited eagerly. To afford her more time in society the visit was to be longer than usual. More important to her, she would meet Dostoevsky. For the first time Sophia was permitted to go along as an emerging young woman. Mother and daughters made the first part of the journey with their own horses through sixty versts (forty miles) of pine forests, the second leg of 200 versts with post horses, and the final leg lasting twenty-four hours on the Moscow to Petersburg railroad. They arrived in Petersburg in early 1865, probably in February.

ii

THE GENERAL'S last instructions to his wife were that she must certainly be present when Aniuta received Dostoevsky. "Remember," cautioned the General, "he is not a man of our society. . . . You must be extremely cautious with him."

That the first meeting was spoiled by the presence of her mother, two aunts, and Sophia made Aniuta furious. The author reacted rudely to all attempts at polite conversation, replying in monosyllables, and on departure shook hands with nobody. He was unimpressive in appearance, with thin reddish hair and a habit of biting his lips in a manner to distort his face.

Five days later, however, doubtless by secret arrangement, Dostoevsky came again when only Aniuta and her sister were at home. The ice thawed immediately. According to Sophia, "Fedor Mikhailovich took

Aniuta by the hand; they sat down side by side on the divan, and immediately began to talk like old and intimate friends." They spoke hastily, interrupted on another, jested and laughed.

"I sat there, taking no part in the conversation," Sophia recalled, "with my eyes fixed immovably on Fedor Mikhailovich, drinking in eagerly all that he said. He seemed to me now quite another man, quite young and very simple, amiable, and clever. 'He can't be forty-three already,' I thought. . . . 'One can treat him just like a comrade.' And then I felt that he had become indescribably dear and near to me." Sophia was then fifteen years of age.

Sophia continued in her *Recollections*:

" 'What a splendid little sister you have!' said Dostoevsky all at once, quite unexpectedly, although a minute previously he had been talking to Aniuta of something entirely different, and seemed to be paying no attention to me.

"I flushed all over with joy, and my heart was filled with gratitude to my sister when in reply to this remark, she began to relate to Fedor Mikhailovich what a good, clever little girl I was; and how I was the only member of the family who sympathized with her. She grew animated, praised me, and invented unheard of merits in me. In conclusion she even confided that I wrote verses—'Really, really, not bad at all for her age!' And despite my feeble protest, she ran out and brought a thick copybook of my rhymes, of which Fedor Mikhailovich immediately read two or three fragments, smiling the while, and which he praised.

"My sister beamed with satisfaction. Heavens! how I loved her at that moment! It seemed to me that I would give my life for these two dear people.

"Three hours passed unperceived. All at once the bell rang in the vestibule. It was mama returning from the bazaar. Not knowing that Dostoevsky was with us, she entered the room with her bonnet on, all laden down with packages, and excusing herself for being a little late for dinner.

"On seeing Fedor Mikhailovich thus at his ease alone with us, she was dreadfully startled and even alarmed at first. 'What would Vasily Vasilevich say to this?' was her first thought. But we threw ourselves on her neck; and seeing us so happy and beaming, she thawed also, and ended by inviting Fedor Mikhailovich to dine with us informally.

"From that day forth he became an entirely different man when he was in our house; and in view of the fact that our stay in Petersburg was not to be long, he began to come to us very frequently—three or four times a week.

THE DOSTOEVSKY AFFAIR

"It was especially pleasant when he came in the evening, and when there were no other visitors. Then he brightened up and became unusually agreeable and attractive. Fedor Mikhailovich could not endure general conversation; he talked only in monologues, and that only on condition that all present were in sympathy with him, and listened to him with strained silence. On the other hand, if these conditions were fulfilled, he could talk better, more picturesquely, and more vividly than any person I ever heard.

"These monologues were about his fiction, his life as a political exile, his last minute pardon when already before the firing squad, his experiences as a common soldier, and his political views. As an anti-nihilist, Dostoevsky belonged to the Slavophiles, who were as free in thought as the western liberals but who remained definitely religious, although his views, like those of many other Slavophiles, were not strictly orthodox."

It was not long before Dostoevsky proposed to Aniuta. She accepted tentatively, on condition that the engagement for a time be kept secret between them. Not even Sophia knew. Aniuta was well aware that Dostoevsky was an epileptic and widower but probably did not know that he had recently traveled through Europe with a young mistress. She appreciated his many good qualities and above all was impressed by his literary ability.

At about this time Dostoevsky was invited to an evening party at the House of Shubert. Guests were numerous. Dostoevsky's appearance in a badly fitting evening suit was in sharp contrast to the garb of others and made him feel uncomfortable. He barely responded to introductions and soon monopolized Aniuta in a corner even grasping her hand to prevent her from rising at the request of her mother to circulate among the other guests. One guest was a second cousin on the German side of the family, Andre Ivanovich Kosich, a colonel on the general staff, who was then very much interested in Aniuta. Handsome, educated, clever, polished, welcome in the best society, able to please the right people without toadying, he had already advanced beyond his years as a guards officer. He later became an influential general and governor of a province. His uniform was faultlessly cut, his manner with Aniuta charming, and, as Sophia observed, Dostoevsky immediately "hated him to madness."

In an ensuing general conversation, the Russian church was being compared with Protestantism. Elizabeth with her Lutheran background favored Protestantism because of its greater emphasis on the Bible. This gave Dostoevsky an opportunity to vent his ire over Aniuta's officer suitor, obviously favored by Elizabeth. Dostoevsky

[73]

launched into a tirade about Christ and marriage, castigating Russian mothers as having no thought for arranging the best marriage but rather the most profitable marriage for their daughters. The other guests remained silent until this awkward situation passed, and then they ignored Dostoevsky for the rest of the evening.

iii

FROM THAT time on Aniuta's manner toward Dostoevsky changed. She saw him with new eyes, less as a writer, more as an imperfect man she could tease and contradict and make jealous. He for his part began demanding an account of her time when he was not with her. Under these strained conditions he paid more attention to Sophia, with the result that she soon developed romantic notions, because he showed obvious pleasure over her interest in him. He even praised her personal appearance to the disparagement of Aniuta's.

"I drank in this unprecedented laudation of my beauty with rapture," wrote Sophia, who even thought it might be true.

The sisters, who slept together in Petersburg, usually shared confidences while undressing. "What ridiculous things Fedor Mikhailovich said today," Sophia began one night.

" 'What were they,' asked my sister, having evidently forgotten the conversation that was so important to me.

" 'About my having gypsy eyes and being destined to become a beauty,' I said, and felt myself blushing to the ears.

Aniuta paused while combing out her hair. Then gazing mysteriously at Sophia, she remarked, "And you believe that Fedor Mikhailovich thinks you handsome—handsomer than I am?"

"This cunning look, those gleaming, green eyes, and the disheveled golden hair made a perfect water nymph of her. Alongside her, in the big full-length mirror, which stood exactly opposite her bed, I beheld my own small swarthy face, and could make the comparison between us. I cannot say that the comparison was especially agreeable to me, but my sister's cold, self-confident tone vexed me, and I would not yield.

" 'Tastes differ!' I said angrily.

" 'Yes, some people do have strange tastes,' remarked Aniuta calmly, and went on brushing her hair.

"When the candle was extinguished, I lay with my face buried in the pillow and continued my reflections on the same subject.

" 'But perhaps Fedor Mikhailovich has such a taste that I please him more than my sister does,' occurred to me, and I began to pray mentally: 'Lord God, let everyone, let the whole world, go into raptures over Aniuta, only make me seem pretty to Fedor Mikhailovich!'

"But my illusions on this point were destined to a speedy and cruel destruction.

"Among the accomplishments that Dostoevsky encouraged was music. Up to that time I had learned to play on the piano as the majority of little girls learn, without feeling any particular liking or particular hatred for it. My ear was only moderately good" but "a certain amount of execution had been developing" with "a tolerable touch and a faculty for sight-reading.

"It happened that once, at the very beginning of our acquaintance, I had played for Dostoevsky a piece of music in which I was remarkably successful—variations on the themes of Russian songs. Fedor Mikhailovich was not a musician. He belonged to that class of people whose enjoyment of music depends purely upon subjective conditions—on their mood at a given moment. . . .

"It chanced that, on the occasion when I played, Fedor Mikhailovich was in just one of those sensitive emotional states of mind, for he went into ecstasies over my playing, and allowing his feelings to run away with him, as usual, he began to lavish on me the most exaggerated praises—I had talent and feeling and God knows what all!"

Consequently, for some time Sophia practiced assiduously Beethoven's *Pathétique* sonata as a surprise, and even took several lessons from a qualified teacher. When the opportunity permitted playing this composition for the author, she launched forth, confident of the keen pleasure it would give him. While absorbed in the music she did not see Aniuta and Dostoevsky leave the room; but after the last note, instead of the anticipated applause and praise, there was only silence. What a disappointment to have been left alone. Nobody was in the adjoining room, either, but peeking into the room beyond, she saw the pair sitting in a dimly lighted niche.

"They were sitting side by side on the little divan. The room was dimly illuminated by a lamp with a huge shade. The shadow fell directly on my sister, so that I could not distinguish her face; but Dostoevsky's face I saw plainly; it was pale and troubled. He was holding Aniuta's hand in his hands and bending toward her. He was talking in that passionate broken voice, which I knew and loved so well. Sophia eavesdropped and heard:

" 'Anna Vasilevna, my darling, do you understand? I loved you from the first moment that I beheld you; and before that I had already had a presentiment of it from your letters. And my love is not the affection of friendship, but passion—the passion of my whole nature.'

"Everything swam before my eyes. A sensation of bitter solitude, of deadly insult, suddenly took possession of me, and all the blood in my body seemed to rush first to my heart, and then to pour, in a burning flood, to my head.''

The writing is perhaps exaggerated, but without doubt Sophia felt consumed by hurt pride and jealousy, as she withdrew in silence. Her infatuation continued, however, now accompanied by a near hatred of her sister.

All ended well, nevertheless, when several days later while preparing for bed, Aniuta took the sobbing Sophia into her arms, exclaiming, "Come, stop that, you little goose," and then explaining that Dostoevsky was far too old for Sophia and that she herself did not intend to marry him.

" 'Of course I love him,' she admitted, 'and I have a frightful respect for him. He is so kind, so clever, such a genius!' "

But then she went on: " 'How can I explain it to you? I do not love him—in short, not in the way to marry him. You see, I am quite astonished myself that I cannot love him. He is such a fine man. At first I thought that perhaps I might come to love him; but he does not need such a wife as I, not in the least. His wife ought to devote herself entirely, entirely, to him; give up all her life to him, think only of him. And I cannot do this. I want to live myself. He seems to be constantly grasping me—sucking me into himself. I was never myself with him.' "

For once Aniuta was ready to return to Palibino. Sophia's *Recollections* end at this point in her life, but not her friendship with Dostoevsky.

iv

ALTHOUGH ANIUTA had rejected marriage, Dostoevsky did not give up hope. Perhaps his motivation had become more mercenary than otherwise, because he was in financial difficulty. Apparently he proposed staying at Palibino during the summer of 1865, but obviously he was not encouraged to do so. Instead, to get away from his obligations, and to satisfy once more his compulsive craving for roulette, he went abroad for the third time, from July to October of that year, part of the time in the company of his former mistress. She was Apollinaria Suslova, a captivating nihilist, daughter of a former serf. In 1863 he had carried on a turbulent affair with her in Russia and Germany. He had met her in the same way he met Aniuta, through a story sent to him as an editor.

Apollinaria's sister, Nadezhda Prokofevna Suslova, later Sophia's good friend, earned an M.D. degree in Zurich and became one of Russia's first woman surgeons.

Incidentally, in the winter of 1864-65, while courting Aniuta, Dostoevsky had also been engaged in a secret affair, which was only disclosed by a letter printed half a century later, with one Marfa Braun-Panin.

When leaving Petersburg, Aniuta had recommended to Dostoevsky, as one who could be trusted, her friend, Anna (Zhanna) M. Evreinova, daughter of the adjutant-general in charge of the Tsar's palace at Peterhof near Moscow. This friend, in a letter to the author in late November of 1865, offered to exchange messages without the knowledge of Aniuta's father. Whether either party resorted to this stratagem is unknown, but Dostoevsky, having returned from gambling in Europe, early in the New Year proposed visiting Palibino during the coming summer of 1886 to write a novel.

Earlier that year the Korvin-Krokovsky women were about to leave again for Petersburg—for one reason so that Sophia could study with Strannoliubsky. The General wanted to prevent further intimacies with Dostoevsky. Therefore on 14 January he sent the author a letter that was a masterpiece of polite praise and ironical indirection but with a clear underlying message. He apologized for his original reaction to Dostoevsky and asked a frank opinion of Aniuta's literary ability, "since we, having experienced life—that is, 'being old men,' know from experience that much appears to the young imagination as though through a rosy prism," and expressing the hope to meet Dostoevsky some day. Although referring obliquely to Dostoevsky's proposed summer visit, he left distinctly vague whether the author would really be welcomed. Certainly Dostoevsky could not have failed to apprehend what the message implied: that he was too old for Aniuta, that only his literary opinions were of interest, and that social contacts were undesirable.

Although Dostoevsky must have realized that there could no longer be any hope for an honorable alliance, he nevertheless persisted. Almost certainly he saw Aniuta in Petersburg after she arrived there with mother and sister on 27 February. Definitely their correspondence continued, for in June of that year he wrote a long letter to Aniuta outlining his financial problems, his contractual obligations, his despair, his difficulty in writing, and again angling for an invitation. "I would like very much to visit with you in Palibino," he wrote. "But would I be able to work there as I have to? For me this is a question. And it's impolite for me to come and work whole days. Write me about everything. Please don't leave me."

That suggests that Aniuta invited him. At any rate, his letter came to the attention of Aniuta's mother and through her to the General. His impulse was to announce that Elizabeth and daughters should leave at once for Europe. He confronted Aniuta in a stormy scene. Disregarding her plea that it would be instructive for her to observe closely a novelist at work, he ordered her to have nothing more to do with that criminal journalist, lest she be sent to the stable to herd cows! At that point he gasped for air and had a heart attack that kept him in bed for two weeks.

Thus Aniuta and Palibino did not witness the writing of what some persons consider Dostoevsky's masterpiece, *Crime and Punishment*, which he began in July, interrupted to write *The Gambler*, and then completed in November. The proud and demoniacal Pauline in *The Gambler* apparently was based on the mistress Suslova.

Elizabeth made Aniuta write Dostoevsky that she was ill and that the doctor had ordered her to take the waters in Europe, and that her sister and mother would accompany her. For one reason or another, however, the women remained through the summer in the country, only leaving for Europe in the autumn.

That ended Dostoevsky's pursuit of Aniuta, for in October, only one month and four days after a young shorthand student, Anna Gregorevna Snitkin, had become his first stenographer, Dostoevsky proposed to her and was accepted. Married in February of 1867, they went abroad for a stay that was to last until July of 1871. During the early part of their honeymoon his wife recorded his daily casino losses, the dissipation of the settlement she brought to the marriage, his frantic borrowing, and his pawning or selling of her jewelry, her dresses, and even their wedding rings.

V

DOSTOEVSKY'S WIFE made a stenographic record for her husband of his broken romance with Aniuta: "Anna Vasilevna is one of the finest women I ever knew. She is extraordinarily intelligent, mentally developed, well-educated in literature, and she has a wonderful kind heart. This young woman has high moral standards, but her beliefs are diametrically opposed to mine. She is too single minded. It is doubtful therefore that our marriage could have been happy. I returned her promise to me and with my whole soul wish that she may meet somebody with similar ideas with whom to be happy."

Anna Grigorevna later wrote that her husband had the warmest of relationships with Aniuta throughout the remainder of his life, and that there were times, after Aniuta's own marriage, when he called upon her almost daily. When eventually the two women met in 1873, they became good friends. The wife found Dostoevsky's description of her fine qualities to be true and considered her, moreover, to have become an excellent wife and tender mother. She was only jealous of Apollonaria Suslova, the ex-mistress, who married a young man after Dostoevsky's death. She probably never knew about Marfa Braun-Panin.

To assess the advantages versus the disadvantages of the friendship of Aniuta and Sophia with Dostoevsky is impossible. He had an extremely complex character. In his writing he parodied the "nihilist woman," making it appear that higher education and careers for women caused coarseness and sexual promiscuity. At the same time he maintained respectful and warmly friendly relations with such well-educated and liberated women as the Korvin-Krukovsky sisters and others. His friend and first biographer, in a letter to Tolstoy, described the novelist as malicious, envious, conceited, debauched, and alluded (falsely, Dostoevsky's widow asserted) to his serious molestation of a girl child through the collusion of a governess, as described in *The Possessed*. Yet he was often inspiring in conversation, spiritual in outlook, and of course a great novelist. An epileptic who was often ill and irritable, he long was beset by financial problems, and suffered much for his beliefs.

Aniuta did not profit as a writer from knowing Dostoevsky but perhaps benefited as a woman. Her association with him, however, caused much family discord and perhaps prevented a marriage, in which she might have been happy, with the liberal Colonel Kosich, happiness she did not enjoy with her eventual mate. As for Sophia, the Dostoevsky relationship, to the extent that it was not counterbalanced by her being the daughter of an influential general, doubtless in later years, when she sought preferment, prejudiced the authorities against her, because unknown to any of the parties, from the time of his discharge from the army until the year 1875, Dostoevsky had been under surveillance by the secret police.

CHAPTER 10

Nihilistic Marriage

i

EARLY IN 1868, when Sophia had just turned eighteen, the family moved to Petersburg to further her education and that of her brother. It is probable that at this time Aniuta occupied her time at the Smolni Institute, a school for noblewomen specializing in languages. The family rented a comfortable apartment.

In connection with Sophia's studies under Strannoliubsky, it is necessary to go back briefly to her earliest days at Palibino to something that first sparked her interest in higher mathematics.

"When we transferred our abode to the country the whole house had to be done over afresh, and all the rooms were papered," she wrote in *Recollections.* "But as the rooms were many, there was not enough paper for one of the rooms belonging to us children; it was a great undertaking to order more from Petersburg, and to order for a single room was decidedly not worthwhile. They kept waiting for an opportunity, and in the interim this ill-treated room stood for many years with nothing but common paper on its walls. But by a happy accident the paper used for this covering consisted of sheets of Ostrográdsky's lithographed lectures on the differential and integral calculus, used by my father in his youth.

"These sheets, spotted over with strange incomprehensible formulas, soon attracted my attention. I remember how, in my childhood, I passed whole hours before that mysterious wall, trying to decipher even a single phrase, and to discover the order in which the sheets ought to follow each other. By dint of prolonged and daily scrutiny, the external aspect of many of those formulas was fairly engraved on my memory, and even the text left a deep trace on my brain, although at the moment of reading it was incomprehensible to me.

"When many years later . . . I took my first lesson in differential

[80]

calculus from the famous teacher of mathematics in Petersburg, Alexander Nikolayevich Strannoliubsky, he was astonished at the quickness with which I grasped and assimilated the conceptions of the terms and derivatives, 'just as if I had known them before.' I remember that was precisely the way in which he expressed himself, and in truth the fact was that at the moment when he began to explain to me these conceptions, I immediately and vividly remembered all that had stood on the pages of Ostrográdsky . . ."

How it happened that Strannoliubsky was recommended to the General by a neighbor has already been mentioned. He came to be considered the foremost Russian teacher of mathematics during the last third of the nineteenth century. He was then only twenty-seven and quite handsome, with piercing eyes; his good features were partially obscured, at least in later years, by a great forked beard and a full drooping mustache. He gave Sophia private lessons at her parents' apartment. These sessions might last five hours at a time. They covered in rapid order analytical geometry and differential and integral calculus.

From Strannoliubsky she not only learned mathematics but by her unusual aptitude she greatly encouraged him—as he in turn definitely influenced her—in furthering the movement for women's education. He later took an active part in organizing first class gymnasium schools for women, and for fourteen years was a member of a committee that raised money for such schools. For several years, while living in Petersburg after completing her education in Germany, Sophia served actively on that committee. Much earlier, while still a university student, Strannoliubsky with other members of a student group had formed and funded and largely staffed, during off time, a free school for sons of poor parents, a school unique not only in its advanced pedagogy but also in that it gave no grades, no prizes, and no punishments. While teaching Sophia, Strannoliubsky was also a civilian tutor at the Naval Academy. There he became in 1886 a faculty member for the remaining thirteen years of his life, while at the same time carrying on his extensive writing and lecturing on education.

Crusading activity was mostly in the future, however, for both Sophia and her tutor. In 1868 Sophia wrote a joint letter to her sister and Anna Mikhailovna Evreinova, who was always called Zhanna, in which she referred to her tutor: "I was terribly happy to see him. He is very, very kind, and I liked him very much." And in another letter she stated: "He was not angered when I told him that in addition to mathematics I am planning to study physiology, anatomy, physics, and chemistry. Just the opposite. He himself agreed that mathematics alone is too dead and advised me not to dedicate myself exclusively to science but even to occupy myself with some practical activity."

But I have anticipated. After studying with Strannoliubsky, Sophia was ready for a wider world than she could enjoy in Russia. Unfortunately Russian universities were officially closed to women, as in fact were those in most countries, including nearly all in the United States. Although Oberlin College in 1837 became the pioneer coeducational institution in the United States, as late as 1910 three state universities, including that in Virginia, were still closed to women. The common argument against coeducation was that the free intercourse of university life would produce bold, aggressive, competitive women lacking the qualities to make them the refiners of home and society. That same argument had been advanced as early as 1697 when Queen Anne, influenced by a book written by Mary Astell, was successfully opposed by her advisers when she wanted to open English universities to women. Sophia approached this problem of a higher education in collaboration with her sister.

ii

WHILE SOPHIA studied mathematics, Aniuta made acquaintances among young women in nihilist circles. She herself, as she must soon have realized, lacked the formal training necessary to enter any university. Nevertheless, she harbored the illusion of obtaining a university education as her excuse for escaping abroad. She fired Sophia's hopes by telling how one girl or another, nominally married, soon would leave for foreign study; and she urged her sister to arrange a marriage for her, no matter with whom, just so the man would leave immediately after the marriage and make no claims upon her. The sisters presumed that Sophia would be allowed to go abroad if chaperoned by a married Aniuta supposedly accompanied by a husband.

The first attempt to satisfy Aniuta certainly was ill conceived. It was direct in the manner typical of Sophia and therefore was probably her idea. With no preliminary groundwork Sophia, her sister, and their 24-year-old friend Zhanna, called upon some young professor known to be sympathetic to the women's movement—it may even have been Strannoliubsky—and asked point blank if he would be willing to marry Aniuta and escort the three of them to Europe, leaving them there. The manner of this proposal sounds rather ridiculous, but the professor listened seriously before politely declining the honor. Whereupon the three young women thanked him and departed. They must have learned something from the experience, for they made no more unexpectedly direct approaches to prospects.

Zhanna was then studying ancient languages, probably with Aniuta at an institute for noblewomen. Two years earlier Zhanna's father had promised that after three years he would permit her to attend a foreign university, but she doubted that such would come to pass and in any event was impatient. She moved in nihilist circles, considering parties, dancing, and social calls an unbearable waste of time.

Sophia, referring in later years to her days in Petersburg, declared to her close Swedish friend and first sketchy biographer, Anna Charlotte Leffler: "Oh, what a happy time it was! We were so enthusiastic about the new ideas; so sure that the present social state would not continue long. We pictured to ourselves the glorious period of liberty and universal enlightenment of which we dreamed, and in which we firmly believed. . . . Besides this, we had a sense of true union and cooperation. When three or four of us met in a drawing room among older people—where we had no right to advance our opinions—a tone, a glance, even a sigh, were sufficient to show one another that we were one in thought and sympathy. And when we discovered this, how great was the inward delight at realizing that close to us was some young man or woman, whom we had never seen before, and with whom we had apparently exchanged some commonplace remark, yet whom we found to be devoted to the same ideas and hopes, ready for self-sacrifice in the same cause."

Sophia as much as Aniuta became a "girl of the sixties." That term referred to those involved in the new women's movement, individuals seeking equality of the sexes and social reform but not upheaval, individuals sometimes indifferent to religion and in any event believing that the social sciences would free mankind, and individuals agitating for admission to the universities to qualify them for careers in the professions.

Not all "girls of the sixties" could be termed nihilists, but it is uncertain where to draw the line. Even among nihilists there were two main types and many variations. The "brown" nihilists, drawn mainly from the lower ranks of society, included only a few young men and women from landowning families. The "browns" were willing not only to talk but to act; they produced the revolutionaries devoted to militant materialism. The "clean" or "salon" nihilists, on the other hand, came predominantly from the higher class, persons willing to break away verbally but not quite actually from their families and class. Such individuals usually turned into liberals. As time would show, Sophia belonged to the "salon" category.

At this time, as well as before and after, the major responses to the women's question were those of the progressives (essentially feminists as in Europe and America), the nihilists (some of whom, such as Sophia, interacted with the progressives), and the revolutionists (with whom the extreme nihilists interacted).

The progressives sought solutions within the existing social system and were influenced by such as John Stuart Mill and Alexander Herzen, believing that women themselves should improve through moderate means the position of all women and of society in general. Among their activities was the advancement of education for women, such as by establishing Sunday Schools where those of the lower class could learn religious doctrine and the three Rs. They were, after Sophia had already gone to Germany, responsible for the establishment of Public Lectures for Men and Women, which were popularized university courses; and they were partly responsible for the Military Medical-Surgical Academy which the Minister of War, the Korvin-Krukovsky friend, Baron Miliutin, would found in 1872 in order to improve the military medical service, and at which ninety women would enroll for the first semester.

As distinguished from progressives, nihilist women had more concern for personal emancipation, as from parental control and from the pressure to marry. They wanted equality of the sexes, freedom in marriage, a room of one's own, and divorce if considered desirable. This did not mean free love but one committed relationship at one time, perhaps for life. At first popularized by Turgenev in *Fathers and Sons*, the term nihilist signified the negation of differences between the sexes as far as biologically possible. Only later, when nihilism as such reached a dead end in the seventies, did the meaning become synonymous with assasin. In education the nihilist stress was on individual effort from books and tutors and participation in discussion circles. The nihilist did not so much have formal beliefs as a set of attitudes and values, even extending to manners, dress, and friendships. They tended to avoid organized movements. The nihilist woman usually wore a plain dark wool dress with white collar and cuffs, short hair to avoid the eroticism of long hair and elaborate coiffures (although bobbed hair soon became a widely adopted style). Sometimes they wore blue-smoked glasses. Many were direct to the point of rudeness.

These two movements, then, progressive and nihilist, formed Sophia's outlook at this time and to some extent throughout her life.

The nihilist marriage, the fictitious marriage, as a means of seeking their goals was adopted by some women nihilists of whatever camp. Parents of a daughter entering such a marriage might disown her but could not prevent her from living on her own, nor from receiving a passport to go abroad. In such marriages the principals were supposed to go their separate ways immediately after the ceremony, which was frequently a civil one. Obviously in such sham unions the parties seldom had much in common and no particular physical attraction for one another. Later, if one or both parties wanted to enter a real family relationship together or to marry somebody else, there were serious problems. Marriages not solemnized in church created additional complications, such as the fact that children of such unions were excluded from all government schools or only accepted after much difficulty. Divorce was possible but far from easy. If the nihilistic marriage occurred in church, annulment was a possibility, but only after long delay for the legal establishment of facts difficult to prove. Therefore an early nihilistic marriage could be disastrous for persons whose ideas might change with time.

One couple entangled in such a predicament were the Bokovs. The Korvin-Krukovsky sisters had become friendly with Maria Alexandrovna Bokova, daughter of General Obruchev and at first the fictitious wife of P. I. Bokov, a revolutionary physician with a large practice. Bokov through his influence had secured special permission for his wife to attend lectures and demonstrations at the Medical and Surgical Academy of the university in Petersburg. Several years later in Zurich she completed her training and became a surgeon but was not allowed to practice in Russia until 1871. What the sisters did not know was that while at the academy in Petersburg Maria had fallen in love with Ivan M. Sechenov, professor of physiology, and that all three principals were then discreetly living together. This domestic arrangement supposedly is what Chernyshevsky described in his novel *What is to be Done?* (Maria being Vera Pavlovna). He wrote this influential work in jail following the student riots of 1862, attempting to show how young socialists should act as opposed to Turgenev's portrait of a radical in *Fathers and Sons.* Dostoevsky in *Notes from the Underground* declared Chernyshevsky's novel to be naive.

Knowing that Maria Bokova had helped other young women toward their educational goals, Sophia turned to her for help in obtaining a partner for Aniuta. Maria in turn approached a friend of Sechenov's, Vladimir Onufrievich Kovalevsky, who knew the position of the Korvin-Krukovskys in the general area where his own family had lived. On that basis he apparently agreed to "free" Aniuta, although they had yet to meet.

iii

KOVALEVSKY, AGE twenty-six, whose mother had recently died, was the son of a deceased landowner whose greatly diminished estate originally had comprised about 1,890 acres and about 140 male serfs in a swampy region of Vitebsk, about eighteen miles from Dvinsk, in what is now Latvian S.S.R. The Emancipation and mismanagement had left Vladimir an income of less than 500 roubles a year as his half-share from what remained of the property. Highly adept in languages, he was endeavoring to eke out a living by publishing, on credit, a series of texts and popular studies on the natural and other sciences. During his lifetime he published altogether about fifty books, mostly translations, including major works of Darwin, Agassiz, Brehm, Lyell, and Fogt.

Maria Bokova must have praised Aniuta highly for Vladimir to have agreed sight unseen to the proposal, because several years earlier he had rejected a proposal on behalf of a radical journalist.

Before that, Vladimir had in 1864 been engaged to Maria Ivanovna Mikhaelis, daughter of a woman who in the 1840s had been a real pioneer in the women's movement, having supported the liberal publicist A. I. Herzen, with whom Vladimir had lived in England. Maria Ivanovna herself had spent much time assisting Colonel Peter Lavrov in organizing the Society for Encouragement of Women's Work. A mathematician and philosopher, Lavrov taught at the Artillery Academy, had been an early friend of the Korvin-Krukovsky family, and later in France would influence Sophia's thinking. When Vladimir fell in love with Maria Ivanovna, the mother was much pleased, because she already looked upon him as a son.

About that time occurred the public sentencing, after two years in jail, of the philosophical revolutionary journalist, Nicholas G. Chernyshevsky, whose articles in *Sovremennik* (*The Contemporary*) the Palibino priest's son had brought to Aniuta. Chernyshevsky opposed both authoritarian rule and Western capitalism, favoring instead a democratic socialist society of agrarian and industrial communes, based on philosophical materialism and the enlightened self-interest of individuals. His influence had largely supplanted that of Herzen, whom young socialists had come to consider a tired liberal. Today in Russia he is considered a forerunner of Lenin. In the crowd at his sentencing stood Vladimir and Maria Ivanovna. The prisoner was placed on a scaffold surrounded by mounted police while sentence was pronounced: hard labor in the mines to be followed by exile to Siberia, where as it turned out he would remain until 1883. Then took place the civil "execution," symbolized by the breaking of a sword, weakened by saw-cuts, into three pieces over the prisoner's head.

Among those who tossed him flowers as he was driven away in a carriage was Maria Ivanovna, whose bouquet landed squarely on his lap. Police having observed her action, she was taken off to jail. In trying to protect her, Vladimir was roughed up. The girl's father, a respected member of the establishment, went at once to call upon Prince Suvarov, the Governor-General of Petersburg. The governor agreed to release Maria Ivanovna on condition that she go to her father's country estate and remain there. Later he denied permission for her to return to Petersburg for marriage to Vladimir, saying, "Let her get married in the country; then she will become stable, and I shall permit her to live in the capital."

A quiet marriage therefore was scheduled for September of 1864. During the summer Vladimir visited the estate regularly, but the parents noticed that the pair frequently argued while out walking and that Vladimir would return to the house depressed. Still, it was a great surprise when, only two hours before the church ceremony, the young couple having secluded themselves in a room for some time, emerged to have Maria announce that the marriage was off. Vladimir departed in dignified silence. Maria had simply decided that Vladimir, who following marriage wanted to devote himself exclusively to science, no longer held political beliefs sufficiently militant to match her own.

The fact was that Vladimir had spent many indecisive years in study and travel and agitation. He had come to believe wholeheartedly that only science could eventually improve society. Quite likely he had also decided that his role, as soon as possible, should become something more than that of a mere popularizer.

In youth both Vladimir and his brother Alexander, two years his senior, had studied under house tutors and then at the university in Petersburg, where the brother became originally a civil engineer and where Vladimir in 1855 entered the exclusive Imperial School of Jurisprudence. He completed the course in 1861 with first honors, qualifying him at once for what other law graduates would have to work ten years to achieve—namely, a position as titular councilor (ninth of the fourteen government grades) in the Department of Justice.

While a student, however, Vladimir had become active in a circle of young men that grouped around his brother. They met with leaders of the revolutionary democrats, including the aforementioned Chernyshevsky, and passed around *Sovremennik* (*The Contemporary*) and other publications, including Herzen's forbidden *Kolokol* (*The Bell*). At that time Vladimir had become excited by the ideas of Darwin and other natural scientists and resolved to abandon law. When entering law school, however, he had promised to work for at least six years in the Department of Justice. He wanted at least to postpone this service. Therefore he obtained a sick leave for four months and left to join his brother in Heidelberg.

Once there he resumed his political activity and developed considerable skill as an orator. Others urged him to advance reform in Russia through the law, but he decided upon biology as possibly his life work. Consequently he went to London in 1862 to study English law and political ideas, but more especially to meet Darwin and to read in the London Museum the latest works on biology, meanwhile living with Herzen and tutoring his daughter.

Because Russian agents were active in London he lived under an assumed name until warned by Herzen to leave England. His request for an extension of sick leave had been refused, and he had, moreover, been dismissed from the Department of Justice with an official reprimand that limited most future possibilities of government service. So he moved on to Lemberg and in 1863 reportedly had some part in the Polish rebellion. Afterward he apparently reentered Russia illegally, but after the broken romance with Maria Ivanovna he probably went abroad again, because in 1866 he presumably participated in the Italian uprising under Garibaldi.

iv

SUCH THEN was the background and experience of the young man that met the Korvin-Krukovsky sisters at an evening social affair where they could look one another over. Idealistic though he may have been, Vladimir must also have had financial expectations and perhaps even the hope for a real marriage. A marriage with parental approval would mean a dowry to permit both parties to study abroad. Doubtless he asked Aniuta about her ideas, hopes, and plans, quickly apprehending that disciplined study was not for her. Also, in her embarrassment, the usually impulsive Aniuta was aloof and withdrawn. Neither party impressed the other.

Sophia did attract Vladimir's attention, however. She was lively and talkative, taking the initiative that should have been Aniuta's, and obviously she was a serious student.

A few days later the intermediary reported to the sisters that Vladimir was unwilling after all to marry Aniuta, partly because her response to his offer had been hesitant and because she lacked the courage to tell her father she wished to marry—but that he would marry Sophia.

Although loving her sister more than her mother, Sophia nevertheless had always, consciously or otherwise, felt jealous of her—not jealousy of the kind that belittles but rather that of seeking to emulate —and to be preferred over pretty Aniuta must have pleased her considerably. As for Aniuta, obviously it damaged her ego for Sophia, the Little Sparrow, to be chosen even by such a one as Vladimir, over herself who had always been the princess of the family. In fact, she now became uncertain of her own course of action and proposed abandoning the whole idea, until Sophia persuaded her that there were other men nihilists to fish for, if only she would be patient. From this time onward the positions of the sisters gradually reversed, Sophia becoming the dominant one, or at least Aniuta permitted her to appear so.

Of course the sisters discussed all aspects of Sophia accepting Vladimir's offer. Sophia argued that if she married, then Aniuta could probably get permission to accompany her abroad—as Sophia had intended to do had the original plan worked out—although that would be necessary only if Aniuta herself did not find a willing partner. Sophia must have realized that if she were the one to marry, it was certain that she could get a passport to go abroad, whereas if only Aniuta married, no passport would be granted without her father's doubtful permission.

One problem remained, however. In those times the older daughter customarily married first. Could family permission be obtained for Sophia to reverse that order? The sisters decided an effort to gain such permission was worthwhile, while meanwhile continuing to seek a partner for Aniuta. Sophia contacted Vladimir and discussed with him frankly all aspects of the problem. Several secret meetings of this sort took place by arrangement in a church.

How did Sophia appear to Vladimir at that time? Sophia had recently formed a lifelong friendship with Zhanna, later to be the first Russian woman to earn a doctor of law degree. Zhanna left a description of Sophia as she was when Vladimir met her:

"Among all the women devoted to politics to some degree, women exhausted by life, she made a completely original impression with her childish appearance, the reason for her endearing nickname, Little Sparrow. She had already passed her eighteenth birthday but appeared much younger. Small, slender, with a rather round head covered by short curly chestnut hair, she had an unusually expressive and mobile face, with eyes constantly changing expression, either brilliant and dancing or deeply meditative. Her expression mixed childish innocence with the appearance at times of deep thought.

"She attracted the hearts of everyone by her unaffected charm, which distinguished her in this period of her life. She charmed old and young, men and women. Completely natural in manner, without a shade of coquetry, she seemed not to notice the adoration she aroused. She paid not the slightest attention to her general appearance and dress, which was always unusually simple, even betraying a certain disorder that lasted throughout her life."

From photographs of this period it is obvious that Sophia, while no beauty, was very good looking. Her chin was dimpled, her lips full, her eyes compelling, her fingers long and tapering. Presumably she was immature, although corset pads would have augmented her figure. Not improbably her puberty had been delayed and she was still developing. She was physically and emotionally a child-woman, mentally a genius. Doubtless her brother was correct when he wrote of her in after years that in disposition and coloring she much resembled her father, and therefore had his practical outlook and his tendency to view people and events with a certain detachment, while resembling her Shubert grandfather in intellectual development. Withal, at age eighteen she was imbued with a girlish charm and a youthful enthusiasm so appealing to Vladimir that he soon lost his heart.

Vladimir wrote to his brother: "My Little Sparrow is such a marvelous being, I won't describe her, as you'll think I'm captivated. It should be enough for you to know that Maria Alexandrovna [Bokova] . . . after two brief meetings with Sophia, fell absolutely in love with her." He described Sophia's education and observed that she worked "like an ant from morning to night" and yet was "lively, kind, and very attractive."

From Sophia's viewpoint it mattered little that Vladimir, if not actually ugly, definitely was not handsome. He had reddish hair and beard, a high forehead, a large nose, and lively blue eyes. He was friendly, intelligent, cultivated in manner, idealistically unselfish, and expressed himself well. In him she saw a man of her own class, reserved, serious, with a brotherly respect for women, and with ideas similar to her own; one already experienced abroad—for they had decided to travel together—a man who could be depended upon to be a gentleman and she hoped a true friend. Also there was the fortunate fact that he had the profession of law to fall back upon if necessary, which would make him more acceptable to the General.

Elizabeth Fedorovna Litvinova, the young woman with whom Sophia would later become friendly in Switzerland, thought Sophia acted hastily in deciding upon a nihilistic marriage. She observed the General not as an autocratic tyrant but as an elderly and worldly-wise man who deeply loved all his children and desired the best for each. She stated that the General was proud of Sophia and believed she had a brilliant future. Since that could only happen if she studied abroad, it perhaps suggests that he had this in mind for her eventually. Litvinova believed that the General—certainly in preference to an early marriage —would have permitted Sophia to go abroad chaperoned by the old English governess, who then lived with the Shuberts. Some Russian girls, apparently including Litvinova herself who became a mathematician, went to Switzerland or Germany under arrangements made for their protection by approving parents.

If Sophia considered such a possibility she apparently rejected it. She could not wait! In any event, she presumably would hardly have wished to be under the eye of the old governess, the tyrant of her early life.

About this time a curious incident occurred. A young nihilist named Ivan Grigorevich Rozhdestvensky, son of a priest, approached the General to ask for Sophia's hand. In nihilist circles he was not taken seriously, being something of a character, rather bear-like in appearance, who usually lived with one friend or another while earning a few kopecks by giving lessons to adolescents. It happened one evening that Sophia's search for a fictitious husband was being discussed by one group of nihilists, but none would volunteer except Rozhdestvensky. When approached with his offer, Sophia and her sister would only agree that he could go as a decoy to test the nature of the General's reaction. This he did, in borrowed top hat and frock coat. Since his manner clearly indicated his origins, there was no real need for the General to ask his position in the world, but the young man answered the query with aplomb: "I am occupied with free pedagogy." Having thanked him for honoring his daughter, the General explained that Sophia was too young to marry. One can only wonder about Sophia's response when the General questioned her later about that individual.

As for Vladimir, Maria Bokova told him that Sophia would not be permitted to marry before her sister, for not only was Sophia much younger than Aniuta but also she was physically younger than her actual age, and the custom for the older daughter to marry first was deeply established. Therefore, Maria urged him to reconsider marrying Aniuta. But he firmly asserted that, although he much respected Aniuta, he was not willing to give up his freedom and a family life for her. Doubtless he hoped, even expected, that physical intimacy with Sophia would develop naturally and that love for him would flower, although from the beginning she made no secret of the fact that she shared the scorn of most nihilist girls for the occasional couple that entered into a fictitious marriage and ended up sleeping together.

At one point, despairing of gaining permission to marry Sophia, Vladimir wrote to the mother of his former fiance, and from her received assurance of a refuge for Sophia if she fled her paternal roof. For a man of his age and experience, Vladimir obviously, not only in his business dealings but in this plan, lacked ordinary good sense. What could come of Sophia's running away? How could she get to Germany? How be accepted in a university? How could she live?

At least Sophia herself realized the futility of such a plan. Confidently she assured Vladimir that one way or another she could persuade her father. If a direct approach failed, she had another plan, one she would not disclose to anybody.

As the first step she and Aniuta convinced their mother to favor Sophia's desire. The mother felt that the best procedure would be to introduce Vladimir simply as a Vitebsk nobleman, which would be immediately in his favor. Vladimir should then make repeated visits to the apartment where the Korvin-Krukovskys lived, so that the General could observe Sophia's interest in him. Then in due time Vladimir could ask to marry her.

This stratagem was carried out, but not without delay, because it was deemed essential for Vladimir's introduction to come through some prominent Petersburg family. Vladimir called upon the friendly son of such a family to assist. Whether the first meeting occurred on the regular reception day of the chosen family or that of Sophia's family is uncertain. But the General was cordial with Vladimir. This cordiality diminished somewhat, however, as Vladimir took advantage of the introduction to call at the apartment on a number of occasions to study with Sophia, who in the General's view did not know how to behave. In her unsophisticated way she was attempting to display to her father a growing affection for Vladimir.

Eventually Vladimir made his proposal, to which the General listened politely, pretending to believe Vladimir's optimistic calculation of his financial position, consisting of his interest in the estate, the list of his unsold publications, their selling price, and the splendid profit he would make when all were sold.

The General knew little about publishing, except that debts came before uncertain profits in the future, but he did know the problems and uncertainties of second-grade or third-grade estates in the Vitebsk area. Nevertheless, he remained silent about his doubts and with great reluctance said he would not oppose Sophia's desires. But he added that she was still young. Therefore the two should become better acquainted. He invited Vladimir to visit Palibino for that purpose. After all, a wedding could wait. Obviously he expected time to be on his side.

This greatly perturbed Vladimir, who wrote that the General obviously considered Sophia worthy of a titled nobleman, and while outwardly polite when speaking with Vladimir or when observing Sophia and Vladimir planning their future together, the General's lips could sometimes be seen "trembling with rancor." Vladimir feared that the General would somehow break up the wedding plans.

But Sophia had no doubts. Her close Swedish friend and literary collaborator in later life, Anna Charlotte Leffler, described Sophia's reaction to the imposed delay: "The tender young girl, who could not bear an unkind glance or a word of disapproval from those she loved, at this critical time became like steel. For though of a delicate, sympathetic, and affectionate nature, she had within her a vein of sternness and flint-like inflexibility, which came to the fore in any crisis. . . . This arose from her intensity of will. For her will was so strong that it became an overmastering force, even when it had to do with a purpose entirely unconnected with feeling. What she desired, what she wished, she desired with such intensity that she was almost consumed by it. Now she wanted to leave her parents' home and continue her studies, cost what it might."

V

THEREFORE, WHILE the General temporized, Sophia decided the time had come to force the issue according to her plan. She chose a day when a dinner party was scheduled. While her mother was out shopping, her father at the club, Sophia slipped out of the house at early twilight. Hurrying along darkening streets, she soon reached a dilapidated house on a back street, ascended a dark stairway, and rapped three times on Vladimir's door, which opened by prearrangement.

Meanwhile at home the Shuberts, the Korvin-Krukovskys, and guests (including an old diplomat, two academics, and three generals who had been artillery school comrades of the General's) sat down for dinner before Sophia's absence had been noted. The maid sent by Elizabeth to summon Sophia from her room, returned to report that mademoiselle was not there. Aniuta when questioned murmured something inarticulate and distracted attention by requesting a napkin.

Of what happened next two accounts exist.

According to Anna Charlotte Leffler (who made occasional errors in relying on her memory of conversations with Sophia), a footman brought the General a note found on Sophia's dressing table. It consisted of the words: "Father, I am with Vladimir and beg you that you will no longer oppose our marriage." Having read the words in silence, the General excused himself and departed. Ten minutes later Sophia heard heavy footsteps on the stairs just before the door was flung open by her angry father. She had been compromised. The three returned together to the House of Shubert, where the General presented the young man as Sophia's fiance.

It seems unlikely, however, that the General even knew where Vladimir lived. A more probable rendering of what occurred had the

General's man Ilia enter the dining room to announce: "Your Excellency, Sophia Vasilevna ordered me to tell you that they won't come to the dinner. They are busy at Vladimir Onufrievich's preparing plans for the wedding." Sophia had persuaded Ilia to make the announcement aloud in the presence of everybody. The General had no honorable alternative except to smile and remark as calmly as possible that such a reason excused his daughter from dinner.

Within a few days it was agreed within the family that the wedding would take place at Palibino sometime in the autumn. Vladimir was invited to visit as Sophia's fiancé. The General left for Palibino on 3 May, to be followed by the rest of the family on 10 June when the school term ended for Fedor.

vi

On 25 June Vladimir left Petersburg for Palibino and on arrival there wrote to his brother: "I've come for three weeks to the parents of my bride. Personally I am very happy that I can see her, but our affair isn't progressing rapidly, and I can't in any way get the date set for our wedding. My life here is very good and even intellectual, which happens infrequently in the country. Sofa and her sister rise at 6:00 A.M. and I also; bathe, drink tea, and at 8:00 A.M. we start work—that is, she teaches me mathematics; I've gone through much of it already. My time not only isn't wasted but during the courtship period I succeeded in preparing myself solidly in mathematics and physiology. Her ability and character, perseverance, energy, and determination place everything else in the background."

A few days later, having discovered new virtues in his bride-to-be, Vladimir again wrote to his brother: "I'm sending you a portrait of my Little Sparrow. It's very bad; the expression on her face is usually more serious." The photo to which he referred probably is the one showing Sophia seated in profile, her lips showing a slight smile; one would judge the picture to show her not at age eighteen but at about the age of fourteen.

Vladimir's letter continued: "I've had the opportunity daily to be amazed at the abilities that can fit into such a young head. Various chemical facts are already known to her, and she knows all of physics [elementary], of course, one hundred times better than I."

In fact, in the light of his hopeless love, Sophia's ability began to make Vladimir feel inferior. "With all my experience in life, with learning and social polish," he continued to his brother, "I can't even half as quickly understand and analyze the different economical and political questions she can; and be assured this is not due to infatuation but to cold discernment. I think that this meeting will make a decent person out of me, that I'll drop the publishing and start studying again, although I can't conceal from myself that this person's character is one thousand times better, wiser, and more talented than mine. In fact, she is a little phenomenon, and how she fell to my lot I can't imagine."

Very likely he was too proud and too hopeful to disclose to his brother the real nature of the coming marriage, or that Sophia was physically indifferent to him, or that he had very tactfully to repress his feeling in order not to provoke her anger, or that he was worried about the General's sharp observation of his daughter's reactions.

Also Vladimir was distressed to have learned from his brother that their late father had sold the little village of Pelech, and that almost the entire forest had been cut down and sold. Ownership of the village Shustianka and some mostly barren acreage and lakes with fishing rights apparently remained, under doubtful title, but the income was woefully inadequate for two heirs.

Apart from his doubts because of Sophia's immaturity, the General sensed something not quite right about the marriage, without suspecting its true nature. As long as possible he delayed agreeing to a date for the union, hoping something might occur to change the situation, but under pressure from all sides he finally consented unwillingly to a September 11 date.

When Vladimir left about 30 July Sophia declared that in letters she would address him as "brother." He was charged with finding a husband not only for Aniuta but also one for Zhanna. They agreed that candidates for fictitious husbands would be called "good people" or "doctors" or "preserves," the latter word because Sophia's mother had given him preserves to take home. They also decided that "Baden" and "Stuttgart" could safely be mentioned in connection with their German plans as actual code words for particular Shubert relations. Sophia had not forgotten how years earlier her Shubert uncle had helped torpedo Semevsky's prospects with Aniuta and feared to have Vladimir's background probed with damning results. Therefore Vladimir was cautioned to call upon the various Shuberts and gain their friendship. He left Sophia something by Darwin to be translated for publication, but during their separation she was so busy writing lengthy letters, and studying, that, because of her passion for exactitude, she only managed a few pages.

vii

EN ROUTE to Petersburg Vladimir detoured to the Kovalevsky estate to see if conditions there were as bad as reported. Then about August 5 when leaving Shustianka for Petersburg, he wrote Sophia: "I have a whole week of visits to my future relatives, and on Monday I shall go to Peterhof to fulfill your mutual request to Zhanna. In Petersburg, of course, as you desire, my first business will be the observation and selection of the better examples for the preparation of preserves; we'll see how this new product will come out."

The mailbag that arrived and left Palibino each Thursday contained numerous letters; most of Sophia's have been preserved, several of Vladimir's. Sophia expressed surprise that she was permitted to write him without censorship and that the General did not ask to read Vladimir's letters. "With my father," she confided, "I meet only at dinner and supper, and these brief meetings are passed exchanging sharp remarks; however, mostly we remain silent." Vladimir's letters she did read aloud to her mother, skipping portions with double-meanings.

The post office had trouble reading Vladimir's addressed envelopes. "To improve your handwriting," she wrote, "I advise you to write more frequently, naturally to me." She closed her letters with "Your sister" or "I shake your hand" or simply "Goodbye," but in one she anticipated events by signing herself "Sophia Kovalevsky" and in another she confessed that "I really never thought I'd ever be friendly with someone so firmly as with you!"

In general Sophia conveyed a warm affection, expressing her loneliness without him, her eagerness to start their studies together, and her assurance that while she studied "quite a lot of chemistry" but "most of all mathematics," still he should not be concerned that she had gotten ahead of him in other subjects. She warned him of her determination to teach him mathematics. "Don't imagine that you'll succeed in avoiding mathematics; if you're flattering yourself with this hope, then throw it away. In general, my poor, dear V.O., you will lead a hard life and I pity you with all my soul." How prophetic!

One letter contained news of a "great misfortune"—the "charming red caterpillar" had escaped from its cardboard box and "nasty worms" had developed in the aquarium with the pike, which died. She also reported talking to Vladimir's old wet nurse, then living in nearby Nevel, who had declared she had never had such a crybaby as he had been. Sophia reported that a she-bear had come to stay, probably the General's sister; that she herself was using compresses of cold tea on her tired eyes; that many persons in the district were ill; and that some days as many as ten persons came to her for medicine, which she selected by referring to a healing manual. She told Vladimir not to be anxious about wedding attendants. "We'll find some lads here."

Earlier, at the end of July, from Petersburg, Vladimir had written: "Here it's a whole eternity since we parted, my dear, wonderful friend, and again I'm starting to count the days until our next meeting. However, I have very little time to spend on this partially arithmetical and partly sentimental occupation, as my work and cares swallow up time. First of all, I started looking for an apartment. Our apartment is frightfully high and bright to an extreme, in fact the interior is extremely pleasant, despite several exterior inconveniences." He went on to state that he had a pleasant evening at the Shuberts but made no mention of "preserves" or "good people."

In replying on August 8 Sophia soon came to that significant topic: "I am glad that you have already taken an apartment; in fact everything makes me very happy, whatever refers to our future life. I can't tell you with what impatience I am awaiting the month of September; however, I hope that August won't pass in vain; I would so like to have the fate of my sisters decided quickly; it will be terribly vexing if before September nothing has been arranged for them!"

viii

THE HEART of every letter to Vladimir, in fact, concerned Aniuta and to a much lesser extent Zhanna. On 23 August Aniuta and her mother went to Petersburg, Aniuta to stay at the summer *dacha* of the Shuberts, where unfortunately she was somewhat remote from Petersburg, while Elizabeth's stay was only a short one to purchase things needed for Sophia's trousseau. Nevertheless, Sophia pulled what strings she could, arranging for Zhanna to take her friend, Peter N. Trachev, to Vladimir to propose nihilist husbands. It should be realized that young people, while holding diverse political and social views, were friendly with anybody who might advance their own special goals. Thus Trachev, age forty-two, a dedicated revolutionist who was then helping to organize in Petersburg the forthcoming student revolt that S. V. Nechaev was directing on a wider scale from Moscow, attracted Sophia and Zhanna because he supported women's rights. Sophia was much opposed to the revolt when it later occurred, but both girls had been much influenced by his article, "People of the Future and Heroes of the Common People," in which he expounded the utopian ideas of Spielhagen's novel *In Rank and File*, George Sand's *Lady Merkem*, George Eliot's *Felix Holt*, and Andre Leo's *Rebellious Marriage*. Sophia eventually became friendly in England with George Eliot and Aniuta in France with Andre Leo.

Apparently Trachev did produce a certain Petrov as one of two potential husbands, about whom Vladimir wrote to Sophia. The other may have been I. I. Mechnikov, who will be introduced later. Referring to the two individuals, Sophia promptly replied: "Please my amiable, good, excellent brother, make their acquaintance quickly," so that Aniuta could somehow meet them several times and begin praising them to her mother. Then perhaps the mother would be delighted that "romance is blooming" and would permit Aniuta to live with the Kovalevskys after their marriage.

Earlier Professor Sechenov had been eliminated as a prospect. Both Vladimir and Sophia were upset, in view of Maria Bokova's professed friendship and sympathy, by her strange refusal to proposition Sechenov, not knowing that he was actually part of a *ménage à trois* with Maria.

Sophia was angered, too, by Sechenov's expressed belief that the newlyweds would not be allowed into Heidelberg University. "But we'll still try, isn't that so?" Sophia queried Vladimir. She added: "It seems to me that Sechenov caws like a crow and only predicts all kinds of vileness out of envy. Please don't believe him, my good brother. You'll see how well everything will go for us . . . ."

Sophia wrote that she would be patient until 22 August for something to be arranged for Aniuta but set 29 August as the absolute deadline. Actually, although Sophia urged him to "talk seriously" with Aniuta, who was lukewarm or too particular, Vladimir failed entirely to find anybody willing to join her in a nihilistic marriage.

In two brief letters to her mother in Petersburg, Sophia reported that all but one of the ill peasants had recovered, and she requested her mother to purchase for her a gift for Natasha, her maid, and "baubles for the children." She also reported that a stable fire had destroyed the carriage Elizabeth had left at Vitebsk, and that if she could not hire a comfortable conveyance for the final leg home, the General had arranged for a postal coach to be assigned to her.

It was neither Vladimir nor her mother, however, but Aniuta whom Sophia really missed and to whom she wrote endearingly, beginning letters with such salutations as "My dear, amiable, priceless, best Aniuta." She expressed her delight at having received four letters from Aniuta in one mailbag, including a day-by-day diary. "My dear dove," she continued, "the thought of you and your future solitude never leaves me for a minute." She also wrote, "Please don't lose heart, my wonderful little sister."

In another letter she declared: "Yesterday while reading your letter a terribly frightening feeling came over me, as if I were simply becoming one person with you, understanding each of your perceptions even more than expressed in your letter; never before had I realized to what degree we are necessary to each other and what an unbreakable tie exists between us. Dear priceless sister, whatever should happen to us, no matter how fate may debase or mock us, still as long as we're together we are stronger and more steadfast than anything on earth—in this I firmly believe." Although her own future had been arranged, she nevertheless confessed, "whether from fear for you or from my increased studies and loneliness," that at times she felt "dark forebodings" which she found difficult to dismiss as nonsense.

Regarding those studies, she disclosed to Aniuta her unusual self-discipline, as though still under the vigilant old governess or the guidance of Malevich. Throughout each day she progressed by the clock from mathematics to physiology to chemistry to translations, earning at day's end an hour of reading from *Little Dorrit* by Dickens; but if at any time she had been lazy or lacked understanding, she deprived herself of the reward.

She went on to spin a long dream of an ideal future with Aniuta, when the latter, accompanied by young women she had "freed," joined Sophia in Heidelberg. The two of them would live in a snug little room, Sophia writing her dissertation, Aniuta writing a story. The fantasy then jumped to Siberia where Sophia would go to be useful to exiles, after which she would return to her own laboratory for important work in physics and mathematics. Together with Aniuta she would organize a gymnasium for girls and one for boys. She would make great scientific discoveries, while Aniuta wrote marvelous stories, until both turned gray and had the satisfaction of having many protégés.

"Now isn't such a life heavenly," she asked, "and yet it is the most ascetic I could imagine, and it depends only and exclusively on us two. I have purposely eliminated Zhanna and amiable, good, and kind good brother from these dreams; just add them and what a good life it would be. For me it is difficult to live alone; it is absolutely necessary for me to have somebody to love every day, but you know what a little puppy I am.'

How little *that* was Aniuta's idea of a perfect life!

ix

ANUITA WAS to arrive at Palibino just in time for the wedding, accompanied by Zhanna and probably by Shubert relatives. Vladimir had already arrived early in September and at Sophia's request agreed to a brief delay in the wedding, although they agreed not to tell their parents in advance lest it appear that they had quarreled. Sophia simply wanted some time with Aniuta. "Judge for yourself," she wrote her sister, "four days won't make the slightest difference in my studies, but it is very important for me to spend four extra days with you and our priceless Zhanna. When you arrive, then it will be quite natural that I've become emotional on seeing you."

She went on to state that following the wedding she would be separated from Aniuta for only one month. Her timetable called for Vladimir to return to Palibino for Aniuta and Zhanna on October 15. "The relatives must let you go; if you don't break them down to this, then the fault will be yours; if worst comes to worst, brother will take you away by force. During the interim we'll arrange everything in Petersburg—that is, a husband."

Sophia in letters to Aniuta expressed her genuine affection. Having felt rejected by her mother, she had turned to Aniuta as a surrogate and having been isolated in the country, she had also found in Aniuta her only girl friend, valuing her sister all the more because the English governess had kept them apart for so long. More than that, Sophia's letters at this time betrayed a certain apprehension over her coming marriage, certain fears regarding Vladimir, even uncertainties about her own emotions. She was after all a Victorian girl, only chronologically 18 years of age, who had never danced with a man much less held hands or been kissed, and who was not even in love with the man eight years her senior to whom she had agreed to trust herself. No wonder she stressed again and again her need for Aniuta to be with her. "You are absolutely necessary to me; without you I am in constant fear that I'll become spoiled or will in general deviate from our close, ascetic, only true path." And again: "My spiritual mother, remember, if you have spoiled me, then it is your fault if now I am unable to get along without you." The references to asceticism and spiritual motherhood perhaps originated in Aniuta having introduced her several years earlier to the *Imitations of Christ* by Thomas à Kempis.

X

MEANWHILE NEW dresses were being fitted on Sophia, her trousseau completed and packed, and relatives were arriving to be greeted. Among the latter was Sophia's great-aunt on her mother's side, Alexandra Alexandrovna Briullova, from Petersburg. She privately considered Sophia too young to marry and her mother wrong in having favored the union. From Palibino the great-aunt wrote to the German relations that the wedding would not be a merry one, as it would not be followed by the usual ball; and she expressed disapproval of Sophia's complete withdrawal from sociability with the relatives that had come so far to be with her, of her absolute refusal for several days to attend a dinner honoring the bridal pair at the estate of the General's sister—apparently because this individual had joined the

General in advising a long engagement—and of her sulky manner en route to the dinner when finally she did agree to go. Obviously the old lady considered Sophia spoiled and her mother irresponsible. She could not be aware, of course, of the mixed emotional feelings that distracted the bride-to-be, her resentment against her father, her great reluctance to part with Aniuta, her desire to spend with Aniuta every possible minute of the time remaining, and her doubts and even fears as she entered into a strange relationship. The relative was more favorably impressed by Vladimir, however, than she had been in Petersburg, considering him amiable and trustworthy, although impecunious. Nevertheless it would appear that she, like the General, suspected something lacking in the marriage but hoped for the best.

Vladimir's brother did not come. He was in Italy with his new common law wife. So the bridegroom had no relatives or friends to stand beside him. Had he brought male attendants they would, of necessity, because of the remoteness of Palibino, have had to accompany the bridal pair back to the railroad and Petersburg, and Sophia didn't want that.

In letters to Stuttgart dated 22 and 28 September, Great-Aunt Alexandra related wedding details. The night before the ceremony the servants, according to peasant custom, gathered outside Sophia's bedroom door to sing an epithalamium and sang there again to awaken her on the important day itself. After a leisurely breakfast the aunt arranged the bride's hair in curls and helped dress her. The gown "though very simple was very pretty," made of white silk with ruffles and applique. She wore a long veil with a wreath of myrtle and orange blossoms. It was Sunday, 27 September 1869. About eleven o'clock the family and servants clustered in the entrance hall for the blessing, performed according to patriarchal tradition by the General with his wife beside him. This was done with the ikon that Grandfather Shubert had given Sophia at her birth. The bridal pair knelt at the doorway and were admonished to love one another always. The General charged Sophia with the importance of obeying her husband for their mutual happiness and then kissed them both. The family and Malevich then kissed the pair, after which the older servants kissed them on the shoulders.

The parents did not observe the custom of that district, which would have kept them at home while the marriage was solemnized in church. Instead they entered a waiting carriage with Sophia and Aniuta. In the second carriage Vladimir followed with two young male neighbors as attendants. In the third the great-aunt, several other relatives, and Malevich took their places. Other carriages followed and finally came several servants in whatever conveyances were available. En route to church the party saw autumn foliage of birch and beech in flaming reds and yellows against the blue sky and the dark green of the pine trees. As the procession passed through the village on the estate, the peasants waited for a glimpse of the bride, and girls sang wedding songs.

In the Orthodox manner the inside of the church had no pews, only a few seats at one side for notables and the infirm. A solid screen-like *iconostasis*, painted with religious figures, and having a door at each side and double "royal" doors at the center, separated the altar from the open area where the ceremony took place. Vigil lights flickered before the large ikons of Christ on the *iconostasis* to the right of the royal doors and the Virgin on the left. Before smaller ikons on the walls little vigil flames added their odor of burning oil to the scent of old incense that permeated the church.

On entering, the principals and members of the wedding party, in the customary manner, kissed the ikon of the crucifixion on its stand before the royal doors. Sophia's ikon was placed on a small table. By her wish the ceremony was short, lasting only twenty minutes, without choir or chanter to intone liturgical responses in Old Slavonic. The couple stood before a small pink rug, as the priest in cope, assisted by a deacon, blessed and incensed them and their ikon and intoned prayers. Heavy brass crowns were held over their heads. Vladimir's best man and another young man for Sophia performed this arm-tiring task. Each of the principals held lighted candles during part of the ceremony. These were specially decorated to be taken home and preserved. Finally the marriage pledges were exchanged and rings slipped over fingers.

Sophia, according to her great-aunt, appeared in "such loveliness that all those present declared they had never seen so attractive a bride."

As the ceremony ended, Sophia teased Vladimir by stepping first onto the pink rug. This, according to superstition, foretold that she would be the head of the house—an accurate prediction.

Did Sophia, in effect, keep her fingers crossed during the marriage vows? Certainly she had mental reservations that made the marriage invalid in the eyes of the Russian Orthodox Church. It is unclear what formal religious views if any Sophia held as an adult. She never addressed this subject in print. It would seem that she hovered between Russian Orthodoxy and a watered-down Christianity but rarely entered a church. In the family the outward forms of the Russian religion certainly were observed, such as the celebration of saints' days, attendance at church (at least in clement weather), participation in the sacraments occasionally, and the keeping of lent by the elimination in the Polish manner of milk, eggs, cheese, and butter from the diet. Presumably for some years to follow, Sophia abandoned outward evidence of belief. As for Vladimir, it is to be supposed that he was sincere in his wedding promises and hoped desperately for the best, although it is doubtful that his early beliefs in the tenets of Christianity had survived the supposed conflict of that period between religion and the Darwinian thought that he so wholeheartedly embraced. At any rate, for both, the marriage was one of outward form only.

When all had returned to the house, about forty persons sat down at 2:30 P.M. for a dinner lasting for about two hours. Probably at some point Malevich played his violin; the great-aunt characterized him as stiff and pedantic, which she attributed to his early education under Jesuits. The size of the party required that the meal be served in the upper hall at two long flower-decorated tables. The chef outdid himself, and champagne flowed freely. But through it all Sophia was only anxious to depart, for to have remained overnight would have required the newlyweds to share a bedroom in order not to betray the nature of their union. At one point she sent Aniuta off to supervise the loading of the luggage for a quick departure. The previous day Sophia had been entirely unconcerned about last minute packing, so that her maid had to consult Vladimir. The meal no sooner ended than Sophia rushed off to change into her traveling costume.

Then began the farewells. Sophia shed tears, but principally because of parting from Aniuta. She made one last appeal for Aniuta to accompany her but met refusal. Her father did suggest that Sophia in her letters try to convince Aniuta that happiness for her could only be found in marriage. One can imagine Sophia replying, "Then let her come with me, papochka, and I'll try all the time to convince her," and the General laughingly rejecting that argument by pointing out that she was really too young to guide her older sister, adding moreover, that when Aniuta did visit Petersburg she would be staying with her mother and aunts. Neither he nor his wife, of course, could imagine that Vladimir would really want Aniuta with them during the early period of such a marriage as they supposed Sophia to be undertaking.

As the carriage with the newlyweds drew off, Elizabeth doubtless watched tearfully from an upper window and made toward it the sign of the cross for a safe journey, but she did not feel the sorrow of separation that she would have experienced had it been Aniuta or Fedor in the disappearing carriage.

Sophia, in her joy at being released at last, really was only sorry to be leaving Aniuta. In verses written later she highly dramatized her feelings at the time of departure, in prose translation as follows:

[103]

LITTLE SPARROW

No sadness has the heroine in leaving her native places, and neither dear nor precious is the view of her family home. In her these bring forth only enmity and anger. She recalls years of life filled with passionate striving and struggle, of unheard and secret suppressed desires. Before her gloomy images of slavery file by. From the house she flees as a prisoner from jail.

CHAPTER 11

The Good Life Begins

i

THE KOVALEVSKYS arrived in Petersburg on the third day after the wedding. Oblivious to the fatigue of the tiresome journey, Sophia kept repeating joyously. "Now begins the good life of work."

Not all work, of course. Now as a married woman free to go whenever and wherever she wished, Sophia at last could really enjoy the planned city of St. Petersburg, which Dostoevsky called the most premeditated place on earth. Founded by Peter the Great, subject of its famed bronze horseman statue, Petersburg occupied a site on the Neva River delta, its population of about 600,000 living on the mainland bank and on the various islands linked together by bridges. Nevsky Prospect was perhaps the world's finest street. The city attracted nobles and the newly rich bourgeoisie, high society and the demimonde; it embraced colonies of Germans and other Europeans and was the bureaucratic, political, business, educational, and cultural center of the nation. Created as Russia's effort to catch up with Europe, it was, as Gogol said, a foreigner in its own fatherland. Among its several hundred churches the five gilded domes of St. Isaac's Cathedral could be seen from everywhere in the city. Its palaces and public buildings had been designed by the best French and Italian architects in classic and baroque styles, with columns, pilasters, and porticos on every hand, structures such as the Tsar's Winter Palace, the largest palace in the world, and the Hermitage. Typical European buildings of a later period, though of inferior design, gave evidence everywhere of the flourishing capitalism. Petersburg was the center for scientists, writers, musicians, artists, the theatre, and ballet. Through it all endlessly flowed the Neva and its branches, controlled by granite revetments, connecting the city with its bustling harbor several miles away on the Gulf of Finland.

As the Kovalevskys drove from the railway station down almost the entire length of Nevsky Prospect, past cathedrals and buildings, Vladimir pointed out the Medical and Surgical Academy conveniently situated just across the river ahead. Influenced perhaps by her recent work with the ill peasants at Palibino, Sophia had decided she might become a physician. The carriage turned from the main thoroughfare into quiet Sergievakaia Street, and there at Number 24 stood the House of Buturlin. Vladimir's friend Prince Vadbolsky, having lived there himself, had suggested this house after Vladimir's long search had been unsuccessful elsewhere. It was suitably located so that it could be taken over in March by Nadezhda P. Suslova when she returned from Zurich with her medical degree. The sister of Dostoevsky's former mistress, Suslova had been introduced into the academy by Sechenov but in 1864 had been expelled. Her father, a former serf, had then financed her Swiss education. She eventually developed a large gynecological practice in a provincial city.

The Kovalevsky quarters consisted of five rooms on the second floor, pleasant front rooms with high ceilings and large windows. Sophia expressed delight with the arrangements, although to Aniuta she wrote: "I was shocked when I saw my bedroom. Where was my little Heidelberg cell? But that will come later." In the room where Sophia would study, Vladimir had placed between two windows her large desk on which stood a clock and two candlesticks. Nearby was his wedding gift, a fine bookcase containing leather-bound copies of all the books he had published. On the half-bindings the titles appeared in gold, with lines beneath in smaller type reading: "Library of Sophia Vasilevna Kovalevsky." The book by Darwin had its title in English and a reproduction on the cover of his signature taken from one of his letters to Vladimir. Other miscellaneous books had also been selected, including Herzen's novel *Who is to Blame?* In one corner hung a complete skeleton, loaned by Dr. Bokov as his contribution to aid in her anatomy studies. Maria Bokova had helped Vladimir furnish and decorate the rooms.

Sophia, weary as she was, could not sleep that night before dashing off a long letter to her "dear, darling, priceless sisters" at Palibino, in part as follows: "Today we arrived in Petersburg at 12 o'clock; I need not tell you how happy I was to come here; this is an entirely new feeling to come to Petersburg freely, not to visit but to start an industrious life of which we had dreams all these years; this feeling you'll understand easily, and I confess that at first it overwhelmed me.

"But then I became very sad when I thought that you, my dear lovely sisters, and especially you, wonderful Aniuta, with whom we had always fantasized about this, are now at Palibino alone, lonely, and weary of the tedium—whereas I, who until now had always shared everything with you, both sorrow and happiness, now I alone am free and happy with that happiness that previously was possible only in dreams."

After describing the apartment, she continued: "Dear Aniuta, I need you now more than ever before; write me darling, more more; the thought of you must not leave me for a minute; I know that it is very difficult for you, but for Our Lord's sake love me deeply, deeply; after-all, it is not my fault that I am happy and not indifferent to this happiness. All this is so new, so temptingly good for me, that I can restrain myself only by recalling you and our last farewell in mother's room behind the screen; my only prayer is that my ideal will remain as chaste and inviolable as it was during the period of our sorrow and loneliness."

She then went on to say to Aniuta that "my brother" will mail eighty pages of the German book to be translated; that Bokova had them to dinner the first night; that the evening was very gay. Those present included Dr. Sechenov, Dr. Bokov "whom I definitely like very much," and as an impressive surprise, Dr. Nicholas A. Bologolov, prominent surgeon, radical journalist, and friend of Herzen's. "At first I was very embarrassed in the august company and remained discreetly silent," she wrote. "Everybody of course was very kind and friendly to me, though I don't know why." Before leaving to attend his patients Dr. Bokov told Sophia that Strannoliubsky was in despair that she hadn't taken his advice but would nevertheless be delighted to give her further lessons. What that advice may have been is uncertain—possibly not to enter into a nihilistic marriage, possibly to pursue higher mathematics rather than medical studies.

According to descriptions of the dinner companions from various sources, Bokova was "elegant and tightly-corseted and slightly stern"; Dr. Bokov had "a personality of surprising honor and purity, with amiable features in a kind quiet face"; and Dr. Sechenov, author of a book on the brain, had an "extremely thin pock-marked face, sparse small beard, and wonderfully lively and wise eyes."

At this time (and in subsequent letters) Sophia wrote that she would audit physiology under Sechenov and have the use of his own laboratory, would study anatomy under Gruber, and physics if some professor could be induced to accept her. Strannoliubsky came to the apartment for sessions lasting as long as five hours in spherical trigonometry, which she found less interesting than differentials and analytical geometry. Since women were excluded at the university, she would be unofficially an auditor and could not obtain a degree. Sechenov advised her to take the final examination at a gymnasium, because a certificate of maturity (diploma) would be essential in applying to any foreign university. Therefore Sophia had to review history and geography and asked Aniuta to send all the books on these and other subjects from their Palibino library. She later expressed regret when one book could not be found, "because I always become personally attached to books that I study."

Still not knowing the secret triangular relationship in the Bokov household, she wrote Aniuta that she would try again to arrange something between Sechenov and Aniuta. She lamented that Vladimir was not a Mohammedan so that he could add both Aniuta and Zhanna to his harem. With this last remark Sophia finally suspended her first letter after arrival, but only to add next day a report of her first experience at the academy.

She was escorted to Sechenov's lecture by Dr. Bokov, Vladimir, and her beloved Uncle Petinka (who probably had accompanied Sophia's brother to the capital for the new semester). They entered by a back stairway known to Bokov, so as not to be seen by the authorities. "Everything went smoothly," reported Sophia. "The students behaved excellently and didn't stare." An elderly woman in yellow ribbons was also there, perhaps a student midwife, such being permitted to attend certain lectures. In case of future challenge, Sophia later arranged to obtain a student midwife certificate, probably through her anatomy professor.

In a subsequent letter she added that the lecture hall—the first school room she had ever been in—was like an amphitheatre seating about 200 students and that she and her husband sat on the last bench in order to be less conspicuous. Again she was pleased that the men did not stare at her or even seem to notice her presence. On one occasion she feared she had been spotted by the school authorities but nothing happened.

ii

ABOUT THIS time Vladimir's brother arrived in Petersburg from Italy and advised Sophia, should she be expelled, to return dressed as a boy. This advice she had no intention of following. Having entered the university by a back door was bad enough, only justified because it gave the administration an excuse for official blindness—because her presence would inevitably become known—but to deny her sex by disguise was out of the question.

That was Sophia's first meeting with Alexander, age twenty-eight, who had abandoned engineering for a career in biology and had just received an appointment as a sub-professor of biology in Kazan. She found him better looking than Vladimir but was turned off by his advice, spoken to Vladimir but intended for her ears; namely, that it was important for children to maintain ties of love with their parents. Sophia attributed this to the fact that he was himself a new parent. Otherwise she found him to be a good nihilist. Soon she met his wife, Tatiana Kirillovna Semenova. She also saw their baby daughter, Olga, and all of Alexander's live biological specimens, some of which he had collected in Italy.

In a letter she described the wife as pretty but stupid (then crossed out "stupid" and substituted "undeveloped"). With this second meeting Sophia's attitude toward Alexander changed to one of friendliness that lasted many years. He even offered to assist her in her studies if she wished. She now wrote to Aniuta that she liked him best of all her new acquaintances, including Bokova, although she confessed that "in general I love women much more than men, because it is easier to be severe with women and to control them."

As an older man Alexander could see that Sophia was unreasonably biased against parents in general, especially against her own. Doubtless he considered this an obstacle to parental support, especially in view of Vladimir's finances. More than that, however, he must have realized—what is clearly evident—that Sophia would be happier and the marriage would have more chance of becoming a real one, if Sophia did not cut herself off from her parents and relations. She felt close at that time only to Aniuta, her brother, and Uncle Petinka. Her other relations included Madame Briullova, her great-aunt, who about this time called on the Kovalevskys unexpectedly with wedding gifts. She found Sophia after two weeks of marriage apparently happy and observed nothing unfavorable in Vladimir, as she promptly wrote to her niece, Sophia's aunt, in Stuttgart, adding that nevertheless she "feared for the future of my little Sofa." She declined in a letter to be more specific, preferring to wait to "speak openly and frankly" when next they met. The old lady may have observed something suspicious in the living arrangements of the apartment.

At this very time, despite all the excitements of Sophia's new life, so long desired, the first crack in her relationship with Vladimir did become evident.

She wrote to Aniuta: "Brother is very amiable, good, charming, and I am sincerely attached to him, although my friendship, naturally, has lost every trace of exaltation." She went on to add: "You won't believe how solicitous he is about me, how he waits on me and is ready to subordinate all his desires and caprices to mine. I'm terribly ashamed to be so indebted to him; I love him really with my whole soul, but a little as one does a younger brother. I would be most sorry if he knew that something in our present life doesn't satisfy me, and I depend upon you completely, Aniuta, that you won't even hint of this when you see him; because . . . I am dissatisfied only and exclusively with myself," dissatisfied without reason, inasmuch as with regard to platonic love "everything has fallen together to make me good. But without you, Aniuta, I cannot live."

The marriage, in other words, had not really provided the joyous freedom she had expected. Moreover, she admitted feeling a certain falsity in her position. Nonetheless, she enjoyed being treated by professors and others with the respect due a married woman.

iii

As FOR her boast about controlling women, Sophia had not been very successful in controlling Aniuta, who kept eluding her snare. In several letters Sophia referred to the mysterious Petrov who had been under consideration for months. Because of birth or perhaps a police record, Petrov obviously would have been unacceptable to the General, for in urging him as a nihilistic husband, Sophia declared that within a year the parents "will forgive you, no doubt about that, while we, working together, will be able to live for that long in comfortable financial circumstances." Aniuta vacillated in this as in other proposals.

The facts obviously were that Aniuta did not greatly miss her, as Sophia supposed; that her attitude toward her parents was more loving than Sophia's; that she was changeable and more timid than Sophia, or more cautious; that she was not about to burn any financial bridges behind her; and that, although she never so much as hinted the truth, she no longer wanted a nihilistic union. She would not agree to any date for Vladimir to take her from Palibino. She still was a princess in her tower, dreaming of real romance, and especially of reaching Paris to pursue an exciting literary life.

Nevertheless, she permitted the search to continue in Petersburg. Sophia was determined. A zoologist long considered as a prospect came directly into the picture.

Vladimir's brother introduced to the Kovalevskys his friend, Ilia Ilich Mechnikov, who taught biology at the university while working for his doctor's degree. On their first meeting, however, Sophia decided against Mechnikov, because all during dinner he spoke of the importance of family happiness—obviously signaling that he would only enter a real marriage with the wealthy landowner's daughter. Later he conveyed indirectly his definite refusal. Nevertheless he continued as a friend. He gave Sophia permission to attend his biology lectures and sought to have her permitted to audit lectures in physics. The man he approached, however, refused to bend the rules. Instead Sophia made arrangements for private study under an individual named Bobylev, who could only see her on Sundays. She knew too little for a special course and too much for an elementary one. In consequence, she and Vladimir studied on their own and then on Sunday Bobylev clarified any difficulties and helped them perform the necessary experiments. On Fridays, also, Sechenov repeated for them all the experiments done during the regular lectures and gave them additional tutoring.

With Mechnikov the newlyweds went one evening to the French theatre, where for the first time Sophia sat in the cheap seats of the pit; there she found observing the people to be more interesting than the plays, which were "very bad, and one very indecent, although I didn't understand this until the end." Another evening the trio attended the Russian opera *Troubador*.

Besides the persons already mentioned, the Kovalevsky's circle of friends or acquaintances included N. A. Nekrasov, the writer who then ranked not far below Tolstoy and Turgenev; M. E. Saltykov-Shchedrin, a literary satirist; S. P. Botkin, clinical scientist; and Evgeniia Ivanovna Konradi, wife of a surgeon, translator of George Eliot, and crusader for women's education. Through Dr. Bokov they also met the family of Chernyshevsky, who was then in Siberian exile, following his public sentencing at which Vladimir's former fiancé had been arrested. Sophia already had fiction-writing in mind as a sideline and contemplated a novel with Chernyshevsky as the central figure.

Nevertheless, although Petersburg intellectual and political life was exciting, Sophia continued to feel a certain dissatisfaction. In part, at least, this centered on her chosen course of study. When the first enthusiasm wore off she found anatomy "terribly dull." Having learned the Latin names for the bones in the skull, she joked to Aniuta, "Who could believe there is such nonsense in the head?" She especially missed the exhilaration she felt when tackling a problem in mathematics and soon decided that in mathematics, a science followed only by men, she might do more for women than in medicine. Therefore, having passed the examination for the gymnasium certificate of maturity, in anticipation of going abroad, and while continuing at the academy, she devoted more time to her lessons with Strannoliubsky at her apartment. That Sophia had obtained not a women's but a men's gymnasium diploma made her an instant heroine for Litvinova, her future close friend.

iv

SOPHIA HAD not long been at the university before she joined about 400 other young women in signing a petition, promulgated by Evgeniia Konradi, seeking permission for women to attend all university lectures and to take degrees. The first girls' gymnasium had opened in Petersburg in 1858, the year Sophia began studying with Malevich, but after ten years the scholarship there remained second-rate, so that to advance to the level of the average boy, a superior girl upon graduation still had to take additional lessons, privately if her family had means, otherwise by pooling funds with other girls to hire a common tutor. However, for the few girls that could be accommodated, a second gymnasium had been opened to offer better training. Thus the time seemed proper for qualified girls to enter the university.

At this time, and for many years to come, Sophia not only believed women deserved equal education but also supposed such education would bring about gradual social reform. Sophia definitely opposed revolution and the elimination of her aristocratic class, as advocated by many persons she knew. This explains her exasperation over the revolt of male students at the university, just when prospects seemed brightest for women to undertake university life.

Actually the university trouble in late 1868 and the early months of 1869 was part of a larger movement, instigated with revolutionary aims. The official reaction was to impose the discipline of a military educational institution. The old government inspector was replaced by a colonel, who prohibited long hair, careless dress, and the smoking of cigarettes. Several professors to whom students violently objected were retained, and the courses and procedure continued as before. One student leader was expelled, but when this provoked violent student reaction, the colonel agreed he could return at some future time. After such an initial taste of power the students were further inflamed by a speech by Bakunin, urging them first to free the people through revolution and in that way to attain full freedom of education. Passions were also raised by a London letter from Herzen that was widely circulated, although actually the letter was quite moderate.

The result, as Sophia wrote 19 March 1869 to her friend Julia Vsevolodovna Lermontova in Moscow, was that the University of St. Petersburg temporarily closed; many students were arrested and several of them exiled to distant places within European Russia. Sophia observed that "what is saddest for us is that women were almost admitted to the academy and now, of course, are again refused. All this is terribly sad and even sadder because the reason for the entire affair is most insignificant." She clearly was duped as to the underlying aims of student agitation.

V

JULIA LERMONTOVA was Zhanna's cousin and a relative of the famous poet, M. I. Lermontov. Her father directed the First Cadet Corps in Moscow. In 1868 Julia and two friends, who were daughters of a General Federov, had applied to the Agricultural Institute of the university of Petersburg to be accepted as science auditors, but despite the approval of several professors there, the request was rejected. Julia then decided that despite all obstacles she would somehow get to Europe to study medicine or chemistry.

Although Julia and Zhanna were the daughters of sisters, they had not seen one another since early childhood. When Zhanna learned that she had a cousin eager to study science, she began a correspondence. This in turn led to an exchange of letters between Julia and Sophia, resulting in Sophia's closest lifelong friendship. Wanting to meet Sophia, Julia in late 1868 persuaded her father to take her to visit their relatives in Petersburg. There she met Sophia as well as her cousin, who had returned to the capital from Palibino.

On 31 January 1869, Sophia having characteristically resolved to "free" her new friend, wrote Julia that eight young Russian women were already studying in Zurich. "I myself can't wait until I can go to Europe, and how I would like, Julia, to study there with you. I can't imagine a more happy existence than a quiet modest life in some forgotten corner of Germany or Switzerland among my books and studies. I think that such a life seems to you also the height of happiness." Apparently Sophia had learned that Aniuta would not be living with her in Europe.

Julia was attached to her parents and didn't want a nihilistic marriage. Therefore Sophia concentrated, in an undated letter, on stiffening Julia's desire for parental permission to study abroad. Sophia urged her to withstand with courage and even harshness the "tears and despair" of her parents, declaring "your gentle parents would become all the more gentle after a brief separation from you. . . ." She went on to assert that the parents were using their "most powerful ammunition" of material dependence, but that according to Suslova it was possible "to live quite decently on 500 to 600 roubles a year" (about 400 to 480 dollars in 1870) in Switzerland. Consequently she urged Julia to estrange herself from her parents, comparing them to animals being vivesected for a greater good. "If you are going to be affected by your parents' disappointment, then think about the dogs that you'd have to dissect if you achieved your goal and who could look at you with pathetic weeping eyes."

Julia was not inclined to dissect her parents, but she did show them a letter that Sophia enclosed requesting permission for Julia to accompany the Kovalevskys abroad. As this letter from a person almost unknown to them was not favorably received by the Lermontovs, Sophia in her next letter to Julia offered to go to Moscow upon completion of her studies at the end of March to meet the parents and make a personal appeal. This strategy having been agreed upon by further correspondence, Sophia left Petersburg on 2 April for the day-and-night train ride to Moscow.

Julia met her at the long wooden station so that they could talk things over before meeting the parents. In arranging this meeting Sophia, who had been suffering from eye strain, wrote to Julia, "We must be careful that we don't miss one another due to our nearsightedness." To help identify herself Sophia stated she would be wearing a black silk cloak, a white Caucasian scarf, and a grey hat. Fearing that she might not recognize Julia at first sight, she confessed that she had difficulty remembering faces.

The appearance and sincerity of Sophia must have been reassuring to the parents and her arguments unusually persuasive, because, contrary to all expectations, the Lermontovs agreed that their daughter could join the Kovalevskys once they had been accepted at some university abroad. The fact that Sophia's father had been a general and marshal of nobility and her grandfather a general and outstanding scientist must also have been a deciding factor for Julia's military father.

vi

How or when Aniuta left Palibino to join the Kovalevskys is uncertain. Obviously she neither ran away nor was taken off by Vladimir, as impatient Sophia had proposed. Very likely she simply wheedled her parents into permitting her departure. At any rate, without assuming the complications of a nihilistic union that she had apparently come to consider demeaning, Aniuta gained all that she wanted—that is, permission to go abroad without breaking with her parents, and an annual allowance of 1,000 roubles (then about $800), the same amount allocated to her brother in Petersburg. The General further obligated himself to send a like allowance to Sophia during her university career. The girls—despite Sophia's assurance to Julia that one could live decently abroad on 500 to 600 roubles—considered their allowance parsimonious, being as always unaware of the declining financial position of the family. At that time an estate steward might receive about 300 roubles annually, plus housing; 500 roubles a year was the approximate salary of a minor government clerk. Thus each daughter received twice that latter amount to supplement the funds Vladimir supposedly would provide. The General assumed of course that Aniuta would live with the Kovalevskys, so that the 2000 roubles combined for the girls was really a substantial sum.

On 15 April 1869, after months of delay, the Kovalevskys with Aniuta finally left Petersburg for Vienna. This was only possible because a portion of the 20,000 first-installment of Sophia's 50,000-rouble dowry permitted Vladimir to extricate himself partly from his publishing problems and to finance the journey. In a letter written two days before departure to her husband's brother, Sophia had written: "As you predicted, Alexander Onufrievich, we remained in Petersburg longer than we thought, and now Volodia's publishing affairs are so mixed up that he'll barely succeed in leaving day after tomorrow. These last days he was completely confused and had to pay off many old debts; he, of course, became completely downhearted and just sighed the whole day. We leave day after tomorrow. I'll go to Heidelberg with my sister. Vla.Onu. will remain in Vienna. My sister is traveling with us but will leave soon and go to Paris."

In a postscript Vladimir complained about his problems: "Business is very bad, that is debts of 20,000, and although there are publications worth 100,000, their sale is so problematical that it's frightening, but the debts are real."

CHAPTER 12

Heidelberg At Last

i

SOPHIA FOUND Heidelberg to be a charming town, stretching in a narrow line along the Neckar River, flanked by woods and hills, with the university occupying a prominent site. Founded in 1387 on the plan of the University of Paris, the university produced many scholars through the centuries but did not become world famous until the nineteenth century, when the excellence of its library and its faculties of theology, science, medicine, law, and philosophy, together with romantic stories of lively student life, drew students from many countries.

The first account we have of Sophia's arrival is contained in a letter to "Dear Julenka" (Julia Lermontova) dated 28 April:

"I am writing you upon returning from a lecture in Heidelberg. I suppose you are becoming impatient, not having heard from me for such a long time; but I couldn't write sooner, as my fate was decided just yesterday.

"From Petersburg we went to Vienna, where I immediately went to Lang, professor of physics, to ask him to let me attend his lectures. He agreed quite readily, and probably the other professors would have agreed likewise, but nevertheless I decided not to remain in Vienna, as it would have been inconvenient in many respects: first of all, mathematical courses there are inferior; secondly, it is expensive to live there. Therefore, before deciding, I wanted to try my luck in Heidelberg.

"I went there alone with my sister, V. O. staying in Vienna, since if unsuccessful here I would have had to return there. The first day I almost despaired, everything went so badly. Professor Frederick, with whom I was somewhat acquainted, was not then in Heidelberg. I went to Kirchhoff (physics); he is a little old man who used crutches. He was amazed at such an unusual request from a woman and stated that it didn't at all depend upon him to permit my entry, but that I must ask permission from the pro-vice-chancellor, Kopp.

"At this point Professor Frederick returned from his travels, which was a great happiness for me; he responded sympathetically to my request and gave me a card to Kopp. He in his turn said he couldn't assume such an unheard of permission and left it to the will of the professors.

"I again dragged myself to Kirchhoff, who said that he personally would be happy to have me among his auditors, but that it was still necessary for him to discuss it with Kopp. You can imagine how tormenting these delays and half-answers were. The following day Kopp announced his new decision—he would present my affair for consideration by a special commission. Again I had to wait with folded hands.

"I learned that information about me was being gathered in the town. One woman whom I had never laid eyes on told a professor I was a widow. He of course was amazed by such a discrepancy with my own words; I had to send V. O. to him—V. O. having arrived by this time—to convince them that I really had a husband, which seemed important to them. Finally the commission decided to let me hear several lectures, namely mathematics and physics. That was all that I needed, and today I started my studies.

"Now I have 18 lecture periods a week, and that is quite enough, as the largest part of my work is done at home. One thing is sad—that the permission was granted to me as an exception, so that in the fall when you arrive the same permission will have to be obtained again for you; of course, the second time will be easier.

"I can imagine with what impatience you are awaiting autumn, dear Julenka. Just so your parents don't change their minds. However, it seems to me that now it would be quite difficult for them to go back on their word. Write quickly and describe in detail what you are now studying. From bitter experience I advise you to pay attention to the German language. I am now experiencing inconvenience from not knowing it better. It is completely easy for me to listen to the lectures, because scientific German is known to me, but when I have to speak with the professors, then I always feel very inadequate."

Sophia interrupted her letter and did not resume writing until 2 May.

"I started this letter several days ago but didn't mail it and then couldn't find time to finish it. I'm very busy going to lectures; the students behave wonderfully well and don't show any amazement at the presence of a woman.

"I am awaiting autumn with impatience. How good it will be for us

[117]

to have you here. You'll be able to study very well; you'll hear physics from Helmholtz, chemistry from Bunsen. It will be especially good for you with the latter. I'm told that he spends all day guiding students in his laboratory and only in the evenings finds time for his own work. In fact, from all that I hear about Bunsen it appears that he is simply an astonishing man.

"Goodbye. I embrace you fondly and wait impatiently. Assure your parents of my esteem. I forgot to tell you that my sister is now with me but is going to Paris tomorrow, where she probably will remain until the first of July."

Actually, Aniuta remained in Paris much longer and concealed her whereabouts from her parents by sending letters addressed to them for mailing by Sophia. Vladimir, having come at first only to see Sophia, remained to attend the university also, taking subjects that would be useful in his chosen field of geology. Sophia's new surname actually had helped her to be accepted as an auditor, because the biological work of Vladimir's brother, Alexander, was known and valued by several of the professors. In writing to Alexander on June 20, Vladimir characterized the Germans in Heidelberg as Pharisees and Philistines and stated:

"The papers here are writing all kinds of nonsense about Sofa, and all the professors and especially the docents are gossiping terribly. All the gossip reaches S. Lamansky, who from time to time brings us the latest. My studies are going well enough; interest is arising and will grow; it is only sad that Petersburg affairs disturb me. My whole soul isn't in the place." S. I. Lamansky, 28, brother of a prominent Russian financier, had been a leader of student activities in Petersburg in 1861 and was then studying in Heidelberg. His attentions to Sophia aroused Vladimir's jealousy.

Sophia added a note to the letter to Alexander: " . . . How is your wife's health and the little animal's [his daughter]? Give them my regards. I am well situated here; I have 22 lecture periods a week and among them 16 on pure mathematics. Devoted to you."

Pure mathematics was precisely that, whereas most mathematicians in those days usually combined mathematics and physics; that is, pure mathematics and applied mathematics. In maturity Sophia worked in both fields.

During her three semesters at Heidelberg, 1869-70, Sophia attended lectures and seminars in physics and mathematics under Gustave R. Kirchhoff, who made numerous contributions to physics and was joint inventor with Bunsen of the spectrascope. It was he who fully explained the Fraunhofer lines in the solar spectrum, thus leading to knowledge of the chemical composition of the sun, stars, and terrestrial matter. She also attended lectures on physics or mathematics by Herman von Helmholtz. The latter was one of the first to grasp the principle of the conservation of energy and was discoverer of the principles of vortex motion. Most importantly, she studied the theory of elliptic functions under Leo Konigsberger, one of the first students of Weierstrass.

At Heidelberg students could elect what courses they pleased without any requirements, and attendance at class lectures was optional. Although Sophia and most others were serious students, some young men had come primarily for beer and swordplay. Approximately every tenth student wore a cap of one color or another, indicating the fraternity-like corps to which he belonged, and was devoted to dueling, perhaps to acquire a facial scar as a badge of bravery to carry through life. Rules of student behavior were strict, however. Rowdiness in town or disturbing the peace in a beer hall, or being seen in public with an unsuitable woman, could result in several days or longer in the university jail, where the inmate paid for his own food, fire, and light and had ample time for study. A professor took a friendly personal interest in his students but required respect; for failure to salute him politely when meeting on campus or in town, a day or two in jail could serve as a reminder.

ii

THE KOVALEVSKYS had promised to visit Sophia's parents during August but deceived them, causing the parents to be angry when informed that the pair would go instead to Switzerland. Actually they went instead to see Aniuta in Paris. She lived there on 150 francs a month and was studying typographical composition by which she hoped to double her income.

From there the Kovalevskys went to London, where Vladimir introduced Sophia to such men of science as Charles Darwin; Thomas Huxley, the proponent of scientific humanism; and William Carpenter, the naturalist and physiologist. While moderately impressed by such individuals, Sophia was much more interested in making the acquaintance of the famous woman novelist, George Eliot (Mary Ann Evans). Although she very much wanted to meet the woman she so greatly admired, she hesitated to impose herself. She remembered that her own great uncle by marriage, O. I. Senkovsky, author of many stories and sentimental novels, had enjoyed such popularity that strangers became a positive nuisance by calling upon him and introducing themselves with some such remark as this: "I considered, sir, that I hadn't used my time in Petersburg properly if I hadn't been to see the great Senkovsky."

Sophia feared being such a nuisance, but Vladimir's friend, a Mr. Ralston, head of the Slavic section of the British Museum, while informing Sophia that the novelist was reclusive because she lived with G. W. Lewes, a married man, nevertheless urged that a letter be sent. A prompt reply came back, stating that Sophia's name was known to her through an English mathematician who had met Sophia at Heidelberg, and that for a long time she had wanted to meet Sophia personally.

In her "Recollections of George Eliot" Sophia years later wrote: "She set the day when I could visit her and talk with her heart to heart. How happy I was to hear this. George Eliot had thought about me as long as a year ago! There were few things in my life of which I was so proud."

After meeting Sophia, the novelist wrote in her diary for 5 October 1869: "On Sunday an interesting Russian pair came to see me—M. and Mme Kovalevsky, she a pretty creature, with charming modest voice and speech, who is studying mathematics (by allowance, through the aid of Kirchhoff) at Heidelberg; he, amiable and intelligent, studying the concrete sciences apparently—especially geology; and about to go to Vienna for six months for this purpose, leaving his wife in Heidelberg!" In the same diary entry Eliot noted that she had begun a long-meditated poem, "The Legend of Jubal."

Sophia recorded that Lewes and Eliot at that time occupied a house in St. John's Wood Road, "a very pretty part of London rich in private gardens." A maid led Sophia into a fairly spacious living room furnished in "typical English" fashion. "Mr. Lewes and G. Eliot were already waiting to greet me politely. I must confess that at my first sight of G. Eliot I desperately hoped that I was mistaken, that this wasn't she but somebody else: to such a degree did she appear to me old, unattractive, and quite unlike the image I had formed in my imagination . . . But alas, it was true, that my mental image was quite unlike actuality. A small, extremely thin little figure with a disproportionately large and heavy head, a mouth with enormous protruding teeth, a nose straight and beautifully contoured but too large for a woman's face, some sort of old fashioned hairdress, a black gown of light transparent material that emphasized the bony neck and more sharply defined the yellowness of the face—that is what I beheld to my dismay. I had no time to control my confusion before G. Eliot came up to me and began speaking in her soft, wonderful, velvet voice. The first sounds of this reconciled me with reality and resurrected G. Eliot to me as she had lived in my imagination. Never in my life have I heard a softer, more ingratiating and bewitching voice. When I read the famous words of Othello about Desdemona's voice I involuntarily recall the voice of G. Eliot.

"She seated me on a small divan beside her and at once began quite naturally such a sincere and simple conversation that I felt we had been acquainted for a long time. I can't recall now what we talked about at our first meeting; I can't say there was anything wise or original in what she said; but I know that not even a half hour had elapsed before I had surrendered completely to her enchantment and felt already that I loved her terribly, and that the real G. Eliot was ten times more wonderful than my imagined one. I positively am unable to explain in what existed her peculiar fascination, to which everybody involuntarily submitted . . .

"Turgenev, who was a great admirer of women, once remarked to me about G. Eliot, 'I know she is ugly, but when I am with her I don't see this.' He also said she was the first woman to make him understand that it was possible to lose one's mind and fall in love with a woman who was unquestionably not beautiful." Sophia continued on to describe her delight in conversing with the novelist, who had a talent for drawing a person into conversation and guessing the person's thoughts, and that her charm lasted through the years.

Sophia described Lewes as a lean and lively person, witty and voluble, who asked whether Eliot's writing and his own were valued in Russia. He was especially pleased to hear that his *Physiology in Common Life* was at that time so popular that, as Sophia jokingly told him, "Among us a young girl need only to read this book, or merely have it adorn her writing table, to become known at once as modern and advanced." Unfortunately his novel *Ranthorp* enjoyed no such popularity. He also wrote plays and biographies.

Sophia devoted several pages to psychological speculation about the curious English pair, who were mutually supportive, and about Eliot's later union with the young J. W. Cross; to her own analysis of several Eliot novels, and to her later conversations with Eliot about her novels. Sophia, whose own life experiences were so much a part of what she wrote, obviously found it psychologically puzzling that Eliot's inner life and motives and experiences, as apprehended by those who knew her, found "no echo or explanation in any of her novels."

Sophia and Vladimir before leaving England were again guests of the Lewes. "One of their regular visitors on Sunday afternoons and one of their most devoted friends was Herbert Spencer. There I had an opportunity to meet him and must admit that our acquaintance began in a very original way.

"There were already about twelve persons in her sitting room. The company was rather mixed: there were, as I recall, a very young lord, who had just returned from some little known country, several musicians and painters, and two or three others not having any specialty; apart from me there was just one other woman guest, the wife of a painter. . . . Very few women from respectable English society ventured to appear at G. Eliot's. Mr. Lewes presented each guest to me and usually mentioned those qualities about an individual that would interest me.

"I was there for some time when an elderly man with grey sideburns and a typical English face entered. This time nobody mentioned his name, but G. Eliot at once turned to him. 'How happy I am that you came today,' she said, 'because I can present to you the living refutation of your theory—a woman mathematician. Allow me to present my friend,' she continued, turning to me but still not mentioning his name. 'I must however tell you that he rejects even the possibility of the existence of a woman mathematician. He is willing to allow that in an extreme case there might appear a woman who through mental ability rises above that of the average man, but he affirms that such a woman will always direct her mind and acuteness to the analysis of her friends' lives and will never let herself be chained to pure abstract thought. Please try to change his views.'

"The elderly little man sat down beside me and peered at me with some curiosity. I didn't suspect at all who he was, particularly since there was nothing imposing in his manner. The conversation centered on the everlasting and unending theme of the rights and abilities of women and whether it would harm or profit humanity if more women dedicated themselves to science. My companion made several partially ironical remarks, which as I now judge were mainly meant to bring out my refutation. I must say that at this time I was only twenty years old . . . and that I felt the enraptured ardor of the neophyte, and that all timidity left me when I had to break the pike for a rightful cause. Besides, as I have mentioned, it hadn't even occurred to me with what an adversary I was competing, and G. Eliot on her part was doing everything she could to incite me to argue. This was not hard to do. Carried away by the argument I soon forgot my surroundings and failed to notice how the other guests little by little grew silent, listening curiously to our conversation, which was growing more lively.

"A good three-quarters of an hour our duel lasted before G. Eliot decided to stop it. 'You have defended our mutual interest well and courageously,' she said to me with a smile, 'and if my friend Herbert Spencer still isn't convinced, then I'm afraid he is incorrigible.' "

Could Sophia, after so short a time in the country, actually have employed English conversationally well enough to argue as well as she seemed to remember? She did like to be considered clever! Nevertheless, she did have a quick ability to pick up a language well enough to be understood, as was the case later with Swedish, and she could read English; so perhaps she managed well enough in broken English with Spencer. The latter was then at work developing his *Principles of Psychology*, one of his books attempting to formulate the theory of evolution in general terms embracing philosophy, psychology, ethics, sociology, and educational theory. His thought influenced American philosophers and educators more than it did their British counterparts.

Sophia did not see Eliot again for eleven years, although they exchanged several letters and sent messages through common friends. Although Sophia visited London in 1870 she did not meet Eliot again until November of 1880, at which time she hesitated to see the novelist. Lewes had died and Eliot, at the age of sixty-one, had just married an American who was half her age and who had been in love with her for a long time. To Sophia the situation seemed so inappropriate that she preferred to remember the novelist from an earlier day. When informed, however, that Eliot knew of her presence in London and would be hurt if she did not visit, Sophia renewed her acquaintance. She found the novelist as charming as ever, happy in her marriage, the relationship neither abnormal nor laughable but one of mutual sincerity and satisfaction and common tastes. Several weeks later Eliot died of pneumonia.

iii

AFTER RETURNING to the continent in September of 1869, the Kovalevskys became stranded in Paris without funds to proceed farther. As Aniuta could not help them financially, Vladimir appealed to his brother. After recounting again the lack of income from his books in Petersburg, he continued: "To a certain extent I'm fearful that some creditors may cause unpleasantness, and most of all I'm concerned lest they threaten the estate. Therefore it occurred to me to sell my part of the estate to you. Then at least you could be completely calm and I also." No sale took place.

Vladimir's letter continued: "Despite economy exercised to the highest degree we don't have enough money. My wife does not receive an allowance from her parents until November, and so we are here with only fifty francs and nothing with which to return to Heidelberg, where we could live on credit until she receives her allowance and whatever moneys I might get. But the problem is that we owe our landlady there 120 gulden, which must be paid immediately upon our return . . .

"If you have any possibility of getting this sum prior to November, then for God's sake send it immediately in the name of Sophia Kovalevsky to the old Heidelberg address: 3A [?] Untere Neckarstrasse. We will pawn the watch here and get out of Paris, but it is necessary to pay the landlady at least part of the 120 gulden."

He expressed his desire to go to Vienna for the best course in geology but as events developed had to remain in Heidelberg for another semester. He reported that in Paris he had seen Gregory N. Vyrubov, prominent naturalist and sociologist, whose Russian estates supported him generously while he studied science abroad. Vyrubov was coldly polite but did not respond to hints for a loan. Later Vladimir learned that this individual had reacted to an old and false rumor that years earlier Vladimir had been a spy for Herzen. It is a curious fact that educated Russians of the period were unusually tolerant of the ideas and beliefs of others in political matters, however, antithetical to their own, but of course the company of a supposed spy was another matter.

Finally the Kovalevskys managed to reach Heidelberg, where happiness awaited Sophia in the person of Julia Lermontova. Supplied with funds by her parents, Julia rescued the Kovalevskys from their temporary financial predicament, although Vladimir also borrowed fifty gulden from their friend Lamansky.

Obviously the Kovalevskys would not attempt to live within their income. On 25 October Vladimir again dunned his brother: "If you become a professor in ordinary then perhaps I'll ask you to give me 250 roubles a year, if nothing can be had from the estate. One needs to have 1,000 roubles to work practically in the laboratory and make distant excursions in the spring, which for geology is necessary. In England I became acquainted with Geksli [Thomas, zoologist, president of the Royal Geological Society]; he praises your work highly and was terribly kind to us, invited us for an evening, introduced my wife to mathematicians and me to geologists. Send him, Sasha, all your work. . . In fact you've become well known; Lewes, Carpenter, and others know your work. If you go to Europe visit London and you will be well received."

iv

FROM THIS time onward, Julia Lermantova's "Recollections of Sophia Kovalevsky" provide most of what is known about Sophia's life in Heidelberg and Berlin. She wrote about Sophia at the request of Anna Charlotte Leffler when that Swedish woman was preparing her *Sonya Kovalevsky: Our Mutual Experiences, and the Things She Told Me About Herself*, in which Julia is called "Inez." Julia's manuscript came into the hands of Vladimir's brother, who eventually deposited it in the Russian state archives.

Julia's parents were well-educated Russians with a large library. For their children they hired not one tutor but different ones qualified in various fields, which they were able to do because they lived close to Moscow. They even kept a special equipage with horses to transport tutors between central Moscow and their property on the outskirts. From an early age Julia had done experiments in chemistry. Her parents did not oppose a scientific career for her and approved of her efforts to study at Moscow University. But they did object to the dangers of her studying in a distant land. These objections Sophia had overcome, initiating a close friendship with Julia that lasted throughout Sophia's life. Julia was plain of face, with a no-nonsense hair-do severely parted in the middle, somewhat drooping eyelids, sharply prominent nose, large mouth, prominent teeth, and receding chin— not by any means ugly but far from beautiful.

Julia remembered that upon Sophia's return from Paris she was "as fresh and attractive as at our first acquaintance, except that there was more fire and sparkle in her eye." Julia continued: "She was animated more than ever before by eagerness to resume the studies she had begun. This serious search for knowledge did not interfere, however, with her finding pleasure in other things, even it seemed trivial ones. I recall the day after her return when the three of us went walking. We went quite far through the environs of Heidelberg and found ourselves on level ground. Together Sofa and I began running, racing one another like two small children. Dear Lord, how much jollity and happiness there is in my recollections of that first period of our university life! Then Sofa seemed most happy, happy in a different way than before.

"Nonetheless, when later on Sofa had occasion to speak about her youth, she recalled it with a bitter feeling of displeasure, as if, for her, youth had flashed by uselessly. But when I recall this early period in Heidelberg it seems to me that Sofa had no basis for complaint. Her youth was full of the most noble feelings and aims; besides this she lived hand in hand with a man who loved her with restrained passion. She apparently treated him with the same gentleness. To both of them, seemingly, that painfully unalterable passion that ordinarily is called love was still foreign. It was only in this first year that I remember Sofa as happy, however; the following year was not the same."

Julia commented further: "Sofa's outstanding abilities, her love for mathematics, and her unusually sympathetic personality attracted everyone she met. There was something in her absolutely adorable. All the professors under whom she studied were enthusiastic about her

[125]

talents; besides that, she was hard-working and could sit at her desk by the hour doing mathematical calculations. Her moral image was completed by a deep and complicated spiritual psyche such as I never encountered again in anybody."

Weekdays Sophia spent at the university and evenings studying, leaving only Sunday for long walks or for an occasional visit to a theatre in Mannheim, about fifteen miles away, or for a social call upon some professor's family. The girls also ascended to the brownish-pink ruins of the old castle, its scars partly covered by ivy, its tower crowned by a growth of small trees and shrubs. Together they investigated its dungeon and cavernous rooms, marveled at its famed wine cask as large as a cottage, examined its antiquities and historic manuscripts in the museum, and sauntered along its terraces and through its leafy groves.

Julia recalled that Sophia's professors spoke of her as "something extraordinary" and that news about the "surprising Russian girl spread through the entire small town, so that often people stopped on the street to look at her."

Julia added: "Once, having returned home, she told me laughingly how one poorly-dressed woman with a child in her arms stopped at the sight of her and said loudly to the little one, 'Look, look, there's that girl that goes to school so diligently.' "

Understandably Sophia was not displeased by such attention; to gain unusual recognition was one motivating force in her life. Yet she retained her quiet manner, and in her relations with professors and students "always felt great shyness and even anxiety."

Furthermore: "She never entered the university except with lowered gaze, as though not daring to look directly at anybody. She spoke with classmates only when it was absolutely necessary for her studies. This modest deportment pleased her German professors very much; they generally attributed great significance to a woman's reserve, especially in one so outstanding as Sofa, who moreover was occupied with such an abstract subject as mathematics. And this modesty was not at all assumed at this period of Sofa's life. I recall how once, having returned from the university, she told me that during the lecture she noticed that one of the professors or students had made a mistake in his calculations on the blackboard. The poor fellow was in misery over the problem, not realizing the nature of his mistake. After hesitating for a long time, Sofa finally gathered courage and with pounding heart went to the board to point out the error."

But the life together of Julia, Sophia, and Vladimir—"so happy and so maintained, thanks to Kovalevsky, who responded with lively interest to every question, even to such as had no relation to science"—was not destined to continue.

V

MEANWHILE, JULIA encountered less difficulty in gaining permission to attend classes than had Sophia, because a precedent had been established by a person of approved demeanor, obvious seriousness, and demonstrated ability; and Julia was her friend.

Nonetheless, Julia did not gain entrance to the laboratory of R. W. E. Bunsen. The reason given was true enough; she was unqualified. An experimental chemist, Bunsen was the first to discover how to produce magnesium in quantity, developed spectral analysis, and incidentally invented the Bunsen burner still found today in every chemical laboratory. He was a rather crusty bachelor and for years had proclaimed that no woman would ever profane his laboratory. Then he encountered Sophia. Julia had qualified herself by studying qualitative analysis in a private laboratory during her first semester in Heidelberg, but Bunsen's sacred precinct still remained closed to her, until Sophia called upon him to exert successfully her powers of persuasion. When the effects of her charm had worn off he realized fully what had happened. Several years later when Weierstrass of Berlin visited Heidelberg, Bunsen related the incident, proclaiming Sophia a dangerous woman who had made him eat his own words. He was given to exaggeration, and Weierstrass wrote Sophia to ask if the story really was true.

Apparently Sophia also spent some time in Bunsen's laboratory. Julia, under him, learned his methods of quantitative and qualitative analysis of ores and the separation of rare metals. She also studied chemistry under Herman F. M. Kopp, who besides being vice-chancellor devoted his research to the correlation between physical properties and chemical compositions. She studied physics under Kirchhoff and other subjects under others.

vi

JULIA CHARACTERIZED Vladimir as a "very talented and hard-working man, completely without pretentions in his habits, and never feeling the need for recreation." She observed: "Sofa often said that 'he needs only to have a book and a glass of tea to feel completely satisfied.' In this peculiarity of his character there was something that really offended Sofa. She became jealous of his studies, as it seemed to her that they excluded her or relegated her to the last place in his affections . . . But still she somehow could not reconcile herself to live apart from her husband and began to disturb him with endless demands. She would insist that she could not travel without him and would ask for his company without regard to his important studies, or she would force him to do all kinds of errands and to help in trivial affairs, all of which he always readily and politely took upon himself despite the urgency of his own work.

"When Sofa many years later discussed with me her past life, she with utmost bitterness always expressed the following complaint: 'Nobody ever sincerely loved me!' When I retorted, 'But your husband loved you so deeply,' she would answer, 'He loved me only when I was with him, but he could always get along perfectly well without me.'

"She couldn't tolerate failure. No sooner did she think of a goal than she would strive with all her strength to achieve it, using every means at her command. For this reason she always achieved what she wanted, except on those occasions when emotion interfered, at which times, in some strange fashion, she lost the acuteness of judgment habitual to her. She demanded too much always from the one who loved her, and whom she loved in turn, always wanting to take by force what the person loving her would himself have given willingly if she had not used such passionate insistence.

"She felt always an irresistible need for gentle intimacy, a need for having a person always with her to share everything with her, and at the same time she made life impossible for the person in such a close relationship. She was too restless in character, too lacking in harmony, to find satisfaction for very long in a quiet life full of the affection of which she apparently dreamed. Besides this, she was too individual in character to pay sufficient attention to the yearnings and inclinations of the person living with her [as Julia herself over many years discovered]. Kovalevsky likewise had an extremely restless nature. He was constantly being carried away by new ideas and plans. Only God knows whether these two beings, so richly endowed, under any circumstances could have lived together happily."

Obviously the emotional dependence Sophia in her early years had felt for her nurse, and then especially for her sister, had at this time largely been transferred to Vladimir, and in his absence partially to Julia. All her life Sophia's nervous nature feared loneliness and future uncertainty. Yet she would not—perhaps psychologically could not—take the step Vladimir desired to bind him to her in an intimately physical way.

vii

WHILE SOPHIA and Julia were enjoying the relative academic freedom of Heidelberg, the latter's cousin and Aniuta's close friend,

HEIDELBERG AT LAST

Zhanna (Anna Mikhailovna Evreinova) already was twenty-five years of age and had not been able to begin her higher education. When in 1866 she had asked to go abroad, her father, who had been in charge of the court system of Pavlovsky, and then was adjutant-general in charge of the imperial palace at Peterhof on the Gulf of Finland twenty miles from Petersburg, had promised to reconsider her request after three years. When in 1869 she approached him again in the matter, however, he angrily denied permission.

Learning of this denial, Sophia in characteristic fashion resolved to act. It seemed to her some urgency existed, because Zhanna wrote that she was afraid of being kidnapped and forced to be the mistress of the Grand Duke Nicholas Nicholaevich, brother of the Tsar, who on two occasions had accosted her in the park near the university. Stories circulated of some ballet dancer or actress having suffered that fate at the hands of a powerful nobleman, but Zhanna's fears doubtless were greatly exaggerated if not imaginary. Her cousin Julia characterized her as eccentric. Zhanna scorned society life and did not dress well, although she was quite good looking, being tall with a good carriage and having a good profile and thick dark hair. Since on both occasions when encountering the royal personage she had been without a chaperone, and unattractively dressed, it is possible he mistook her position in society. More probably he was merely saluting a young woman whose identity he knew by sight because of her father's position with the palace.

However, true or false, gossip did circulate in Petersburg. E. A. Shtakenshneider, daughter of the court architect, recorded third hand in her diary that the Grand Duke paid court to Zhanna very seriously, that her father encouraged her, and that in her helpless position Zhanna wrote Sophia that she would drown herself unless she could escape the country.

In any event, the Kovalevskys hastened to make arrangements for Zhanna to join them. Having himself in his younger days crossed the border illegally several times by a smuggler's route through a swamp, a route by which illegal publications entered the country, Vladimir directed Zhanna to obtain 200 roubles from V. I. Evdokimov, who had been left in charge of his publishing affairs, and who would introduce her to the necessary individuals to effect her escape through the swamp. Although she came under fire by a border guard she crossed bravely and successfully, arriving in Heidelberg on 2 November 1869. She then telegraphed her parents of her whereabouts and later wrote her sisters. Unfortunately for Evdokimov, a former army officer turned nihilist, who came under suspicion as the friend of a suspect in a political murder case, Zhanna's letter of thanks compromised him. He was arrested,

LITTLE SPARROW

along with A. A. Cherkesov, a wealthy landowner who operated book-shops to spread nihilist ideas, and who also sold Vladimir's scientific books. This put a financial clamp on Vladimir, because for a consider-able time his publishing enterprise closed down entirely.

While the younger girls studied, Zhanna had a companion in Aniuta, who had recently returned from Paris, somewhat disillusioned regarding a literary life. The presence of the two new arrivals over-crowded the Kovalevsky apartment, so that Vladimir was forced to find a room elsewhere. At first, relations between him and Sophia remained much as before. She visited him often and took long walks with him. Aniuta and Zhanna, however, were impolite to him, thinking that since the marriage was fictitious he should be off somewhere else. "This interference in the life of the young couple," Julia observed, "led to small disputes and soon spoiled the good relations that existed among the members of our small circle."

After several weeks spent in this manner Vladimir decided to leave Heidelberg. He wished, moreover, to devote himself wholeheartedly, without the distraction of Sophia, to scientific study in his chosen field. Before settling down in Munich for that purpose he first spent inter-semester time in Tubingen and Jena, presumably with Sophia, for at that time they made a journey together that gave her great pleasure. The calendar of German universities afforded ample time for travel. The scholastic year began in the spring, the first semester extending from early May to early July, followed by about three months of summer vacation; the fall semester ran from early October to early March, followed by another vacation of about six weeks.

One winter day not long after Vladimir's departure, good news came for Zhanna in the form of an insured letter from her parents. This con-tained a Russian passport for her to be in Europe and a draft for 70 gulden. It also contained a letter from her sisters, rebuking her gently for her actions but stating that neither they nor her parents were angry with her. Her mother had grieved terribly until the telegram had ar-rived, and now she was distressed that Zhanna had taken nothing with her. Therefore Zhanna should write at once to specify her needs in clothing from home and should state how much money she needed in order to live in Europe. The family only asked that she write to them frequently, sharing her sorrows and happiness with them, and turning to them in every need.

Concerning this turn of events, Sophia in a letter to Vladimir com-mented: "How do you like this! Just try to figure them out! If Zhanna had lived with them ten more years they would have continued to tor-ment her and wouldn't have let her leave for any reason; but she ran

[130]

away—and they have softened! Now Zhanna can start studying at once. You can imagine in what a state of rapture we are! It is needless for her to concern herself about getting accepted by the university until spring, as she will have enough work getting that nasty Latin into her head. . ."

Looking forward to her own departure for study elsewhere, Sophia very much wanted Zhanna to be admitted so that she could remain as a companion for Julia should the latter not accompany Sophia. Aniuta had returned to Paris and would not return; she had become associated with the socialist writer Andre Leo on a periodical called *Women's Rights*.

Encouraged by the reaction of Zhanna's parents, which Sophia— who considered them ogres—still could not understand, Sophia resolved to "free" yet another Russian girl, Julia's cousin, Olga. Therefore in her letter to Vladimir she added: ". . . today I am going to write to Olenka Lermontova, so that if possible we can draw her here to us. From all that Julia told me about her I am beginning to feel great sympathy for her, despite her reserve and unsociability which maddened me so in Petersburg." She then went on to magnify Olga's sufferings and disappointments and character defects, "but it seems to me that she can become a very good woman." She outlined to Vladimir a plan for one Sonechka Ushakova, who was returning to Russia in the spring, to have Olga leave home and live with her until arrangements could be made for her to cross the border as Zhanna had done. Then she could receive money from her parents, and Julia and Olga together could get by on 1,000 roubles a year. There is no indication that Olga had the slightest interest in this proposal.

In concluding her letter Sophia indicated her definite emotional need for Vladimir, at least in his absence: "Goodbye, dear one. I'll come as soon as the holidays begin. . . . I'm awaiting the time with impatience, as I want to talk and dream with you, especially since there is happiness in my soul that I want to share quickly with you. . . . Write more often and love your Sofa."

CHAPTER 13

Adventure in Paris

i

MEANWHILE IN Paris, having become involved in friendships with revolutionary Russian emigrés, Aniuta had formed an attachment with Victor Jaclar, a man of French peasant background who was exactly her own age, twenty-seven, and who had become a revolutionary leader following his expulsion from university for political activity. A tall individual, bespectacled, with the appearance of an artist, he had long black hair, a small beard, an uncertain walk, and a nervous manner. When in mid-1870 he fled France to avoid deportation, because of reprisals over the murder of a police official, Aniuta accompanied him to Geneva, presumably as his supposed wife. Actually it is not clear whether she had already joined Jaclar in an intimate relationship, depending upon one's interpretation of her lamentation in a letter to Sophia that she seemed destined, for lack of necessary papers, to remain an old maid for life.

Her difficulty probably involved lack of birth and baptismal certificates, a passport being insufficient for even a civil marriage. Therefore she sent Sophia a letter to be mailed from Heidelberg to her parents, mentioning her desire to travel to Switzerland to marry Jaclar, and requesting that the essential papers be sent to her. So that the union would be legal everywhere in Europe and also in Russia, she planned a civil ceremony to be followed by a Russian Orthodox marriage.

When no response came from her parents, she speculated to Sophia, ". . . perhaps they have learned something about our life in Paris and are so angered that they won't answer." She proposed writing again to state that she had joined Jaclar in Geneva but had found her Russian passport inadequate and that papers from Russia were essential to end her untenable position. She did not send such a letter, however, or at least not for a long time, if ever—because when parents pay they have their say, and Aniuta wanted a dowry and depended upon the continuation of her allowance.

As a matter of fact, Jaclar had no money, and those installments on the 1,000-rouble yearly allowance constituted their principal support, supplemented in Switzerland by what the couple could earn by giving lessons, Jaclar in mathematics and Aniuta in Russian. As a favor to a woman friend Aniuta also translated into Russian some tracts by Karl Marx. Evenings she taught English to Jaclar, using *The Subjection of Women*, the only book they owned in English, as a sort of text. Both pawned their watches. Near the end of their time in Switzerland Jaclar obtained a temporary teaching post.

Aniuta's attitude toward events in France is clear from her statement to Sophia. She wrote: "Jaclar impatiently awaits definite words from his friends about the disposition of the brains. It would be desirable to undertake something in case of an overthrow [of the Bonapartists]— but then, the devil doesn't joke; perhaps they will be victorious, in which case farewell to the revolution for several years. Confidence would be restored, the merchants and bourgeoisie and chauvinists would be on the side of Bonaparte [Napoleon III], and perhaps we will simply have to regret that the opportunity was lost while Paris was free of army troops."

No papers came from Palibino. Having asked Aniuta to give up her idea of such an unsuitable marriage, and receiving no answer, the Korvin-Krukovskys ceased writing to her. They presumed she would do nothing without the papers and did not learn until the following year that Aniuta was not all that time with Sophia in Heidelberg.

Jaclar finally addressed a letter to the General in which, as Aniuta wrote Sophia, he "simply and frankly, without concealing his beliefs or position, said that he was sorry to be the cause of the rupture" between Aniuta and her family, but asked the General whether it would be humanly possible for him to give up the thought of marrying Aniuta when he saw her complete attachment to him. Jaclar also explained his material position but hoped always to be able to give Aniuta at least a life secure from want. Apparently there was no reply.

ii

AT THE end of the university term in Heidelberg the Kovalevskys had planned to visit Paris, where Sophia wished to meet certain mathematicians, and where Vladimir intended to examine paleontological specimens in museums. These plans were upset by the disruption of railroad transportation and the clogging of roads during German mobilization for the Franco-Prussian War, which did not erupt into hostilities until 2 August 1870. Prior to that the borders of France and Belgium had been closed.

While the Kovalevskys remained indecisive, Julia, as always during her holidays, went to visit her parents in Russia. Zhanna's father at the threat of war wrote that he would come for her. Being fearful that she might not be permitted to return unless a definite arrangement for her further education had been made, Zhanna hastened to Leipzig, where she desired to study law. The professors rejected her, however. Under a change of plan her mother instead of her father arrived in Heidelberg to find her gone and proceeded to Leipzig. Through the mother's influence with the Russian ambassador, or perhaps at the request of that grand duke Zhanna had suspected, John I of Saxony overruled the professors and assured the Russian girl a place at the beginning of the autumn semester, whereupon she returned to vacation in Russia. The Saxon ruler even was present several years later in 1873 when Zhanna passed her oral examination brilliantly. Subsequently she traveled in France, England, and Italy. Then at monasteries on the shore of the Adriatic she studied the ancient laws of the southern Slavic peoples and eventually published her findings. Upon returning to Russia as that country's first doctor of law, she became an ardent advocate of women's rights. Her lectures on such rights were printed in Russia, Europe, and the United States. In 1885 she became co-publisher of *Severny vestnik* (*The Northern Herald*) in which Aniuta's last story appeared.

Meanwhile, on 25 July 1870, the Kovalevskys finally set forth for London, hoping to visit Paris later. By train they could only get as far as Mannheim, but there they fortuitously secured passage on a Dutch vessel going down the Rhine, debarking at Cologne to travel overland through Aachen into Belgium, and thence via Ostend to London. They took an apartment close to the British Museum where Vladimir spent his days while Sophia renewed acquaintances with mathematicians she had met the previous year.

The departure of Aniuta and Jaclar for France was delayed first by the latter's illness and then by the turn of political events. General Trochu of the Orleanist party became military governor of Paris and then in September temporary head of the national government. Aniuta consoled herself with the thought that the peace the Orleanists would have to arrange with the Prussians would be so humiliating to France that it could be used as propaganda for a revolution. She advised Sophia against going to Paris, saying it would soon be under siege and would be no place for peaceful scientists. She looked with ironical disbelief upon Vladimir's plan to study in Paris during all the turmoil;

but, if that was his plan, she intimated a certain distaste for ivory tower scholars.

Actually Vladimir snorted somewhat like an old warhorse, but not for long. As he wrote from London to his brother: "The war really interferes with my studies; it distracts my attention to be always waiting for the newspaper with dispatches. I think that by the time we reach Paris it will already be a Prussian city, and this will be good for the French; it will perhaps knock out their desire to be a military nation and most importantly will overthrow the Bonapartes forever." His personal concern was that the war might prevent German universities from opening in the autumn.

Jaclar, ignoring personal danger, could no longer delay returning to France. Early in September he and Aniuta arrived in Lyon, just in time for the proclamation of the provisional republic declared after the capture of Napoleon III. Publicly Jaclar was chosen by the new government to sit on the Lyon committee for public safety. Secretly he was chosen by the Marxists of the International in Lyon to represent them in Paris.

Aniuta from Paris advised Sophia in England that libraries were closed and books stored in basements in anticipation of Prussian bombardment of the capital. Research would thus be impossible. Nevertheless, right up to the siege, the Kovalevskys planned to go to Paris. If well received by the mathematicians Sophia might remain there through the winter.

During his last weeks in London, at the request of his brother, Vladimir asked Darwin to loan a certain biological work. In answer Darwin sent two heavy volumes as a gift, flatteringly inscribed to Alexander. "I am sorry for poor Darwin," Vladimir wrote his brother. "I know that he hadn't any copies of his own and simply bought both volumes in order to present them to you." In gratitude Vladimir translated several recent lectures by Alexander into English and took them to Darwin. Within a few years Darwin would consider Vladimir, not Alexander, as the outstanding Russian in the field of evolutionary science.

Then the Kovalevskys finally abandoned their Paris plans and set forth for Leipzig, where Vladimir expected to study, but en route Sophia decided on Berlin instead.

· · ·
iii

BEFORE PROCEEDING chronologically with Sophia's pursuits in mathematics, it seems best to jump ahead several months in order to conclude with the experiences of the Kovalevskys and Jaclars under the Commune and thereafter.

In the spring of 1871 Sophia abruptly interrupted her studies in Berlin. Perhaps no episode in her life is so clouded by uncertainty as that concerning the part she and her father and Vladimir played in the escape of Aniuta's lover from jail. For obvious reasons pertaining to Sophia's position in Berlin and her sister's future residence in Russia and her father's reputation, the involvement of the family was kept as secret as possible. Years later in Russia when her former suitor, Semevsky, asked Aniuta to enter into his autograph book her comments on the Paris uprising, she merely shrugged and handed back the book with no more than her signature.

The soviet academician Nechkina, and others, by interpreting facts and suppositions to suit the party line, concluded that Sophia rushed to Paris to participate in the uprising. Actually she had no interest whatever in revolutionary participation; in fact, she firmly withstood the influence of the propagandist, Natasha Armfeld, who had been in Heidelberg before going underground. Sophia did deeply sympathize throughout her life with Poland's struggle for freedom from Russia and Germany, and she was tolerant of persons with revolutionary ideas if they supported the women's movement, but she had no sympathy for Marxist revolution. At that period, in fact, she was not even concerned about women's rights in general but only about quality education for young women. She never scattered her energy but rather directed it to one goal for maximum effect, like a good general. In going to Paris Sophia's only concern, and with very good reason, was for the safety of her beloved sister!

Sophia had worried about Aniuta for months, although letters arrived assuring her of her sister's well-being. Then letters stopped during the siege of Paris. Finally, following three weeks of intense bombardment, the provisional government sued for peace on 28 January 1871. Thenceforth Sophia supposed Aniuta would be safe. But then word reached Berlin of the rising on 18 March of the Paris Commune, the flight of the republican government to Versailles, and soon rumors of poor Parisians having to eat dogs and cats. Each commune, the smallest political subdivision in France, had a considerable measure of self-government, with an elected council presided over by a mayor. The Paris revolt was a revolutionary assertion that the Paris Commune should have full autonomy and the nation be merely a federation of many communes, instead of being controlled by a strong central government. This "divide and conquer" approach, planned by a small group in secret contact with Karl Marx, took advantage of the fact that Parisians had arms and were discontented by hardship and defeat.

One of the most active of the leaders was Jaclar, who helped direct the civil aspect of the uprising, who for a brief time during the fighting was colonel of the Seventeenth Legion, and who then became inspector-general in charge of strengthening the defenses of Paris. He is mentioned in the correspondence of both Marx and Engels. Wholeheartedly following her lover's views, Aniuta became a prominent member of the Vigilante Committee for Montmartre and became a committee member of the Women's Union. She also helped organize the daily paper, *La Sociale*, that published for 48 days.

In early April the Kovalevskys reached the Versailles headquarters of the Republican government, then headed by Adolphe Thiers, where they requested a passport to visit relatives in Paris. Upon being denied this they supplicated Bismarck, at Prussian headquarters in Versailles, who stated he had promised to permit nobody into Paris without French approval. Thereupon the Kovalevskys boldly crossed the German line at night. They then walked along the Seine until they found a rowboat and crossed into Paris, where active fighting had begun two days earlier between the Republicans and the Communards.

Hostilities lasted for ten weeks. Of that period the Kovalevskys were in Paris for thirty-eight days. Despite the turmoil Vladimir managed to examine fossil specimens that excited his interest. According to word he later sent his brother, they lived very well thanks to Jaclar, although those doing the fighting and dying often subsisted on no more than two hard crackers a day.

The political organizations to which Aniuta belonged on 6 May ordered removed from hospitals and jails all the nuns who served as nurses, on the pretext that they were counter-revolutionary. Therefore inexperienced women had to be pressed into tending the sick and wounded. Thus it was that Sophia with her sister spent one night in such service. According to a different account, it was with the ambulance corps that the sisters served. The experience left Sophia with a strong aversion to armed combat that produced such suffering and death.

Having failed to convince Aniuta to accompany them, the Kovalevskys left Paris by some undisclosed means on May 12. In so doing they escaped the peak hostilities, which occurred between 20 May and 30 May, when about 6,000 revolutionists fell and over 38,000 became prisoners. Several persons mistaken for Jaclar were summarily shot, but he and Aniuta hid out until order had been restored, so that by the time of his arrest he was merely jailed to await trial.

Years later Sophia related her experiences to Anna Charlotte Leffler, who wrote: "She was still at an age of intense fervor of feeling, and the events of worldwide historic interest that were taking place around her impressed her more than the most exciting romance. She watched the explosion of bombs without the slightest trepidation; they only excited a fluttering of the heart and a secret delight that she was in the midst of the drama. For her sister at this time she could do nothing."

iv

FOLLOWING THE return to Berlin of the Kovalevskys and the defeat in Paris of the Commune, a letter arrived from Aniuta indicating she was still free but in peril and begging Sophia to intervene with their father on behalf of Jaclar, who had been arrested and faced certain death. So Sophia addressed the General, confessing Aniuta's actions and sorry plight, begging his forgiveness for their mutual deceptions, and imploring his advice and help. As Leffler commented: ". . . one can easily realize what a terrible blow it was to him to learn the whole grim truth of the deception of his children, and the fact that his older daughter had taken her own course in a manner calculated to wound most deeply all his instincts and principles." Nevertheless, the General responded at once. Both he and his wife hastened to Paris. The Kovalevskys also headed for Paris.

The day Sophia left Berlin an article in a newspaper there confirmed the arrest of Jaclar, erroneously reported the arrest of Aniuta, and stated that Jaclar would probably be sent to the penal colony on the French island of New Caledonia in the South Pacific. On arriving in Paris the Kovalevskys immediately sent Aniuta to safety in Heidelberg, where her mother's Adelung sister arrived to care for her. Aniuta was so exhausted that she spent eight days in bed, only awakening to take occasional nourishment.

Although Jaclar's trial was not to take place for several months, the Kovalevskys had good reason to think he would be sent with other leaders to New Caledonia and that Aniuta would want to follow him. Therefore the ever-generous Vladimir agreed with Sophia that he would give up his studies and escort Aniuta, while Sophia would return to complete her studies before joining them. To that end Vladimir promptly wrote to ask his brother to agree to help repay from his professor's salary and from their joint-estate a loan of 2,000 roubles that Vladimir proposed to obtain for expenses as soon as the General arrived.

On 1 July the Korvin-Krukovskys arrived in Paris, taking a hotel room adjoining that of the Kovalevskys. Adding to their new knowledge that Aniuta had been living with a man she had not married was the surprising discovery that their younger daughter although married had never really lived with her husband. The immediate problem, however, centered on Jaclar. During July, August, and September various plans were considered and abandoned, while Jaclar occupied an underground cell in Chantiers Prison in Versailles. Finally, as the time for his trial approached, the General decided to go to the top man, Thiers, the French statesman and historian who headed the French government. Supposedly they were acquainted.

In civilian dress but wearing one of his medals, as was customary in Russia on special occasions, the General called on Thiers. What transpired between them is unknown. Aniuta later told Dostoevsky that a bribe of 20,000 roubles (then about $16,000) went to some person or persons. In any event, the General left Thiers after having obtained the information that three days later, on a Sunday, Jaclar would be transferred from prison along a certain route, to a jail in Paris. Vladimir received permission to visit Jaclar in his cell and presumably briefed him on the escape plan.

As Anna Charlotte Leffler later recalled hearing the story from Sophia, the prisoners were to pass a certain building where an exhibition was in progress and many persons would be milling about. Vladimir went to the spot and mixed with the crowd. When the prisoners appeared he slipped in among the soldiers, and taking Jaclar by the arm guided him unobtrusively through the crowd into the exhibition. From there they left by a rear door, hastening to the railway station. Then Jaclar used Vladimir's passport to get into Switzerland.

A much more likely variation was that related to Marie Mendelson, Sophia's Polish revolutionary friend of later years. It had been arranged through Thiers that a single soldier would transfer Jaclar to Paris. At an appointed place he entered a tobacco shop to chat with the woman clerk, turning his back on Jaclar who simply stepped into an adjoining room where Vladimir awaited him with a change of clothing. From there they hurried to the train bound for Switzerland.

Since Vladimir then lacked a passport, the General presumably obtained temporary identification for him at the Russian embassy. That embassy in early July had reported to Petersburg that the violent Russian-born wife of Jaclar, known only by a pseudonym, in her widowhood probably would be sentenced to New Caledonia. The embassy of course little suspected her relationship to the General or that she was already safe in Heidelberg.

At the request of the General the resourceful Vladimir accompanied the family as far as Frankfort. From there the others doubled back, covering their tracks to join Aniuta, while Vladimir returned to Paris to finish his drawings at the museum while awaiting the return of his passport. Disregarding Vladimir's need, Jaclar retained that document until finally Aniuta, generously supplied with funds, joined him in Switzerland and mailed it back. After Aniuta's departure the Korvin-Krukovskys accompanied Sophia to Berlin and then continued on, weary from the worries of their long adventure, to the peace of Palibino.

The entire episode was costly for the General in both money and physical exhaustion from his weak heart, but as Leffler remarked: "His daughters, who knew they deserved quite other treatment, devoted themselves to him from that time on with a tenderness never before evinced."

CHAPTER 14

Prótegée of Weierstrass

i

W HEN S OPHIA, while en route from England with Vladimir in the autumn of 1870, decided to go to Berlin instead of to Leipzig, she knew that she probably would not be accepted as an auditor in the Prussian capital, even though several Heidelberg professors had warmly recommended her to friends on the faculty. She wished, however, personally to appeal to Professor Karl Theodore William Weierstrass (1815-1897) who taught at the University of Berlin. Again the general's daughter would make a frontal attack.

Weierstrass was the foremost teacher of mathematics in Europe at that time, perhaps of all times, and fathered modern mathematical analysis. His better pupils readily obtained faculty positions at other universities. Because his institution had more traditional rigidity than prevailed in some other places in Germany, Sophia rightly expected him to have a bias against feminine students. Very likely, moreover, he would be too busy with his own mathematical investigations to bother with private lessons. Nevertheless, she considered it to be well worthwhile to approach him boldly. Why not at least attempt to study with the best man in her chosen field? And so she bearded the lion in his academic den.

Weierstrass agreed to receive Sophia and set a time in the late afternoon where he lived at No.40 Potsdam Street. While Vladimir waited in the carriage, Sophia with some trepidation approached the door to pull the bell-handle. One can imagine that the door was opened by the longtime family maid, dressed neatly in gray with a white apron; that Sophia followed her through the parlor, with its heavy furniture and steel engravings, into a sitting room where, by the dying light from a window, the professor's two middle-aged sisters sat knitting, probably socks or mufflers for militiamen in the Franco-Prussian War. The spinster ladies in their plain and somber dresses, Elisa and Clara, aged forty-four and forty-seven, must have paused between stitches to nod and smile as Sophia passed through to the professor's study. Weierstrass put down his pen and arose from his large writing desk to greet his guest, inviting her to be seated in a leather-covered chair, one of several that sometimes were occupied by the professor's mathematical colleagues, some of them former pupils, when they visited from other universities for a courtesy call or an evening of conversation.

The professor himself recorded that he definitely was not impressed. Sophia became shy in his presence and, as was usually the case at this time in her life, appeared badly dressed in a cloak with tassels that concealed her girlish figure. To help her courage she wore a new bonnet of black silk, but its floppy brim half-concealed her eyes, shadowed her face, and in the dim light made her appear much older. Weierstrass later told Anna Charlotte, who queried him for her memoir of Sophia, that he had no idea at this first meeting of Sophia's extreme youth, nor did he then notice the eager intellectual expression of her eyes that so impressed most observers. He told Sophia flatly that it was absolutely impossible for her to attend his lectures, this being against university rules. To her proposal for private lessons, thinking perhaps to be easily rid of her, he only agreed to test her ability by asking her to solve several problems that he had assigned to his more advanced students. She departed in disappointment but firmly resolved to prove her ability.

Although Sophia had been recommended to Weierstrass by his former pupil, Königsberger, who also assured him that she had not been among those Russians involved in political activity at Heidelberg, the Berlin professor really had not expected much in a woman. Therefore when Sophia a week later returned to his residence with the mathematical solutions he was at first suspicious. With considerable disbelief he asked her to sit down and explain her work point by point. In her eagerness of exposition Sophia removed her bonnet. Her short curly hair fell over her brow. She blushed vividly under the professor's obviously approving eyes. The 55-year-old bachelor soon became not a Prussian lion but more like a faithful watchdog during their future association. He recognized at once that the intriguing Sophia possessed an intuitive gift seldom found even among his very best students. Therefore he generously accepted her as a private pupil without charge, giving her two or three lessons weekly at his house or her apartment, and soon became her friend and counselor for life.

Sophia's early biographer, Elizabeth Fedorovna Litvinova, the young woman who looked upon Sophia as a model and who studied mathematics in Switzerland, had somehow learned, whether as truth or as myth, that Weierstrass as a young man had a blighted romance. During his early period of poverty he fell in love with a young woman so far above him in wealth and position that marriage with her was impossible. Nevertheless, she encouraged him to persevere in mathematics. With great difficulty he had reached his eminent position. Hampered by an entirely inadequate education, he began his teaching career in secondary German schools, leading an impoverished existence while supporting two younger sisters, until eventually his mathematical capability came to the attention of persons that recognized his genius. The academic ranks gradually parted to admit him to its innermost circle.

According to Litvinova, he saw in the childlike Sophia a strong resemblance to his lost love and soon received her into his family like another sister or a daughter.

The name of Weierstrass is inseparably connected with the theory of functions, especially elliptic and Abelian functions. He constructed a theory of analytic functions based on their representation as infinite series. He also wrote and lectured on the foundations of analysis, on the calculus of variations, and on the theory of minimal surfaces. His theorem of approximation by trigonometric and rational polynomials will be found expounded in texts, together with his theorem that every bounded infinite sequence of real numbers has a convergent subsequence.

In Berlin Sophia and Vladimir took separate apartments. During most of her Berlin period Sophia resided at 27A Potsdamerstrasse. Berlin in 1870, with its bridges over the River Spree, its triumphal Brandenburg Gate, its broad avenues, and its famed statue of Frederick the Great, had almost one million inhabitants; and the following year, when King William I of Prussia became Emperor of Germany, his capital city attained the importance of London and Paris. Its university, although founded only sixty years earlier, had attracted the best faculty in Germany and occupied as its main building a former palace on Unter den Linden. Although under the ministry of education, the university operated freely under its rector and faculty senate, even to the point of having police and judicial powers over professors and students.

For a time Vladimir busied himself by examining specimens in museums and studying the literature of geology and the new branch of paleontology. He delayed his formal studies for lack of money; and also, as he wrote his brother on 21 December 1870, he could not leave Sophia, "as she cannot stay alone even for a day." Being shy about her relations with Vladimir, Sophia didn't discuss him with the professor or his sisters. For a long time the closest the family came to meeting him was on Sunday evenings, at the hour when Sophia left the Weierstrass place after lesson and dinner; Vladimir would knock at the door and inform the servant that Madame Kovalevsky's carriage awaited. Vladimir had also been kept very much in the background at Heidelberg; on the occasion of several chance meetings with professors Sophia had introduced him vaguely as a relation.

Soon Julia arrived from Heidelberg, permitting Vladimir to leave for Vienna, although he returned for visits during at least three of the nearly four years that Sophia studied under Weierstrass. The Kovalevskys customarily vacationed together between semesters and in the summer, and of course had the Paris adventure already mentioned.

Vladimir's stay in Paris during and after the Commune shaped his entire future. On a previous visit he had met a professor of anatomy who interested him in tertiary mammifers. While studying such specimens at the Museum Jardin des Plantes he decided to make them his specialty. A scientist who died during the siege owned a nearly complete skeleton of a particular mammifer; this passed into the possession of the aforementioned professor, who in turn gave it to Vladimir. His two years of study and omnivorous reading paid off. With the specimen to work with initially and the drawings he made of other specimens he opened a new area of paleontology, providing ideas in his scientific papers for research by others during the next decade and assuring for himself a place in the history of Russian science.

ii

JULIA DESCRIBED life in Berlin as more routine and solitary than in Heidelberg. "Sofa spent entire days at her writing desk doing mathematical calculations, whereas I worked from morning to night in the [private] laboratory," she wrote. "V. O. Kovalevsky who was then studying at Jena University visited us infrequently. We took advantage of no entertainment opportunities, such as the theatre, and had no acquaintances. Our only consolation was Professor Weierstrass and his family who always treated us kindly and warmly; as if for their children, they had Christmas trees and invited us for evenings and for dinner. They lived in a retired way, however, so that we met no other visitors there."

Julia further described their life during the Berlin years: "Apart from Professor Weierstrass not a single soul crossed our threshold. Sofa was in a most unhappy mood the entire time; it seemed nothing gladdened her; she was indifferent to everything except her studies.

The visits of her husband enlivened her somewhat, but the happiness of their meeting was frequently darkened by mutual reproaches and misunderstandings. They took long walks together.

"When Sofa was alone with me she didn't want to leave the apartment for any reason, not to walk or go to the theatre or make necessary purchases. One Christmas the Weierstrass family had arranged a tree especially for us, and Sofa absolutely had to have a new dress, but she wouldn't go out to obtain it. We almost quarreled over this, because I didn't want to buy it alone. [If her husband had been there, everything would have been arranged easily, because he always took care of all that she needed, choosing not only the material but also the style of dress for her.] Finally our argument was resolved by assigning the housekeeper to buy the material and order the dress, as Sofa would not budge from the place.

"Her ability over many hours to devote herself to concentrated mental labor without leaving her desk was really astonishing. And when, after having spent the entire day in pressing work, she finally pushed away her papers and arose from her chair, she was always so submerged in her thoughts that she would walk back and forth with quick steps across the room, and finally break into a run, talking loudly to herself and sometimes breaking into laughter. At such times she seemed completely separated from reality, carried by fantasy beyond the borders of the present. She would never consent to tell me what she was thinking on such occasions.

"She slept very little at night and frequently had disturbing dreams. Often she would awaken suddenly from some fantastic dream and would ask me to sit with her. She readily related her dreams, which were always very original and interesting. Not infrequently they were like visions to which she ascribed prophetic significance and which often actually came true. In general she was distinguished by an extremely nervous temperament. She was never at peace, always setting difficult goals for herself, always wanting passionately to obtain them. Despite this, I never saw her in so depressed a state of mind as when she had achieved a particular goal. It seemed the reality of achievement never corresponded to what she had imagined.

"While working she caused little pleasure in those around her, being wholly immersed in her work. Yet when one observed her, melancholy and sorrowful in her complete success, one involuntarily felt a deep sympathy for her. These constant changes in disposition, from sadness to happiness, made her most interesting to know.

"On the whole, our life in Berlin, in an ugly apartment, with bad food, in foul air, with tiring work and no entertainment, was to such an extent joyless that I think of our previous life in Heidelberg as of a lost paradise."

iii

ONE MAJOR problem disturbing Sophia during her years of university study was that of her relationship with Vladimir. At first the relationship concerned only the two of them, and they were reasonably happy together. Then Aniuta and Zhanna in Heidelberg caused trouble, and Vladimir went elsewhere. In 1871 during the Paris Commune episode, Sophia's parents for the first time discovered their younger daughter's marriage had remained platonic and were greatly disturbed. The loving response of the General and his wife to Aniuta's plight, and Sophia's own growing maturity, had considerably modified if not eliminated Sophia's hostility to her parents, so that she found it distressing to have to withstand their advice to consummate the marriage. During Sophia's years in Berlin the parents several times visited her there, and in 1872 she accompanied them to Palibino for the summer. The family also spent time together in Switzerland, as in the late summer of 1873. Therefore the efforts to bring the Kovalevskys together continued over a long period and for just as long caused Sophia great annoyance, especially as Aniuta, happy in her union with Jaclar, added her voice to that of the parents, her attitude to Vladimir having changed after he had rescued Jaclar.

How is Sophia's marital enigma to be explained? Some answers are hidden in the individual natures of each of the principals. Sophia presumably never disclosed her innermost thoughts regarding the relationship. On her side only inferences can be drawn from her actions. Vladimir did reveal his viewpoint, however, in a long letter to his brother written from Paris on 11 November 1871, stating in part:

"Since you want me to write about something besides geology, I'll talk to you now about Sofa. As I already wrote, she had gone to Berlin with her parents and is studying there with Lermontova. It must be very hard and lonely there for the poor little one, but it is absolutely impossible for me to go there, as I must finish my drawings . . .

"I hope that what I write to you, Sasha, about my relations with Sofa will remain only between us two, and since this question interests you I shall discuss it in detail. I love Sofa excessively, although I can't say that I am what is called in love; at the very beginning real love seemed to be developing, but now a quiet attachment has replaced that.

"During our life together, of course, I have wanted this very much. I could have been her husband, but I was always positively afraid of this for many reasons. First, inasmuch as we had been united for a particular purpose, it somehow wasn't right to turn the marriage into a reality; that would be as though I had stolen a wife, something unpleasant for me. Second, in my opinion, Sofa absolutely can't be a mother; this would simply ruin her, and she herself fears this; it would tear her away from her work, making her unhappy, and besides this I think she would make a bad mother; there isn't a single maternal instinct in her, and she simply hates children. Third, I myself can't assume the responsibility of being a father, especially with such a person as Sofa. She is a person one must care for as for a child. She simply cannot spend an evening alone and would stop loving anyone not with her constantly and upon whom she could rely never to leave her.

"In my character and in my work I am something of a nomad and a wanderer; she detests this; trains create in her a revulsion. I can't promise that I will change and become a Simon-dapifer [i.e., a noble devoted to the personal service of a tsar]. Feeling tied to one place I would be deeply unhappy. She wouldn't accompany me, or having done so of necessity would be melancholy.

"She needs quiet but also at times a merry life in one place with many intimate friends. I can't give her that. . . . Besides this, her intimate friends are beginning to tell her how unsuited we are to each other. This is of course unpleasant, although I am conscious of the unsuitability myself. I think we should not tie our lives together permanently, for we would make one another unhappy, but rather we must just remain good friends.

"Besides this, our work is so different. For her no other science exists except mathematics; nothing else attracts her in the least; and this kind of situation will certainly separate people when each sincerely loves his own subject. The society of mathematicians is necessary for her, whereas in such society I would be unneeded and comical, having no interest in mathematics.

"I am unsuitable to be a father, and no matter how hard it is at times to be so solitary, still I am consoled in that nobody is suffering on account of me; and, yes, the thought of you, Sasha, and the fact that we are indeed friends and love one another, deeply consoles me. I can always depend upon you and know that you will forgive me everything and will stand up for me in front of others and generally will be concerned about me more than I am of myself.

"Sometimes it is very difficult for me to be alone, but I don't think that I shall ever marry; I certainly would not make a wife happy unless she were a gypsy and liked to move about.

"We both now regret our marriage. I am sorry for her because the married state constricts her terribly and can do so even more in the future. Of course if she fell sincerely in love with somebody and that person was good, I would take all the blame in order to get a divorce and free her.

"All in all, I love her very, very much—more than she loves me—but I cannot assume the role of a constant male nurse (for which she would love me completely); for that price I could be her husband, but I'm afraid I could not maintain the role, and then what would the poor thing do.

"In fact I don't think she will be happy; there is much in her character that won't allow that, unless she should meet an exceptionally good and talented person, a rarity unlikely to be found."

In another November letter in 1871 Vladimir felicitated his brother on the formalization of his common-law marriage: "I congratulate you and Tania on your wedding; this is how all we nihilists fall into legal ties, despite all protests against them; accessory conditions always force us, the pressure of society being so strong that we can't overcome it, and we have a church ceremony."

It would appear that Vladimir set forth his views regarding Sophia very well, although on a minor point, that she did not like to travel, he was surely mistaken. Throughout her life she traveled widely in Europe—as she said, to every country except Spain. Doubtless what she disliked was having to interrupt her work when Vladimir wished to travel; also, when they traveled together there was the occasional embarrassment over sleeping accommodations. In Vladimir's analysis of their relationship he understandably overlooked several possibilities, such as that she might have found him unattractive in physical characteristics or in some personal habit. There is no more evidence for this in the record anywhere than there is that she might have had lesbian tendencies.

Very possibly, apart from a real fear of pregnancy, Sophia had simply never been sexually aroused, and she never attained real respect for the man who gave in to her every selfish whim, who entirely lacked her firmness, who abandoned law at the onset of a promising career, who failed in publishing, who still vacillated in his scientific goal, and who, as time would tell, demonstrated repeatedly his lack of an essential balance wheel. While realizing that he was indecisive and her intellectual inferior, she cannot have been unaware of his fine qualities of ready generosity, deep kindness, obvious patience, constant understanding, significant intelligence, gentlemanly behavior, and genuine idealism. Yet, self-centered as she was, such attributes must have been insufficient to awaken her passion.

Moreover, she had no nest-building instincts. She had grown up expecting to be waited upon by many servants. She was deceptively shy but actually the proud daughter of a proud father. She perhaps felt that a real husband would be a leash on her freedom—but did not, of course, hesitate to restrict Vladimir's freedom. In her nature she had, for an ordinary human being, too much love of science and too little science of love. She was not ordinary, however, but a genius.

Vladimir's brother presumably advised him, for his own good, to see much less of Sophia, for he had his own studies and career to pursue. He may not have seen her at all during the year 1872. That was certainly not what Sophia wanted! Vladimir received his doctorate from Jena University on 11 March 1872. Thereafter he presumably visited his brother and went into the field in pursuit of his specialty. At any rate, Sophia, having vacationed alone at Palibino during the summer, returned to Berlin lonely and depressed.

iv

PART OF Sophia's lack of obvious joy during her Berlin years resulted from her rigorous study and her unhealthy life, apart from the tensions involving her marriage. In the experience of Felix Klein, a pupil of Weierstrass who became a mathematics professor at Leipzig and Göttingen, it was difficult to be a student of the mathematical master because his intellectual superiority depressed many students rather than impelled them to individual creation. He had absolute and unquestioned authority in his field, Klein stated, so that "we did not listen to his lectures in a spirit of contradiction."

Sophia was exposed to Weierstrass on a one-to-one basis. He certainly challenged her comprehension. Yet he did not overwhelm her. Rather, he found in her that rarest of creatures for a dedicated teacher; that is, one of those who make worthwhile a lifetime of often tiresome and frequently fruitless efforts with mediocre intelligences. At times during their later time together she challenged and even exceeded his own insight, so that ideas flowed in both directions. As she advanced he treated her not as a pupil but as another mathematician. With her he experienced some of the zest of discovery since she acted as a catalyst in his own mathematical inquiries. He gave her of his very best, and considering her industry and ability, it is not surprising that she became his favorite pupil.

Unfortunately the letters Sophia wrote Weierstrass over a period of twenty years he burnt, along with other correspondence and papers, some time after her death. However, over eighty of his letters to her have survived. Some were mere notes arranging times for meetings, many concerned mathematics or mathematicians, a few were personal in nature. The salutations of the letters changed from "Dear Madam" of the first letter dated 11 March 1871 and several subsequent, to "My dear Sophia," "Dearest Sonya," "Dear, dear Sonya," and then usually "Dear Friend" or "Dearest Friend" for many years after. In the German of the romantic period "dearest" was less intimate than it sounds in English today.

On 14 November 1871 Sophia had advanced to the point where the professor assured her: "In the future you can turn to me in all mathematical questions that interest you without fearing to trouble me. It will always be a great happiness for me to have the opportunity to help you in your work." At that time Weierstrass obtained for her the privilege of using the university library. By October of the following year he could address her as "Sofa," that being the name used only by family and closest friends, although later this changed to "Sonya," apparently the name by which she preferred to be called the rest of her life.

By November of 1872 a marked change in the teacher-pupil relationship occurred. From that time onward Weierstrass used the intimate form of "you," the second person singular. His letter of 4 November ended: "I wish you all the best, my heart, until our new meeting. And occasionally when you are engrossed in my formulas turn your thoughts to your faithful friend. W."

What happened to alter their relationship so markedly? Almost certainly it pertained to her marital situation. Sophia had just returned from a summer visit, alone, to Palibino, where doubtless she received more advice than she wanted. She had not heard from Vladimir for months and didn't even know his whereabouts. It is possible that Weierstrass, seeing her troubled and depressed after a vacation that should have rested her, took the initiative and invited her confidence. Or she may simply have approached him for his views. Either way, for Sophia to have discussed so personal a matter with a man would not have been out of character. Emotionally and intellectually, with the exception of her close feelings for Aniuta and her childhood dependence on her nurse, she had always been closer to men than to women— to Uncle Peter, to Malevich, to Strannoliubsky, and in varying degrees to the General. She was never really intimate with her mother. She so much resembled her father in nature that during her late adolescence this constituted an actual barrier between them, as often happens when such pairs see their own faults as though magnified in one another. It was, therefore, as though she found in Weierstrass a surrogate father, causing him to react to her as to a foster daughter, perhaps with faintly sexual overtones.

If indeed Sophia at this time did disclose to Weierstrass the fictitious nature of her marriage and its unhappy consequences—as seems almost certain—he must have advised her to continue on as before and let time remedy the situation. Most certainly, if Vladimir could be brought round to a continued close friendship, that was what she wanted. It may have been at this time that Sophia gave her tutor permission, to which he referred on another occasion several years later, to counsel her like a spiritual father. This would account for his use thenceforth of the intimate form of "you" in addressing her, although it is most unlikely that she would have used the same form in addressing him. Quite apart from similar German custom, in Russian upperclass families the parents and relatives used the intimate form with children, but only in some families were children permitted so to address their parents; tutors used the form unilaterally with younger charges, rarely with older ones, and never young male tutors with girl students.

It is even possible that Weierstrass discussed Sophia's situation with her parents, whom he met in Berlin, or with her mother, with whom he had a limited correspondence. Any German professor was much respected, and an outstanding one was a prestigious figure who shared honors at court with generals. His right to speak to parents in the matter would have been respected.

On 27 December 1872 both Sophia and Julia accompanied the professor and his sisters, Clara and Elisa, to a concert. On 5 April the following year Sophia fell ill, and Weierstrass became most solicitous. He himself suffered from the flu at the same time and so had recourse to the pen. He urged her to keep him informed of her condition and to give up study entirely to store up energy for her forthcoming trip to Zurich, cautioning her to dress warmly if the doctor permitted her to go carriage-riding. The professor apparently also wrote Sophia's parents expressing concern over their daughter's health.

Accompanied by Julia, Sophia arrived in Zurich to stay with the General in rooms he had taken in Hotel Bauer while Sophia's mother stayed in the Jaclar's small apartment. It annoyed the General that Elizabeth tired herself by waiting on Aniuta and heating milk for the new baby at all hours, but for Elizabeth it was a pleasure to be with her best-loved daughter and her first grandchild. Litvinova, who had been drawn into intimacy with Aniuta and thus with the family, recorded that the General's gloom changed into cheerfulness only with the arrival of Sophia. Seeing her again offset his depression caused by a crying baby and a disheveled Aniuta living in cramped quarters with a slovenly maid and a penniless husband. But at the hotel he laughed and joked with Sophia, Julia, and Litvinova who gathered there for long hours at a time. Sometimes they walked of an afternoon through the parks and promenades of Zurich, an old city situated at one end of long Lake Zurich. From its site on a hill, the old cathedral where Zwingli preached still overlooked a city divided by a river, its older portion having many narrow and crooked streets laid out in the Middle Ages.

Weierstrass, upon receiving word of Sophia's safe arrival in Zurich, wrote on 18 April 1873 a letter that indicates the nature of their warm relationship by this time:

"My dear friend: You gave me so much happiness with your dear little letter, which I had not expected so soon, as I feared that the journey you had undertaken with insufficient recovery would tire you, so that on arrival in Zurich you would need at least a week of rest. Having heard from you I am that much happier that my concern was without basis.

"You say, but unconvincingly, that you are completely recovered. Since you mention long daily walks that gladden you, however, I must assume you find yourself sufficiently strong for this. If only the weather during your visit there would remain as constantly wonderful as when you arrived, then you could be more out-of-doors to experience personally the truth of the opinion of one of our medical lights here that 'besides camomile tea only one other medicine exists that is firmly known to act beneficially—namely, clean and soft air.'

"Don't forget that you promised me during our farewell to return fresh and blooming. Imagine the happiness it will give me when upon meeting you I can see my dear Sonya has indeed kept her word.

"If you are really determined to be here by the first of May, then I advise that until that time you avoid all serious work, if in fact during the busy life you are now leading you can even think of work. You must conserve your strength for the study we will resume upon your return. I hope you will achieve at least this—that you will get together enough material during the summer months for our project [her thesis] to be completed in the fall."

He reported that he continued to be indisposed but had been cheered during the holidays by repeated visits of mathematical friends, especially Heine from Halle and Baltzer from Giessen, who "unlike my little favorite, whom you know," disagreed with his views on the geometry of finite space. He closed by saying: "My heartfelt gratitude for the polite regards you send me. Saying to you, my heart, at this time, goodbye, I must importunately add that wherever you may be I shall think of you always with a feeling of deep affection. Your faithful friend. W."

V

MANY MONTHS had elapsed since several caustic letters by each party had halted correspondence between the Kovalevskys. Vladimir kept track of Sophia through Aniuta, however, and having learned Sophia would be in Zurich expressed the intention of going there. Sophia, not knowing his whereabouts, addressed him in care of his brother, stating that his arrival would be "extremely unpleasant" because the abnormality of her position caused both the General and Aniuta to counsel her on that "very painful" subject. "Recently," she wrote, "from conversations with Aniuta and from reading your letters to her, I have had the tormenting thought that you are as distressed and constrained by our position as am I. Believe me, I am ready to do everything that depends upon me to somewhat lighten [crossed out: 'and to return to you at least part of that freedom that you were deprived of on my account'] and to make a family life possible for you." She suggested that instead of meeting in Zurich he might come to Berlin in May to clarify their future relationship. She wanted some decision, no matter what, so that she could resume her studies in a calm manner.

In another letter, undated but obviously from this period in 1873, Sophia commented: "I received your letter, which pleased me very much, but I must admit that it made me laugh. Truly it seems to me that gossip about my 'friend' [Weierstrass] has invaded your imagination. . . . although this distresses me, still I must correct your mistake: in my new friendship there is much that is poetic, ideal, open-hearted, and it gives me a terrible amount of happiness and delight; but, alas, there is nothing of romance in it! Really, it is so unpleasant for me to write you this that for the past two days I have wracked my brain to see if I couldn't make a minor romance out of my friendship; but, no, [in German] 'it doesn't work'; and my love for truth forces me to point out your error."

To anticipate events, the Berlin meeting did not occur, nor did Sophia accept Vladimir's counterproposal to meet in Munich. That prompted a spiteful letter from him, but on 2 May he wrote to apologize and, trying to separate her from Weierstrass, he suggested that she prepare for her doctorate in Paris or London.

During Sophia's Easter visit in Zurich the rector of the university there, Herman A. Schwarz, having heard about Sophia from his former teacher, Weierstrass, who had sent some of her papers, very much wanted to meet her. Mistakenly thinking he might develop another Kovalevsky, he had offered to give Litvinova private lessons. Several times he asked her to introduce him to Sophia, but Sophia put off such a meeting. It would seem she wanted first to make up her mind whether she wanted to remain in Zurich, primarily to be close to Aniuta, partly to stifle Vladimir's jealousy over Weierstrass, partly to study for a time under somebody other than the Berlin master. She had greatly respected the work of R. F. A. Clebsch at Göttingen University and had hoped to receive her doctorate through him, but his recent death had so disappointed her that she had put aside entirely her treatise on elliptic functions. In Zurich she could obtain a doctorate on the same basis as a man if Schwarz would sponsor her. Therefore meeting him could become a turning point in her life. Schwarz did important work in partial differential equations and analysis, advanced to Göttingen, and eventually succeeded Weierstrass in Berlin.

Sophia and Litvinova held long conversations about Schwarz and mathematics. Litvinova recorded Sophia as having declared: "I feel that I am meant to serve truth in science, but also to work for justice by breaking a new path for women. I am very glad I was born a woman, as this gives me the opportunity to work at the same time for both truth and justice. But it is not always easy to persevere."

When finally Sophia and Schwarz did meet, their conversation lasted for three hours. The attraction was mutual. They held similar thoughts and shared the same mathematical outlook. At a second meeting, during which Sophia mentioned her indecision about returning to Berlin, he offered to tutor her if she remained in Zurich. Without having warned Aniuta in advance, Sophia impulsively invited Schwarz and his wife to dinner the next day. Accustomed only to such visitors as Jaclar's rather scruffy friends, Aniuta was ill-prepared for such a surprise but made hurried preparations. In the cramped quarters with a crying baby in the next room, the dinner was a social disaster, quite unlike what the guests had expected from a Russian noblewoman. But between Schwarz and Sophia it made no difference.

Still Sophia remained undecided. She had been estranged from Vladimir for many months and in Aniuta found love and support, despite the disturbing presence of Jaclar. Also, Aniuta needed her, because she had not regained her strength following the birth of son Urey on 18 March, second anniversary of the Paris uprising. Sophia knit a blanket for her new nephew, although she felt no attraction to the infant.

Then Sophia learned from Schwarz what Weierstrass had modestly refrained from mentioning—that the latter had been chosen rector of Berlin University. In writing to congratulate him she also suggested, in view of his recent illness and new duties, that to continue with her lessons might be too great a burden. He responded promptly, mentioning his improved health and assuring her: "You will remain my pupil in the best sense of the word as long as you wish and can learn from me. . . . You suggest that if not as a friend then as a student you can burden me—that is how you used the ugly word. Amiable dear Sonya, be convinced that I shall never forget that I am in debt to my pupil in that I possess in her not only my best but my dearest friend. Therefore, if in the future you maintain your former attitude to me you can be firmly confident that I shall also devotedly support you in your scholarly aims."

Thus Sophia felt an obligation to return. She was displeased to hear Litvinova's expressed hope of studying with Weierstrass herself. This jealous reaction may have been the deciding factor in her decision to return to Berlin. Soon she obtained a pledge from Weierstrass that he would not accept another woman for private study.

At the end of the term Sophia promptly rejoined Aniuta in Zurich. By prearrangement or otherwise, Vladimir showed up there. Within a day or so of his arrival Litvinova called at Aniuta's to find him combing Sophia's hair, which she had allowed to grow out and had been wearing in a careless braid pinned to her head. Vladimir asked the visitor for the names of various shops and next day bought Sophia gloves, shoes, and an umbrella. He did not want her to go to Palibino, as planned, because mistakenly he thought that the Korvin-Krukovskys opposed him. It is true, they were well aware of his indecisive character, but this was not opposition. They did think the marriage should be a genuine one but had ceased to pressure Sophia. She did cancel her Palibino plans. Instead the couple, after entertaining Dr. and Mme. Schwarz at a suitable dinner at a hotel to compensate for the one at Aniuta's, left for Lausanne and remained there for several weeks.

Although it is doubtful that Sophia discussed her personal life with Litvinova, the latter had sharp eyes, and when years later she wrote about Sophia she also had the opportunity of talking with Julia and Sophia's brother. Thus she could write of Sophia's "moral suffering" in connection with Vladimir and that he cared for her with "gentle consideration." She felt no passion for him but at the same time was "terrified" that he might fall in love with another woman. While fearing "total singleness," she had no other "suitable man" in view. Consequently, "what happened was that they were constantly drawn one to the other. She was happy in the first period of their meeting, but then something would go wrong, and they would separate with bitter feelings, each devoting full energy to his own work. From year to year the same story was repeated, and this drained the strength of them both."

Sophia thought no more of abandoning Weierstrass. A letter from her caught up finally with him where he vacationed at a hotel on the Baltic island of Rügen at Sassnitz. In his reply he quoted parts of a letter from his friend, F. J. Richelot, citing the latter's views about numerous mathematicians that had worked on Abelian functions. These were named for a Norwegian mathematician, N. H. Abel (d.1829), an originator of the theory of functions, whose own labors filled two volumes. Sophia was attempting further to clarify aspects of this subject.

Because of cholera in Berlin, Weierstrass warned Sophia to stay away until he had returned and sent her word of safety. He promised that during the autumn he would see her every Sunday and otherwise whenever he could spare the time. From the beginning it had been his practice for the meetings to be twice weekly, but more often if required, and occasionally even on successive days if they were engaged together on a line of reasoning that might be obscured for him by his other activities. Now, of course, Sophia had for some time been doing independent and original work and needed less guidance.

In a more personal vein Weierstrass wrote from Rügen: "While here I often think of you and imagine how beautiful it would be if I could spend several weeks with you, dear friend, among such wonderful surroundings. How excellent it would be for us—for you with your soul full of fantasy and for me enlivened by your enthusiasm—to dream here over the many problems we have to solve: about finite and infinite distances, about the constancy of the world system, and about all the other great problems of mathematics and physics. But long ago I resigned myself to the fact that not every wonderful dream is realized."

On 8 October Weierstrass chided Sophia for not having written to him for six weeks, although he knew from her mother's letter that she would be returning to Berlin. Although Julia had already arrived, he cautioned Sophia to delay, because cholera still raged, and because he would be busy anyway, as rector, through most of October with visits by persons "high, higher, and highest." Apparently the Emperor and others were to inspect the university and be entertained. Outside of Russia various European monarchs took a personal interest in educational institutions and sometimes even attended university lectures.

Despite word from Berlin that eight persons were dying daily of cholera, Sophia finally appeared there on 1 November. Through the rest of 1873 and into the summer of 1874, the professor's letters and notes, written for same-day delivery in the absence of telephones, mostly had to do with setting appointments. One meeting he had to cancel because he was commanded by the Emperor to dinner, another because of a dinner honoring the Crown Prince. Sophia was busy on her thesis, so that often when they met it was to exchange ideas on the professor's own work, as between mature mathematicians. After Sophia had left Berlin for good, Weierstrass in his first letter to her reported having finally put aside a problem on which he had worked for two weeks, lamenting that "in conversation with you I would have more quickly brought some thoughts to a complete development than can be done alone with simple reasoning." This suggests that she was sometimes intuitive and leaped beyond the ordinary sequence of reasoning.

Sophia during her last two years in Berlin had been working intermittently on determining the shape of the rings of Saturn but did not put her conclusions into final form. Laplace had examined this problem and concluded that a transverse section of the previously presumed axi-symmetrical rings would not be stable to slight perturbations and therefore that the ringlets must have variable width and density, that is, a shape about which both axes are differently curved. Sophia determined that the stable form would be a somewhat egg-like oval. She had followed Laplace in assuming the rings to be liquid. When some years after her death the astronomer James E. Keeler showed experimentally that the rings are actually composed of orbiting solid particles, her assumption became invalid. Nevertheless, her mathematical approach using power series continued to be of value.

A number of years elapsed before she put this Saturn study into form for publication. She was not at that time eager to publish and in fact tended to lose interest in the final presentation of a problem once she had solved it to her own satisfaction. In this she was like Weierstrass, much of whose thought remained unpublished and first was put in print by some of his students, because he himself would submit nothing for the press unless it could be presented with the utmost clarity. Some of his work did not get into print until a quarter century after his death.

vi

BETWEEN 27 JUNE and 21 July of 1874 Weierstrass wrote four letters to his old pupil, Lazarus Fuchs, at the University of Göttingen, asking him to mediate with the faculty for Sophia to receive a doctorate *in absentia*. (One letter in which, as one mathematician to another, he explained her mathematical accomplishment appears as an appendix.) At first Fuchs objected that Sophia was a woman; that there was no indication that she needed a degree in order to teach; and that degrees were never awarded without an oral examination.

Weierstrass reminded Fuchs that the late Karl Gauss (d.1855) of Göttingen, who in his day had been considered the foremost mathematician of Europe, had stated that a woman is just as capable of scientific accomplishment as a man and therefore should not be denied a diploma. Because he himself opposed the general admission of women into universities, he assured Fuchs that he had been far from inclined to lighten the testing of his pupil. He mentioned Sophia's outstanding ability and her unusual power of will, combined in a person extremely feminine in nature. He gave assurance of her married respectability, her inheritance of mathematical ability from her artillery-general father and her astronomer grandfather, her struggle against opposition for a higher education, her five years of study in Germany without the comforts to which she was accustomed in Russia, and he stressed that she had never been involved in the disorders of Russian students in Zurich. He predicted for her a great future.

Of course he described to Fuchs in technical terms, as one mathematician to another, Sophia's work involving certain differential equations, a problem "I myself, speaking frankly, was afraid to go into"; her work correcting Laplace on the shape of Saturn's rings; and her work on certain elliptic functions. Any single one of these treatises he himself would have accepted for a degree, although she would only be submitting the first.

Weierstrass wrote Fuchs that he had advised Sophia against taking an oral examination, "not because I lack confidence in her knowledge —I repeat that on the contrary she possesses in mathematics and physics such knowledge as only a rare candidate has—but . . . because . . . she has led a very secluded life devoted only to study. Here in Berlin she has seen only me (whereas her friend living with her, Lermontova, worked in Hofmann's laboratory and came in contact with many people). Consequently she is very shy and doesn't speak easily with persons unknown to her. Add to this, that with her surprising mental acuity her thoughts are always going more rapidly than she can verbalize them in German, in which, however, she can express herself very well in writing." He went on to state that if she became agitated under questioning she would become so disconcerted that the examination would not reveal her true knowledge. He believed that if she had to be orally examined she would not seek a degree there or anywhere, which would be unfortunate for science.

Weierstrass also put in a word with Fuchs for Lermontova but wrote separately to Professor Hans Hübner at Göttingen asking him to sponsor Lermontova. Hübner declined, because he said Hofmann of Berlin had already approached Mühler of Göttingen to act in the matter. Because of his own prejudice Hübner was perhaps glad to have so ready an excuse.

As her official doctorate dissertation Sophia submitted what turned out to be her most important work: *The Theory of Partial Differential Equations (Die Theorie der partiallen Differential-gliechungen)*. The problem she examined was Augustin Cauchy's problem of 1842 in mathematical physics. She used as a theoretical example one involving the conduction of heat. Her proof was more simple than Cauchy's and gave to the problem its final form, as covered today in higher mathematics under "The Theorem of Cauchy-Kovalevsky."

Ever since the invention of derivatives by Newton and Leibnitz in the seventeenth century, differential equations have been studied by mathematicians. Natural laws often take the form of such equations. Usually an individual physical event depends not only on the laws but on additional pieces of information or "data." Thus, for example, in order to predict where a falling body will land, it is necessary to know not only the law of gravity but also from where and with what initial speed the body started, the so-called *initial data*. The general problem consists in determining what amount of additional information is just adequate to lead to a unique solution to the differential equation. An answer was suggested by Cauchy, a leading French mathematician. Roughly speaking it states that the number of initial data one can prescribe is equal to the order of the equation. It remained to show that this so-called Cauchy problem actually has a solution and that the solution is unique. A proof was given by Cauchy for the case of ordinary analytic equations. Sophia extended the proof to the more general analytic *partial* differential equations, requiring the data also to be analytic. The restriction to analytic data somewhat limits the value of the theorem for applications, as Hadamard pointed out in the early twentieth century.

Together with the manuscript of her dissertation Sophia also sent to Göttingen in Latin both her official petition and a brief account of her studies and qualifications. Without delay she was granted *in absentia* her degree, *summa cum laude*. Julia, however, had to defend in person her right to a degree—more than that, she had to prove her comprehensive knowledge of chemistry.

Early in 1874 Julia had submitted her dissertation: *On the Knowledge of Methylen Compounds (Zur Kenntniss der Methylen Verbindungen)*. Then all summer she studied at home in Moscow preparing for her ordeal, which would be the first school examination she had ever taken and was a frightening prospect, added to which she had to travel alone to a foreign land to face unknown professors. Her account of what took place indicates what Sophia escaped through the influence of Weierstrass. Julia spent what she described as "three terrible weeks" in Göttingen while awaiting her testing, during which time she lost her appetite completely and could hardly sleep. She was to be quizzed on inorganic chemistry, organic chemistry, physics, and minerology.

"I was very surprised by the arrangements for the examination, which took place at night," she recalled. "A table was set with pastries and wine. I was examined alone for two hours [before the faculty]. For the major subject, chemistry, I was examined rigorously. . . . Professor Hübner questioned especially strictly; without exception his questions covered the most difficult parts of organic chemistry. . . . Wöhler as an old man examined more easily [inorganic chemistry]. The questions for the secondary subjects were shorter and easier. At the end we all ate and drank, and I was informed that I was worthy of the title Doctor of Chemistry, *magna cum laude.* To remember the occasion Professor Wöhler gave me a small faceted stone of the mineral in which he first discovered the element titanium. How I came out alive after all this I can't even remember.

"After such an examination it is customary in Göttingen to visit all the examiners. One of them, Professor Listig [physics], and his very pleasant wife and two daughters, invited me to move into their home to await the printing of the diploma and dissertation. They surrounded me with such attentions and kindness as can never be forgotten. I lived with them for several weeks."

Julia had expected after the examination to feel great satisfaction but experienced only a hard letdown. "I never felt so unhappy as when going home with the trophies in my suitcase." En route she stopped with Sophia in Petersburg, where she was honored at a reception and dinner given by D. I. Mendeleev, professor of chemistry at the University of St. Petersburg. Those attending included a number of Russian professors and chemists, one of whom, A. M. Bulterov, invited her to work in his laboratory; but in order to be with her aging parents, the first year she worked in a Moscow laboratory.

Following the award of her own doctorate Sophia had remained until mid-August in Berlin, sharpening up for publication the text of her dissertation to meet Weierstrass' standard of clarity and, with his help, polishing her German. The granting to a woman of the first doctorate in science created a sensation among German scholars. Today's glut of doctors of philosophy did not then exist. To be designated a doctor in any field really set the person apart, and for a woman to achieve the honor in science was almost unbelievable. Some individuals in the academic world, jealous of the position of Weierstrass, concluded that he had lowered his standards in judging Sophia. However, the awarding several months later of a second doctorate in science to Julia, protégée of a different Berlin professor, must have caused even such doubters, together with the greater number of academics who were prejudiced against women but confident of Weierstrass' probity, to have shrugged their shoulders in despairing defeat.

Sophia left for Palibino before the printing of her dissertation, leaving Weierstrass to distribute most of the 350 copies to various mathematicians and institutions.

Sophia Vasilevna Kovalevsky (*née* Korvin-Krukovsky), age about 37

Lt. Gen. Vasily Vasilevich Korvin-Krukovsky, father

Elizabeth Federovna Korvin-Krukovsky (*née* Shubert), mother

Sophia Vasilevna Korvin-Krukovsky, age about 16

Anna (Aniuta) Vasilevna Korvin-Krukovsky, sister

Joseph Ignatevich Malevich, house tutor

Alexander N. Strannoliubsky, mathematical tutor in St. Petersburg

Fedor Dostoevsky, Sophia's friend and her sister's suitor

Vladimir Onufrievich Kovalevsky, husband

Karl Theodore William Weierstrass, Berlin professor

Julia Vsevolodovna Lermontova, closest friend

Gösta Mittag-Leffler, Stockholm professor and friend

Maksim Maksimovich Kovalevsky (1880), lover and fiancé

CHAPTER 15

Married Life in Russia

i

AFTER THEIR long separation during much of 1872 and 1873, Sophia during her last year in Berlin saw Vladimir at fairly frequent intervals, although their marriage continued on the same unsatisfactory basis as before. About the middle of August, 1874, they arrived together to vacation at Palibino, joining Aniuta and Fedor who had arrived from Petersburg about two months earlier. Jaclar remained in Petersburg to complete a pedagogy course so that he could teach French. Once more the great house contained the entire family, including its newest member, Aniuta's year-old Urey, beloved by his grandparents.

Sophia had grown thin and dispirited but in the familiar surroundings of Palibino, in her new close relationship with her father, she regained some of her physical and emotional well-being.

She showed her old tutor the embellished velvet case, a gift from Weierstrass, that protected her diploma. Malevich examined with greater interest the diploma itself, all in Latin. In remembrance of his teaching, Sophia then presented him with a vellum copy of her diploma, which pleased the elderly man immensely, since his dreams for her had so far been realized.

Malevich, having just directed a play in the village with amateur actors, proposed staging a family play at Palibino to honor Sophia's mother on her name's day, 17 September. On that date, as it turned out, Aniuta would have to bring Jaclar from Vitebsk to Palibino. In becoming a Swiss citizen Jaclar had adopted the name Jaclar-Korvin, so that Russian authorities in permitting him into the country very likely were unaware of his revolutionary past. According to one report he had resumed his university training in Switzerland and according to one probably erroneous report had become a physician, although this seems unlikely. He never practiced medicine in Russia.

Since the play could not be given as planned, it was decided to present it instead on 29 September, Sophia's name's day, and as a surprise for her to have a ball. A search began in the estate and the village libraries for a suitable play having five parts. Aniuta found one in French that satisfied everybody, a comedy called *Murderer* that had been presented in numerous European theatres. To make this understandable for all rural guests it had to be translated, however; so Aniuta and Fedor set to work, each doing half; then Malevich added his polishing touches; and finally Sophia's mother copied out the parts in her legible hand. Malevich played the role of a prosecutor, Aniuta of a widow, Vladimir of a gardener, Sophia of his wife, and Fedor the remaining part. Having once wanted to be an actress, Aniuta began rehearsals with real enthusiasm, persuading her sister to enter into the carefree spirit of the affair. Vladimir was wooden but willing.

On the great day guests from neighboring estates and the two nearest towns arrived by seven o'clock in the evening. The play began at eight and was received with much laughter and applause. Following that, when the General opened the ball, Sophia asked Malevich for the first quadrille, assuring him that a short walk over the parquet wouldn't torture him excessively. Sophia herself had rarely danced and very likely was glad to have a stiffened elderly man as her first partner of the evening.

Several hours after midnight the guests entered the large dining area where Sophia's wedding dinner had been held. The General himself had arranged a platoon of champagne bottles at one end of a side table and a similar array of still wine bottles at the other end. He directed the serving at table of food and drink. As dessert was served and goblets refilled, Malevich arose to ask the host's permission to say "several words on the occasion." He said more than several—in fact went on for hundreds, in an address he printed in his recollections. Sophia was abashed at first by this surprise but regained her composure after her mother embraced her. The address followed the form to be expected on such an occasion, fullsome praise for Sophia, her parents, German universities, Weierstrass, and of course the glory reflected on himself as her first mentor. Finally he proposed a toast to the first Russian woman to receive the highest degree in mathematics and physics. Sophia responded with a toast to the health of her first teacher and received his bouquet.

Thus ended the holiday. Next day the Kovalevskys paid farewell visits to the closest neighbors and the following day left for their new life in Petersburg.

ii

AND FOR them it was a new life, filled with new interests, new and old friends, and with living continuously together, although in the old fictitious relationship. Several Shubert relatives in Petersburg conveniently departed at this time for a stay of six months in Germany, turning over their apartment to the young couple. Until they could become established financially the General continued his monthly allowance to both daughters. He had already shown his liking for Vladimir, whose materialistic philosophy he managed to ignore, and for Aniuta's sake he tolerated her revolutionary peasant-born husband.

Sophia began a social whirl of receptions, dinners, plays, and other diversions, which she described to Weierstrass. In reply he took advantage, as he reminded her, of her permission to scold her at any time like a strict teacher. This new phase of Sophia's life worried him. He felt she had spent enough time recovering from her years of study and should not betray science by delaying too long in rededicating herself with renewed strength to her life work.

He also asked her to write him about Julia, who had been so "lively" in Berlin and had "pleased me and my sisters very much." Then months later he reported academic gossip that Julia had advanced the cause of women's emancipation by having withstood Hübner's aggressive questioning at Göttingen, thereby converting the historian, R. Pauli, who had entered the examination room firmly resolved to vote against her. Pauli considered Hübner's questioning unfair and later told him so; the circle of academic wives also chided Hübner for his attitude toward the young woman.

One letter from Weierstrass closed with the words: "Goodby, dear heart, and don't force your friend to wait so long for signs of life from you. You must see that he is an indulgent spiritual father, the welfare of whose child often agitates him, and to whom are known the weaknesses of human nature."

The plain fact was that at the age of twenty-four Sophia had wearied of mathematics. She had left all her mathematical papers at Palibino in a trunk, in which she found some old verses that had reawakened her interest in writing. She began literary work in a small way by reviewing plays for *Novoe vremia* (*New Time*), edited by a friend. However, the arrival of each new letter from Weierstrass, and the tutoring she gave her brother, then still studying at the university, kept Sophia's interest in mathematics from withering entirely.

In a letter of 14 December 1874 Weierstrass reported having received favorable reactions to her dissertation from G. R. Kirchhoff, Edward Heine, Wilhelm Scherer, Herman A. Schwarz, and especially from P. DuBois-Reymond, who was "extremely delighted" and would doubtless write her an "enraptured letter." Then came the publication in the journal of the French Academy of Science of an article by some mathematician along the lines of Sophia's published dissertation. Weierstrass called upon the Academy to publish official recognition of Sophia's prior publication. It would seem, although this is unclear, that plagiarism occurred. Eventually Sophia's dissertation was reprinted, a significant honor, in Crelle's journal for mathematicians.

Weierstrass asked Sophia to spend a week putting into final shape her work on the rings of Saturn, as several of his friends wanted to read it, but she did not do so, and several years passed before she finally revised and published it.

He tried again to rekindle her interest by his letter of 12 January 1875, congratulating her on her twenty-fifth birthday, 15 January, and sending condolences to Julia on the death of a sister. He mentioned the mathematical work he had begun two years earlier on her birthday and had discussed with her. Although he had completed 600 pages, it remained unfinished; but he promised she would be the first to read it. After several pages of equations in the letter he added: "I do so much like to develop my ideas before you."

His efforts did stir an interest in Sophia. She asked him to outline a program of further study. He recommended lower mathematics, analytical mechanics, and new aspects of physics including electrodynamics. After referring to the work of Poisson, Cauchy, the two Neumanns, Hamilton, Saint-Venant, and others, he commented: "Among the mentioned authors you will be unpleasantly surprised by the lack of precision in their conclusions." He urged her, in order to sharpen her own thinking, to rework as practice some of those conclusions into better form. In one letter he referred sadly to a new book on elliptic functions by his oldest pupil, a book "in which it is hardly possible to find a page that should not be done over." He observed that any scientific work should have unity, according to a definite plan, with details clearly worked out to show the stamp of independent research. He praised the precise if sometimes superficial work of most French mathematicians, clearly urging her to seek both content and precision in her own work. He posed for her several mathematical problems.

It is probable that Sophia read several of the recommended books,

[178]

but it is unlikely that she followed his other advice. The tug of pleasures long denied was too great. During 1875 they exchanged a number of letters, however. He wrote her at least eight in which he worried about her health, discussed academic appointments in mathematics, mentioned that he had been chosen a cavalier of the Order of Merit, conveyed a request from the University of Göttingen for her photo, and added his own request for a recent photo. When several years later he finally received the photo, he complained that the camera (short focal length lens, doubtless) made her nose look too large and asked for a different pose. The unacceptable photo he mentioned may be the one of unknown date showing Sophia wearing a dark puff-sleeved dress, cut with a deep V at the bodice, the V filled in by a heavily-embroidered, high-collared jabot, having cuffs to match. Her hair is becomingly coiffed high on the head to show the ears. Her fingers are slender, her bust still slight, her eyes large, her expression serious and perhaps superior.

In one letter of 1875 Weierstrass first mentioned a new Swedish student he liked very much, one named Magnus Gösta Mittag-Leffler, who later was to play a key role in Sophia's life. Weierstrass wrote that the Swede and a companion, students at the university, began taking additional private lessons from him but that he had soon terminated these, because he could not tell whether they understood him clearly and therefore he could not establish a closeness of thought with them. Mittag-Leffler already had his doctorate from Uppsala and had subsequently studied in Paris and Göttingen.

In another letter he lamented Sophia's absence: "During four years I had become accustomed to see my thoughts and aims reflected by you, with whom I could speak as to a close friend. I have never found anyone who expressed so well the highest aims of science, who so happily responded to all my views, as you did. Oh, we should never have been separated. You should have worked with me another year or two."

Understandably Weierstrass was positively delighted, therefore, when Sophia proposed visiting him for several months beginning at the end of June, 1875. Sophia had exacted a promise from Weierstrass that he would not study mathematics with any other woman. Now, however, she intended to bring as her traveling companion and his potential pupil a talented young woman. He wrote back that true to his promise to her, to which he wished to adhere, he had already rejected a woman who asked to study geometry with him. One must suppose that actually he had not time to spare for anybody involved with elementary mathematics, or indeed for anybody but the most gifted, and that his old promise offered a gracious excuse for refusal.

His plans to have somebody rent an apartment for her and to see her himself every day were dashed, however, when Sophia came down with measles, the effects of which lasted until September. Weierstrass asked her to write three lines at least every eighth day to let him know her condition, but she apparently left him in suspense until the end of summer, although a letter of hers may have miscarried, as several of his to her certainly did. As often as not, throughout their correspondence of many years, Sophia failed to date her letters, much to her mentor's annoyance. Careless she may at times have been, but also, because she traveled so often between Russia and Europe, with their confusing difference in calendars, and because, too, she often became absorbed entirely in her work, Sophia probably didn't happen to know a date and didn't bother to find out.

iii

FINANCIAL TROUBLES continued to burden Vladimir in connection with his tottering publishing business. Partly this was because the period from 1873 to about 1877 was one of depression and industrial crisis. A loan was called that the General had guaranteed; only at the last minute could Vladimir secure a new loan to avoid embarrassment. Evdokimov as manager wanted to carry on the business and found support in Sophia, who saw it as a chance for Aniuta to earn money translating new works to be published, while she herself could take over entirely the finances from Evdokimov. One book to be published was a French anthology by the Jaclars of classic French authors. Although wishing to have no active part in the business himself, Vladimir agreed to continue the venture. His eye, however, was on a professorship.

Vladimir's Jena thesis had been published in French by the University of St. Petersburg and then reissued in a revised Russian version by the university at Kiev. His subject was the paleontological history of the horse. He was the first to attempt to construct a genealogy of hoofed animals. He advanced the idea of adaptive radiation, developing Darwin's views on divergency, as a means of evolutionary transformation. Despite his credentials, despite his German doctorate, to be certified for teaching in Russia he needed a Russian master's degree. Several years earlier he had sat for this in Moscow and been rejected, apparently because of academic opposition to his materialistic scientific views. He passed the master's examination, however, early in March before a somewhat hostile faculty at the Petersburg university. Subsequently, reflecting an altered opinion about him in Moscow, he was offered a sub-professorship there. In rejecting this he deferred to Sophia's wish to remain in Petersburg close to relatives and her circle of friends there. In time he became a sub-professor in Petersburg.

When Sophia had sufficiently recovered from measles to be able to travel, the Kovalevskys vacated their apartment for the returning Shuberts and set out for Palibino. In her weakened condition Sophia's heart rather than her brain now ruled her actions. She felt a new security in her closer relationship with her father. Having put mathematical work aside entirely, she spent her time reading in the old library, playing cards with the family, walking around the estate as in childhood, sharing the social life of the neighborhood, playing charades and forfeits, and best of all talking in the evening with the entire family gathered around the singing samovar in the large drawing room with its familiar red-damask-covered furniture, its mirrors, and candle-laden chandeliers.

Then quite unexpectedly this peaceful existence was shattered. As "Sophia" was a popular name at that time, many families observed the name's day on 29 September. Exactly one year earlier the dinner and ball had feted Sophia. This year it had been decided to hold a progressive celebration honoring several Sophias in the vicinity. Lunch would be at one house, dinner at another, and the evening would be spent at a third. On his usual morning walk it happened that the General sighted thick smoke pouring from a barn, and he shouted for all the servants to come. Actually, only a flue had been left closed, causing the alarm, but the stressful excitement caused the General to suffer a collapse.

While the family made him comfortable, a trusted servant rushed to Velikiye Luki for the nearest physician, who diagnosed the trouble as paralysis of the intestines. What he called the trouble didn't much matter, because the General was fatally stricken and within twenty-four hours died of an aneurism on 30 September 1875 at the age of seventy-six.

Malevich recorded that Sophia was overcome by such grief that "for several days we were afraid to leave her alone and took turns trying to distract her or at least quiet her a little." Summoned by telegraph from Velikiye Luki, Fedor and Vladimir and Jaclar arrived from Petersburg. A throng of relatives and friends attended the funeral and the burial on the estate.

For Sophia her father's death was tragic. Sophia felt that Aniuta's affection for her had been lost to Jaclar and their child, while she had never enjoyed her mother's affection, which now was centered on Fedor and on her blond grandson, so that Sophia had turned for family affection to her father. Surely it was not only the sundering of so egocentric a relationship, however, that caused her such acute distress. She must also have felt a residual guilt for her hostility to the General during adolescence and afterward. In his old age she had come to understand and love him, recognizing his generosity, his noble qualities, and his real concern for her happiness that she had mistaken for tyranny. She had come to realize that in letting Aniuta as a girl have her headstrong way in so many things the General had not indicated greater love for Aniuta but, on the contrary, evidenced that he had given up trying to direct her energies in an orderly and constructive manner, and that by concentrating as he did on Sophia's training he had shown his real interest and hope for her.

Sophia wrote at length to Weierstrass of her loss. He commented in reply that for the first time in their correspondence her letter revealed personal insight into her deepest feelings, and he was gladdened that "from the very moment of your return home you had such excellent relations with your father" and that "you reached the conviction that you had been the favorite of his heart, although as you once said to me, in former years he showed this very little." He advised that she find surcease from grief in work, if she felt able physically, and tried to whet her interest by asking if she wished to be informed about his excellent new theory of integrals.

Mathematics offered cold comfort, however. Instead, Sophia really turned at last to Vladimir. If earlier in Petersburg they had come together physically, which is possible, now all psychological barriers Sophia had maintained crumbled at last. She no longer needed to fear pregnancy as a hindrance to study or a career. During her period of sorrow, after seven years of denial and evasion and subterfuge in a fictitious marriage, it seemed natural to ease into a full relationship with Vladimir. She had nobody else.

The General's will left Palibino to his wife Elizabeth in trust for Fedor, while the Moshino estate went to the son directly. Apparently Elizabeth also held in trust the cash bequests of 50,000 roubles to each of the three children, of which, however, Sophia had received 20,000 when she married, and Aniuta had sacrificed a like amount as a bribe to rescue Jaclar.

Following the funeral the widow departed Palibino to spend the winter in Petersburg but returned the following summer to initiate the construction, in a shady grove on a hillock, of a stone chapel over the General's grave. Eventually she would rest by his side. Malevich remained in the country to supervise the completion of the chapel and its decoration after Elizabeth returned to Petersburg. She never lived again at Palibino, much preferring city life and the company of Shubert relatives. She leased out the Palibino estate with its associated properties.

Elizabeth took a large apartment on Vasilevsky Island, Sixth Line, No.15. This island lay between the Great Neva and the Little Neva branches of the river and was the largest of Petersburg's several islands that, along with the mainland portion, were interconnected by bridges. With Elizabeth lived Fedor and the Jaclars. Fedor, at age nineteen, who so much resembled his sister in various ways that the family described him as "Sofa in man's clothing," had already under his mother's lax supervision begun the wasteful life of a young nobleman about town. Jaclar as a Frenchman was popular in Petersburg—but Sophia called him a cat. His attitude toward family members, even toward his adoring wife, was one of indifferent detachment. Elizabeth, being an accomplished pianist and having a pleasing manner, attracted many friends to her regular musical evenings, which Sophia usually attended but which Vladimir, having little liking for such gatherings, frequently avoided. The Dostoevskys sometimes attended. When in Petersburg the writer, with the full approval of his wife, sometimes spent several afternoons a week in long conversations, or monology, with Aniuta. Presumably he discussed his work in progress, but mostly she provided an intellectual friendship for a man with few sincere friends.

Where Aniuta put on too much weight and began to show her age, Sophia in gaining a little weight became more attractive. Vladimir wished always to see her well dressed and developed in her a certain taste for fashion. In the view of Litvinova, "He inflamed her vanity and wished to see her shine in society."

By this time Sophia's friend, Litvinova, had completed her mathematical studies in Switzerland and had returned to Petersburg. She wrote that for a time the Kovalevskys lived in a separate house with a garden in which they kept a cow and in a glassed forcing bed raised melons and other vegetables. During most of their Petersburg years, however, they lived in an eight-room apartment in which, it seemed, new furnishings and knicknacks continuously appeared, usually as presents or surprises from Vladimir. The result was a disordered clutter rather than a cozy arrangement. He also showered his wife with sweets, which she loved. Some friends thought that by compensating for Sophia's Spartan years in Germany, Vladimir tried to develop in her unnecessary wants that he could satisfy in order to attach her more firmly to himself. Litvinova thought he did not do this consciously. At any rate, everything in their new life was now at Sophia's service.

Sophia herself described her new life in Petersburg, in the first person autobiographical part of the initial Russian edition (prior to later editing) of her posthumous novel. At the age of twenty-five (she wrote twenty-two, to correlate with the fictitious age she later claimed), after five years of almost hermitical study, the joy of living positively "inebriated" her. "Forgetting for a time those ideas about analytical functions, space, and the fourth dimension, which so recently had filled my inner world," she wrote, "I now with my whole soul entered into new interests, making acquaintances on the right and the left, attempting to break into the most varied circles, and with greedy curiosity observing all the aspects, so attractive at first glance but so empty in substance, of that hurly-burly known as Petersburg life. Now everything interested and gave me delight. The theaters amused me, and the benefit evenings, and the literary circles with their endless arguments on abstract themes. . . . I gave myself to everything with the enthusiasm to which a naturally talkative Russian is capable, after having lived under several specialists, each occupied with his own narrow and all-engrossing work, without understanding how it is possible to waste precious time in leisurely babble." She had attained a reputation as a scholarly woman and brought her own enthusiasm to her friends and acquaintances. "In a word, I was in the best of spirits, living my 'honeymoon' of fame, and at this time was ready to exclaim: 'Everything is for the best in the best of worlds.' "

iv

AFTER INFORMING Weierstrass of her father's death, Sophia sent him nary a line for twenty-four months. If she had any justification for such seeming ingratitude it is not evident. When urged by her mother or sister to write the professor, she would reply that she would do so as soon as she returned to mathematics. Perhaps she simply wanted to escape constant reminders that she had strayed from her true course. Presumably she found real marriage after seven years of delay to be so much to her liking, and became so involved with Vladimir in plans to make money, that she had all but abandoned thoughts of an active scientific career. Obviously Weierstrass could not understand what had happened. Had her father's death silenced her? Had she serious marital problems? Was she ill?

Weierstrass therefore prevailed upon his Swedish protégé, Gösta Mittag-Leffler, to travel to Petersburg for a first hand evaluation of the situation. It is not impossible that Weierstrass, supposing that Sophia's marriage was still fictitious and would be annulled should she take a fancy to a brilliant young mathematician, had matchmaking in mind. This seems improbable, however. In any event, the young Swede met Sophia for the first time on 10 February 1876 and was greatly attracted to her. Of Sophia he wrote to his old professor in Sweden, Carl J. Malmsen: "Today I spent several hours with her. As a woman she is charming. She is beautiful, and when she speaks her face is animated with such an expression of feminine kindness and high intellect that the effect is blinding. Her dealings with people are simple and natural without the slightest trace of pedantry or pretense. In all respects she is completely a well-bred woman. As a scholar she is characterized by unusual clarity and precision in expression. The depth of her knowledge becomes clear then, and I understand completely why Weierstrass considers her the most talented of his pupils.''

Doubtless he tried tactfully to learn her future plans, and doubtless she realized he had not really come so far merely as a sightseer. Perhaps she decided Weierstrass was imposing a pressure she could not tolerate. Mittlag-Leffler left with the impression that she had given up mathematics.

Actually, Sophia had not given up her broad interest in science but had combined it with her awakened interest in literature and life. As an accomplished conversationalist she moved in a circle that included the novelists Ivan Turgenev and Dostoevsky—but did not see them together, as the pathologically jealous Dostoevsky had spitefully caricatured Turgenev in *The Devils*. Apart from other literary persons, friends included Julia's friends, Professors A. M. Bulterov, who contributed significantly to structural chemistry, and D. I. Mendeleev, who discovered a predictable periodic system for elements. With one exception Sophia had no friends among Russian mathematicians, the reason being twofold: either that her political views were too liberal or that the mathematicians did not look with favor on the direction taken by German and French mathematics. The exception, predictably, was the foremost figure in nineteenth century Russian mathematics, P. L. Chebyshev. He made the first advance since Euclid on the theory of primes, developed the theory of approximate solutions, and in general worked on integrals and probabilities.

Sophia did spend some time with Chebyshev, who urged her to continue her mathematical studies (doubtless at the suggestion of Weierstrass) and even offered to work with her; but she found she could not enter into a scholarly association with him as she had with Weierstrass, although this may have been because she was unwilling to devote the time and effort required for concentrated thought.

She was diverted, for example, between November of 1876 and July of the following year, by her writing of theatrical reviews and science news articles for a Petersburg periodical in which she and Vladimir had some financial interest. She reported on such new developments as a solar-powered steam boiler, a new photometer, an artificial eye, a conic reflector, a flying apparatus, a talking telegraph (telephone), an American writing machine (typewriter), and Pasteur's new researches.

She was further distracted by money problems, which had continued since her father's death about a year earlier. As a sub-professor Vladimir earned 600 roubles, and he received about 600 from the estate he held jointly with his brother. Sophia received interest of 900 roubles annually from her bequest held by Elizabeth, about the same sum as her previous allowance. Thus the Kovalevskys' income totaled about 2,100 roubles yearly, a sum they found inadequate for their new way of life. Their apartment cost 300; and 600 went for housekeeping services; this left 1,200 for other living and entertainment expenditures. As a suggestion of prices at this time, an ordinary restaurant dinner without wine cost one rouble. The Kovalevskys moved among affluent friends who supposed them to be equally favored, whereas they maintained their position only by borrowing. To keep his publishing business afloat Vladimir borrowed from one source to pay another; then instead he diverted funds into costly clothing for Sophia or cash gifts to poor acquaintances. He had a genius both for generosity and for financial mismanagement. He arose early, dressed carelessly, ate little, read little, and frequently had the appearance of one pressed from all sides.

When Vladimir's brother advised him to cut his losses, abandon publishing, and seek a better paying teaching post in the provinces, Sophia on 25 November 1875 wrote the brother:

"In what manner should we act in the future in order to make our common life happier? Mathematically we would have stated this question in this manner: given a definite function (in this case, our happiness), which depends upon many variables (namely our monetary resources, the possibility of living in a pleasant place and society, and so forth)—in what manner can the variables be defined so that the given happiness function will reach a maximum? Needless to say we are unable to solve this matter mathematically."

Unfortunately. But by ordinary reasoning they had decided not to seek a post in the provinces for Vladimir, because what would be gained in security and time for scientific work would be overbalanced by the loss of "pleasant company" and for Sophia the separation from all her relatives and close friends.

Nor did Sophia want to live carefully in Petersburg on their available income, perhaps to be supplemented by translations. Instead the couple decided to concentrate on the publishing business, believing that in two years it could gross 10,000 roubles or more. Toward that end Vladimir had already obtained a loan of 2,500 roubles from his brother. "He swears by all the saints that he will return it to you," Sophia had written Alexander.

Within a year the Kovalevskys wanted to buy a three-or four-story house as an investment. One could be obtained near the university for 15,000 to 17,000 roubles and could be remodeled into apartments. It appears that Vladimir mortgaged some of his books (such as *The Birds* by Brehm that was selling well) and with 1,000 roubles from Sophia's mother and a sum from Julia managed to make a down payment on a house.

It became Sophia's aim quickly to arrive at financial security so that they could live in comfort and be entirely free to concentrate on scientific careers. She argued that Chebyshev was a great mathematician and yet managed to acquire for himself a fortune in property. Why could she not do likewise? "On every street I'll have a house," she would say jokingly, yet not without some serious intent.

In a letter of May in 1877 Sophia wrote Alexander that the house they had obtained was nearly ready for tenants. They had themselves rented a summer apartment in the center of a large park near Petersburg. Julia who had been living with them left for suburban Moscow. Various friends scattered for the summer, the Sechenovs departing for the Crimea. Dr. Sechenov had married Bokova, breaking up that *ménage à trois* with her fictitious husband.

V

SOPHIA FREQUENTLY met Dostoevsky in Petersburg, as already mentioned, and also sent him occasional letters during 1876 and 1877. In one letter she reminded him of his promise to aid the niece of Pushkin's wife in contacting her fiancé jailed incommunicado. To that she added a postscript concerning his wife: "Everytime that I speak with her I begin to love her more and more." Another letter hoped for the novelist's quick recovery from an illness and his early visit to see her. A third recounted how during her own illness she had developed at great length an idea he had related to her about a planned novel to be called *Dreamer*, which was never written under that title. In February of 1877 she cancelled a meeting with him because an elderly aunt, presumably Alexandra Briullova, had died. A letter of May 1877 indicates that Sophia was the first to introduce Dostoevsky to Tolstoy's *Anna Karenina*. She greatly admired the novel, but Dostoevsky later pronounced it over-rated.

During these years, of course, Aniuta continued her close relationship with Dostoevsky and his wife. In a letter sent late in 1878 to his wife, when the Dostoevskys were relocating in Petersburg following a period in Moscow, Aniuta urged that they settle close to her residence so that the families would not have to travel so far for visits and so that their children could play together. Life had become easier for the novelist. He had a settled income as editor of a journal and had achieved literary popularity. Of his important novels only *The Brothers Karamazov* had yet to appear.

During the Petersburg years of 1875-1877 Sophia occasionally met Turgenev socially in her apartment or elsewhere. *Virgin Soil* was then taking form in the mind of the grey-bearded cosmopolitan novelist, who at that time divided his time between Paris and Russia. Years earlier Sophia had been the supposed prototype for Dostoevsky's Alexandra in *The Idiot*. That identification is uncertain, but there can be no doubt that she was the physical prototype for Marianna in *Virgin Soil*. Marianna had precisely Sophia's round face, her curly chestnut hair in a round crop, her large and very bright eyes, her thin eyebrows, her small hands and feet, her "sturdily supple little body that reminded one of a sixteenth century Florentine statuette," a "very nervous creature" with "tendency to blush" and an "unsociable air," who in serious conversation was impatient with trivialities in place of causes and facts. The novelist, however, gave Marianna a "large aquiline" nose, whereas Sophia's was more dough-like than classical. Marianna, a proud woman like Sophia, is also the daughter of a general, though of civilian rather than military rank and of blemished rather than upright character. Marianna is interested in the emancipation of women and the education of girls, and from her whole being there emanates in connection with her beliefs a "strong and daring and passionate and impetuous element." It is not surprising that the man with whom Marianna runs off has hair of a peculiar red shade such as Vladimir had, although in other respects the character of Nezhdanov has no physical resemblance to Sophia's husband.

All this is not to suggest any parallel in the life of the Kovalevskys with the story of *Virgin Soil* beyond the facts that it deals with the nihilist movement of the sixties and seventies in which they participated, and that the Kovalevskys' marriage had been fictitious. In his novel Turgenev ridicules liberals and conservatives alike, aiming to avoid literary stereotypes of young persons as being either scoundrels or saints. "I decided," he said, "to choose a middle course in order to approach closer to the truth; to show young people as they are, for the most part, good and honest, but to show that despite this their course is so false and impractical that it must lead to complete fiasco."

Virgin Soil appeared in 1877. A month after its publication many young men and women were arrested for revolutionary conspiracy. Sophia described their trial in *Vera Vorontsov*. Students misunderstood Turgenev's message, however; and following acts by terrorists against the Tsar, students at the university reacted to the consequent repression by making Turgenev a symbol of protest. Following an address he gave at the university, girls impulsively kissed him, all cheered him wildly, and finally students wreathed him in laurel.

vi

IN MOSCOW, meanwhile, Julia contracted typhoid fever. This affected her brain, so that the gentle Julia acted like a madwoman, attacking those trying to help her, especially relatives. Nurses would not stay, not even for extra pay. Sophia responded at once by hastening to Moscow to try her influence.

In the dead of winter it was cold on the train despite the iron stove. Through the windows stretched forests of pines with snow clinging to branches. Areas of open countryside appeared deserted of all life, only occasional spirals of smoke from huts betrayed life within. At night the lanterns illuminating the train coach cast unsteady shadows. Upon arrival in Moscow a narrow sleigh stood waiting with straw for her feet and a wolfskin laprobe. The driver slapped reins against the horse, which was eager to be moving again and exhaled vapor as it jogged along with harness bells jangling. En route to the Lermontov's they passed idle cab-drivers warming themselves at bonfires in the streets. Naked linden trees gleamed with dull hoarfrost.

Unfortunately Julia rejected Sophia as "that monster," so that Sophia became afraid even to enter the sickroom. This she wrote to Vladimir on 24 January 1876. The nursing situation was solved when Julia submitted meekly to a family friend, a woman whom she very much disliked in normal times. Sophia returned then to Petersburg.

Following Julia's slow but complete recovery she moved in 1878 to live again with the Kovalevskys. Professor Bulterov accepted her in his private laboratory and permitted her to attend his university lectures on organic chemistry. In working with him she derived real pleasure, especially as his new wife included her in their social life. This arrangement ended, however, with the illness of Julia's parents which called her home, and upon the death soon after of both parents she abandoned chemistry entirely to manage the estate left to her and her younger sister.

March of the following year saw the birth in Wurtemburg of Albert Einstein, who changed man's concept of creation and whose work, and the work of so many others, became possible because of the mathematical contributions of nineteenth century workers, including Sophia. As E. T. Bell commented: "It may be said that without the theory of power series most of mathematical physics (including much of astronomy and astrophysics as we know it) would not exist."

In 1878 Higher Courses for Women began in Petersburg as the result of long planning. Sophia participated as a member of the supervising committee, guided by her old teacher Strannoliubsky; the committee consisted of women educated in foreign universities. From a modest beginning they hoped a private university for women would develop; this never happened, although eventually they did obtain a large house as a center. Sophia felt disappointed that she was not invited to lecture, as she had begun to tire of her unproductive life. Nevertheless she zealously devoted herself to the planning and administration, and Vladimir donated copies of the many scientific works he had published.

In the spring of 1878 the life that had become gray for Sophia brightened with anticipation when she became pregnant at age twenty-eight. Six months in advance she began preparing baby clothing and a nursery and engaged a prospective wet-nurse. During the long days of waiting she turned again to mathematics, probably carrying out the study Weierstrass had recommended and when about seven months along finally wrote again to him in early August. Once more she wanted advice. Her forwarded letter reached him on vacation at Rugen Island. He replied promptly on 15 August, rebuking her for her long silence, stating that he had heard about her only twice, once from Mittag-Leffler and once from Chebyshev, both of whom had affirmed that she had given up mathematics. Nevertheless, he brought her up to date on his recent work on periodic functions and on the theory of partial differential equations.

On 17 October 1878 Sophia became the mother of a daughter named Sophia but called Fufu and later Sonya. The new mother expressed satisfaction to Weierstrass that she had not exhausted her strength with excessive mathematics to the possible harm of the child who would, she confidently expected, inherit strong mental capabilities. Actually Sophia did not regain her strength until the following spring.

The birth was a difficult one, labor lasting 12 hours. In the end chloroform and forceps had to be used, and there was a double placenta. Fufu was "terribly large," as Vladimir informed his brother, adding: "Apparently learned women are starting a new breed, *biplacentia*, with a 10-month pregnancy! Sophia, thank heavens, withstood all this bravely." And: "I am very happy that we have a daughter; this is the first production from two scholarly nobles, and we are very curious about the result; already the second day of her life she has begun to display diverse talents and gives promise." Vladimir closed his letter by observing that the child should give stability and solidity to their marriage and that they were consolidating their separate finances.

Although Vladimir had urged artificial feeding, the wet-nurse arrived, and a physician came regularly on a yearly retainer to examine Fufu. Julia was godmother and Sechenov godfather. Arrangements for the infant took over much of the apartment—Fufu had to have separate rooms for sleeping, bathing, and eventually exercise; Julia had her room; the nurse, wet-nurse, cook, and maid had to be accommodated— so that for Sophia, raised in the spaciousness of Palibino, eight rooms for six or seven persons and a crying baby tried her patience. In everything involving Fufu she was fussy, so that the nurses often went about with sulky faces. When emotional explosions occurred Vladimir would persuade Sophia into admitting she had been wrong, but a nurse had only to kiss Fufu in her presence to have her flare up jealously, saying the woman might have tuberculosis or something else. Fufu had the thin dark eyebrows of her mother and the meek blue eyes of her father.

Sophia's old governess, Margarita Frantsevna, then a family pensioner in the House of Shubert, again entered upon the scene with mostly unwelcome advice and assistance. Sophia's mother had little chance to become acquainted with her first grandaughter, inasmuch as her interest centered firmly on Aniuta's son. Relations with the mother had been somewhat strained because she disapproved of the Kovalevskys' speculations and predicted bankruptcy, although she overlooked her son's extravagant lifestyle. Then in February of 1879 Elizabeth died unexpectedly of a heart attack at age fifty-nine. This did not greatly affect Sophia emotionally, because she always had been denied a full portion of her mother's love. It did affect her financially by giving her full control of her inheritance.

Another incident that affected the Kovalevskys just at this time was an article, a masterpiece of sarcastic innuendo, accusing Vladimir of being a government spy. The spiteful article was written by Vladimir's former longtime friend, V. A. Zaitsev, editor of *Obshchee delo* (*Common Work*) published in Geneva and distributed in Russia and Europe. Zaitsev reasoned that Vladimir, formerly the young "cock" hero who "scuttled about like a whirlwind on revolutionary causes," had changed into a wealthy apartment landlord with many friends among the upper class of Petersburg. Since most of his erstwhile revolutionary acquaintances had been jailed or forced to flee Russia, while he alone remained free and prospering, therefore it followed that he must all the time have been a paid informer. Not all of Vladimir's politically active friends had disappeared, of course, but the article seemed logical enough and caused those remaining to distrust him in the future. In fact, some years later the article also caused Sophia to be received with caution by Russian emigrants in Paris. To be called an informer certainly pained and humiliated Vladimir but actually may have been beneficial in deflecting official suspicion from him in the political climate of the period.

In January of the following year, 1880, very likely at the behest of Weierstrass, Chebyshev stirred Sophia's renewed interest in mathematics by inviting her to report on Abelian integrals before the convention of Russian Naturalists and Physicians. From a dusty box in the attic storeroom she withdrew her mildewed mathematical papers, brought there from the trunk when Palibino was vacated. The appropriate paper she translated into Russian in one evening and presented it before the naturalists, winning the approbation of Chebyshev, and also that of Mittag-Leffler who made a special trip to be present. Again, enmeshment by Weierstrass may be presumed. Apart from his affection for Sophia, he knew her potential and didn't want it to be lost to science.

More of Mittag-Leffler later.

vii

THE PERIOD from 1878 to 1881 was one of political unrest and terrorist acts in Petersburg and elsewhere in Russia. This inspired Zaitsev's aforementioned attack on Vladimir. Encouraged by the general disillusionment over the unsatisfactory peace treaty with Turkey, the revolutionists, who had been silenced by wartime patriotism of the public, again became active. Although relatively few in number, the terrorists created confusion with leaflets, pistols, and bombs. Many arrests, mass trials, and hunger strikes advertised the movement. Plotters engineered prison escapes. When juries feared to convict, the government eliminated jury trials for offenses against officials. In September of 1878 the terrorists proclaimed a death sentence for the Tsar and over a period of several years attempted to carry this out by blowing up an imperial train and by dynamiting the dining room of the Tsar's Winter Palace in Petersburg.

The Tsar put in charge of all the ministries a tough soldier, General Loris-Melikov, who personally nabbed a terrorist who tried to kill him. Loris-Melikov replaced the conservative ministers of education and finance with liberals and proposed reforms that attracted peaceful liberal support. This the terrorists feared more than anything else. As in all such violent movements, they wanted no peaceful solution of problems but only complete revolution. They intensified plotting against the Tsar. On 13 March 1881, having approved his dictator's plan for publicly elected representatives joining in the government's legislative work, Tsar Alexander II rode in his carriage along the

Catherine Canal. En route a terrorist threw a bomb that injured several guards. When the Tsar alighted to speak to the wounded men, a second assassin threw a bomb between his legs. He died one and one-half hours later at the palace.

The bomb that killed him ended the beginning of Russian constitutionalism and sent many innocent liberals of the peaceful type, such as the Kovalevskys, scurrying off to escape the retributive measures expected to follow.

viii

TWO DEVELOPMENTS caused the Kovalevskys to leave Petersburg early in 1880, a year before the assassination. The first was the aforementioned political unrest. Considering the stripe of some of their friends and acquaintances, the Kovalevskys could have come under grave suspicion by association. The real, compelling reason, however, for preparing to leave Petersburg was the failure of their real estate projects and the desire of Vladimir to seek again the once-offered subprofessorship in geological sciences at the University of Moscow.

Not only had the publishing business languished and the entire stock of books been consigned, but also creditors pressed them in connection with large loans. The death of Sophia's mother had freed the principal of Sophia's bequest, and the Kovalevskys had lost no time in sinking nearly all of this into building public baths adjacent to their stone apartment house on Vasilevsky Island. To utilize heat as effectively as possible, the three-story bath structure had a bakery in the basement in front and a steam laundry behind, while in the attic a greenhouse received warmth rising from below and from steam piping. It was all very scientific but not profitable.

In a letter to Vladimir's brother on 16 January 1880 Sophia wrote that cold weather discouraged customers, making the baths a losing proposition, and that they could not get a mortgage for 100,000 roubles or even 50,000 to tide them over. Petersburg has a damp and cold climate, with snow or rain falling about 150 days of the year, snow often on the ground into May, and only three or four months of equitable weather out of twelve. The Kovalevskys considered leasing the baths and apartment house to a merchant for ten years but doubted his honesty. In the end they had to call creditors together to reach a settlement. The baths were lost. Apparently Sophia's brother and the Jaclars advanced money to become part owners of the heavily mortgaged apartment structure, in which, however, the Kovalevskys retained a minor interest but very little income during future years. Worldwide economic conditions, which caused a deflation of about twenty-five percent between 1870 and 1875 did not help matters. All the Kovalevskys' apartment furnishings and some personal possessions went at public auction.

Vladimir at this time became deeply depressed. Sophia reported to his brother that twice she had him see the Sechenovs, both being physicians, and that he made a good impression on them both, but that nevertheless she had an appointment for him with a Dr. Sikorsky, recommended by Sechenov as a specialist in nervous troubles. The outcome of that consultation being inconclusive, Sophia upbraided Vladimir for his melancholy as showing lack of character in adversity. Nobody realized, least of all Sophia who had been reassured by medical advice, how tenuous was his grasp on complete reality.

Presumably the move to Moscow, leaving all troubles behind, brightened Vladimir's outlook. But Sophia, who could never give herself by halves to anything, and who had been drawn again to science by the success of her appearance before the convention of naturalists, now found herself bound to an actual and ineffectual husband, rather than a merely fictitious one, and by the demands of an infant daughter. Her 30,000 roubles had vanished, and Vladimir had no job. The wealth she retained was that characterized by the words of an ancient philosopher: "All that is mine I carry with me."

ix

IN MOSCOW the Kovalevskys settled with Julia in her rather small apartment. This was Sophia's third time in Moscow as an adult, but previously she had come alone and remained briefly only to see Julia. Now that they had come to stay she had time to see something of Russia's ancient city, which had become important as a manufacturing center. Doubtless the Kovalevskys viewed the city from the eminence of Sparrow Hill. From there they could see the gilded and colored domes of dozens of churches, with flights of pigeons circling about, the various palaces, as well as the pinkish walls and towers of the Kremlin. Through the city flowed the serpentine river, spanned by numerous bridges and frozen solid five months of the year. Vladimir's goal, the university, had been founded in 1755 to supplement the Corps of Pages in training young men for leadership and now offered four faculties.

Sophia had known in Petersburg a young man trying to perfect an electric light bulb and had subsidized him to the extent of fifty roubles monthly. That subsidy had ended, of course, but not Sophia's interest in the matter. Now she decided to work on the problem herself in an effort to repair their fortunes. She interested Vladimir and Julia in this also, and the trio began spending their days, each with his own apparatus, attempting to produce incandescent light. Over meals and in the evenings they exchanged their thoughts, while Julia's merry sister, Sonya, who supervised the housekeeping, made fun in a good-humored way of the three serious doctors of science who sought to produce light from invisible electricity when the world already had perfectly satisfactory candles, oil lamps, and gas jets. Nothing came of these experiments.

In the summer Sophia and Fufu accompanied Julia to her estate with its village of Samotechno-Sodovia near Moscow. There the modest house little resembled that at Palibino. Among other products the estate produced in large quantities a French-type white cheese similar to Brie and Neufchatel. Vladimir remained in Moscow. Through the efforts of his brother he was a candidate for a modest position in the University as keeper of the cabinet of specimens in the geology-zoology department.

At this point, however, he was offered what appeared to be a golden opportunity to join a firm producing naphtha or kerosene from a petroleum springs at Konstantinov. Dr. Bokov in Petersburg had recommended Vladimir to a wealthy patient from Moscow, Victor Ragozin, head of the firm in association with his brother Leonid. The refinery stood on the bank of the Volga and was overlooked by Ragozin's castle-like house on a hill. Vladimir could become administrative director of the technical department, at an annual salary of 10,000 roubles if he invested in the firm, or an annual salary of about 4,000 if he became an ordinary employee. What Ragozin wanted was the prestige of Vladimir's doctor's degree to impress customers and potential investors in European cities to which he would be sent.

Vladimir agreed to decide after making a planned visit to see his brother in Odessa. The more he thought of this project the more fevered he became, except that he had no money to buy shares, and a salary of 4,000 roubles was less than needed for the life he had in mind. Alexander thought he should continue with his scientific work, but the hook had been firmly set.

Upon Vladimir's return to Moscow the Ragozins in August encouraged him to buy into the company. With what? No problem. He assigned to the firm part of the 10,000-rouble salary he hadn't earned in return for shares at 1,200 roubles each, shares supposedly selling on the market for 1,500 roubles. Additionally he borrowed from the firm enough to establish his family appropriately in Moscow and a further sum of 6,000 roubles to pay off a Petersburg mortgage. A promise of future shares was somehow tied to the loan, and all shares in his name were held in the treasury as security. Within about three years, when the shares could be sold and the loan paid off. Vladimir privately intended to sell all the shares then and devote himself thereafter entirely to science. Meanwhile, the Ragozins convinced him, the shares would pay dividends of twenty to fifty percent the first year and eighty percent the second. In this way, by a modest outlay by Ragozin standards, Vladimir was entangled in the operation in such a way that he could not resign.

Sophia assented to this murky involvement, and both Julia and Alexander were willing to accept title to some of Vladimir's shares in the treasury as repayment for the money he had lost of theirs in Petersburg. Alexander even sent 2,400 roubles for two extra shares.

The Kovalevskys proceeded to rent a spacious apartment and purchased expensive furniture in order to resume a life similar to that in Petersburg. This mirage of success fooled the Moscow professors and apparently enhanced Vladimir's prospects for a better position than that originally under consideration. The Couple entertained university professors in the fields of literature, mathematics, physics, botany, anthropology, and geology. Vladimir viewed the naphtha business only as way of keeping his wife and child in comfort while accumulating money for the future. For several months he became cheerful again, remaining so even after noticing signs of business irregularities, about which he consulted Alexander. They decided it was needless to be concerned, because as Vladimir pointed out, truly the "business was golden." And in fact its growth had been rapid, from a gross of 320,000 roubles the first year to 1,200,000 the second, with 2,300,000 projected and to be achieved the third year.

Even so, the experience of Julia's friend, D. I. Mendeleev, the Petersburg professor of chemistry, should have been a warning. Several years earlier he had gone to the United States to study the production of naphtha and had later supplied Ragozin with details of the process, in return for a vague agreement that he would share in the profits. Then Mendeleev had developed apparatus for the continuous distillation of naphtha and in the laboratory had learned how to produce additional petroleum products. He felt that these and his earlier services entitled him to a half interest in the company. This the Ragozins refused. Therefore he severed all connections with the firm.

From early October until January of 1881 Vladimir traveled in Europe, first with Ragozin to Berlin, and then alone to visit customers, and old friends of his own, in London, Brussels, Paris, Basel, Prague, and Munich. Having stretched out his absence for his own pleasure, he felt relieved upon his return that this had not chilled the Ragozin brothers' warm regard for him.

Shortly after returning he entered into a partnership with a merchant who was somehow associated with the Ragozins. This involved a kerosene refinery of which future production to the extent of 100,000 roubles had been sold, although not a brick had yet been laid. That Vladimir would become a merchant's partner set him apart from those noblemen who, if required to do business with a member of the mistrusted merchant class, even if with a millionaire, only admitted him through a side or rear door and would not shake his hand. The mischief the merchant meditated for the gullible Vladimir must therefore have given particular pleasure.

X

MEANWHILE, INTENDING to seek a Russian teaching position, Sophia had spent the summer preparing herself on subjects needing study or review, so that she could sit for the necessary master's degree. At age thirty she was a much more experienced person than the young woman Weierstrass had feared to subject to doctoral examination in German six years earlier. She delayed applying for the examination, however, lest she arouse opposition among the Moscow faculty to Vladimir's pending appointment. Moreover, already there was one Kovalevsky on the faculty, a distant relation of Vladimir's, one who would at a later time occupy a central place in Sophia's life. Then in October, during his absence from Moscow, Vladimir finally was appointed as sub-professor (state docent with rank of titular councilor). He would begin teaching with the new year, but this would not prevent his continuation with the Ragozins.

Upon learning of the appointment, Sophia applied to the new liberal Minister of Education to take her examination. Both the professors of mathematics and Russian literature endorsed her application. But the new minister was not liberal regarding women in education. He told a mutual acquaintance that both Sophia and her daughter would grow old before any woman would be permitted in a Russian university.

Vladimir's long absence on his business-pleasure trip did not please Sophia. The crack between them, initiated in Petersburg, now widened into a rift. She resolved to seek a future abroad, since she could not teach in Russia. Better to prepare herself for a foreign position, for which published evidence of competence was important, she resolved to write as many new mathematical works as possible. This she felt she could do best, with Weierstrass as inspiration, in the isolation of Berlin. Fearful of winter travel with two-year-old Fufu, she left the child and nurse Maria Dmitrievna with Julia.

[197]

LITTLE SPARROW

Anna Charlotte Leffler's memoir mentions an incident that supposedly occurred on Sophia's way to Berlin, which seems improbable, but which should not be overlooked, while keeping in mind that when Sophia related the incident to her friend she may have been telling something she intended to write as a story—for she tried out her ideas on friends—something that Anna Charlotte later mistook in her memory for fact. Yet the incident is not far out of character and may actually have occurred, in view of Sophia's emotional condition, her five years of travel and life during an unconsummated marriage, and her frequent disregard for conventional nineteenth century feminine behavior.

According to the account, after the train left Moscow station Sophia gave way to her suppressed feelings and began weeping. It did her no good to look forward to resuming her mathematical work, for she could envision only the bleak loneliness of a student room. She wept for her brief years of happiness with Vladimir, for her lost hope of happiness with another soul. When her tears turned to sobs, an elderly gentleman sitting opposite her in the compartment sought to comfort her, supposing her to be a young woman leaving her country, alone for the first time, perhaps to become a governess. Seeing that her identity was unknown, she let him continue in his illusion and after a time even began to enjoy the mystification.

After some time the sympathetic gentleman proposed that they stop in a town that they were about to pass through in order to see whatever was interesting. She consented, and they spent two days sightseeing there and then parted, without ever having learned one another's name or position in the world. Whatever may have been the man's expectations in such an episode, if it was anything other than quixotic kindness, Sophia, supposing she so wished, well knew how to draw the line at nightfall. This episode worked wonders for her, and she proceeded to Berlin with a firm resolve to make a future for herself.

CHAPTER 16

Search for Fulfillment

i

On 1 November 1880 Sophia arrived in Berlin. She had informed Weierstrass of her coming but had not awaited his reply, in which he suggested delaying her visit until spring. His burdens had multiplied, he complained, without mentioning that he was also growing old. His closest friend, Karl W. Borchardt, had recently died, so that the editing of Crelle's mathematical journal had devolved upon him, jointly with Leopold Kronecker, a quarrelsome mathematician on the Berlin faculty. Additionally he had become guardian of Borchardt's six children (one of whom he later took into his home to raise as his adopted son); he was editing for publication the complete works of Karl Jacobi, Peter Dirochlet, and Jacob Steiner; his lectures tired him; and he felt unwell.

Consequently, although Weierstrass welcomed Sophia sincerely upon her arrival, rejoicing over her return to mathematics, he could give only very limited time to her. Since he had laid aside temporarily all his own work to edit that of others, he could not discuss his thoughts with her as before. He did devote one entire day to going over possibilities and suggested she investigate the refraction of light in crystalline media. Sophia found Berlin conducive to work, away from marital distractions, and began on the crystal problem.

That she had not given up hope on the incandescent light invention is indicated by the fact that she several times called upon Siemens to discuss electricity. He may have been the German physicist, Sir Karl W. Siemens, who lived in England and was involved with solar energy and electricity, and who may have visited Berlin at that time; otherwise she saw one of his brothers, who were active with him. Probably she learned then that Edison the previous year had succeeded in making an incandescent lamp by using a vacuum bulb; the following year his first commercial lamp appeared.

In March of 1881 she noted in her new diary that seventy patents had been granted to women around the world in 1880. Into this small leather-bound, gold-edged French diary Sophia made occasional entries during coming years, such as mathematical calculations, housekeeping memos, titles of books, as well as notations of a more personal nature.

Early in January of 1881, lonesome for Fufu and also for Vladimir, Sophia returned to the Moscow apartment. Vladimir was about to take up his teaching duties but had his attention continually distracted by the naphtha business and by Sophia's unaltered intention to return to mathematics.

From Berlin Sophia had brought home a Weierstrass manuscript on linear differential equations, hoping to overcome the difficulties that had halted him. This may have been the manuscript that she lost, the return of which Weierstrass occasionally requested. He was always most generous in loaning his unpublished papers to other workers, and not infrequently these were never returned; in one or two instances his material was rewritten and presented as the work of the borrower. This did not annoy Weierstrass so much as the fact that his ideas were distorted in the process, to the detriment of mathematics. Sloppy work in mathematics saddened him, and incompetent work with errors infuriated him. Sophia tried to compensate for her own carelessness by urging the master to be more careful with his unpublished work, much of which he customarily carried together with his working notes in a large wooden box when he traveled. In 1880 that box had been lost in transit and never recovered.

During the tense period between the Kovalevskys, Vladimir became unresponsive to Sophia and withdrew physically from their intimate relationship. At first, overlooking her own share of responsibility, Sophia, who had developed a strong aversion to the Ragozins, blamed them for Vladimir's depression in the evenings and wanted him to break off that relationship and concentrate on teaching. Victor Ragozin met that threat by hinting to her that Vladimir's attitude was because of another woman. While such could have been true, much more probably only overwork and Sophia's own divisive plans were at fault. This Sophia's reasoned judgment should have suggested. She reacted, however, with consuming jealousy. The thought of another woman taking her place in Vladimir's affections was unbearable. Consequently, to escape the humiliation of being a supposed neglected wife, instead of remaining with Vladimir for several months as planned, she abruptly decided to leave. Shortly before midnight on 30 January she hurriedly packed her bags, and next morning Vladimir saw his wife and daughter and nurse off by train to Berlin. She took an apartment at Potsdamstrass 134A.

So abrupt had been her departure that the abandoned Moscow apartment appeared as though the occupants had stepped out for only a few minutes, leaving samovar on the table and glasses half-full of tea. It fell to Julia to pack and store everything and to sublease the apartment. Vladimir moved into a furnished room and at his first opportunity, during Easter vacation, traveled to Odessa to seek consolation with his brother.

ii

DURING THE summer of 1881 Vladimir came down with a serious case of spotted fever. For nearly two weeks Julia directed his care and herself did much of the nursing. In order not to cause worry Vladimir asked that neither his wife nor his brother be informed. After his recovery, when Sophia learned of his illness, she felt hurt that she had not been called to his bedside.

In an undated letter that summer from Berlin she addressed Vladimir: "What is this happiness of ours indeed? We no sooner entered the business than the dividends fell from fifty to twenty percent and your salary from 10,000 to 5,000. As long as you will continue to send me money I shall live in Europe and shall work as much as I am able and not rail at fate. You know that one gets drawn to European life. Moreover, your last illness showed me clearly that you have no need for me at all, which significantly opposed whatever eagerness I had to return. In regard to the apartment, please do not decide anything. The old one in any case did not suit us and moreover has become so distasteful to me that I will not return to it under any circumstances." Obviously a correspondence had preceded that letter.

In her next preserved letter to Vladimir that summer, Sophia remarked: "Apparently it is necessary for me to live alone and develop in myself those signs *d'une femme forte* which are so lacking in me. Now I am again myself and determination has returned. The Weierstrass family was terribly upset by my refusal to go with them to Marienbad. Therefore, in order to console my little old people, I decided to go there for two or three weeks. The journey won't cost much.

"You write truly that no woman has created anything important, but it is just because of this that it is essential for me, while still I have energy and tolerable material circumstances, to position myself so that I may show whether I can achieve anything or whether I lack brains.

You as a person are energetic and talented in your temperament, whereas I by contrast am gifted by passivity and inertia, so that by living with you I involuntarily become an exemplary wife and good mother and forget completely that I myself should achieve something. Of course it is great credit to your side that you give me the means, while you live a prisoner's life; and when I think how you would value the opportunity to live a whole year without care in a circle of scholars, then my conscience is so troubled that I can't even tell you. If you, like others, treasured the peace and comfort of family life, I would not have the courage to ask such a sacrifice from you; I would instead have meekly donned a dress of soft linen and would have allowed the mire of bourgeois family life to suck in even those few talents that nature has given me.

"In view of the fact that you in every way have fired my egotism, I consider it right to take your words at face value; and also, since you are refusing to send me money to live with a light heart, without concern, in the place most favorable to my work, I shall try not to think at all of how you are alone in Moscow. That I am working and will continue to do so to the extent of my abilities you may be confident. But good mathematical work is not done quickly. Up to now I have had three months, and despite obstacles it really seems to me that I have accomplished a great deal, although not yet with final result. Weierstrass says my present work (in case of complete success) will be among the most interesting of the last ten years. Therefore, little friend, I beg you not to be too impatient. Do not expect from me such quick results as you have in your work, and let me live and work according to my nature; that is, without hurrying and by doing things little by little. Goodby, little friend. Write me more often . . ."

While writing her next letter Sophia obviously felt lonesome and ready for a reunion: "How happy I would now be if we had occasion once more to travel together. Before I didn't know how to evaluate anything, but now it would be different. Is it really true that you are leaving Russia in August? It is so bitter for me to think this [presumably because she had planned to visit in August] that I have almost, in that case, decided to return home for the winter. Would you allow me to go to Paris for two months at least in order there, if possible, to bring my work to its conclusion? Goodby my dear and amiable friend; I embrace and kiss you many times and await a substantial letter from you. *Ach*, if only we could see each other soon in Europe. It is awful how I want to see you. It seems we have been apart for a whole year. Write to me what to do; as you decide, so will we do. All your Sofa."

It is obvious that in the manner of so many marital separations, in which the bond had stretched but not broken, the parties sometimes relished their freedom and sometimes felt lonely and eager to reconcile. In the exchange of letters, one letter containing real or imagined affronts would provoke outright or implied rebukes, raising recollections of earlier discord, while another letter would produce memories of happiness together and a loving response. Gradually, emotions of hurt feelings and blame would overbalance more tender affection, and the tone of letters would become colder.

In early August from Marienbad, where she rambled with the two Weierstrass sisters and the professor, Sophia wrote: "We live peacefully. Having awakened and dressed, we all go into the forest. We drink coffee in some cafe and then go farther until we tire and rest in a shady spot until one'clock. We have dinner at the first restaurant we come upon and then again walk until evening, returning home only to sleep. Fufu climbs wonderfully over the hills and could shame other children. She goes almost everywhere with us and rarely complains, even when Maria Dmitrevna [nurse] can barely drag her feet."

Earlier from Berlin she had addressed a number of letters to Vladimir without reply and then was surprised by a letter forwarded from Berlin, saying he was lonely and asking her to return to Moscow.

Within several days she responded: "My dear little friend, not having received an answer to my letters and telegram for a long time, and not knowing that you were at the factory, I understood that actually you were not especially desirous of our coming and for this reason decided to go to Marienbad, where as you know I am presently. But from your letter I see that, on the contrary, you had counted very much on our coming, and actually if you consider it wiser not to come to Europe in August, then I consider it absolutely necessary for us to come to you, at least for a time, and I am ready to sacrifice reluctantly my hope to visit Paris."

It seems that Vladimir changed his mind again, or sought perhaps to test Sophia's real desire to return, for while still in Marienbad she wrote him once more with a quite different tone: "Your telegram of yesterday confirms my suspicion that you are keeping us here only to give me an opportunity to lecture about mutual freedom. Well, is it possible to imagine anything more comical, like a caricature, than keeping one's family here a whole extra week simply to be able to say that you don't want to constrain us in any way? Why these sophistries? . . . had you simply telegraphed, 'Pay no attention to my previous letters and go where you wish,' then this would have been human; but to force me to wait a week and then give me a dissertation on free will, about which you know I am so fond, this really surpasses all imagination. Of course I must be consoled that this will serve me as a good lesson. Only these lessons are terribly hard, and it is shameful for a man of forty to give his wife such lessons.

"Life in our hotel is terribly expensive. Every triviality costs three prices. Write from where I should take money in case of need. For August I have already received 700 marks [about 400 roubles] but these have almost all been spent. Goodby. Excuse the sharpness of this letter. If you only knew how revolting is Marienbad when it rains without stopping all week. Probably you had something good in mind, but heavens, will you never stop being a sophist. Your Sonya." Not the intimate "Sofa."

When Vladimir did not respond positively regarding her return to Moscow, Sophia resumed her work in Berlin. Correspondence all but ceased. In November she queried him about accepting an anticipated offer from Mittag-Leffler to teach in Sweden. "Shall I accept the invitation or not? The honor is great. It is lonely always to live alone." What Vladimir replied, if at all, is unknown.

iii

IT WILL be recalled that Mittag-Leffler had gone in 1876 to meet Sophia in Petersburg and had been enamoured of her as a woman and impressed by her as a mathematician. Chiefly to see her again the Swede had traveled to Petersburg four years later when she addressed the meeting of Russian scientists. Still a bachelor at 34, Mittag-Leffler was at that time professor of mathematics at Helsinki University. Following this meeting a correspondence developed between them. In all, Mittag-Leffler saved about 420 letters and notes from Sophia's hand during the next ten years.

In a letter from Moscow on 14 October 1880 she asked whether his university admitted women, and he replied that women could audit but not take examinations. She therefore sent him a young woman named Pokrovskaia, who remained in Helsinki only briefly before returning to take private instruction in Russia.

Then late in 1880 Mittag-Leffler had attempted to open a place for Sophia in Helsinki but met faculty opposition, not so much because she was feminine as because she was Russian. Although Finland had been annexed to Russia, it still retained considerable internal autonomy. The assassination of the Tsar had created shock waves throughout Europe. In Helsinki it was feared Sophia might attract nihilist students, who were then under pressure in Russia, and that such students would cause trouble in Finland as they had through the years in Switzerland and Germany. "All my university people know about your exceptional talent," wrote Mittag-Leffler. "So if you were a Finn, or belonged to any other nation except Russia, you would without doubt be invited here."

Soon the professor obtained the chair of mathematics at the new Stockholm University and in June of 1881 asked her to accept the position of sub-professor, at first without pay. On 8 July from Berlin she accepted with all her heart, saying that she had means of her own, did not expect a higher position, and wished to use her ability to further feminine education. She feared, however, that her coming might harm him or the new university and asked him to determine exactly how the faculty would react to woman students. Her obvious goal was not only a position for herself but to open the university to women.

Letters also passed back and forth between Mittag-Leffler and Weierstrass, who expressed the opinion that it was too soon for Sophia to teach. The first woman professor of mathematics needed better credentials than a man, he said. He also expressed this view to Sophia, who asked Mittag-Leffler to delay her appointment until "I have shown by purely scholarly work of what I am capable."

Actually her doctoral dissertation which remains significant today was important enough, but other works were lacking. Yet it may seem odd that Weierstrass would oppose her career. Her ability had changed his mind about having women in universities, although during his term as rector he had been unable to lift the ban against them. He had always advanced his capable former students and others by using his influence with the right persons in several countries. He was then favoring the career of the Frenchman, Poincaré. Why should he hold back his favorite pupil who was already thirty years of age and well qualified? As her spiritual father he had his reason, but his good judgement would not permit him to disclose it until June of 1882 when the event he envisioned had actually occurred.

Therefore in 1881 Sophia pressed on with her work on light refracted by crystalline substances. She also returned off and on to the problem that had been naggingly demanding a solution since her earliest days with Weierstrass; namely, that involving the motion of a rigid body about a fixed point, which also involved the pendulum, and which had baffled mathematical-physicists for many years. This she hoped to solve but made no immediate progress.

Regarding Vladimir's business with the Ragozins, Sophia began to have suspicions and complained to Alexander: "It appears that fate will not let us rest; at the slightest success Volodia so bites at the bait that it is really as though he tempts fate to send us another blow." She found the future "terribly frightening."

iv

AT THE beginning of 1882 Vladimir, supposedly on business for Ragozin but probably more to see Sophia and Fufu, arrived in Paris, where Sophia had gone at the suggestion of Weierstrass to meet the best mathematicians there, headed by their dean, Charles Hermite, of the Sorbonne, whose specialty was elliptic functions.

Hermite like Weierstrass deplored a growing tendency among younger workers toward nationalism in science. When Mittag-Leffler, already a Ph.D, had applied to him in 1874, the Frenchman characteristically remarked: "You have made an error, monsieur; you should have followed the course of Weierstrass in Berlin; he is the master of us all." Against his inclination Mittag-Leffler did take the "great" course in Berlin, which determined the direction of his entire career. Hermite became Sophia's friend and advisor whenever she was in Paris. He trained among others Paul Appell, Gaston Darboux, Emile Picard, and most importantly Henri Poincaré. He was somewhat of a mystic about numbers, believing they have an objective existence and that mathematicians occasionally succeed in penetrating the realm of numerical existence. While this view has few if any followers today, his algebra became essential in mathematical physics, as in the quantum theory.

In Paris the Kovalevskys seemed at first to get along together but not for long. In February they had a common worry in the illness of Fufu, who had been exposed to measles while playing with the children of Olga Monod, the daughter of Herzen. Vladimir had tutored Olga as a girl in England, and she had married a Frenchman. Although ill, Fufu did not develop a rash. Sophia wrote Vladimir's brother to ask if she might bring Fufu and her nurse to stay with him in Odessa, for which she could contribute fifty roubles monthly of the 200 Vladimir allowed her. This would permit her to finish the work upon which all her future hopes depended. Fufu did go to Alexander's, remaining there for over a year until the summer of 1883 when she became Julia's charge. For a period of five years she saw her mother only for a few weeks annually during holiday periods.

When Vladimir left Paris to return to his university, the separation became final. Sophia remained to live frugally in Paris, occupying a student-type apartment at St. Mandé, Grand Rue 7. She could walk in the Bois de Vincennes not far away, or if she went to the Sorbonne to see one of the mathematicians could take time to stroll or sit in the nearby Luxembourg Gardens with their alleys, terraces, vistas, fountains, and sunshine. There were cafes for refreshment and bookstalls along the Seine. It was the Paris of Flaubert, Zola, the Goncourts, and Maupassant. She viewed Parisian extremes, from men and sometimes women dragging heavily-burdened carts through the streets, to men in top hats and women holding parasols gliding by in carriages drawn by spirited horses. Between those extremes there were the double-decked omnibuses pulled sedately by great Percherons. For the privileged, especially, Paris was the most lively and sophisticated city in the world, the mecca for artists, poets, and expatriates. For Sophia, even in her reduced circumstances, life was not unpleasant and sometimes was exciting. She delayed seeking a teaching position in a French higher school for girls until her future became more clear.

On 11 April Weierstrass chided Sophia gently for having written him only one letter from Paris and for not confiding in him as her spiritual father, so that he had to draw conclusions about her from vague hints instead of frank disclosure. Therefore in early June she did finally indicate to him that she and Vladimir had separated, probably permanently, and that Fufu had been put under the care of Alexander.

Not until receiving this did Weierstrass comment upon her obvious marital difficulties and upon his principal reason for opposing her Stockholm career. On 14 June he wrote:

"Several hours would have been enough of an acquaintance with Kovalevsky to convince me that an interior crack had appeared in your relations and was threatening a complete break. He doesn't have an understanding of your ideas and goals, and you cannot adjust yourself to the restless manner of his life. Your characters are too diverse for you to hope to find in him that which is essential for a happy marriage—somebody to support you with firmness of character and to perceive in you a fulfillment of his own being. Otherwise even certain mistakes on his part would not have interfered with your reconciliation. If I considered it my duty to protest against your plan—that is, against taking the place in Stockholm while he occupied a position in Moscow—this was due to my conviction that it would be unnatural for spouses to live apart. In any event, it would be impossible to make me believe that such a separation would have occurred to you had you been sincerely attached to your husband and loved him as every husband wants to be loved. I cannot chide him for having refused your plan, and perhaps this is why he opposed even more your mathematical learnings. Under present conditions your former relations apparently have become impossible. I would wish only that everything would be resolved, so that you could become free from worry, freedom necessary for your existence. You must as soon as possible come out of your shell and have little Sonya near you. Concern about her and observation of her development will occupy your time worthily and will gladden you."

After adding that she could turn to him any time for advice or support, he touched on mathematics: "About your association with Hermite, I have heard from him directly. He wrote me with great delight about this and enumerated all the questions you discussed. You will probably come into contact with other mathematicians, among whom the younger ones will be the more interesting: Appell, Picard, Poincaré. In my opinion Poincaré is the most able in mathematical thinking, if only, considering his exceptional talent, he would give his investigations time to mature." He indicated that the work of Jules Henri Poincaré had opened a new path in mathematical analysis.

Sophia found Poincaré, four years her junior, to be a gentle and kind individual with a deep musical voice that became at times highly animated. In conversation he was inclined to shift subjects abruptly, sometimes rising and pacing briefly as he talked, and then reseating himself. He was similar to Weierstrass in idealism and dedication to truth but quite different in his mental approach to problems, tending to plunge to the very heart of a problem, as though intuitively, leaving details to be worked out by others. This approach obviously annoyed Weierstrass, who nevertheless recognized Poincaré's unusual ability. As a young mathematician he had been inspired by the functions of Fuchs, pupil of Weierstrass and sponsor of Sophia at Göttingen. During the years to follow she would exchange views with Poincaré whenever she visited Paris; she would also lecture on his differential equations. When first they met he was on the threshold of a career that would make him the uncontested master of geometry and analysis. As a mature scientist he would help shatter the foundations of Euclidean geometry by demonstrating that other geometrical systems can also be valid. He would move with ease from analysis to mathematical physics to celestial mechanics to philosophy. He held that science can never penetrate the absolute but is supreme in discovering whatever is relative. He would come close to anticipating Einstein's work.

On 26 July Weierstrass wrote asking Sophia in Paris to receive politely his Alsatian student, Jules Molk, who eventually became a professor at the University of Nancy and co-authored a four-volume work on elliptic functions. Weierstrass at the time of writing to Sophia was expecting a visit from Mittag-Leffler to introduce his new wife. He suggested that Sophia meet the Weierstrass family in Baden-Baden, but she declined and remained in Paris.

There, it would seem, she actually did little creative mathematical work. Rather, she spent most of her time either with French mathematicians or with Polish and Russian political emigrants. One of the latter was Peter Lavrovich Lavrov, son of a general and former colonel-instructor of mathematics at an artillery school. A heavy-set man at age fifty-nine, he had gray-frosted hair and full beard and mustache and wore glasses with small lenses. He had been a family friend when Sophia was a child, but later she had known him only slightly in Petersburg, where he organized the short-lived Society for Women's Labor. After Sophia left to study in Germany, the force of nihilism with its policy of rejection had largely spent itself. Lavrov had been unable to attract nihilists of the two extremes to his central unifying position; namely, that the world could be changed by education and persuasion and that service to the people was the justification for the nihilist cult of individualism. After he became active in the populist Land and Liberty party he was arrested and banished to a military post in the Urals. He ran off to Switzerland in 1870 but was too intellectual and idealistic to influence Russian students in Zurich with his moderate views, when opposed by the burning revolutionary appeal of Bakunin. Then in Paris he had represented the French Commune in Belgium and England, was on friendly terms with Marx and Engels, and for a number of years edited in French a socialist periodical called *Forward*. His *Historical Letters* (1879) had a considerable influence among students.

Other friends of Sophia's in Paris included Vladimir V. Lutsky, Russian ex-naval officer, and most notably Marie V. Mendelson, daughter of a Polish nobleman, Vikenti Zalesky. Marie was at that time still married to a Polish landowner named Iankovsky, but after his death she married Stanislaus Mendelson, who had published a socialist newspaper in London, had been arrested in Germany and deported to Russia, and had then bribed his guards and escaped to France. In his later years he abandoned the Polish socialists to be welcomed back into Russia as a leader of conservative Jews. To avoid confusion Marie will be constantly identified by her Mendelson surname, by which she is best remembered. She is mentioned in the correspondence of Marx and Engels. Marie was a very attractive woman of means, who dressed in the height of fashion, whose Paris apartment was a frequent meeting place for members of the large Polish clique. An ardent agitator for Polish freedom from Russia, she had been arrested in Warsaw, escaped to Germany, spent time in a Prussian jail, and finally settled in Paris. She helped revolutionaries escape from Poland and bravely visited there herself on false passports. Within a very short time she became Sophia's intimate confidante and one reason that in future years she would return so often to Paris. According to Anna Charlotte Leffler, Sophia so greatly admired Marie, who was exactly her own age, that she would never fault her in any way. "This friend," wrote Anna, "possessed several qualities that Sophia herself desired and envied—

beauty, a rare beauty of fascination, and an equally rare talent for dressing in perfect taste."

Marie in her recollections of Sophia described the setting in which they first met when both were invited by Lavrov to an evening gathering. The elegant Marie alighted from a horse cab in front of a nondescript old building on a dirty street in the Latin quarter. She mounted a grimy staircase to the second floor, noticing as she ascended the odor of dampness and musty books. She entered a two-room apartment, illuminated by two smoke-blackened kerosene lamps, and could sense the dust in the air, indicating that the room had recently been swept. Lavrov greeted her with a tender smile and after introductions seated her in the only comfortable chair, opposite a divan on which sat Sophia and Varvara Nikitina. The latter wrote political articles under the name of B. Zhandr for a periodical edited by Georges Clemenceau, later to become the Tiger of France. Sophia was seen as lively and quick, with sparkling eyes; but what Marie especially noticed was her large head, covered by short curls, on her rather small body. Another woman had been invited, one who used a false name, but fearful of betrayal by the newcomer Sophia, she failed to appear.

Present also were several men students, who hovered around the samovar and presently served the ladies tea in cups, while the men had to drink from glasses with chipped rims. From a table drawer, from atop papers therein covered with his neat script, Lavrov extracted a gold-rimmed plate of pastries, sufficient only for the ladies. All signs indicated his purse was very thin indeed, but this bothered the emigrant nobleman not at all.

At first Sophia came on too strong with Marie. Knowing that Marie had been in jail for revolutionary activity, she sought to probe her experiences and reactions while behind bars. Unwilling to have her psyche dissected by a stranger, Marie avoided such revelations, so that Sophia backed off to join the general conversation about socialism. Marie listened while Lavrov and the two women conversed animatedly about equal rights to happiness, the need for enlightening the lower classes, and of social change to solve all difficulties. "All this sounded very beautiful but at the same time very indefinite," wrote the practical Marie. "It was easy to understand that the subject was as dear to them as it was foreign; they spoke of dreams as of realities and tried to quench the thirst for political freedom with theories mostly removed from all reality." Of Sophia in particular she remarked that, although Sophia confessed that economics were totally strange to her, she nevertheless expressed her opinions with great fire. "The more I listened to her the more I liked her straight-forwardness, her honest attitude, her sincere

[210]

search for truth. . . . It was obvious that she wanted primarily to clarify the questions being examined and was not in the least offended by jokes or derision at her expense but on the contrary laughed heartily. Her behavior completely vanquished me."

Anna Charlotte Leffler wrote that Sophia at this time had a platonic romance with a young Polish revolutionary mathematician, and that Sophia told her they often spent whole days until two o'clock in the morning, together in Sophia's quarters, talking earnestly, composing verses, and writing chapters of a romantic novel. "Nobody had ever understood her so well and sympathized with her so much as he," wrote Leffler. "They indulged in the idea that every human being has its twin soul, so that every individual man or woman is but half a creature. The other half, which is to complete the soul, exists somewhere on earth, but rarely in this life do they meet." Of course Sophia and the unnamed individual fancied that their twin souls *had* met. Sophia was not free, however, and the infatuation did not survive a tragic event soon to occur.

Marie Mendelson asserted the romance existed only in Leffler's imagination and was really nothing more than a close friendship, but she may not have known the actual circumstances. It is possible, also, that Sophia exaggerated to Leffler the nature of her relationship to the Pole. Neither Marie nor Leffler named the individual. He could have been the ex-naval officer, Lutsky. He probably was not Sergei Ivanovich Lamansky, a Pole who as a student at Heidelberg had admired Sophia greatly, knowing she was only fictionally married, and had caused Vladimir some jealousy, and who remained Sophia's devoted friend for life. Very likely the unknown individual was somebody else entirely.

Sophia called upon Marie on the day after their introduction. Soon the two women, being from the same class and having a common love for Poland, established an intimacy that was to grow and endure. One day, deeply troubled, Sophia confided in Marie that she feared she had caused the arrest in Russia of a 16-year-old girl to whom she had sent her passport and who was long overdue. The girl, Zoia, was the sister of a mathematician friend and wanted to study science in Paris. Rather than advise a fictitious marriage, difficult to achieve and perhaps unfortunate in consequence, Sophia had arranged for a friend to spirit the girl away from home secretly, in order to get her safely off before a telegram from her parents could stop her at the border.

Marie pointed out the difference between supplying a genuine or a false passport. With the former, if the girl was caught and if Sophia subsequently returned to Russia, she would be linked with the crime

[211]

and prosecuted for cooperating in the abduction of a minor girl, or at least could face serious passport difficulties. Sophia replied that she could not act otherwise, could not refuse to help somebody who didn't want to follow the usual path into marriage but thirsted for knowledge and might become an outstanding scholar.

When eventually Zoia did arrive in Paris, having only been delayed in the execution of the escape, Sophia took her into her rooms. Zoia showed much more interest in mathematicians than in mathematics. She was a beautiful girl with heavy black braids who found Paris delightful. Sophia's tutoring to prepare Zoia for the Sorbonne did not last long, because Zoia found mathematics too hard and too dry, preferring to adorn herself, or visit Paris shops, or chatter with the students and young professors who visited Sophia. Although disenchanted with Zoia as a student Sophia became warmly attached to her as a person, and as Marie observed, Zoia "simply worshipped" her new friend. As events were to prove, it was extremely fortunate that Zoia lived with Sophia.

V

MEANWHILE THE situation with Vladimir had been dragging on; although there was no final separation, the prospect of reconciliation receded with time. Each party held off, waiting for the other to act. Sophia had made her marriage requirements clear: she would pursue a career, and Vladimir would have to cease his aimless wanderings. With all the uncertainty, Sophia felt emotionally adrift, worried over the present and uncertain of the future. At such a time many a woman might have turned to the consolations of religion, but for her this had no attraction. Her religion, although in her adult years she still clung to the externals of Russian Orthodoxy and belief in God, mostly consisted of trust in science, for Darwinian thought was then viewed as incompatible with revealed religion. She longed, however, for something besides her science in which to believe. She therefore turned to socialism as to a new religion, or the expansion of an old one. This was the preoccupation of many of her Polish friends in Paris, and she had long had a deep sympathy for Poland in its struggle for freedom from Russia, a sympathy first engendered during her impressionistic years as a girl at Palibino during the abortive Polish uprising. In that regard Sophia never tired throughout her life in repeating the story of her one hero, a Russian officer named Serakov, about whom she had learned as a girl from her family's friendship with the Minister of War, Baron D. A. Miliutin. The Tsar had just approved Serakov's reform of the military code and had personally congratulated him when the Poles revolted. Refusing promotion, Serakov instead handed the war minister his resignation, giving as his reason his intention to join the revolt. "Poland needs her sons," he declared. "Within several weeks you will sign my death warrant, but you will not stop respecting me." And, indeed, several weeks later he was taken prisoner and hanged. More than anything else his heroism conditioned Sophia to accept the socialism of her Polish friends, that and her passion for women's equal education, denied under nearly all existing European regimes.

Her conversion she expressed in a letter to George von Folmar, an activist exactly her own age who headed the right wing of the Social Democrats in Germany and who opposed the extreme views of Marx and Engels. Probably she came to know him in Paris. In a long letter to him dated 4 May 1882 she expressed her pleasure in his friendship and her belief that the times did not permit a person to dedicate himself exclusively to intellectual interests. She stated that at the time of the French Commune and afterward she considered it more important to be a serious scholar, but that her association with socialist nationalists during her recent five months in Paris had changed her views.

While remaining always sympathetic to socialism, Sophia's enthusiasm would gradually wane, however, as she returned to her former attitude; namely, that as a serious scholar she was capable of "doing something better" by furthering science and women's education rather than by being a political activist.

vi

MEANWHILE, VLADIMIR in Moscow had begun to suspect the Ragozins of genuine duplicity and was not getting along with them. Teaching he found burdensome. In April of 1882 he had again become restless. Letters to his brother from this time onward indicate a dark cloud increasingly affecting his outlook. He longed for holidays. He regretted that he had "killed 14 years" from the date of his wedding. He considered being officially ill for six weeks in order to visit his brother.

At about this time he proposed some change in the naphtha firm's finances, just what is unclear. As there was to be a meeting of shareholders, mostly Moscow investors eager to acquire additional shares, Ragozin apparently thought it best to have Vladimir out of the way and therefore dispatched him to Europe for two months.

In Paris, where he contracted to sell naphtha valued at 200,000 francs monthly, he met Sophia at the Jaclars', Aniuta then being a Paris visitor. Although it would seem Sophia had hopes for continuing the marriage, on her terms, Vladimir considered their separation to be final. As he wrote to Alexander: "I understand this and in her place would have done the same. . . . but for me it is hard. Oh, how hard is solitude at age forty and how frightening to look around and not see a single friendly face."

He left Paris for other cities and then spent considerable time in Marseille following his own interests, until Ragozin appeared to show him off in various French cities as his technical director, mentioning his scholarly achievements and his scientific friends. This was in preparation for an offering of shares on the Paris exchange. After that he wandered alone to London, where he spent time with several paleontologists. He wrote his brother about fossils there from huge flying reptiles.

In August from London he also wrote his brother about going to the United States. ". . . one must make this last effort; perhaps something sensible will come of it; but somehow I feel little courage or enthusiasm. Of course if I am able to collect good plaster reproductions at American museums, then this could yield a good work with important results." He could not forget his wife but left her in ignorance of his whereabouts. "From Sonya I have had no news for a long time. Have you? Is she happy? That is the major thing. All the rest can be arranged. The fear of being alone falls more and more on me now. Here I am very unhappy."

He did go to the United States, where he remained for a month or longer, visiting various cities and museums. He stayed for a week with a Philadelphia paleontologist owning an extensive fossil collection. Only a letter from his brother, warning that he would lose his university position, brought him back to Russia.

He bought a large case to display all his new specimens at the university.

Alexander also received letters from Sophia. In one she declared: "I positively do not understand your brother during this last period. My anxiety for the future grows daily. . . . What does it mean that he does not write or even inform one of his address? From Julia I yesterday received a letter with strange news. She writes that V. O. is terribly merry and exalting . . . although both to her and to me his position appears completely unsatisfactory. . . . He is planning to rent in Petrovsky Line [in Moscow] a large apartment to settle there Madame Janeuval, the wife of a genial Italian who is living now at his expense in Paris while inventing some system for heating, and the other rooms he intends to rent. What all this signifies I positively do not understand. . . . If only V. O. would settle down and limit himself to the university, then it would be essential for me to return to Russia. This wouldn't be so terrible if only he would come to rest and not destroy himself with his eternal projects. . . . Sometimes for whole days I am unable to do anything except walk back and forth in my room like a caged animal. Just any decision, but this indecision is simply murderous!''

Vladimir's letters to Alexander continued. "I just now realized," he wrote in one, "that I am a totally worthless person and how much pure love such persons as you and Sofa have wasted on me." On 3 November 1882 he reported the bankruptcy of the Ragozins and his fear that criminal responsibility would be shifted to him. Three weeks later: "Everything will go on public sale. Today I went to my lecture as to a torture chamber; to such an extent have I become weak." A fellow professor recorded that Vladimir was often late and sometimes inaccurate in his lectures at this time—yet on one occasion, he entered the hall with the wing from a dead crow he found on the way and gave a brilliant improvisation on the ability of vertebrates to fly.

At the end of the year he thanked Alexander for supporting him and resolved to follow his brother's advice to hold to his university post. He admitted that it was taking him an hour to prepare only one lecture page to be read in three minutes and that therefore he sometimes pasted into the manuscript printed pages torn from books. He wished he could do physical labor, "the best occupation for a man," if only it paid more than thirty kopecks daily. "What is hard are the thoughts that revolve in my head and give me no peace."

During the Christmas holidays Vladimir fled once more to Odessa; from there he wrote to Julia that "living with the family I became calm and forgot to some extent those threats hanging over me. . . . Fufu recognized me at once and was very happy. She has developed greatly although she has not grown very much. She has taught herself to read and doesn't miss a single printed word. She also knows how to count and loves that. In fact it is very consoling that her abilities remind me more of Sofa than myself." Fufu was then four.

Upon his return to Moscow the correspondence with Alexander resumed. Vladimir was engulfed by the thought of the trial of the Ragozin brothers. Sophia's position concerned him, as he could no longer send her money, and she had to rely on her sister. His ultimate intention becomes clear from a letter written to Alexander on 1 February but not mailed: "My dear invaluable friend Sasha. I am afraid that I shall grieve you very, very much, but from all the clouds that have gathered from all sides over me, this was the only thing left for me to do. Everything for which I was preparing has been broken up by this, and life is growing terribly difficult . . . Write Sofa that my constant

[215]

thought was about her, and how very wrong I was before her, and how I spoiled her life which, except for me, would have been bright and happy. My last request was to Aniuta—to take care of Sofa and little Fufu; she is the only one now who is able to do this, and I beg her to do so. I am asking forgiveness from your dear wife Tania for all the sorrow I am causing, but I fear that were I to remain among you I would cause even more grief; I kiss all your children, Vera, Volodia, and Lida, and a thousand times I press poor Fufu to my heart. I embrace you, dear, invaluable friend Sasha. Your Vladimir."

At the same time he left notes for his old friends, Bokova and husband Sechenov, asking if they wanted to raise and educate Fufu, and one for Julia simply stating: "Forgive me, I could not do otherwise."

He delayed the act, however, until 15 April 1883, when he wrote a last letter to Alexander regretting the long chain of insane actions in his life and reporting that on the advice of two friends, lawyers like himself, he composed a note for the court officials explaining his actions in the Ragozin affair.

The following day the police informed the university rector of Vladimir's death. Two days later the *Moscow Gazette* reported his suicide in his furnished room. Failing to rouse him, his servant had summoned police. With a bag over his head, Vladimir had inhaled chloroform. The corpse was denied to Julia because she was not related. It went for autopsy to the university, which then appropriated 250 roubles for burial ten days after his death.

Among the last to learn of Vladimir's death was Alexander, because Julia, knowing of the deep attachment between the brothers, temporized for two days before writing to a mutual friend in Odessa, asking him to contact Alexander's wife so that she could prepare him for the blow. She observed that Vladimir's mind had been so tormented that in her opinion death was a saving outcome.

vii

THE SUICIDE prostrated Sophia. Refusing to eat, she shut herself in her room. Fortunately Zoia was there and with tearful eyes admitted Marie when she called the second day. But Sophia would see nobody, nor would she admit Marie on the following day. Marie called a physician, but he could accomplish nothing through a closed door. For four days Sophia ate nothing and on the fifth, exhausted by fasting and despair, lost consciousness. A physician then force-fed her and put her to sleep. After several days under Zoia's loving care she sat up in bed, asked for paper and pencil, and plunged into a mathematical problem. As once she had said, "I have only to touch mathematics and I forget everything else on earth." She did not forget recent events, of course, but mathematics helped as an anodyne. How different from her reaction following the intense grief over her father's death. Then, after the worst had passed, she had turned to Vladimir. Now she gained strength by relying upon herself. She turned to mathematics with the realization that she was now on her own, that her future lay in science, and that she had best get on with it.

She rebuked herself for not recognizing that Vladimir's erratic behavior, his wanderings, his speculations were symptomatic of his mental state. She asked now to see Marie, who found her pale and thin. During the period of Sophia's recovery their friendship became closer than ever. Sophia welcomed a sympathetic friend and spoke of her childhood, her dreams, her youth devoted to study, and regretted that she had missed real happiness. Such pessimism had become typical when Sophia's Russian pendulum swung in one direction. To Marie she appeared "like a weak little bird fallen from its nest and trembling from cold and fear." Marie blamed the upbringing in wealthy Russian families, which delegated the care of children to nurses, maids, governesses, and tutors, so that they grew up in a servants' quarters atmosphere and witnessed from an early age the "low intrigues, rude betrayals, and all the filth that grows amidst servitude." This she felt distorted love between parents and child and deflected the growing child from loving human relationships, developing a fatal skepticism regarding human nature.

Upon learning that Sophia had been left almost destitute, Weierstrass offered to take her permanently under his roof as a third sister, an offer she declined with great gratitude, and ever after, as she traveled about Europe, Berlin never was too far out of her way for a visit with Weierstrass and his sisters.

Meanwhile, feeling well again, Sophia went to Odessa for Fufu, and then returned to Paris, where she saw Jaclar, who was there with his son, Urey. She wrote Aniuta, whose illness had kept her in Petersburg, to express happiness that Aniuta had taken up writing again and to ask for a lotion recipe, because "due to my grief and work, my hair has started to fall out so much that I am simply terrified."

Sophia always had loved Paris, but personal events had changed her outlook. About this time she wrote Aniuta: "Paris has changed somehow since last year; has become disgusting; I positively don't recognize it. I'm beginning to suspect that I have some evil demon following my footsteps; when I moved to Paris he seemed to lose my trail but suddenly has found me and has regained his own with a vengeance."

In June, having been chosen a member of the Paris Mathematical

Society, Sophia read a paper on one problem among others upon which she had been working. Then she took Fufu to Berlin and wrote Julia that Weierstrass felt satisfied with her work on crystals and no longer doubted that she was ready for teaching. For money she continued to depend upon funds from Aniuta and on irregular payments from the bookseller who in 1880 had taken over on consignment the entire unsold stock of Vladimir's published books.

In August mother and daughter set out again for Odessa, where Sophia was to address the Congress of Russian Naturalists and Physicians. She presented a version of her work on crystals. Foremost among the mathematicians present was Ermakov from Kiev. To anticipate, concerning the crystals treatise, it had satisfied Hermite, and it had met with no objection from Weierstrass, who only asked for more clarity and polish. Both missed an embarrassing error that was finally spotted in 1890 by the Italian mathematician Vito Volterra. As it was desirable for the results of some of Sophia's work to see print, and since it would be too late for her crystal work to appear during 1883 in *Acta Mathematica*, she had earlier dusted off her dissertation written ten years previously on elliptic functions and submitted it for publication. *Acta Mathematica* was the new international journal of mathematics subsidized eventually by the governments of France, Germany, Denmark, Finland, and Sweden and published then in Sweden.

Upon hearing from Weierstrass that the Stockholm appointment was definite, Sophia wrote Mittag-Leffler, expressing her gratitude for his friendship and confidence. "At the same time," she added, "I feel I ought to tell you that in many respects I feel little fitted for the duties of docent, and at times I so much doubt my own capacity that I feel you, who have always judged me leniently, will be quite disillusioned when you find on nearer inspection how little I am really good for." Such self-doubt, uncharacteristic of her younger years, indicated that Sophia had come to realize that paradoxically the more one learns the more remains to be mastered; and the prospect of being on her own, in a strange land with a new language, lacking the accustomed support of Aniuta or Vladimir or Weierstrass, caused her to hesitate.

In fact, she had just written Weierstrass to ask if he did not consider it desirable to prepare herself better by spending several months with him to fill in gaps in her mathematical knowledge. Weierstrass thought not. Her above-mentioned letter to Mittag-Leffler continued: "I am truly grateful to Stockholm, which is the only European university that will open its doors to me, and I am already prepared to be in love with that city, and to attach myself to Sweden as though it were my native home." That full degree of attachment she never achieved, however.

While vacationing in Savoy, Weierstrass on 27 August advised Sophia in Odessa that, in order to have time for adequate preparation, she should not lecture more than two hours weekly. He reminded her, too, that "the mathematician who does not have something of the poet will never be a good mathematician." Two weeks later he again addressed her in Odessa, suggesting she start with lectures on the theory of functions, taking advantage of his work and that of Mittag-Leffler, Poincaré, and others in order to create a base for her own work on elliptic functions. Students would excuse her pedagogical inexperience, he said, if what she presented had real scientific merit. He again reminded her that he considered her more suited for original work than for teaching, but in view of her need for duties yielding a definite income, he approved of her move to Stockholm.

Sophia's letter to him had arrived opened, not the first instance of this. Realizing that the murder of the Tsar had tightened surveillance of mail crossing Russia's borders, he tactfully informed her by asking her to be more careful in sealing her envelopes.

Instead of leaving Fufu at Alexander's in the companionship of his children, Sophia in September took the child to Julia's, partly because Moscow was about 1,500 miles closer to Stockholm than Odessa. Julia had her estate to manage, however, while her sister had duties at her new jointly-owned boarding school for children. Consequently, since Fufu's beloved nurse had been dismissed for lack of funds, and as Sophia would not expose Fufu to certain children she saw at the school, she hired a daytime nurse for a monthly twelve-rouble sum that she could ill afford.

She then proceeded to clear the stain from Vladimir's memory by a frontal attack on the Moscow bureaucracy. She succeeded in getting Vladimir's papers from the examining magistrate and in reading Vladimir's letter to his attorney explaining the limited extent of his involvement in the Ragozin affair. She also obtained from the magistrate his admission that he believed Vladimir to have been a person easily carried away but nevertheless honest. This information she conveyed to Alexander and plainly expressed her feelings about the Ragozins:

"You can't imagine what subtle, poisonous villains these two brothers are. Just think, it appears that they may go unpunished, although moral proof of their guilt is endless. They are trying now to blacken the memory of poor V. O. I can't tell you to what a degree I hate them."

At a later time Ragozin's 18-year-old son, who subsequently committed suicide over the scandal, told her that Vladimir's involvement had been exaggerated by his attorneys, and that the prosecutor had never questioned Vladimir or even suspected him of complicity. Thus Sophia blamed both the Ragozin brothers and the attorneys for Vladimir's suicide and would never fully accept that whatever incidental provocations may have existed—including her own taut relationship—the real reason was his mental instability.

Sophia accepted 400 roubles from the university for Vladimir's plaster casts and animal skulls, rejecting an offer of 1,000 roubles for the other specimens, which she decided to have catalogued by an expert. His books had earlier been sold at auction by the authorities to meet minor debts.

By informing the professors and others of the results of her inquiries, Sophia felt she had done all she could for Vladimir. Now she could feel that the marriage was truly ended.

Despite Vladimir's gloomy assessment of his fourteen years of marriage, without the inspiration and money Sophia had supplied he never would have had the opportunity to become a serious scholar with an assured place in paleontology, a scholar Darwin declared to be the outstanding Russian in evolutionary science. With Sophia he had enjoyed at least a few years of married happiness. With or without her, it would appear, he was fated to experience alternating periods of high and low emotional states, eventually bordering on incapacity, and that sooner or later tragedy would result.

Sophia could now with a clear conscience move on to the next stage in her life. On a frosty day in early November, with a few snowflakes falling, she departed Moscow for Petersburg and watched the fields and villages fly by the train window, all under a gray sky. The constant clackety-clack of the wheels monotonously accompanied her poignant memories of having traveled many times with Vladimir, especially on that first trip to Petersburg as fictitious newlyweds. Now the capital city, upon her arrival, aroused further recollections of their early days there together, and much later of experiencing there the first happy year or two of a finally fulfilled married life. In those times they had been inseparable in Petersburg. Now she must bravely face a lonely future. How very lonely, indeed—as she would more than once complain.

CHAPTER 17

Woman Professor

i

ON A day in November in 1883 a ship nosed out of Petersburg's harbor into the Gulf of Finland and headed due west on a passage to Hanko at the southernmost point of Finland. From there its Stockholm destination lay less than 200 miles across the Baltic Sea. The pleasure of the brisk passage was only marred by Sophia's persistent toothache, but this did not confine her to her cabin. Warmly dressed against the sharp northern airs, she twice watched from the deck as the ship sailed into the setting sun, beyond which lay her future life. On the morning of the third day she scanned for three hours the many fir-forested islands forming the archipelago off Stockholm through which the ship had to pass. Then the Gothic church towers and stone buildings appeared ahead, and the King's waterside palace modeled after that at Versailles. The city's central area occupied a large island, but its 200,000 inhabitants, mostly tall and robust and blue-eyed blonds, overflowed onto other islands and the mainland. The city somewhat resembled a northern Venice, although with more natural attractions.

Sophia debarked on 11 November to be met by Mittag-Leffler and taken to his house, where she met his pretty wife, Signe, daughter of a Finnish general, and their child. Next day she met the professor's sister, Madame Edgren, who used her maiden name of Anna Charlotte Leffler. Anna's difficulty in getting a higher education had made her brother sympathetic to Sophia's goal of opening universities to women, and the two women, of the same age, formed an immediate friendship. The professor and his brother had tutored Anna Charlotte at home, so that she was educated to the level of university graduates. She had become a well-known novelist and playwright as well as an advocate for women's freedom.

[221]

Anna Charlotte described her first meeting with Sophia. "She was standing at a window leafing through a book as I entered. Before she could turn, I had time to see a serious and marked profile, rich chestnut hair arranged in a negligent plait, and a spare figure with a certain graceful elegance in its pose, but not well-proportioned, for the bust and upper part of the body were too small by comparison with the large head. Her mouth was large, her lips fresh and humid and most expressive. Her hands were small, almost like a child's, exquisitely modeled but rather spoiled by prominent blue veins. Her eyes were the most remarkable feature of her face and gave to her countenance the look of lofty intellect that so greatly impressed all who observed her. Their color was uncertain; they varied from gray to green to brown. Unusually large and prominent, they had an intensity of expression that seemed to pierce the farthest corner of your soul when she fixed her eyes upon you. But although so piercing, they were soft and loving and full of responsive sympathy. . . So great was their charm that one scarcely noticed their defect—Sophia was so near-sighted that when she was very tired she often squinted."

Sophia greeted Anna Charlotte with outstretched hands, yet with a certain formal shyness. Their conversation in French soon turned to Sophia's toothache. Therefore Anna accompanied her at once to a dentist. As they walked there Anna, who was plotting out a play, explained the entire story in greater detail than she had up to that point even fixed it in her own mind. According to Anna, this discussion began "the great influence she exercised on my writings afterward. Her power of understanding and sympathizing with the thoughts of others was so exceptional, her praise when pleased so warm and enthusiastic, her criticism so just, that for a receptive nature like mine it was impossible to work without her approbation. If she criticized unfavorably anything I had written, I rewrote it until she was pleased. This was the beginning of our collaboration. She used to say that I would never have written *Ideal Woman* had I not done so before her arrival in Sweden. This work and my novel *At War with Society* were the only books of mine that she disliked."

Anna Charlotte remarked that Sophia's literary judgment was almost purely subjective. If the thought and feeling of a work matched her own she valued it highly, even though it was mediocre; and, on the other hand, if it expressed opinions she did not share, she would deny any merit at all. Nevertheless, she was broad in her views, having few of the prejudices and conventional values common at that time.

Unwittingly Mittag-Leffler had clouded Sophia's arrival in Stockholm. Apparently Weierstrass, knowing the time and effort involved in preparing good lectures and wanting her to make a superior mathematical impression, had urged Mittag-Leffler to try to prevent her from expending her energies in a social whirl as had happened in Petersburg and more recently in Paris. As a result, Mittag-Leffler gave the impression Sophia should be treated rather like royalty; and, wanting nevertheless to insure her acceptance into the provincial society of Stockholm, he had circulated word that due to her position she could not make courtesy visits. Thus gossip went round that a haughty Sophia in ermine would arrive with a lady-in-waiting, and certain women decided that if she did not want to conform to the custom of the country and call upon them first, then they would not go to her.

Sophia herself added fuel to the smoldering fire because upon her arrival, when Mittag-Leffler proposed introducing her promptly at a *soirée*, she asked that he delay until she could learn some Swedish. He did not know that in the quarters she rented she would do nothing but study the new language from morning to night and that within two weeks she would speak it, not fluently or without some errors, but sufficiently well to carry on a conversation. During the first winter, in fact, she mastered the best of Swedish literature, although she never did manage to speak with perfection. Accent and modulation present the principal difficulties in learning Swedish, the most musical of the Germanic languages.

And so the time came for Sophia to meet the Stockholm people that most mattered to her. On the evening of the *soirée* she arrived late. Mittag-Leffler had been nervously circulating among his guests, assuring them she was not proud and asking them to be friendly. Among those assembled to meet her was Baron Adolf Nordenskiöld, the famed Arctic explorer, who was sympathetic to socialism. Finally the drawing room doors opened and a small, animated woman in a dress of soft white flannel entered. She was not truly beautiful, the guests at once decided, but definitely was charming as she moved about naturally and amiably, exchanging pleasantries in their own language with the benefactors of the university and other prominent citizens and their wives and with the professors and some of their wives.

Sophia's effort with the language at once created a very favorable impression. When this and her friendly manner became known in the wider Stockholm society, and that far from having a lady-in-waiting the learned newcomer was humble enough to occupy only a rented room in a house at Kommandörsgaten 10 occupied by two respectable old ladies named Vidmar, she became the pride of most of those in the university and of those who supported it.

Nevertheless, as Sophia several months later wrote to Folmar, many persons, because she was Russian, suspected her of nihilism ("which in the given case is not far from true"), and that lacking a husband she was in an ambiguous position. She noticed particularly that a number of Swedish mathematicians, including some from nearby Uppsala University, although they "visit me assiduously and shower me with gallantries and compliments," did not introduce her to their wives. She had encountered this same attitude in Paris, but to have it happen in Stockholm worried her. She told Folmar that she mentioned this to the wife of one mathematician who laughingly answered that the particular wife of the outstanding local mathematician would never receive in her house a young woman who without a husband lived in a furnished room.

Obviously some of those women who would not have accepted her as a wealthy princess now found reason to scorn her as a poor widow.

ii

THE UNIVERSITY on its large tract of land had been created entirely through private contributions of several million *kronor*. Such public interest in education was quite unlike anything elsewhere in Europe. Once the university had become established, the kingdom together with the city agreed, without imposing any academic interference, each to supply half the operating expenses. Apart from providing higher education for the fast growing city of Stockholm, the university had a secondary reason for its founding. This was to offer greater academic freedom. Classes were open to auditors of both sexes, and there were no examinations unless and until a student decided to sit for a degree. In the beginning King Oscar II, a former Uppsala student who spoke many languages and was a competent historian, had been in accord with the goals of the university; but at this time he had turned away, fearing that it would become a center for militant freethinkers. When this did not happen he again favored the institution.

The progressive Young Sweden party had led the drive to create the university in order to free science from the limitations of the older Swedish universities at Uppsala and Lund. As Sophia later remarked, Uppsala suffered from several hundred years of aging, as though all its vitality had frozen, so that the professors there were hostile to new ideas. New concepts were changing man's way of thinking in science, especially in those disciplines influenced by Darwinian thought, but also in physics and mathematics.

The progressives supported women's rights and therefore Sophia; the politically conservative would oppose her. As Mittag-Leffler stated in an article years later about Sophia: "For Sweden, for the young

Stockholm University, and for the educated men and women having concern for the university, it was a great happiness that Stockholm University attracted such a great light as Sophia Kovalevsky. Was anything like this possible at this time in any other European university? But on the other hand, it would be unseemly to pretend boastingly that the invitation to Sophia was evidence of a more advanced view of the women's question in Sweden than in other countries. Her invitation succeeded mainly because the opposition had no chance to get organized. Actual difficulties arose later."

In truth, the position of the Scandinavian woman at that time was less free than in some other countries, as witnessed by Knut Hamsun, the Norwegian novelist and eventual Nobel Prize winner, who returned in 1889 from a lecture tour of the United States and complained of the freedom bordering on tyranny of American women.

In general, however, Sweden was politically and socially more free than most other European countries, and the drive for financial gain was less pronounced. Wealthy families led a rather simple life without a show of elegance. Moral truth and personal responsibility had real significance. About a year after her arrival Sophia wrote: "Here in Sweden one really feels that in life there exists a definite connection between conviction and action. Generally speaking it is not an easy matter to convince a Swede of anything; but once this has been accomplished, he does not stop halfway but immediately puts his belief into practice in a material way."

Although welcomed by the progressives, a woman mathematician seemed strange to the conservatives; and petty gossip, if it died down briefly, would rise again at some later time. When Sophia reported such bourgeois gossip to Weierstrass, he assured her that this was natural with Swedes and that he likewise had experienced the same in the past. Sophia wrote both Marie Mendelson and Alexander on the same subject, declaring that when her lectures were officially announced, the mathematical students and certain professors at Uppsala "spent an entire evening in slandering me; they denied that I had any scholarly achievements, hinted at monstrosities," and advanced unworthy reasons for her coming to Sweden. Doubtless a romantic relationship with Mittag-Leffler was rumored. Without doubt he did greatly admire her as a woman, as well as a mathematician, and had he not married too soon their relationship might well have been different.

One politically sympathetic newspaper, however, was rhapsodic over her coming. "For your amusement," Sophia wrote Alexander, "I will translate what was written about me . . . : 'Today we must inform you about the arrival not of some trivial foreign royal prince or similar person knowing nothing. No, a princess of science, Mme. Kovalevsky, has honored our city with her visit and will be the first woman sub-professor in all of Sweden.' " At that time, incidentally, Sweden also embraced Norway. "You see," Sophia added, "now I am become a princess! If only they would assign me a salary. Well, perhaps they will do so." She confessed to Alexander that she dreaded the moment when she must stand at the podium, because her entire future depended upon her success.

With the beginning of the new year of 1884 and the start of her new career, Sophia resolved to be regular in keeping her diary, a resolution she kept for about two months before becoming spasmodic. She simply was not constituted to be much concerned about dates. During the holidays she had written many friends, but all except Weierstrass seemed to have forgotten her. Then for Russian Christmas (7 January at that time) she received gift books from Julia and Marie and letters from Alexander and Jules Molk and also candy from Professor Gulden, all of which cheered her somewhat.

During early January she spent one day looking at apartments with Mlle. Amelia Vikstrom, a young woman who sought her friendship. She dined with the Guldens and Mittag-Leffler's parents, read Poincaré's thesis, had callers, and received letters from the mathematicians Kronecker, Lipman, and Hermite. The latter again asked to print her crystals work in *Comptes Rendus*, a publication of the French Academy of Science, but she did not want to distress Weierstrass by agreeing without his knowledge. Eventually the study appeared in the French journal, in *Acta Mathematica*, and in a Swedish publication.

Finally came 30 January, the day of her first lecture. Nineteen students were on hand to give Sophia an ovation as she entered the classroom. Several of them presented bouquets. Also present were several benefactors of the university and a number of the professors. Since the semester would be devoted to "The Theory of Partial Differential Equations," it came as no surprise that no women students were present; in fact, there is no evidence that the champion of higher education for women ever herself had a woman student at the university.

Wearing a simple black dress, one she had worn in mourning for Vladimir, Sophia mounted the podium and arranged her lecture pages on the lectern. Fortunately the lectern being high and she rather short, she could easily read from the pages without squinting to betray her short-sightedness. For a moment, as she later related, it seemed that her lips completely froze, and she could not speak a word, but outwardly she gave the impression of calm deliberation. She spoke in German, partly from memory, and chalked equations on the board as required. At the conclusion of the class she received another polite ovation. Mittag-Leffler among others remained behind to compliment her on her confident manner and clarity of presentation.

At the end of the first day Sophia confided to her diary: "Don't know whether it was good or bad but do know that it was very sad to return home and feel so alone in the world. At such moments one feels very strongly that [in French] 'one more stage of life is left behind.' "

Since as a sub-professor or private docent that first semester Sophia received no university pay, students individually contributed for her course of instruction. Offered in advance their choice of lectures in French or German, the students preferred the latter, although in the second year she felt comfortable with Swedish. Later on, as students came also from Finland and Germany, she may have reverted to lectures in German, but as she later remarked: "In mathematical work the language plays a very secondary role. For the most part—for the subject, the ideas, the comprehension—mathematicians have their own language of formulas." Her students and auditors included graduates of Uppsala, Lund, and other universities. Outsiders, especially professors, continued to visit, although some came less for enlightenment than to appraise a woman teaching at university level.

Having been briefed by Mittag-Leffler, Weierstrass was prompt in congratulating Sophia in having succeeded with her first lecture. He expressed his conviction that she would overcome the inevitable difficulties to be encountered in the first semester of university teaching. "I am only concerned," he cautioned, "lest such concentrated work affect your health." He urged her not to give more than two one-hour lectures on the same day—she lectured two days a week—and to preserve some time for her own important work. He stated that Mittag-Leffler thought she would become a professor in ordinary (a five-year appointment). Such a position would give her a solid and honorable post from which to pursue science with real freedom, Weierstrass observed, adding that he had recently recommended her to the Swedish minister of education.

iii

BRIEF DIARY entries in February accented Sophia's loneliness, although she went on sleigh rides with Amelia Vikstrom and Amelia's suitor and with others, visited an observatory, and frequently was invited out for dinner or evening affairs. It was being alone in her room that depressed her. One day she returned home "terribly sad and sat thinking of my loneliness" until she was given a letter from Berlin. It was obviously from the individual soon to be introduced as the "unknown mathematician," who quickened her heart. In the diary entry for 21 February Sophia vaguely referred to failures and was so tired that she felt like running away. "It is difficult to live alone in the world." As a girl she had leaned on Aniuta, as a woman—in varying degrees at different times—on Vladimir, Julia, Weierstrass, Marie, and briefly on Anna Charlotte.

But Anna in December had gone to London to be away for months, so that Sophia could not turn to her. Much of Sophia's fatigue, as she confessed in writing to Anna, came from the many dinners, suppers, *soirées*, and receptions that followed one another so rapidly that, as Weierstrass had foreseen, she had trouble preparing her lectures. She looked forward to letters from Anna Charlotte. "Your letters," she confided to her, "are read, commented upon, and make quite a sensation. The leading ladies of Stockholm seem to have very few subjects of conversation, and it is really a charity to give them something to talk about." These Stockholm petticoats, as she sometimes characterized them, really bored Sophia; yet she did her best to be agreeable in the society in which she must live.

She could not forget Vladimir and on 21 February wrote Alexander that it was a disgrace that no worthwhile obituary about him had appeared. She had provided details to a Stuttgart geologist who asked to write about him. At the same time, "Now that my name has begun to be dragged through different journals, I live in constant fear that they might dig up some story that would harm me here. Through acquaintances here I requested all the editors of the major newspapers, as a personal favor, not to write more about me until I gave permission to do so; the newspapers here are very decent and have fulfilled my request, excepting for two of little importance. . . . When I become a professor in ordinary, then it won't matter to me, but until the matter is settled I live in constant fear for my reputation." Doubtless she had in mind, apart from her social life as a widow that might cause suspicion, the Ragozin affair, Vladimir's suicide, the earlier Petersburg financial debacle, and her Parisian political friendships.

iv

IN LATE February Sophia received a welcome 100 roubles from Aniuta. For a time also she received occasional payments from the consignment of Vladimir's unsold stock of published books. But her need for a regular salary was acute if she was to live and travel in what she considered a bare minimum of comfort.

By the end of April, following her last lecture, the students complimented her and as a memento presented her with a framed group photograph of her first class. She lost no time in sailing for Petersburg, visiting there with Aniuta and other relatives before proceeding on to

Fufu and Julia in Moscow. Arriving there on 29 April, she commented in a letter to Mittag-Leffler: "In Sweden I found a new native land, a new family, and that exactly at the moment when I most needed support and sympathy."

That apparently was in response to a letter awaiting her Moscow arrival, which announced her appointment as professor in ordinary. The salary would be 4,000 *kronor* (about 2,300 roubles or $1850), a sum which in later years would become 6,000 *kronor*. Actually the university could pay only 3,500 *kronor*, but private individuals had pledged the additional 500 *kronor*, surely evidence of the regard she had earned in the community—and evidence, too, of the efforts of Mittag-Leffler, who had to overcome determined opposition within the university by several anti-feminists. In fact, it was necessary for Sophia's supporters, Professors Mittag-Leffler, Nordenskiöld, and Gulden—to compromise by finally agreeing to promote two other sub-professors, of no particular ability, who previously had been denied advancement.

Upon receiving word of the appointment Sophia hastened to share her happiness with Alexander, knowing there was no need to inform Weierstrass who would be informed directly from Sweden. Two sentences will suffice: "You can't imagine how pleased I am! It is only awful to think that Vladimir will never know of this." In a subsequent letter she asked to know the reaction of Mechnikov to her appointment. He was the biologist who had declined to marry Aniuta fictitiously. There is the suggestion that about this time he had a romantic interest in Sophia, which she did not share.

While in Moscow Sophia heard from Teresa Gulden, wife of the professor, urging her to bring Fufu back with her to Stockholm. In reply Sophia explained to her friend that she considered it to be in Fufu's best interest to remain another year with Julia, where she was happy in the care of Julia's sister, who had traveled much in Europe to study pedagogy. Then, when she herself became suitably housed to care for Fufu, she would bring her to Stockholm. Regarding Mme. Gulden's warning that "there will be talk" if Fufu did not live with her mother, Sophia pointedly replied: "I am completely willing to submit to all the trivialities of life in Stockholm's society in regard to my dress, the manner of my life, the choice of my friends, and assiduously to avoid everything that might offend a stern judge—more exactly, a judge of feminine gender—but when the subject concerns so important an issue as the welfare of my daughter, then I must act according to my own reason." She planned to bring Fufu to Stockholm in the autumn of the following year. In preparation for this, and obviously to mark her new position as a professor, she asked Mme. Gulden to lease for her, if possible, a sunny apartment, large enough to house a servant, and located somewhere between her two magnet points—the Guldens and the Mittag-Lefflers—at a yearly rental of about 700 or 800 *kronor.* "I rely completely upon your choice." Sophia did obtain a suitable two-bedroom apartment at 14 Ostra Hummelegardgäten, and a maid.

Having never learned to economize, Sophia felt pinched despite her professor's salary. On 10 October 1884 she mentioned certain matters to her friend Sergei Lamansky, who was then managing affairs for her in Russia. An impractical physicist, he had no ability in business matters but had been her admirer since Heidelberg. "Life in Stockholm is very expensive," she wrote him, "and against my preference I have to be part of a circle of ministers, ambassadors, and millionaires. Although there is little to gain from them, one inevitably incurs needless expense." She remembered a locked cash box of Vladimir's left somewhere in Petersburg and hoped Lamansky could locate it and find money therein. She likewise wondered whether it would be worthwhile to bring from Moscow, for sale in Sweden, a collection of Korvin-Krukovsky and Shubert engravings. She hoped Lamansky could somehow forestall a possible lawsuit over some of her brother's debts and authorized him if necessary to divert some of her share of rental money from the apartment house. Later on Lamansky became a science professor in Warsaw but soon resigned rather than participate in the required program of Russian indoctrination, after which he could not get another university post in Russia.

V

AT SOME time, probably during her 1883 period in Berlin, Sophia had met a German mathematician, of uncertain name, to whom over coming years she would address no less than twenty letters. It is certain that she had romantic expectations, because obviously he came under her charm as Mittag-Leffler had done. "I want to see you very much," she wrote him in one July letter in 1884, "and I must tell you some happy news: I received a dispatch from Stockholm that my appointment as professor in ordinary has been officially confirmed." In another July letter a few days later, she wrote in part: "One must have great will power, truly, to refuse your polite proposal, but it is highly necessary for me to work on what I must present to Weierstrass on Sunday. In any case, I am very grateful and console myself with the hope that during the winter I shall be able to go with you to see *The Pauper Prince.* With warm regards, your Sofa Kov." "Sofa," significantly—not Sonya or Sophia.

The unknown mathematician had to leave Berlin shortly after her arrival. Wherever he may have gone, she wrote him before her departure for Sweden in August: "I tell you frankly that I have a feeling rather like that of a child who must leave his home and return to school. Of course I am inexpressibly happy that such an excellent occupation awaits me in Stockholm. There are persons there who have treated me most kindly and during my short stay showed me many favors, but nevertheless I feel myself a complete stranger there, and I feel very sad when I think of the long period of time that I shall have to be away from others that I value. Actually, more than anyone else, I should have become accustomed to loneliness, but just the same I don't succeed in this. The fewer of my friends that remain on earth, the harder it is for me to part from them."

It had been Sophia's expectation that now as a university professor, although a woman, she would be permitted at last to audit classes at Berlin University. It was common for one professor to broaden his knowledge by attending lectures of another. Weierstrass even petitioned the ministry but received word that permission must come from the rector, a position he had given up. The new rector and others didn't want women in the university, and its doors remained forever closed to Sophia. Not long after Sophia's death an American woman did succeed in getting special permission from the then rector, but the ministry soon canceled this permission.

Sophia therefore left Berlin to make a short visit to Paris before heading back to Sweden, where she rented a summer cottage with garden at Söderjelje, near Stockholm, and hired a housekeeper. On 17 August she invited her sickly sister to visit there, suggesting that a sea voyage and a change of scenery would benefit her. She remarked that she bathed daily in a lake and went for long walks among spruce and fir trees in a country resembling that at Palibino except that it was more mountainous. Several times daily she saw the Mittag-Lefflers, who had a place nearby. Aniuta had no inclination to travel, however; so Sophia concentrated on attracting the unknown mathematician to Söderjelje in September.

He gladly accepted her invitation and called on her every day to help redact in German her crystals treatise to achieve the clarity and style suggested by Weierstrass. It would seem that she vacated her cottage for the visitor and moved in with the Lefflers, where they worked on her German text. They spent much time rambling together through the forest and around the lakes.

Anna Charlotte, upon returning in October from London, noticed at once how much younger and more attractive Sophia looked. "At first I thought this was due to her being out of mourning; black was terribly unbecoming to her, and usually she could not wear it. But the change was not only outward. I noticed that the sadness usually visible in her face during her first visit to Sweden had given place to brilliant gaiety. . . ." Obviously Sophia had hopes, although the mathematician had departed for Berlin. Her bright mood lasted through the autumn as she plunged again into the social life of Stockholm.

For some reason the mathematician's name is absent from the records. Marie Bunsen, a high-born German who wrote about Sophia in 1897 and published portions of her letters to the mathematician, called him Mr. X. The Leffler family knew him of course, but Anna Charlotte in her memories of Sophia's Swedish years discreetly avoided naming many individuals and called the mathematician Mr. H—a small clue. Because Sophia in her diary in 1890 mentioned writing to Gustav Hansemann, a Weierstrass friend, one Russian investigator identified him as the elusive Mr. H. At that time Hansemann was fifty-five years of age, however, and for several reasons an unlikely choice. A better identity clue exists in Sophia's diary at the period of the affair. "Another of those strange coincidences that I don't know how to explain to myself," she wrote on 8 January 1884. "On this day exactly I saw his article in Crelle's journal. Returning home the first thing that falls before my eyes is his letter from last year in which he writes that twice already 8 January was such an anniversary for him." This seems to suggest that they had known one another from 8 January 1883, but perhaps from the same date a year earlier.

Crelle's journal (*Journal für die reine und angewandte Mathematik*) appeared twice yearly. The issue for the last half of 1883 would have just arrived at the university. It leads off with an article by Guido Hauck, professor at the Technical Higher School of Berlin-Charlottenberg. Born in Heilbronn, he was just five years older than Sophia, and had his doctorate from Tübingen. Of the two dozen mathematicians with articles in that issue of the journal, only Hauck matches Mr. H. on the basis of surname initial, suitable age, nationality, and location.

A year after the above mentioned diary entry, while in Berlin to see Weierstrass, Sophia sent a note to Mr. H. by messenger at 3:00 P.M. on 21 January 1885: "Light-mindedness has conquered. I am remaining here until the 28th. After the departure of my friends at approximately a quarter to four, I'll come to you in order to perfect my education. Your frivolous friend, Sofa K."

Mention of perfecting her education probably referred to ice skating or dancing. Sophia had never learned to skate in Russia, despite the lake in front of the house at Palibino, and she danced the old steps without grace and the new ones not at all. Although she had reached another plateau of scholarly accomplishment, happiness still escaped her, and in surveying her past life she felt she had wasted her youth. At age thirty-five she realized she had, in her devotion to study, missed many of life's pleasures. Therefore she eagerly accepted the offer of Mr. H. to teach her to skate. As she did not wish her first awkward attempts to be exposed in public, one of her friends arranged for the use of a private rink in the garden of a Berlin mansion. She likewise learned to dance in a private manner with Mr. H. and another admirer.

Presumably the afternoon tryst occurred, but afterward, at 7:00 o'clock in the evening, Sophia sent another note: "The former intention nevertheless holds firm. After much thought I decided still to leave at 3:36 tomorrow. I am sorry but nothing can be done. With my best regards, Sofa K." She offered no explanation, indicating that Mr. H. knew the reason well enough.

What transpired between the two of them during those four hours between messengers? What changed her mind? Did she decide that only something less than marriage was in prospect? Had Mr. H. simply indicated his belief that a woman could not combine marriage and a career? Or, most probably, had he in fact proposed on condition that Sophia become a homemaker and mother? Almost certainly it was Sophia's career that formed an obstacle to marriage, a career she had no intention of abandoning. A reason for this conclusion appears in a letter to Mr. H. in 1889, in which Sophia sent "warm regards" to his children, but with no mention of his wife. This strongly suggests that at the time of the romance Mr. H. was a widower and had at least two children old enough at that time to know Sophia and five years later to remember her. He would have wanted a wife to mother his children. If he had subsequently married and sired children, the oldest in 1889 could have been no more than four, hardly old enough to be the recipient of warm regards from Sophia. In any event, Sophia's serious romance apparently ended that day, although, since she specified the exact departure time of her train, she perhaps had a lingering hope that Mr. H. would appear at the station with a last minute change of mind.

Three days later Sophia wrote Mr. H. from Stockholm: "The fields and trees are totally covered with snow. The road through this brilliant evenness gave me much pleasure. I didn't become the least fatigued; on the contrary, I feel very capable of working. I hope that I shall be very zealous this winter. From my heart I wish you the best and that you don't completely forget your friend, Sophia Koval." That has the air of an end to any intimacy; and she had become "Sophia"—no longer the intimate "Sofa" that she had not wanted even Weierstrass to use.

[233]

The correspondence, marked by a quiet friendliness, continued for several years and mostly dealt with mathematics and scholarly events, with occasional references to recreational activities, as in the letter of early April in 1885. In this she reported to Mr. H. that she had written a short mathematical treatise to be sent to Weierstrass and that she had begun a large mathematical work with Mittag-Leffler. (The first perhaps did not see print, and the second may not have been completed.) She stated that she had met a very pleasant man, editor of the largest Swedish newspaper, who asked her to write short articles for him. (She did write one such article.) Finally she declared, thanks to the Berliner's lessons, that she had developed into an assured performer on ice and could even skate a little backwards. The ice was disappearing, however; therefore she intended to ride horseback at least an hour daily during the Easter holidays. But skating and riding were not the end of her frivolities. She would be among about 100 Swedish women who would conduct a bazaar for the benefit of the Public Museum. As all would dress in costume, she would go as a gypsy, assisted by five young women similarly garbed, to serve tea from a Russian samovar.

Actually Sophia never really became accomplished on skates, perhaps being too fond of male assistance in this pastime. As for horseback riding, her friend Anna Charlotte recorded that Sophia always asked for the quietest horse and while riding would scream if it made any unexpected movement. Aniuta had ridden as a child but the old governess would not permit Sophia to do so. If the Swedish horse broke into a fast gait she would call to the riding master, "Please, good man, make the horse stop!" Her friends teased her about this, but when she talked to other persons she conveyed the impression, which she seemed really to believe, that she was a good rider. Anna Charlotte believed most of her nervous reaction to horses, to cows in fields, and to strange dogs was mere coquetry, for she loved being protected; but actually, according to the recollections of Sophia's brother, she had from childhood been afraid of such animals. Nevertheless, in her person Sophia united, along with a masculine energy and often tough inflexibility, a very feminine helplessness in many things, and wherever she went she managed to attract male assistance.

CHAPTER 18

Twice A Professor

i

IT IS no wonder that Sophia could not feel at home in Sweden. The year 1885 saw Sophia being drawn in many directions at once—romantically (as has already been mentioned) to her Berlin admirer, maternally to her daughter in Moscow, sympathetically to her ill sister in Petersburg, politically to Marie and the Polish socialists in Paris, and intellectually to Weierstrass in Berlin who would soon celebrate his seventieth birthday.

As regards her own age at this time, when life seemed to be passing her by, Sophia in a letter to Mittag-Leffler took occasion to mention her age as thirty-one, a figure accepted thereafter by her friends. She was actually four years older.

During Easter vacation Sophia visited Weierstrass. He had grown temporarily weary of teaching, being fatigued by classes swollen from about fifty to 250 students, many of them foreigners drawn by his fame. He told Sophia he longed for a circle of only twelve really dedicated and inspired auditors to make his work a really priceless occupation. Conflicts with the jealous Kroneker at his own university also sapped much of his joy. When Sophia asked permission to translate one of his unpublished papers for publication in French, he wearily told her to use her best judgement.

Upon Sophia's return to Stockholm he wrote her that he had remained indisposed in his room for two weeks. Having heard from a third party that she too had been ill, he wrote reprovingly: "In general I must tell you that you write stintingly of yourself in your letters to me and my sisters, and yet you know what an interest we have always taken in what concerns you." Having heard that Professor Holmgren, who taught mechanics at her university, was ill and would probably die, he asked her to suggest to Mittag-Leffler that he pause at Karlsruhe to become acquainted with the 28-year-old sub-professor, Rudolph Hertz, as a possible replacement in mathematical physics. He then wrote Sophia several pages of equations on something that interested him, as often he had done in addressing her through the years. It seemed he could never keep his thoughts for very long from his beloved science. His sister Clara once said that while in the grip of mathematics he would sometimes, while eating, pause to write with his index finger on the back of his own hand to fix an equation in his mind until he could put it on paper.

During Mittag-Leffler's absence from the university in June, the rector proposed to Sophia that she act as Holmgren's substitute if he continued ill in the autumn. To this she agreed, but then one professor objected in principle to anybody holding two chairs, and it was even proposed to eliminate mechanics entirely from the curriculum. Three other mathematicians were considered, including the one proposed by Weierstrass, but in the end Lindhagen, the rector, decided definitely upon Sophia. Mechanics would be not too difficult a subject, and he had seen how well she had succeeded the previous spring with the extra burden of a course in algebra that she had given in addition to her advanced lectures.

About this time Mittag-Leffler proposed Sophia for an opening in the Swedish Academy of Science. On 25 June she wrote him: "The vision of the red uniform of the academician now constantly passes before my eyes, and you can't doubt that for my part I shall do everything possible to help you get it for me. I am joking, dear friend, but you can't imagine how much I am touched by every new proof of the interest and friendship that I receive from you." As secretary of the Academy the university rector opposed Sophia as being a woman, so that she then asked Mittag-Leffler to cease his efforts on her behalf so as not to bring forth envy and ill feeling toward her. In later years she did become a Swedish academician.

As for Aniuta's illness, first word of her serious trouble had reached Sophia just before the new year. "Her illness," she wrote Mittag-Leffler at that time, "makes terrible inroads, and now it is her sight that is affected. She can neither read nor write. This is caused by the faulty action of her heart, which gives rise to temporary stagnation of the blood and paralysis. I tremble at the thought of the loss awaiting me in the near future. How sad life is after all! and how dull to go on living!" She went on to speculate that the highest power in a human animal would be the power to die quickly and easily instead of suffering unheard of tortures. She then turned in her letter to a mathematical proposition she had been pondering, and ended by mentioning an article Anna Charlotte had sent her, written by August Strindberg, the Swedish dramatist, who believed social conditions were driving women into selfish and immoral conditions. The article declared a woman professor of mathematics to be an unnecessary and injurious monstrosity. "I think he is right," Sophia commented, "only I wish he would prove clearly that there were plenty of mathematicians in Sweden better than I am, and that it was only *galanterie* that made them select me!"

ii

As ANIUTA failed to get better, and as Jaclar, having received a French amnesty, had left her behind while he visited lingeringly in Paris on her money, Sophia decided to forego Paris and spend the entire summer in Russia. She divided her time between Aniuta's apartment in Petersburg and Julia's estate with Fufu near Moscow. For Aniuta she could do little except offer loving emotional support. They talked of politics and friends but mostly about mutually shared experiences during their girlhood and early womanhood.

With two-fifths of her patrimony Aniuta had rescued Jaclar from the French prison; the other three-fifths he had managed to waste away almost entirely. All that remained was their interest, along with that of Fedor and Sophia, in the heavily mortgaged apartment house. After loan payments, the rents did not amount to much; apparently at this time Sophia turned over her share of the income to Aniuta. Ill as she was, Aniuta endeavored to supplement her income with her pen, without much success. Jaclar had failed in Russia as a teacher and journalist and was no more successful in France as a journalist or later in politics as a would-be deputy. He still lived mentally in the days of the Commune and had become, except for a few young student leftists, rather a bore to those who knew him. He seemed unsuited for any work, only for subversion, and on that score was largely held in check by fears, not unfounded, of official surveillance both in Russia and France. He was seen, moreover, to be a rude husband and an irritable father. As early as 1874, in correspondence between Dostoevsky and Mme. Dostoevsky, he had been the subject of gossip over an affair with a married woman. "Ah, such French taste!" exclaimed the novelist, and he wondered that Aniuta seemingly was blind to the situation. In her recollections Dostoevsky's wife wrote that she and her husband were Aniuta's great friends "but didn't at all love her somewhat popinjay and liberal husband."

While in Petersburg, as usual, Sophia also saw elderly relatives and her brother Fedor. Although Fedor had inherited 50,000 roubles in capital and two estates yielding generous incomes, he had plunged heavily in debt from gambling and a fast life. This was a real disappointment for Sophia, who had envisioned a future in mathematics for the talented Fedor as a former pupil of Chebyshev and others.

iii

ON ARRIVAL in Moscow Sophia proceeded by carriage, past the Kremlin walls, the many domes, Ivan's belltower, and across the river to Julia's estate of Semenkov with its quiet village. There she relaxed completely in the bright house, which had an interior mezzanine, a round tower, and glassed-in terraces twined over by climbing roses and grapevines.

Often she read novels by the pond or strolled in the gardens and nearby woods. She even rode horseback, accompanied by sun-tanned Fufu on a pony, with dogs trailing along. On one occasion, having confidently assured Julia that she could drive a carriage without a servant, the carriage hit a tree and overturned, throwing both women into the mud and twisting Julia's leg. "Well, here is an example of the injustice of fate," she wrote Anna Charlotte. "Poor Julenka is suffering whereas I as the instigator of all this came out untouched."

With no thought whatever of mathematics, Sophia indulged her capacity for occasional complete laziness, joked that she would turn into a plant, embroidered, smoked many cigarettes, and in addition to regular meals sipped tea four times a day and consumed jams and pastries. As she later wrote to Alexander: "By nature I am terribly lazy, and nobody suspects what incredible effort I had to put forth, and still do, to keep this laziness in check and to force myself to work, no matter what." One method she used was to deny herself some pleasure, such as novel reading, until she had earned it by working.

Sophia in Paris would usually be introduced as a mathematician, in Stockholm often as a champion of women, but in the environs of Semenkov she was introduced as Fufu's mother. This she found properly diminished her vanity at the very time when her fame as the first woman in mathematics was spreading over Europe and America by way of pictures and biographical material in various periodicals.

It happened that Julia, depressed over the recent death of her sister, had living with her four spinster relatives who wore mourning black and gave the house the impression of being a nunnery. Sophia had agreed to join Anna Charlotte and her brother for a walking tour in the Swiss Alps. But she so enjoyed the relaxed atmosphere, and being with Fufu, that she used the excuse of Julia's bereavement to cancel the Swiss meeting. When it came time for Sophia's departure Julia decided not to accompany her to Stockholm as planned but begged to keep Fufu with her for another year. To this Sophia reluctantly agreed, principally because it would leave her free to visit her ill sister if necessary, partly because Fufu loved the free life at Semenkov and comforted Julia. Sophia described Fufu at this time as a well-developed seven-year-old who read with enthusiasm but was in general wild and frolic-some—a real tomboy.

On 1 September, having paused en route to see Aniuta again for a few days, Sophia arrived back in Stockholm to be met by Anna Charlotte in rather bad humor because Sophia had not come to Switzerland. On her study table Sophia found an announcement from George von Folmar of his marriage. She spent the first evening going over A. Brehm's multiple-volumed *Life of Animals* to be issued in a new edition. First published by Vladimir, this work enjoyed continuing demand, and in coming months Sophia would devote considerable spare time to this project in order to supplement her income.

By this time, if not before, she had deduced Julia's real reason for not coming to Stockholm—namely that Julia really didn't want to live with her. In a letter Sophia implied as much but hoped Julia might change her mind. She described her six-room apartment rented in anticipation earlier in the year at Engellbrecktsgäten No.4. In it two rooms were set aside for Julia, rooms containing completely refurbished furniture. Also Sophia had a cook and a jewel of a maid. In her study, she added, she had a large date palm, a gift from Professor Gulden, and all her books had arrived from storage in Russia. But Julia would not be enticed, for she had now lived too long as mistress of her own household to submit again to Sophia's domination.

Sophia's apartment was in a large two-story gray house in a district of villas, or detached houses, each surrounded by gardens enclosed by picket fences. Teachers of the higher and middle schools and others on limited income lived there, whereas the wealthy lived on or near the waterfront where the foreign embassies were located. Her house had a graveled forecourt. From the entrance hall one door led into a hall connecting with several rooms and kitchen; the other door led into the living room, beyond which lay the study with its large writing table, its divan, and its shelves loaded, among other books, with those of George Eliot, George Sand, and Julia's famous relative, Michael Lermontov, together with copies of Zhanna's Russian periodical *Severny vestnik (Northern Messenger)*. In her bedroom, on the night table, Sophia usually had one of George Sand's novels. Her favorite was *Consuelo*, which had as its chief character the Spanish-gypsy singer who was Turgenev's lifetime friend and supposed mistress.

In mid-September Anna Charlotte visited Sophia, their rift over Switzerland healed. Part of her remaining vacation Sophia spent as a guest of Mittag-Leffler's parents. She also had the duty, as a member of the editorial committee, of reading over articles submitted for *Acta Mathematica*.

iv

AT ABOUT this time Sophia wrote to Mr. H., complaining lightly of trivial household interruptions while she was trying to concentrate on Abelian functions. "These stupid, not to be deferred, practical matters are a serious test of my patience; I am beginning to understand why men place such a high value on accomplished housekeepers. Were I a man I would choose for myself a small pretty housekeeper who would free me from all these tedious duties." On 9 November she again wrote Mr. H., mentioning that she had become twice a professor, as she was lecturing temporarily also on mechanics. At the end of August Professor Holmgren had died. She thought her new assignment might last for two years, by which time some one of the university's graduates should be qualified for the position. Very likely her appointment, despite some opposition, was influenced by the opportunity for saving a new professor's full salary. Sophia received only 2,000 *kronor* (1,300 roubles) extra to add to her previous salary of 4,000 *kronor*.

Besides her household distractions, her social obligations, and her extra lectures, Sophia also was on the planning committee for the birthday dinner honoring Weierstrass. This entailed correspondence that had begun early in the year. Berlin planners engaged a sculptor to create a marble bust of the master, and an album was compiled from all over Europe, containing about 500 photographs of the institutions where Weierstrass had taught and of prominent students and friends, and a record of his honors. His brother Peter supplied early photographs, as did his sisters, and material for a biographical sketch.

Teaching duties prevented Sophia and Mittag-Leffler from being present, but they along with Hermite and Poincaré were among the twenty-five mathematicians that sent him congratulations for 31 October 1875. Mittag-Leffler had stopped in Berlin in September for advance congratulations and presumably to consult on Sophia's competence to teach mechanics.

Weierstrass left for Switzerland on sick leave immediately after the celebration. From there he described to Sophia what took place. Among those present, mathematicians included George Cantor, H. A. Schwarz, Ferdinand Lindemann, William Killing, W. L. Thomé, Paul DuBois-Reymond, and Lazarus Fuchs. The latter, as his first favored pupil, or protégé, spoke, as did the dean of the philosophical faculty and several others, including the quarrelsome Leopold Kronecker, who had not responded to his invitation but appeared at the last minute. After many dinner toasts the party adjourned to a beer hall, where Weierstrass remained until midnight, although his brother and others made a night of it until dawn. In his own student days at Bonn, where Weierstrass studied law and commerce for four years without seeking a degree (having later studied mathematics entirely on his own), many times had he greeted the rising sun in a beer garden. At Bonn he had been so expert in student swordplay with naked blades that he never once sustained a wound, and thus had no facial scar such as so many Germans displayed with pride. Now in old age he had some difficulty in walking. He sent Sophia a gypsum reproduction of his bust, which was displayed in Berlin's art museum, and sent also reproductions of the inscribed medals presented to him from learned societies and governments. As an academician of Berlin, Paris, Russia, and London, he was at the height of his fame. He would return again to teaching and would outlive Sophia, although in a wheelchair.

At a later date, in 1886, in shrugging off continued unpleasantness from Kronecker, he wrote Sophia: "Nobody knows better than I how far I have remained from the goal I set in my inspired youth. But no one can take from me the knowledge that my aim and activity have been useful and that the path I traveled toward the truth has not been a false one." He and his followers were correct in the direction mathematics would develop.

CHAPTER 19

The Longest Journey

i

THE YEAR 1886, like the years before, found Sophia still unsettled in Sweden. However much she tried, she could not feel at home there. She would always say that her longest journey was the short leg from Malmö, her Swedish landfall en route from Paris or Berlin. Sometimes she put it another way: "The line from Stockholm to Malmö is the most beautiful I have ever seen; but that from Malmö to Stockholm is the ugliest and most tiresome I have ever known." As once she had written to Marie, she found Stockholm to be a fairly beautiful city, as indeed it was, with water on all sides and bridges and trees and attractive buildings. She found, however, that the "mixture of new and free viewpoints imposed upon an essentially German patriarchal society" prevented her from orienting herself in Stockholm. Despite all the good qualities of Swedish society, she missed the certain cast of thought and turn of conversation found in the more cosmopolitan atmosphere of Petersburg and Paris. Also, she much preferred keeping late hours; but in Stockholm, as she wrote Marie, "everybody goes to bed with the roosters and, alas, also rises with them." Most of all she longed for Russian friends to share her views and goals.

Part of Sophia's trouble was the language. French she could use fluently, having grown up in a class and family where it often was used in preference to Russian. She picked up other languages rapidly but not really well. Regarding her command of Swedish, as likewise of German, Anna Charlotte observed that Sophia spoke both languages rather brokenly, coined impossible words, but never allowed this to stop the flow of her conversation. "However imperfectly she spoke a language, she always spoke volubly, always succeeding in expressing what she wanted to say and in giving an individual stamp to her utterances." This included English as well as German and Swedish. "One of her characteristics," Anna Charlotte observed, "was that when tired or depressed she had great difficulty in finding words; but when in good spirits she spoke rapidly and with great elegance. Language, like everything else with her, was under the influence of personal moods."

Partly in consequence of the language barrier, Sophia felt she could not identify with Swedes—except for a few close friends—and with the latter, unfortunately, she often could not express nuances of thought but had to use inadequate expressions. "That is why," she told Anna Charlotte, "when I return to Russia, I feel released from a prison in which my best thoughts were in bondage. You cannot think what torment it is to be forced to speak in a foreign tongue to dear friends. You might as well walk all day with a mask on your face."

And yet, despite the handicap of a foreign tongue, Sophia took a lively interest in everything concerning her Stockholm friends. As Anna Charlotte recorded: "She led a social life and was everywhere the center of a magic circle. The strong satirical vein in her character and the deep contempt she felt for mediocrity (she belonged to the aristocracy of the intellectual world and worshipped genius) were, in her, wedded to a poet's ready sympathy with all human conflict and trouble, even the least important." Married women confided to her their domestic worries, young girls consulted her about dress. To them all she seemed simple and unpretentious and in no way supposed herself above other women. But Anna Charlotte knew this to be untrue. Sophia's impression of affability and simplicity was actually an illusion. In fact, she was naturally reserved and considered few persons to be her equal. But the mobility of her nature and the wish to please by becoming a part of Swedish life gave her a sympathetic manner that charmed others. She seldom displayed her ironic or satirical vein to those she considered her inferiors, but she used it freely with those she considered her equals. By upbringing she was, in brief, a gentlewoman in the old and best sense of that term, a person kind and considerate and sympathetic with those lower on the social scale at that time; but frank and occasionally impatiently critical with those of her own social or intellectual class, and entirely willing to be treated the same way by her peers.

"Meanwhile," again according to Anna Charlotte, "it did not take her long to exhaust the social interest of Stockholm. After a time she said she knew everybody by heart and longed for fresh stimulation for her intelligence. This was a great misfortune for her, and accounts for the fact that she could not be happy in Stockholm, or, perhaps, in any place in the world. She was continually in want of stimulation. She desired dramatic interests in life, and was ever hungering for high-wrought mental delights. She hated with all her heart the gray monotony of everyday life." Anna Charlotte further observed, rightly it would seem, that although Sophia's talents were of an original and productive nature, she required the inspiration of other highly gifted persons to overcome her inertia and do productive work herself. Therefore, except in Berlin or Paris she could not find anywhere else the mental stimulus to trigger and sustain worthwhile mathematical work. Mittag-Leffler had done and would do important work, mostly along lines of Weierstrass' thinking, and he was Sophia's faithful friend, but he was no brilliant Poincaré to strike sparks. In Stockholm, however, in Anna Charlotte, Sophia did find the impetus for excellent literary work, which will be considered later.

Consequently, because of her isolation in Stockholm and her teaching and social activities, Sophia had made no progress on the mathematical problem she had set for herself. In January of 1884 she had written Marie: "The new mathematical work, recently started by me, now interests me greatly, and I shouldn't want to die without discovering that which I am seeking. If I succeed in solving the problem . . . then my name will stand among the names of the most outstanding mathematicians. I estimate it will require five more years to achieve good results." Two years had already passed.

Apart from her Swedish isolation, another disturbing factor existed in Sophia's life. This was her longing for a husband to love and sustain and comfort her as Vladimir had done, without her really appreciating him, and to fulfill her new ideal of laboring together in love. According to Anna Charlotte she dreamed of finding a man whose intelligence would complement her own, so that together they could realize, individually or together, the full development of their genius. Belief that she could not find such a person in Sweden was the real basis, in Anna Charlotte's view, for the dislike Sophia had taken to that country and her escape therefrom at every opportunity. This judgement may be valid to the extent that it does not discount the other factors contributing to her feeling of exile.

At one time Mittag-Leffler asked Sophia if she would not be happier married. Probably yes, she replied, but to whom? He suggested a wealthy Stockholm banker who had entertained Sophia with obvious romantic interest on a number of occasions. Her reply was negative; no, if she married it would be only to a Russian and a mathematician. As a matter of fact, both Sophia and Anna Charlotte considered the banker a pompous Philistine. When Anna Charlotte made him a character in a novel, he fortunately did not recognize himself, or dared not say so, but he did recognize her description of his entrance hall as that of the novel's character. At a dinner party he objected to this, but Sophia tactfully convinced him that Anna Charlotte's description was really a tribute to his taste in decoration.

ii

IN EARLY January of 1886 Folmar wrote Sophia that Marie, using the passport of Folmar's new wife, intended going into Poland on revolutionary business. Sophia at once became alarmed and, having obtained Folmar's admission that the journey was not essential, wrote Marie an impassioned letter attempting to dissuade her.

She wrote in part on 25 January 1886: "He [Folmar] is convinced that you are needed more here at present, but that the burden of your seeming activity, the need for self-forgetfulness, and the indomitable urge toward danger pushes you on, and that nothing he or I say will change your intention. You don't consider such influences on your decision as a desire for self-sacrifice, an attraction toward the beauty of martyrdom, and the effect of those irremovable traces of religious ex-altation instilled in you since childhood. . . . Dear Maria, I cannot without emotion imagine you—so nervous, so gentle, so full of life— somewhere in the depths of a Russian jail, condemned for many years to exile in Siberia, in one word subjected to the sufferings of a slow and unavoidable death that awaits political criminals in Russia. This death is worse than hanging, as it is much more torturous, and the hope of escape is minimal. Those few that return from Siberia are physically and morally broken . . ."

She cited the case of a political activist they knew, called Sophia Bardina, who escaped from Siberia and in poor health committed sui-cide in Geneva. A prótegée of Lavrov, Bardina had propagandized among women industrial workers.

Escape from Siberia was infrequent because, although security pre-cautions were at a minimum, few exiles dared cross the vast distances of uninhabited terrain to freedom. The secondary object of isolating persons in Siberia was to populate the country, in the way that England sent so many persons to Australia, and France to its islands. Life in Siberian exile, except for criminals sentenced to hard labor, was, for most, that of pioneers, but for others having sufficient money it afforded a life of relative ease. Some remained when their terms of exile expired.

It would appear that in replying to Sophia's agitated letter, Marie disclosed what she had not told Folmar—namely, that her husband, Iankovsky, had died in Poland. Presumably because of her revolutionary record, and perhaps also for more personal reasons, Marie had not lived with him. Whether or not that was precisely the situation, his death left her in financial trouble, and thus her real reason for going into Russian territory at this time was to seek access to his estate assets. Therefore she needed a safe passport, and she needed to know under what name she was officially listed in the records in Petersburg, whether as Iankovsky or her maiden name of Zalesky.

The real surprise in Sophia's long letter of reply comes in the very last sentence. Marie published it after Sophia's death without date or clarification. In the letter Sophia sent perfunctory condolences, as though Iankovsky's death did not much affect Marie emotionally, and then proceeded to Marie's financial predicament, hoping Marie would not have to appeal to her nobleman father in Poland (from whom she apparently was estranged) and comparing Marie's plight with her own two years earlier when she was cheated in connection with Vladimir's estate. Sophia agreed to have an unnamed Russian, presumably Lamansky, ascertain how Marie was registered in Petersburg. She warned that if Marie used Julia Folmar's passport, even a half-blind border official could see that brunette Marie was not Swedish. Therefore she arranged for Marie to use a passport belonging to Zinaida, the first name of a friend. Finally she closed the letter thus: "Unfortunately I don't have a personal passport: I sent it to Russia, asking that I be excluded from the number of citizens."

Nowhere does there appear any explanation for such an extreme action by Sophia as the attempted renouncement of her Russian citizenship. Nothing indicates, either, that she became a Swedish citizen. Of several possible explanations for her action, perhaps the most likely is that, having secured an honored place for herself in Sweden, she wished to avoid risking trouble while traveling within Russia's borders, where authorities might know of her association in Paris with both passive and active socialists. Possibly, moreover, she had passed along messages in letters to Aniuta for transmission to the underground in Poland. Thus to have Russia acknowledge her as a Swedish citizen would afford a measure of protection when she visited her motherland. Whatever her reasons, the Russian authorities later returned her passport with a polite refusal: "Mme. Sophia Kovalevsky is the pride of Russia, and consequently the Russian government cannot agree to her loss." Apparently that ended the matter.

In any event, with regard to Marie, seemingly the protestations of her friends and her own perceived risk of being snared by Russian officialdom if she surfaced in the estate matter, caused her to change her mind. Perhaps she accepted money from her father, or resolved the

[246]

estate problem when she went into Poland a year or so later, but most probably Stanislaus Mendelson succored her.

In another letter to Marie, a most revealing one, two traits of Sophia's character stand out clearly in her own words—first, her need for constant attention and reassurance and praise; second her domination by reason. She wrote:

"I thank you for your dear letter. It had a beneficial effect upon me. I thank you mostly for your friendship, in which I must believe, judging by the feelings I have for you. Exactly in this is my happiness! You cannot imagine to what extent I am suspicious and unbelieving concerning the attitude of my friends toward me! I demand that they constantly repeat their love, if they want me to believe in it. If they forget this just once, then immediately it seems to me that they are not thinking about me.

"In reality, believe me, nobody has loved me on short acquaintance. In regard even to my closest friends I have the impression that I had to endure much suffering in order to acquire their friendship. But—this is saddest of all—I was forced always to act out a small comedy; that is, to present myself in a somewhat different light. Are you convinced even now, dear Maria, that you would have loved me had you known me completely? Do you know what is the difference between us? You have an impulsive nature, submissive to the first burst of feeling. One feels your nature and without analyzing it loves you just as you are, with all your defects and weaknesses. Yes, dear one, with all your defects, and I shall even add that I think you have an endless quantity of them. I am convinced that you have done many mad acts in your life and were guilty of being foolish. If you had told me the most impossible things about yourself I should have believed you, but loved you for this even more. With me—alas!—everything occurs otherwise. Many times during my life I planned to do something mad but never succeeded. I am so terribly, so incorrigibly reasonable. At the moment when really wanting to do a crazy action I would realize that this would be to act out the part of a madman, nothing else. I feel myself only in the role of a sensible and prosaic commoner—tell me, who can love such a creature? . . . Dear Maria, are you able to love at least a little such a small uninteresting person as I?"

In her letter of 13 June she wrote Marie in part:

"In my official life everything is in order, as it should be, but I confess to you that my personal affairs are in terrible disarray and have left a great emptiness in my life. My small 'I' is demanding and self-willed —often rebelling during the past months and not submitting to reason when confronted with the insignificant and temporary nature of personal happiness. From all this I have a sediment of apathy and indifference in regard to myself. It seems I have attained an ideal of impersonality. Now I am acting out the role of a Sister of Mercy. I am living in a society of many people who really interest me little, but who have at times major or minor unpleasantnesses and for whom my moral support is needed. Worst of all, I know that I can't give them significant help. . . . I completely share your enthusiasm about Paris; it is good to live there, but not to come for several weeks only. How happy I should be if I could find a position of activity there similar to that in Stockholm. But it is needless to think about this. Frenchmen will not accept a woman professor so quickly, although I have not had from anywhere else so many compliments on my appointment as from French mathematicians. They consider that a woman professor is good for elsewhere in Europe but not among them at home."

A small part of the life emptiness of which Sophia complained may have been due to lack of response to her letter of 8 May to Mr. H. "You certainly would laugh if you could see me writing this letter," she wrote him in part, conveying a somewhat provocative picture of herself. "The reason is that I am sitting in a white peignoir, with flowers and a gold butterfly in my hair. Within an hour I must go to a great ball at the Norwegian minister's; the king will be there and all the princes." She seemed to be saying: see what a glamorous creature could still be yours; and, I shall be dancing with royalty.

Sophia actually was a popular personality, often called "Our Professor" by Stockholm society. She one time described the King as a kind and educated man, "in general very friendly with the professors and especially with me." When Marie Lekke, Fufu's playmate and daughter of the professor of zoology, published her recollections in *World of Our Parents* in 1935, she remembered Sophia: "I recall personally, as of a fairy tale apparition from distant times, how my father in a hired carriage accompanied Kovalevsky to a court ball. She seemed to me a brilliant beauty with her dark hair in curls, her myopic, almost unnaturally large eyes, which either sparkled or crossed slightly." She wore a blue taffeta dress with tiers of overlapping cloth having scalloped edges, and slippers to match.

iii

IN LATE June Sophia arrived in Paris and took a *fiacre* to a pension where she had previously stayed, but when notified of her whereabouts, Marie insistently collected Sophia to install her as a guest. The next day Sophia called upon Hermite, Gabriel Lippmann, and Poincaré. The latter, who had just become professor of mathematical physics and the calculus of probabilities at the University of Paris, arranged a dinner in her honor at which several French mathematicians, including Jules Tannery and Joseph Bertrand, were complimentary and very attentive. Bertrand was permanent secretary of the Academy of Science. Hermite praised her work on the refraction of light in crystals. Poincaré wrote a flattering article about her in *Temps*.

Mittag-Leffler, as the force behind *Acta Mathematica*, had given Sophia the diplomatic mission of persuading the French government to join other countries in supporting the journal on a regular basis. Each participating country had several mathematicians on the editorial committee. Mittag-Leffler and Sophia were the Swedish members. Germany through the influence of Weierstrass had already provided an annual grant to augment that of Sweden. Sophia wasted no time in approaching the influential Bertrand, enlisting his successful efforts as her intermediary with French officialdom.

During the course of her stay in Paris, Bertrand one day informed her that a subject had been chosen by the Academy for the prestigious *Prix Bordin*. He recalled hearing that as a Berlin student she had herself been interested in capturing the "mathematical mermaid" that had eluded so many scientists for so long. It happened, he said, that the prize would be offered for the best paper on this very same subject— namely, on the rotation of a rigid body around a fixed point. This problem had already been the subject of three previous competitions and had defied full solution by such as Euler, Lagrange, and Poisson. It is uncertain whether Sophia told Bertrand that she had already during the previous two years made various attempts to snare the mermaid. The problem demanded solution, and its choice for a prize award was fortuitous for Sophia, because it had haunted her for many years and now she had a real incentive. With Poincaré she discussed it in a general way.

She had, as a matter of fact, examined the problem seriously in the fall of 1881. Then it had distracted her from her optics problem involving crystalline substances. Weierstrass had earlier shown that it could not be solved by using differential equations involving single-value functions of time. She had been inspired to try using Abelian functions which avoid the linear functions of time. She thought time could be considered as a complex variable. Soon she had realized, however, that a solution would take her years, and she had resumed work instead on the crystals problem.

Now the year was 1886.

Despite being a professor, Sophia still could not audit classes in Berlin—much less attend sessions of the Berlin Academy of Science.

However, in Paris, despite her sex, she was permitted to attend sessions of the French Academy and in fact was escorted there by the permanent secretary himself. Russian newspapers reported this unusual French honor. Yet Sophia still felt herself to be a social pariah in Paris. It vexed her that still she had never received an invitation to any of the professors' homes. It seemed their wives considered her a notorious person, unworthy of crossing the domestic threshold.

Then, on the morning of 25 June, the mathematician Tannery called to take her to the final oral examinations at a normal school for girls. Seated at the examiners' table with Tannery, Mme. Tannery, and Paul Appell, she listened to eager young women giving their answers and wondered, under the prevailing attitudes toward scholarly women in France, what the future could hold for them in education apart from teaching in lower schools. For many of the girls she had been an inspiration, and all felt that her success offered some distant hope for them. For Sophia, too, the occasion served to inspire her to continue advocating greater educational freedom for women.

Following the session the examiners went to a luncheon as Bertrand's guests. Other mathematicians had also gathered there. Having showered her with praise, they presented Sophia with a manuscript of the great German mathematician of an earlier time, Karl F. Gauss. Mme. Hermite, who was among the guests, appraised Sophia suspiciously. Satisfied with what she saw and heard, at the end of the luncheon she politely invited Sophia to dinner at her impeccably respectable home. So the barrier had finally fallen, but only after so many years that Sophia's reaction was one of ironic amusement when she later discussed the matter with Marie. Nevertheless, her victory over Mme. Hermite was her greatest personal Parisian triumph at that time.

While in Paris Sophia called upon Jonas Lie to give him Anna Charlotte's latest book, *Summer Saga*. The Norwegian novelist, a master of psychological analysis, lived on a writer's pension, being then fifty-three years of age. He returned Sophia's call, and they met on subsequent occasions, especially in future years. He told Sophia he considered Anna Charlotte more talented as a novelist than as a playwright.

Then came the day when Sophia once more had to tear herself away from the city of her heart, and from Marie with whom she had become more intimate than ever. On 3 July she sailed from Havre for Christiania (Oslo), Norway. "Madame Atlantica made fun of me, and for the first two days I felt very unwell," she wrote Marie, "but as soon as we reached the Skagerrak all the suffering ended, and it is difficult to imagine anything more pleasant than the third day of my voyage." On the fourth day she arrived in Christiania, late but still in time for the closing sessions of the Congress of Swedish Naturalists. She was met on the quay by Anna Charlotte and her brother.

A week after arrival in Christiania, replying to a letter from Marie, Sophia on 15 July described her sea passage, as mentioned above, and added: "One's heart barely has time to attach itself warmly and sincerely to someone when again comes the moment of parting. You are very fortunate, dear Marie, in being surrounded by friends dedicated to you, friends who never abandoned you and with whom you are tied by so many common interests! As for me, I feel that I age after each separation. Such a miserable creature am I, an eternal Wandering Jew! And still it is asserted that mathematics requires peace and equilibrium." She wrote that she had been the subject of orations, having been chosen in her absence to head the mathematical section of the naturalists, and that during the official dinner Professor Bierkes gave a long speech in her honor, and that Christiania students raised the rafters with applause.

Although the honor of Sophia's election was a genuine one, the possible politics involved should not be overlooked. Very likely Mittag-Leffler had proposed her name in informal discussions with other members, who could not have been unaware of his position as principal editor of *Acta Mathematica* and of Sophia's influence as a member of the editorial committee. Although the "publish or perish" dictum had not been so formulated at that time, nevertheless printed work was one key to advancement. On the whole, however, most votes must have been cast primarily in real recognition of Sophia's position in Swedish mathematics.

iv

ANNA CHARLOTTE's presence in Christiania was by prearrangement with Sophia, for they had planned a long sightseeing journey through the mountains of Norway as far as the western shore and then back through Norway and Sweden to Stockholm. In a carriage, accompanied by Mittag-Leffler, they set out. The threesome spent a week in the Telemark region. From Sitijord they climbed a mountain, a first experience for Sophia. "She was very brisk and indefatigable in climbing, and delighted in the beauty of nature," Anna Charlotte recorded. "She was full of joy and energy, her pleasure being only now and then marred by fear of a cow near one of the cheese dairies, or by having to surmount heaps of stones that rattled down under our feet, when she uttered little childish shrieks and exclamations that much amused the rest of the party."

Although Sophia did appreciate nature, it was the spirit or mood of the scenery, so to speak, from the light and shadow, the clouds and sunsets, the birdsong and solitude, that appealed to her—because, being near-sighted, she could not clearly see the details of scenery and out of vanity would not wear glasses.

Then Mittag-Leffler departed, leaving the two women to continue their sightseeing alone, afoot and by conveyance. They laughed and sang together happily as they penetrated deeper into the mountains, until they reached a place where a woman friend of Anna Charlotte's was administrator of Ulman's Peasant Higher School. There they remained for several days, as Sophia was greatly interested in the operation of the school, which several years later became the subject of her sketch entitled "Three Days in a Peasant University."

They proceeded on their way, but the trip was taking longer than Sophia had expected; she was eager to solve the mermaid problem, having decided that the way to do this was not with the mathematics of an earlier period but with the new mathematics she had been probing. The more she thought of this the more eager she became to try, especially since the scenery she couldn't see in detail had become boring. She could forego their planned visit with the Norwegian dramatist and novelist, Alexander Kielland, who expected them at Jädern. Thus, with the journey only half over, while they sailed on a steamer along one of the long narrow lakes in the Telemark, Sophia abruptly decided to abandon Anna Charlotte to the companionship of a chance woman acquaintance who had joined their party. A steamer going in the opposite direction took Sophia to Skien; from there she proceeded to Christiania and Stockholm.

While Anna Charlotte was deeply disappointed by this development in their long-planned expedition, she did not remonstrate. In the past she had seen her friend, on a walk or at a party, all of a sudden withdraw from those present, give vague responses in conversation, and then suddenly say goodby, presumably to pursue some mathematical idea at home. As an author Anna Charlotte, in fact, had herself occasionally responded to the call of unexpected inspiration.

V

As IT turned out, Sophia had made not much more than a beginning on the mermaid problem, while staying with Mittag-Leffler's family at Jämtland, before a telegram called her again to Aniuta's bedside in Petersburg. Upon her departure Mittag-Leffler requested her to carry out in Russia the same mission she had successfully fulfilled in France, and which Chebyshev had not yet accomplished in Russia. He asked her to talk with Baron F. R. Osten-Saken, in the Ministry of Foreign Affairs, to seek support for *Acta Mathematica*. In this connection the full sequence of events appears to have been as follows. Possibly King Oscar II of Sweden, that enlightened monarch, but more probably Chebyshev, had written to Tsar Alexander III soliciting a Russian grant. The Tsar in turn, avoiding official channels, wrote unofficially either to Delianov, the Minister of Public Enlightenment, or perhaps to his wife, suggesting that support of the journal be given consideration. It might be presumed that such action from the supposed all-powerful ruler would get results, but such was not the way in Russia. Delianov had taken no favorable action. Therefore other avenues of influence had to be tried. Chebyshev was to see Count D. A. Tolstoy, Minister of Interior Affairs and honorary president of the Academy of Science, but had not done so by the time Sophia arrived. When Sophia had been a Petersburg student it was Tolstoy who had prevented opening the university freely to women.

Sophia had no more than greeted Aniuta before she addressed Osten-Saken, and in their subsequent interview the Baron, a scholar and geographer, reviled Delianov and complained of Russia's stinginess in everything involving science and education. Sophia explained how her national pride suffered because her homeland had not joined the other nations in the international journal. The Baron suggested that Chebyshev go to Count Tolstoy, as originally planned, and if he did not definitely oppose the project, then the Tsar could be persuaded to send him a personal letter that would flatter him into arranging a grant. Chebyshev did see Count Tolstoy and was rebuffed. Russia never supported the mathematical journal which continues active to this day.

Sophia's interview with the Baron had been a lengthy one lasting until nine o'clock in the evening. She then returned to the bedside of her sister. When, after some days, Aniuta showed some improvement, Sophia entrained for Moscow to pick up Fufu at Semenkov. Since Sophia was again in Russia, Julia thus did not have to bring the child to Stockholm as promised but did accompany them as far as Petersburg to see Aniuta and visit friends and relatives.

After again staying for a few days with Aniuta, Sophia returned to Stockholm. Mother and daughter arrived there at the end of August in 1886. Fufu, who was then eight years of age, eventually wrote her recollections of life with her mother. She hated to leave Julia, felt estranged from Sophia, and feared going to a strange land where everybody spoke an unknown tongue, *Svenska*, that her Russian playmates called "Svinska" (swinish). Moreover, during the three-day passage from Petersburg to Stockholm, Fufu was seasick much of the time. On arrival at sunset Sophia hired a cart to bring the luggage, and they proceeded on foot to her apartment. En route they passed through the municipal gardens, where, to the great pride of citizens, a tropical agave plant had bloomed for the first time. But Sophia walked lost in thought, so that Fufu felt forgotten, until her mother noticed her incipient tears and reassured her. The world became brighter for the little Russian on arrival at the apartment, where the maid, knowing how to deal with children, quickly made her feel at home and began teaching her the first necessary words of Swedish.

By going shopping with the maid Fufu quickly enlarged her vocabulary. Sophia always preferred to speak and read to her in Russian, partly for the pleasure of speaking her native tongue, partly because she had thoughts of leaving Sweden, partly because she didn't want Fufu to lose her command of Russian. Later on, however, she would boast to friends that when she gave orders to the servants Fufu sometimes corrected her Swedish.

One day Fufu asked the cause of her father's death, to which Sophia sorrowfully told her never to ask that question again. Thus for many years the child remained in ignorance of her father's suicide. In fact, Sophia didn't want to talk at all about Vladimir. Julia, however, except for not disclosing the manner of his end, had always answered all of Fufu's questions and had praised her father as a good and kind individual. It disturbed Sophia that her daughter seemed to display some of the weaknesses of Vladimir, such as lack of will and direction. Sophia enrolled her daughter in a summer class in gymnastics and accompanied her to participate in the sessions herself. Sophia also was in the habit of taking cold baths to offset mental labors.

By the time the summer holiday ended Fufu had met the children of Sophia's friends and could converse with them to a degree. By then she felt happy in her new surroundings. She liked Mittag-Leffler's gay and kind wife, and the Listers who had no children but had dogs and interesting picture books, and especially she liked the Guldens. "Professor Gulden was an astronomer and had a son my age and three older children," Fufu recalled. "They lived in a house with a tower [with telescope], surrounded by gardens, and I stayed there during my mother's frequent July-August absences. I felt myself a member of the family." She also had friendly recollections of Professors Nordenskiöld, the explorer, and Lekke, the zoologist. She recalled that professors and their families gathered for suppers and walks, had clubs to which they invited prominent actors and artists, or heard reports on scientific subjects.

Sophia enjoyed long walks in the forest-park bordering Stockholm, taking along her daughter and several Gulden children, and afterward having the group to dinner. "She was always merry and joked with us during these walks," Fufu recalled. "We could only go with her on our holidays, however. On weekdays after her lecture she would often walk with Mittag-Leffler and his sister or sometimes with one of her students."

Fufu recalled that their apartment furnishings, besides items purchased in Sweden, included pieces originally from Palibino. Chairs and two divans, from the old drawing room there, were of dark carved mahogany, upholstered in red damask, but the silk had worn in places. Such wear would have been ignored in Palibino, but the tidy Swedes would notice, and so Sophia covered the worn spots with antimacassars. For one old rocking chair that she favored she had embroidered a cover edged with red velvet, embroidery being for her a relaxation from mental work. In regard to this chair cover Sophia sent Anna Charlotte a teasing note: "Last evening I saw the brilliant proof of the assertion that your eyes notice only the ugly and disgusting in life. Every spot, every hole, of my ancient chairs are immediately discovered by you, even if they are covered by tens of antimacassars, but my wonderful, exquisite embroidery on the rocker went unnoticed, despite the fact that I was rocking in front of you all the time in a vain attempt to attract your attention. You didn't honor it with a single glance. Your Sonya."

Another piece of furniture, a cabinet in black wood, displayed on its doors portraits painted on porcelain plaques of Sophia's Shubert grandparents, the general in parade uniform and his wife in ball gown. A large Flemish picture and a mirror also recalled Sophia's Palibino childhood. Everything else came from Sweden.

Fufu remembered, too, how enthusiastic her mother had been over ice-skating. Fufu and her friends would be skating in the children's section and would see her mother skating nearby with Mittag-Leffler and his sister. She recalled the somewhat stiff movements of the threesome. Usually, however, Sophia skated on the so-called King's Rink, where children were excluded.

Maria Lekke, the professor's daughter, in her recollections mentioned often seeing the two professors skating together, and that Mittag-Leffler "accompanied her everywhere as a faithful knight," he with his "thick hair coming out from under his large fur hat," she "with her curls resembling Anna Karenina, wearing a wide skirt with a fur border and a fur-trimmed jacket with many pleats." She added: "It was said of them that they always engaged in mathematical conversations and wrote out mathematical formulas on ice with their skates, but the truth of this I never succeeded in learning."

Worldwide publicity about Sophia caused many persons to write with requests for money, autographs, or portraits. A paleontologist asked for samples of chalk from all parts of Sweden. A Swiss mother asked for her daughter to be found in Russia. Mathematicians sought copies of her work or technical periodicals not obtainable in their own land. One old Russian mathematician wrote that he valued and loved not only her mathematical greatness but her "entire elegant being."

The letters she especially welcomed, however, were those such as the one dated 8 October from Chebyshev thanking her for the photograph of herself and Fufu. "In it," he wrote, "I for the first time saw Sophia Vasilievna II, in whom already for seven years (from the time of the Petersburg meeting of natural scientists) I have been very interested because of the stories of her mother." He gave Sophia permission to translate and print his mathematical letter to her and informed her that the first of the formulas given in the letter had already proved necessary for his new work. He hoped the next holiday period would give him the pleasure of talking with her again about mathematics and mechanics.

Following Sophia's stay in Paris with Marie, their friendship had taken on a new intimacy. In September of 1886, with a Lapland puppy at her feet, Sophia wrote that thenceforth she would only trust the dog as a consolation in her old age, since Marie, that "cunning Pole," had not answered three of her letters. Marie answered at once with a letter that burned Sophia's fingers, with its description of Marie's throbbing heart. Sophia wanted to know whether he was blond or brunette and remarked; "How magnificent this lantern must be, and how strongly he must blind you with his brilliance, that you could overlook his not being a socialist." Earlier the two widows had used "bluebird" as a code word for suitors and "owls" for learned men. Apparently Marie had made some such remark as that the individual in question lighted up her life like a lantern. Sophia asked whether their mutual Polish friend, Pan Genrikh, was jealous and whether poor Mendelson, whom Marie had not yet married, had gone to Switzerland to avoid seeing her infatuation. Sophia assured Marie that she had examined her letter under a microscope and found *febris amorosis* bacteria and therefore pronounced her seriously ill. Then she jokingly admitted she was only jealous. She herself had three lanterns courting her, but unfortunately all three together had an age totaling over 200 years. Although that was an exaggeration, one was a 72-year-old English algebraist at Oxford, James J. Sylvester, who sent her a sonnet calling her "Muse of Heaven." A younger and more serious individual was editor of the most conservative newspaper in Stockholm; and the third was a wealthy minister of state who "speaks very little but when looking at me moves his eyes strangely." Of the latter she would not have believed he was courting her had she not been told so by others. She lamented that unfortunately Swedish males were born married; therefore one could count only on widowers. She ended by imploring "poor, sick, and dear Maria" to take pity on her anxiety and to write many details about her lantern.

During the ensuing autumn semester of 1886, as Sophia concurrently developed her work for the Bordin Prize, she also made "Theory of a Rigid Body" the subject of her lectures, and then continued the same subject through the spring semester. This permitted her to concentrate entirely on her mermaid problem (since her lectures in mechanics did not require extensive preparation). Probably her intention was to spur students into investigating the many aspects of the movement of rigid bodies under various forces, or at least aspects that were byproducts of the particular case being developed by her for the competition. This focusing of her thought on one subject enabled her to make progress in her investigation, and in fact allowed extra time for some literary work. During this period, and in fact always, Mittag-Leffler attended many of her lectures.

CHAPTER 20

Parting of the Sisters

i

AT THE start of the Christmas holidays in mid-December of 1886 Sophia departed at once for Petersburg. The severe weather permitted sailing only as far as Helsingfors. From there a train carried her the rest of the way. Fufu remained with the Guldens.

From Petersburg Sophia wrote Teresa Gulden: "I thank you sincerely for the detailed news that you send me about Sonya [Fufu] and your concern for her. Unfortunately my sister is in a deplorable state. Really nothing is so awful as these diseases that steal up on one. She is suffering very much; all her major organs are affected. . . . Forgive me that I can't write more today. I am myself in a very depressed state; I have just returned from her; she had a very serious attack of asthma and wished for death. It is terrible to see a person suffer and be totally incapable of giving any help. Once more I thank you for everything, my dear Teresa. I wish you all to spend the Christmas holidays happily and pleasantly."

The same envelope carried a letter for Fufu: "I thank you for your little letter, although it was very brief and not carefully written. You say nothing about whether you had fun at the Christmas tree party and what gifts you received? Did you like the hand sled, skates, and Swedish books that I asked Froken to give you? If you behave well I shall bring you several Russian books. Write me in detail how you spend the days. And don't write with such large spaces between the lines; then you will be able to write more in your letter. Also write to Urey [Aniuta's son] who waits impatiently for answers to his letters. Your nurse Mania is now with Ani and is taking good care of her as previously she had cared for you. She kisses you very much. Goodbye, my amiable dear little friend. I embrace you with my whole heart. Loving you, your mother."

Sophia had intended to spend only a week with Aniuta and then proceed on to Paris to meet Anna Charlotte and visit with Marie, before returning in mid-January to her Stockholm podium for the spring semester of 1887.

To Anna Charlotte she wrote on 18 December of her sister's illness and suffering, saying Aniuta was unable to sleep or breathe normally, and of her own longing for Fufu and her work table. Aniuta's ailments included liver trouble.

To Marie she described her sad days at Aniuta's bedside. Aniuta would have periods of relief when they reminisced together about their childhood and youth, causing Sophia to realize the immensity of the loss threatening her. Inevitably she contrasted the appearance of the wasted invalid with the recollection of her as a slender beauty with a mass of shining blond hair, a radiant expression, and expectations of a wonderful future. Now she believed Aniuta's recovery could only be the result of a miracle.

Sophia soon needed rest herself, but Aniuta implored her to remain, saying that Jaclar soon would be leaving for France. Therefore Sophia cancelled her Paris plans and remained until shortly before her lectures began again in mid-January. Fufu remembered that during the ensuing time in Stockholm her mother worried so over Aniuta that she lost weight, became very depressed, and almost didn't speak during dinner. Consequently Fufu attempted to spend as much time as possible with the Guldens.

Jaclar did not leave for France during the holidays as planned; but whether he was in or out of Russia, his long political activity had not gone unnoticed. He was still in Russia on 22 March 1887 when Count Tolstoy, the Minister of Internal Affairs, ordered him to leave the country within three days.

Jaclar appealed at once to Anna Grigoryevna, Dostoevsky's widow, asking her to see the guardian of her children, K. P. Pobedonostsev, to seek an extention of the order until he could put business affairs in order and make arrangements for the care of Aniuta, because he feared she would not survive if forced to accompany him to Paris. Anna Grigoryevna arranged a meeting with Pobedonostsev through his wife; and, as recorded in her recollections, had to listen to reproof for her friendship with persons harmful to Russia. Nevertheless, Pobedonostsev promised to help. This very conservative individual, the Tsar's old tutor, rose to power in 1882 and had a forceful policy influence on Russian affairs under two tsars and was then the cabinet minister in charge of church affairs. That he should have been the one to delay the administrative machinery on behalf of an enemy of the Tsar and

Church shows the influence of women on the leaders of men. He addressed the director of police, and on 4 April received the following reply:

"Gracious sir, Konstantin Petrovich—I hasten to bring to Your Excellency's attention that the Frenchman Jaclar, a member of the former Commune when living in Paris, was in constant contact with the representatives of the Polish revolutionary 'Proletariat' party, the Jew Karl [Stanislaus?] Mendelson, and thanks to Russian connections through his wife was involved in the transfer of Mendelson's letters to Warsaw. He is a friend of . . . many outstanding French radicals. From Petersburg Jaclar sent most false and harmful news into Paris about Russian political affair, and after the first of March (the undertaking of Ulianov) [i.e., terrorist attempts against the Tsar] this information passed all bounds of patience. That is why, at my insistence, the minister decided to send him beyond the borders of our empire.

"Considering the serious illness of his wife, and taking his word that he would send out no correspondence of any kind, I yesterday ordered his exile delayed for ten days."

Jaclar had the grace to thank Anna Grigoryevna by letter, requesting that she express his gratitude to both of the Pobedonostsevs, and at the end of the allotted time he left for Paris.

Aniuta at once called Sophia to her side, and so in late spring Sophia again set out for Russia, taking along Fufu for a holiday with Julia. While with Aniuta, Sophia wrote Anna Charlotte that she was too unsettled to do mathematical work but had been reading treatises "full of genius" by Poincaré. Also she had begun a novel, *Vae Victus*, which as she correctly predicted she would never finish. In mathematics she felt intellectually close to young Poincaré, who had been developing in her field of analysis. A year or two later, in fact, she based her lectures during an entire semester on his work.

For months past Sophia had been writing in collaboration with Anna Charlotte, but as always with anything she did, once the ideas had been worked out, she lost interest in the labor of polishing on which Anna Charlotte was engaged. But she did long for Anna's companionship. "You are the dearest thing I possess," she wrote, "and our friendship must at least last all my life." The friendship did last that long, but what a short life!

In midsummer Aniuta recovered to the point where she could travel. Having put Aniuta and her son safely on the train, Sophia collected Fufu from Julia's and returned to stay out the summer on an island near Stockholm. There once more she applied herself to mathematics and for relaxation read Runeberg's poems that had been recommended by Mittag-Leffler. She found the poems lacked something. "The *devil* is missing," she wrote him, "and without some touch of this high power there is no harmony in this world."

More than once Anna Charlotte had admonished Sophia about her careless habit of leaving letters about for anybody to read. From the island Sophia sent a jesting reaction:

"Poor Anna Charlotte! It seems that it is becoming a regular malady with you to think that your letters are going to fall into strange hands. The symptoms are getting more and more serious each time! I think anybody who writes such an unintelligible hand as yours ought not to be uneasy about this matter. I assure you that, with the exception of the few persons personally interested in what you write, you would hardly find anybody who would have the patience to decipher your scrawl. As to your last letter, it was, of course, lost in the post. When I finally did get it from the Dead Letter Office, I hastened to leave it open on the table for the benefit of the maids and the whole G_____ family. They all thought the letter rather well written, and that it contained rather interesting things. Today I intend to call on Professor Monbau in order to ask about translation from the Polish. I shall take your letter with me, and try my best to lose it in his reception room. I can do nothing better to make you a celebrity. Your devoted Sonya."

Aniuta had arrived ill in Paris. As Jaclar wrote occasionally for the daily socialist newspaper, *La Justice,* he turned for advice to its founder-editor, Georges Clemenceau, the wily politician and future Lion of France, who was then in the process of causing the downfall of General Boulanger, who sought to establish a monarchial regime. Himself a former physician, Clemenceau recommended competent doctors and by his presence at Aniuta's bedside encouraged them to do their best. Two surgical procedures were declared to be immediately necessary. In the first an abscess was removed from Aniuta's armpit; in the second, water was drained from a leg. This gave temporary relief, enabling her to go to Marie Mendelson's apartment with husband and son. Marie had turned over the apartment to them during her own extended foray into Poland. In September of 1887 Aniuta was again back in the hospital, for the removal of an ovarian cyst. As the surgeon was an outstanding one, Sophia in Stockholm felt assured of her sister's safe recovery. While convalescing at Marie's apartment at the end of October, however, Aniuta contracted pneumonia and within two days was dead.

Jaclar conveyed to Sophia the details of Aniuta's last illness, and sorrowing Sophia relayed the information to her Aunt Sophia Adelung and family in Stuttgart. She concluded by observing: "With my

sister's death the last thread that tied me to my childhood is broken."
Perhaps from her childhood nurse or from Palibino servants Sophia
had acquired a belief in dreams and revelations and forebodings. She
maintained, for instance, that she always had troubled dreams whenever somebody she loved was suffering, and the night before Aniuta
died she had very bad dreams. She hoped that her sister would appear
to her in a dream or apparition, but this consolation did not occur.

Perhaps she wished again, as she had recently written to Marie, for
an air balloon to supplant the grimy trains and rolling ships she had to
use on her many journeys. But it was just as well that attending the
funeral was impracticable. At least she could remember Aniuta only as
she had been when alive. Since Aniuta had been ill for so long, and
since death had been anticipated more than once, and since probably
she had not long to live in any case, Sophia's suffering was tempered
by relief that her sister's suffering was over at last. She did not go into
mourning. For Vladimir she had worn black for the customary period;
but she did not look well in black, and she had met, among others, a
charming young arctic explorer.

CHAPTER 21

Her Literary Life

i

SOPHIA'S GRADUAL development as an author will be more clear if overall chronology is interrupted to concentrate upon this aspect of her life.

Her old house tutor had recognized her talent when as a teenager she prepared schoolroom compositions; he had even envisioned the possibility of her becoming another George Sand or Jane Austen. Years of concentrated scientific study, however, followed by her hectic married life and subsequent events, had postponed any serious work in this field. It is true, from childhood on she had composed many verses in Russian, French, and later even in Swedish, and some of these would be printed posthumously; but these were only verses written by one without a true gift for poetic expression. Many verses, moreover, touch upon social themes that might better have been developed in prose. Usually her verses were dashed off as mental relief from scholarly labors, and it is no loss if all are forgotten.

The situation is quite different, on the other hand, with some of her other work, most prominently her *Recollections of Childhood*, which is worthy to stand beside Tolstoy's *Childhood, Boyhood, and Youth* and similar works by Aksakov and Turgenev, with the added advantage that of the four it is the only one portraying a Russian girlhood. Had she as a novelist achieved Tolstoy's or Turgenev's fame, doubtless her *Recollections* would be no less well known throughout the world today.

That Sophia should be successful both as a writer and as a mathematician occasioned some surprise among her contemporaries. One such was A. S. Montvid, a Russian woman who wrote under the name of A. S. Shabelskaia. "I understand your surprise," Sophia wrote her in the autumn of 1890, "that I can work at the same time with literature and mathematics. Many persons that have not studied mathematics confuse it with arithmetic and consider it a dry and arid science. Actually, however, this science requires great fantasy, and one of the first mathematicians of our century very correctly said that it is not possible to be a mathematician without having the soul of a poet. Of course it must be understood that one must abandon the old supposition that a poet must compose something non-existent, that fantasy and invention are one and the same.

"As far as I am concerned, during my life I could never decide whether I had a greater inclination toward mathematics or literature. Just as my mind would tire from purely abstract speculations, I would immediately be drawn to observations about life, about stories; at another time, contrarily, when life would begin to seem uninteresting and insignificant, then the incontrovertible laws of science would draw me to them. It may well be that in either of these spheres I would have done much more, had I devoted myself to one exclusively, but I nevertheless could never give up either one completely."

Sophia actually began her non-mathematical writing during 1876 in Petersburg, but that consisted of purely journalistic reviews of theatrical events and of new technological developments. The only exception was her story "Der Privatdozent" concerning university life in a small German town, based on her observations while in Heidelberg; it is believed that this was published in some obscure European periodical.

Not until years later did Sophia begin more serious writing with her article "Recollections of George Eliot." This appeared in June of 1886 in the literary-political journal *Russkaia mysl* (*Russian Thought*) and later was translated into Swedish, French, Polish, German, and other languages.

Sophia's own literary favorites, those that influenced her writing to some extent, included such foremost novelists of the period as Dickens, Tolstoy, and Turgenev, together with such writers as her friend Nekrasov and Julia's late relative Lermontov; and also such as L'Abbé Prévost, whose *Manon Lescaut* developed the theme of rehabilitation through love and suffering; and Friedrich Spielhagen's *In Rank and File*, in which the hero struggles to create a better world. Certainly she knew the novels of her friend Dostoevsky, although there is no indication that his works were among her favorites. If they were not, perhaps it was because she held the views of many of Dostoevsky's contemporaries who admired his great natural gifts and his ability to create characters but were put off by his limited artistic discipline, his questionable taste for those days, and his misrepresentation of the real Russian life they knew. Perhaps, too, Sophia did not care for his handling of nihilist type characters.

The 1880s marked the great period of Scandinavian romance, which dealt almost entirely with the problem of man versus woman, involving such themes as women's individuality and the double-standard in sex. It was the period of Ibsen, Bjornson, Strindberg, and Lie. In 1879 Ibsen, believing that equality of the sexes was important but that the feminine side of the question needed stronger support, wrote *A Doll's House*. When Nora slammed the door on her husband, leaving him because he valued respectability more than her self-sacrificing love, her act resounded throughout the western world. Two years later in *Ghosts*, Ibsen portrayed what happens when, unlike Nora, a wife remains with her husband and child. At first the message of these and other Ibsen plays met with hostility, but nevertheless exerted a wide influence and won Sophia's approval.

While familiarizing herself with Scandinavian literature and meeting its leading lights, Sophia also spread in Stockholm a knowledge of Russian literature, Tolstoy's work in particular, and likewise Lermontov's. She directed a Swedish translator to the poems of N. A. Dobroliubov and I. S. Nikitin. She thought that her Petersburg friend, the satirist M. E. Saltykov-Shchedrin, who wrote among other things *The God of the Gololevs*, should be known not only in Sweden but by Europeans in general; and in the year of his death, 1889, she wrote an article about him in French. Although this was rejected by French periodicals for lack of foreign interest in the novelist, whose typically Russian satire was not understood, it was published by the Swedish newspaper *Dagblad*. It was not published in Russia until 1934, because Saltykov-Shchedrin was in disfavor before for having shown that the conditions of the peasant had a humiliating influence upon the upper class.

Of her freedom to write in Sweden without regard to possible censorship as in Russia, Sophia remarked in a letter to S. A. Iurev, literary agent and founder of *Russian Thought*: "According to external forms of government Sweden is one of the most free countries in Europe; here one may say or write absolutely anything one wants. But here also, as to some extent in England, the influence of old traditions on society and the pressure of social opinion weigh heavily. Only in recent years have different modern ideas broken out concerning the economic injustice of the social order, the rights of women, the insolvent position of accepted theology, and the like. The lively and passionate feelings on such questions remind me somewhat of such questions as we had in Russia 15 years ago."

ii

DURING THE early part of 1887, confident that she was well on the way to solving the mermaid problem, but being temporarily weary of equations, Sophia felt justified in seeking a change of pace. For a long time she had wanted to collaborate on a play with Anna Charlotte, with whom, during their trip into Norway, she had exchanged ideas of life and love and had formed a closer friendship than ever before.

Anna Charlotte was tall, whereas Sophia was not; fair, by contrast with Sophia's dark complexion; dignified in motion, while the Little Sparrow's movements were quick and restless; cordial on first acquaintance, whereas Sophia frequently had to overcome shyness. Anna was no beauty, facially less attractive than Sophia, and in physique rather angular. Her early marriage having been a peculiar one in which she apparently lived with her husband like a sister, she had full freedom for travel and a literary life; in her person, as an ardent advocate of women's emancipation, she exemplified what was then known as the modern woman.

If her husband was merely friendly, her three brothers all but adored her. The two older ones had guided her higher education, since she was denied entrance to Swedish universities, into the serious study of the Swedish language, literature, and history, so that at the age of twenty she had already published a book of tales under her pseudonym of "Carlot." At the age of twenty-three she wrote her first play, which ran an entire winter in Stockholm. In it, well before Ibsen's work, she wrote that love in a woman must be subordinated to duty, not a limited conjugal duty, but rather a wider duty to self and mankind. In middle age, however, when she entered an exceedingly happy marriage with an Italian duke, her views on love underwent a decided change. Before that, before reaching the age of thirty, three more of her plays had been staged, and not until the fourth appeared did it become known that the author of plays, novels, and stories was a woman.

Anna Charlotte's friend, Lily Wolffsohn, described her as a person void of vanity and pretense, utterly sincere, strong but not violent, and above all kind and loving. More than any other writer of her time she fought with courageous energy for the emancipation of women, her work being translated into Danish, German, Russian, and some into English. No wonder Sophia admired her, although not with the regard she had for Marie Mendelson.

Anna Charlotte seems to have had a mostly just appraisal of Sophia's complex and sometimes baffling character, at least to the extent that she apparently did her best to provide in Stockholm what Sophia needed, a close friendship with intellectual stimulation. She knew that Sophia required contact with the genius of others in order to accomplish productive work on her own. Probably she was encouraged in this by her brother. Although a competent mathematician and Sophia's constant friend, he was essentially a teacher and not an original thinker able to strike sparks from her intellect. In mathematics she missed the intellectual ferment provided by Weierstrass and Hermite and, increasingly, by the young Poincaré. But in literature Anna could and did inspire her.

Thus it happened that during the early part of the year, when ice coated the streets and nights seemed endless, the two women began collaborating on a play. As Sophia later wrote to her cousin, Sophia Adelung, who had produced and illustrated several children's books: "I suggested the theme and the development of the action; the sequence of scenes we planned together; and she wrote in Swedish. By the way, in saying 'play' I am expressing myself incorrectly, as it isn't actually one play—this is the most original part of the work—but two parallel plays under one title, *The Struggle for Happiness* (in Swedish *Kampen för lyckam*). The principal characters in both parts are one and the same, and both parts have the same prologue. The first play represents that which really happened and the second that which might have happened."

For several months Anna Charlotte quite happily put aside work on her new novel, *Unmarried*, to express Sophia's ideas in Swedish. She wrote on 2 February 1887 to a friend that the drama would occupy two evenings. In the first part "everyone is unhappy, because, in real life, people generally hinder rather than further one another's happiness. In the second part, the same personages assist one another, form a little ideal commune, and are happy." She went on to say: "I already see Sonya and myself collaborating on a work that will have a worldwide success, at least in the present, and perhaps also in the future. We are quite foolish about it. If we can only do this, it would reconcile us to everything. Sonya would forget that Sweden is the greatest *Philistia* on earth, and would no longer complain that she is wasting the best years of her life here. And I—well, I should forget all that I am brooding over."

As an experienced playwright, Anna Charlotte had some doubt about the dramatic validity of their project but ignored the question during the enthusiasm of actual collaborative work. During the following week, as Sophia unfolded the plot and scenes of what she had first conceived as a novel, Anna wrote again to her friend: "Sonya is overjoyed by this new project, and the fresh possibility in her life. She says she now understands how a man grows more and more deeply in love with the mother of his children. Of course *I* am the mother, because I am to bring this mental offspring into the world; and she is so devoted to me that it makes me happy to see her beaming eyes. We enjoy ourselves immensely. I do not think two women friends have ever enjoyed each other's society as much as we do—and we will be the first example in literature of two woman collaborators. I have never been so kindled by an idea as by this one. As soon as Sonya told me about it, it shot through me like a thunderbolt. It was a real explosion. . . . When she left me I sat up half the night in my rocking chair, and when I went to bed the whole plot lay clear before me."

After one more discussion with Sophia, she began to write, and within five days—working much faster than she ever had before—she produced the first draft of the first half of the drama, consisting of prologue and five acts.

Six weeks later, to the same friend, Anna Charlotte wrote of the play: "I believe in it because it is Sonya's idea, for naturally it is much easier for me to believe that she is inspired than to believe such a thing of myself. She, on the other hand, admires my work, the spirit and artistic form that I give to the design. It would be impossible to have a better arrangement. It is delightful to be able to admire one's own work without conceit. I have never felt so much confidence or so little misgiving. If we fail I think that we must commit suicide."

In answer to her correspondent's query about their method of work, she replied: "It is quite true that she has not written a single sentence. But she has not only originated the whole but has also thought out the contents of each act. She has given me besides several psychological traits for the building up of the characters. We read daily what I have done, and she makes remarks and offers suggestions. She asks to hear it over and over again, as children ask for their favorite tales. She thinks nothing in all the world could be more interesting."

Anna Charlotte recorded in her memoir of Sophia that each day after finishing work they would walk into the woods, where Sophia would shout with exultation, take Anna into her arms, dance around her, and exclaim that life was beautiful, while cherishing the most exaggerated hopes for their drama.

Alas, on 9 March close friends heard the first reading of the play. Their dampening criticism disclosed serious shortcomings, some due to the feverish haste of composition. Time had come for the tedious process of revision. This continued through the Swedish spring, with its full tidal wave of new growth spreading across the countryside and into villa gardens; and then work continued into summer, when daylight monotonously persisted almost round the clock and one could read the large type of a newspaper at midnight.

Realizing that she had lost her perspective, Anna Charlotte had to forbid Sophia entrance to her study in an effort to doctor the play. "The desire for solitude, so strong in me, has been denied," she wrote to her friend. "My personality has been merged into Sonya's by her powerful influence, and still her individuality has not had full expression. The whole strength of my working power lies in solitude, and this is the chief objection to collaboration, even with such a sympathetic nature as Sonya's. She is the complement of my nature. She is the Alisa in *The Struggle for Happiness*, who cannot create anything nor embrace anything with her whole heart unless she can share it with another. Everything she has produced in mathematical work has been influenced by somebody else, and even her lectures are only successful when Gösta [Mittag-Leffler] is present." This characteristic Sophia herself recognized, as on one occasion when she wrote to Mittag-Leffler: "I shall try to lecture as well as though you were there."

That need for support, for union with another, Sophia expressed in the first part of the play, together with her loneliness and want of self-confidence. She is Alisa seeking common interests with Karl, the character in which she exorcised the ghost of Vladimir. The couple feels little attraction for one another but nevertheless attempts to love one another. Alisa grows bitter when Karl draws back. She will not listen to reason. She tried to force him to be true to himself, to his calling, to their love. In the second part of the drama—as things might have been—Alisa breaks with her past life to live and work with Karl in a garret. There Karl is happy (as Sophia fancies Vladimir might have been), and Alisa dreams about a great labor federation in a state of the future. The burden of the play is that love and love alone means everything in life; that personal growth and strength flows from love; that through love duty can be fulfilled.

Revising the play took much longer than its original composition and had not reached completion by early summer, when the two authors had planned to visit Berlin and Paris together. Aniuta's illness, however, called Sophia to Petersburg, as previously mentioned. When Sophia returned again to her Stockholm apartment, the revision of the play resumed. Golden autumn turned into Indian summer before this was finished. In her sunny room, as she sat at her table concentrating again on mathematical work, gusts of wind blew leaves like birds past her window until the trees were stripped bare.

In late December the drama appeared in print under the pseudonym of Korvin-Leffler and was favorably reviewed by the press but the Stockholm Dramatic Theatre declined to produce it. Obviously it was more a play to be read than acted. A request came to translate it into German, and in 1892 a Russian version came out in Kiev. The play had its first stage presentation as a benefit performance in Petersburg in 1894 and was the first dramatic work to deal with the labor question. Between then and 1905 it was produced in two other Russian cities. Although praised by partisan reviewers, it was not a dramatic success.

Even though Sophia desired further collaboration, on a novel, Anna Charlotte now knew she could only succeed on her own. As she pointed out to Sophia, a play, being somewhat of an artificial creation, permitted collaboration, but for a novel two hearts cannot beat alike. Moreover, Sophia's friendship, with all its exactions, had come to be somewhat oppressive. As Anna observed: "Her friendship, as afterward also her love, was tyrannical in the sense that she would not allow to anyone she loved a feeling, an affection, or a thought of which she was not the object. She wished to have such full possession of the person of whom she was fond that it almost excluded the possibility of individual life in that other person. . . . The very foundation of friendship must be the individual liberty of each friend."

And so it was, more with relief than regret, that Anna Charlotte parted from Sophia at the start of the inter-semester holiday of 1887-1888. She accompanied her brother and his wife to a mathematical congress in Algiers. En route home they paused in Naples to meet Pasquale del Pezzo, Duke of Cajanello, professor of mathematics at Naples University. This was the beginning of Anna Charlotte's romance.

iii

THE NOVEL on which Sophia wanted to collaborate apparently would have been called *Vae Victus*, conceived in the summer of 1887 and perhaps started on her own early the following year. In it the awakening of nature in the spring was to have symbolized the uprising of the downtrodden. It would have traced the loves of various individuals and Sophia's own inner life. This *may* have been the work in which Sophia had intended to include as characters three explorers, two being her friends, the silver-haired Baron Nordenskiöld and the youthful Fridtjof Nansen. She only completed a preface, which was translated from Russian into Swedish and published in *Jul Almanack* in 1889.

Sophia had first met Nordenskiöld on the evening of her introduction to Stockholm society. During part of her time in Sweden he was on the university's faculty. In 1887 he had only recently returned from Greenland. Born a Finn, he had as a young man been expelled from his country by Russia for his political views. Subsequently he had participated in numerous Swedish expeditions, on one of which he had unearthed in Spitsbergen remains of such trees as poplar and magnolia that grow only in temperate climates. From this he theorized that Greenland had not after all been misnamed, but that in some remote valley behind its forbidding mountains, protected from Arctic winds and perhaps warmed by hot springs, he might find a verdant Eden surviving from an earlier age. He found no such Shangri-La, to be sure, but his long snowshoe trek mapped part of Greenland's interior. Before that, Nordenskiöld had accomplished in 1878-1879 what had thwarted explorers for three centuries. He took stout *Vega* from Gothenburg, Sweden, through the fabled northeast passage to Alaska, and home through the Suez Canal, thus circumnavigating Eurasia. But in conversing with Sophia the explorer was interested not in exploration but in the state of socialism in Russia and asked her to recommend books explaining the goals of the parties there. Not knowing such political works, she promised to inquire.

As for Nansen, the second explorer, he apparently first met Sophia early in 1887 when he was in Stockholm planning his 1888 expedition to Greenland, during which he would cross that forbidding land from sea to sea in latitude sixty-four degrees north. His famous exploit with the vessel *Fram* lay yet several years in the future. There arose between Sophia and Nansen a strong mutual attraction. From as early as 1885 he had been interested in meeting Sophia, having in that year read about her in a letter to his literary relative, Peter Nansen, from the Danish novelist and poet, Herman Bang. Later published in Bang's *Wanderings*, the letter described Anna Charlotte's drawing room where pleasant people gathered as a "bit of Europe in a land of barbarians." The letter continued: "Particularly interesting is Mme. Kovalevsky. She is a professor of mathematics but with all her algebra is still a real lady. She laughs like a child, smiles like a mature and wise woman, and she possesses that magical artistry of first disclosing her thought only partially and then remaining silent, and with this silence to say everything. On her face there are such quick changes of light and shadow, that it either flushes or pales; I have never before met anything similar. She leads the conversation in French, speaking it freely, and accompanying her speech with quick gestures. This might have a tiring effect were it not charming; with all that, she resembles a kitten. Listening at the same time to her and to Anna Charlotte one experiences an odd sensation. The measured words of Anna Charlotte, pronounced in a cold tone, cut as with a knife the sparkling lace of Kovalevsky's conversation."

When Nansen and Sophia finally met, their attraction was mutual.

During several meetings he recounted the story of his life, of his boy-hood desire to become a great hunter, how the explosion of his home-made gun nearly blinded him, how fish hook and sharp ice had caused his facial scars. He related the Lapland legend that the spirits of ice age people slumbered in the ice fields of Greenland. But he left Stockholm without indicating to Sophia the possibility of an attachment closer than friendship. He did later on tell Anna Charlotte that under dif-ferent conditions Sophia could have had a deciding influence on his life. His undeclared barrier was his long engagement to another, whom he finally married after returning from Greenland.

Sophia was ironical about his departure. "Such is life," she remarked to Anna Charlotte. "In everything one gets not what one de-sires, not what one considers essential. Everything but not that. Some other person must receive the happiness that I wanted for myself and about which I dreamed. Apparently the dishes are poorly served in the great banquet of life, because some guests take, as though from beneath a cover, portions not intended for them but for others."

iv

OTHER STOCKHOLM friends of Sophia's included Victoria Benedikt-sen, the writer, and Karl Hjalmar Branting, in appearance an ancient Viking, with whom she could speak of political affairs without fear. A man of small means and large family, Branting was connected with a socialist-democratic paper and had been jailed for insulting king and church in print. Not until she felt her position in Sweden to be secure did Sophia join those that gathered at his house.

Apart from Anna Charlotte, Ellen Key was Sophia's first Stockholm feminine friend who was interested in other than housewifely duties. Ellen taught Fufu and the children of other professors at the School of Anna Vitlok. Although she had never attended school herself, Ellen had learned Swedish, French, German and other subjects under home tutors. When her landowning father went bankrupt she became a pro-gressive teacher, whose pupils loved her, partly because she set aside discipline for free behavior. Sophia would argue about this policy when lack of some pupil's discipline caused trouble for Fufu. Sophia had sought a meeting with her, partly because of their common interest in education, partly because Sophia learned that Ellen as a girl had been as enthusiastically in favor of the Polish uprising as she herself had been.

It was Ellen who, in describing Sophia's handshake, unwittingly indicated that Sophia, generous as she was in sharing her learning and ideas with students and friends, yet tended to hold back her essential physical self. "When she greeted somebody," Ellen wrote, "she stretched out her hand with an abruptly quick movement, and then her thin and nervous fingers would slip from the other person's hand, as though they were feathers of a momentarily caught bird."

Sophia introduced Ellen to Russian literature and gave her letters of introduction to such socialist friends as Folmar in Germany and Prince Peter Kropotkin, the geographer who then lived in England. Ellen in turn accepted Sophia into her *Tolfern* (Nineteen), a society of nineteen active women in different professions. This circle, which Anna Charlotte also joined, met regularly to introduce visiting foreign writers and others to Stockholm women.

One of those foreign visitors was Georg Brandes, the Danish literary critic and authority on Shakespeare, who called on Anna Charlotte whenever he visited Stockholm. He was the author of books on Ibsen, Napoleon, and Garibaldi, also on Poland and Russia, and he lectured before large European audiences on nineteenth century literature. In Sophia he took a particular interest, partly because she had been rejected by her own country, as he in his youth had been rejected by Denmark. He found in her a skillful conversationalist who did not hesitate to oppose some of his ideas. Believing that persons of genius were the source of culture, he much admired her logical mind and feminine charm.

This lean and Mephistophelean-appearing individual, with his cutting glance and ironic smile, introduced Sophia to Henrik Ibsen, the Norwegian who spent most of his time in foreign lands. In contrast to Brandes, Ibsen was a short and stocky and quietly serious man. He dressed carefully and had gentlemanly manners. He had a small mirror fastened inside his silk top hat for use when combing his ruff of whiskers and mane of hair. Sophia did not become a close friend of his but did penetrate his austere exterior to the warm and gentle man within. She of course agreed with the themes of his famous plays. It was Ibsen who advised Anna Charlotte, when in later years he learned she was writing her recollections of Sophia, that the latter could only be successfully depicted in a highly poetic manner.

V

SOPHIA'S NEXT published work after the play concerned new methods of treating mental patients in France. "In the Hospital La Charité" and "In the Hospital La Salpetrière" appeared in October and November in *Russkie vedomosti* (*The Russian Gazette*). Jaclar in Paris had escorted her to the first hospital, where she witnessed the hypnotizing of two mental patients. She had been taken to the second hospital, a women's institution with several thousand beds, by a physician friend. They heard a lecture during which the famous Jean

M. Charcot, head of the section for the mentally unbalanced, examined and diagnosed patients for medical students. The scenes she saw in these institutions, the handling of patients as though they were mere deaf and unfeeling animals, greatly depressed her.

Next she wrote her sketch, "Three Days in a Peasant University." This was the product of her Norwegian trip several years earlier with Anna Charlotte and reflected her interest in universal education. It was not published until 1890 in *Severnyi vestnik* (*Northern Messenger*).

The death of Sophia's beloved sister turned her thoughts back to their earlier days together and resulted in the writing of *Recollections of Childhood*. Of all her mother's literary activity Fufu only remembered the writing of *Recollections*, because during this time she overheard many conversations on the subject with Anna Charlotte and Ellen Key at Sophia's apartment. Some chapters Sophia wrote in Russian, some directly in Swedish; the first were translated and the second corrected by the sister of a Stockholm writer. Then each all-Swedish chapter as completed was read aloud to Sophia's friends. Hearing these memories of her mother's early life fascinated Fufu and brought her much closer emotionally to her mother.

In the Swedish version Sophia wrote in the third person, calling herself Tanya Raevsky, and the Swedish and Danish editions were called *Our Russian Life: the Raevsky Sisters*. The book appeared in Stockholm about Christmas in 1889 and had great success. It was read by both children and adults, and Fufu was much prouder of her mother's literary position than of her scientific one. When anybody asked Fufu whether she loved mathematics, she would always reply that she resembled her father and was entirely inept in mathematics.

During the year 1890 Sophia translated the Swedish version of *Recollections* into Russian, eliminating the fictional Raevsky surname, and making numerous revisions and deletions, both to improve the work and to avoid possible trouble with Russian censorship. New chapters were written; the Dostoevsky affair was expanded; mention was made of certain Russian customs or things that Swedes would not have understood. In late summer *Recollections* appeared in successive issues of *Vestnik Evropy* (*The European Messenger*), and Sophia's literary reputation was established firmly.

At age forty Sophia had more reason than ever before to conceal her age. She was madly in love with an elusive Russian. Thus in *Recollections* she was carefully vague or definitely misleading about her age in connection with datable events. For example, she indicated she was only thirteen when she first met Dostoevsky, whereas actually she was fifteen; and he was then forty-four, older by a year or two than she implied. As a result she conveyed the impression that in 1890 she was only about thirty-six years old. Several years after her death it was still supposed that 1854 was her birthdate. Only the disclosure by her brother finally corrected this to 1850.

In writing to compliment Sophia on *Recollections* Marie offered to be godmother for a French edition. Sophia replied that it had already been translated into French by a Stockholm woman and approved for style by the French consul, who had undertaken to have it published in a French periodical. For whatever reason the French version did not appear, however, until 1894 in *La Revue de Paris*. It subsequently came out as a French book with Anna Charlotte's memoirs of Sophia between the same covers. In the same combination it became available in German and English translations. At different times *Recollections* also appeared in Polish (Marie's translation), in Czech, and in other languages, based on translations either from the Swedish or Russian originals.

The first publication in Russia of *Recollections* in book form was in 1893, in a volume that also included "Recollections of George Eliot," the fragment from *"Vae Victus,"* "Three Days in a Peasant University," "Fragment from a Novel Occurring on the Riviera," "Posthumous Poetry," a letter about Swedish life, and recollections of Sophia by her brother and by Julia. These autobiographical and biographical writings were selected by M. M. Kovalevsky, Alexander, Lamansky, and Julia. They wanted to include a *Recollections* chapter on the Polish uprising and a long autobiographical excerpt called "The Vorontsov Family" from her novel *The Nihilist*, but these were rejected by the censors.

In reviewing Sophia's recollections in 1893 in his *Russian Antiquity*, a magazine favored by the Tsar's family and the aristocracy, M. I. Semevsky wrote:

"Lovely days, charming days. I relive them again reading *Recollections of Childhood*. Have you read them? No? Read them unfailingly. These are excellent descriptions of the life of a wealthy landowner's family in the 1850s and 1860s, sketches that are accurate in the highest degree, to which we can witness, since we know the major details referring specifically to the owners of the little village Palibino, sketches drawn with a master's brush by the author-artist. These recollections may be placed beside the best of similar pages from the compositions of I. S. Turgenev and Count L. N. Tolstoy."

vi

Sophia's last literary work was a novel, apparently begun about 1887, of which she left two manuscript versions, neither being titled or quite in final form. One draft had some chapters in Swedish, because she wrote them to read before a Stockholm literary society. Too late she realized that the subject matter of the novel probably would not pass Russian censorship. Thus, having decided to publish in a foreign language, and having tentatively approached French and English publishers, she made a partial second draft in order to make clear certain details and events that otherwise would be understandable only to Russians.

From the two versions Anna Charlotte, Ellen Key, and M. M. Kovalevsky formed one text, and this in 1892 appeared in Swedish as *Vera Vorontsova*, the name of the title character. Later that same year a Russian version titled *The Nihilist* (*Nigilistka*, feminine form) with an anonymous preface by Kovalevsky, came out in Geneva, where subsequent editions were issued in 1895 and 1899. Over a period of eighteen years other editions appeared in German, French, Polish, and Czech. In 1895 as *Vera Vorontsoff* an English edition became available, translated from the Swedish by Anna von Rydingsvard.

For many years only illegal copies of the novel circulated in Russia, however. The one exception was the Czech version, which the censors considered harmless since few in Russia could read that language. Official objection was to the overly sympathetic depiction of political prisoners and the expressed approval of the nihilist movement. When the political climate temporarily changed, permission was granted for a Moscow edition in 1906, with proceeds going to benefit political prisoners. But in 1915 the censors rejected a petition for another edition, so that the novel remained out-of-print in Russia until 1928 when —the term nihilist having lost its former meaning—it appeared as *The Proletary* (*Proletarii*).

The principal characters of the novel were loosely based on Vera Sergeevna Goncharovna, niece of Alexander Pushkin's wife, and probably on Nicholas G. Chernyshevsky, about whom at age eighteen Sophia had resolved some day to write. Chernyshevsky, the philosophical revolutionist, had been subjected to a civil "execution," as already mentioned in an earlier chapter, before being sent to hard labor in Siberian mines. Although Sophia never knew him personally, she had been influenced, by his ideas without accepting his more extreme views.

In depicting Vera's imaginary life Sophia simply remembered her own life at Palibino and drew from incident and description on what she herself experienced. Vera's father, Count Vorontzov, unlike General Korvin-Krukovsky, wasted his substance and encountered financial disaster as a result of the emancipation of serfs. Consequently, unable to continue studying under governess and tutor, the Young Vera receives instruction from a neighbor, the revolutionary Professor Vas-iltsev (Chernyshevsky?), who indoctrinates her in nihilism. (It will be recalled that the professor of physics living adjacent to Palibino, who definitely was not a nihilist, had advised that Sophia be permitted to study higher mathematics.) Vera falls in love with the middle-aged professor and marriage is imminent just as he is arrested and exiled to hard labor. For several years they correspond until the professor dies.

Now quite adult and impoverished, Vera goes to Petersburg to devote herself to the work for which the professor sacrificed himself. There she becomes friendly with the narrator of the novel, who outlines political conditions in the year 1876. At about that time fifty-seven young nihilists actually were on trial, although none in fact was exiled. In the story, however, six ringleaders are to be sent to Siberia. It was customary for men whose wives accompanied them to be sent to southern Siberia to be, in effect, pioneers where the climate was much like that in Moscow. Therefore Vera resolved to marry a Jew who otherwise would be sent to northern Siberia. Having met him in prison for the first time, she obtains his agreement to her sacrifice, uses her aristocratic connections with highest authorities to gain the Tsar's permission to marry, and as the two depart together as exiles, Vera nobly exclaims: "Ah, if only you knew how sorry I feel for all of you who must remain behind."

Except for the marriage theme, very little else in the story came from Goncharovna's real life. Actually in 1877 Sophia had introduced her to a medical student who subsequently was arrested on a political charge. She prepared to accompany him to Siberia, but upon his release they left Russia illegally and married in Paris. There several years later Sophia found the unhappy young woman linked to a tyrannical husband who spent on his own pleasures the allowance sent by her parents. Burdened by a baby, the once beautiful woman had become a sickly shadow of herself. Sophia provided money and her own passport for her to run off to Russia and later outfaced the furious husband when he threatened to disfigure her with acid.

As a novel *The Nihilist* is rather thin, obviously more appreciated in its day for its propaganda content than for character development and believable motivation. It would doubtless have been a better novel, more realistic in the manner of Tolstoy's *Resurrection*, had Sophia followed more closely the actual sequence of Goncharova's marriage and disillusionment, but that, of course, would have blunted her ideological intention. The book as it stands does have merit. Portions describing rural nature and changes of season mark Sophia as an observing individual. The scenes at the time of the emancipation procla-

mation obviously are those of an eye witness. Near the end of the book
the courtroom scenes during the trial of the conspirators also are well
handled, particularly in portraying the interaction of emotions between the accused and the aristocratic spectators, the latter at first
merely curious but gradually becoming sympathetic. The book does
suggest that had Sophia concentrated on writing fiction she might
have developed into a first rate novelist.

CHAPTER 22

Love Again and Glory, too

i

On one of her Paris visits Sophia had become reacquainted through P. L. Lavrov with a liberal Russian jurist and sociologist, Maksim Maksimovich Kovalevsky, a wealthy collateral relation of her late husband, whom they had met years before in Moscow.

It happened that when Anna Charlotte left on a European tour she carried Sophia's letter of introduction to this individual, who was then in London. While there Anna received word of the death of a young Swedish economist whom she had just visited during his last illness in Italy. Partly due to her influence the economist had left his entire fortune of about 200,000 *kronor* to create in Sweden an Institute of Social Science. Its purpose was to further by lectures and new books a better understanding of sociology, political science, agricultural economy, labor problems, credit unions, and so forth. This he wanted done without delay and named a committee of professors and writers, headed by the rector of the Medical Academy and including Anna Charlotte and Sophia among the members. Having been much impressed by Maksim Maksimovich, Anna wrote Sophia proposing that he be considered by the committee to lay the foundation in Sweden for the teaching of the social sciences.

The thought of being joined by a compatriot was of course most pleasing to Sophia, who lost no time in proposing his name to others of the committee, and having obtained favorable reports from foreign scholars regarding the candidate, the committee concurred in choosing him.

Fat Maksim, as Sophia would at first refer to him occasionally in letters to friends, was a bachelor and one or two years younger than she. He was tall, heavy, had a French spade beard, a deep rolling laugh, and

[279]

was as impressive as a lord. After taking a law degree in Russia he had studied in Berlin, Vienna, Paris, and London, and then for ten years had been professor of governmental law at Moscow University. Being witty, ironical, and erudite, he attracted a great many students from all faculties to his lectures; and on Thursday evenings at his apartment, scholars and writers, including Sophia's friend, Turgenev, would gather for gregarious and far-ranging discussions. Maksim's popularity with students, however, drew the jealousy of other professors and official attention, so that his criticism of the "autocratic-bureaucratic" regime caused his dismissal. Deprived of his post, Maksim spent his time traveling or on his estate near Kharkov. Consequently he was free to accept the Swedish invitation, which permitted him to lecture either in French or German and to nominate future lecturers. He also spoke English, Italian, some Spanish, and read classical and medieval Latin and archaic Norman-French.

Upon arriving in Stockholm on 1 February 1888, he immediately called upon Sophia, who briefed him on Swedish politics and personalities. In the evening he returned to 56 Sturegatan, 4th stairway, where she then lived, to meet her friends, Ellen Key, Mittag-Leffler, Professor Gulden, Baron Nordenskiöld, and the socialist Karl Hjalmar Branting, all or most of whom were on the committee.

These first two visits, as Maksim later recorded, were enough to convince him of the important role Sophia played in the Swedish capital. "They sang her praises; they were enraptured with her and proud." After several more meetings with her he also realized "how lonely this woman felt in a foreign country, how everything Russian was close to her heart."

Her friendship with Maksim progressed rapidly, advanced by the fact that he slipped on the ice and twisted his leg; she called on him several times at the Grand Hotel, where under the manipulations of a masseur he soon recovered. Their association in this way was daring for that time and place. Sophia was an aristocrat in a basically provincial and middle-class society. But as Maksim declared in a note inviting her to lunch: "In my opinion, if one is going to break the laws, then do so to the end." And so she did. They saw one another daily, discussing her literary work and his. He had been engaged with questions of comparative ethnology and the history of law and institutions for a book on Caucasia. He found Sophia's quick ability to assimilate new ideas, in these and other areas, and to form independent opinions and to criticize conclusions, to be truly amazing.

The range of Maksim's own expertise may be inferred from the topics on which he had lectured in Moscow: the history of governmental institutions, the characteristics of contemporary political orders, the growth of American institutions, the comparative history of the family and property, the nature of society in Russia and the west, and ancient laws and processes. While he had no interest in mathematics, Sophia was eager to draw him out on subjects in his field. He came to her speaking the language of her homeland, of her beloved sister, of her childhood, and with the approach of spring her lingering emotional involvement with Nansen had been replaced by an attraction to Maksim, which at first she tried to regard with a rather ironical detachment.

Because of him, however, she could not concentrate on her mathematical work. The deadline approached. She wrote a note to Mittag-Leffler remarking on her inability to bring her work to a conclusion. "The worst is this," she said, "that I am so exhausted that I just sit and think for entire hours about some simple thing that under other circumstances I could easily solve in one hour."

Mittag-Leffler intervened at once by requesting Maksim to go to Uppsala for at least a week so that Sophia could complete her work.

Anna Charlotte was by this time in Italy again and from Rome inquired about Nansen vs. Maksim, to which Sophia responded: "You ask me questions that I do not even want to answer myself. I am afraid of making plans for the future. The only thing that is unfortunately certain is that I must spend two months and one-half in Stockholm." Anna Charlotte replied that she had learned from Scandinavian friends that Nansen had been engaged for two years.

To this news, Maksim having just left for Uppsala, Sophia replied: "[In French, from *Rigoletto*] 'Woman changes very often, and the one who believes her is crazy.' If I had received your letter with its awful news a few weeks ago, it would no doubt have broken my heart. But now I confess to my shame, that when I read your deeply sympathetic lines yesterday, I could not help breaking out into laughter. It was a hard day for me, because fat Maksim was leaving that evening. I hope some of the family have already told you of the change in our plans, so that I need not mention that subject now. On the whole, I think this change to be good for me personally. For if fat Maksim had stayed longer, I do not know how I should have got on with my work. He is so great, so *grossgeschlagen* . . . that he really takes up too much room on the divan and in one's mind. It is simply impossible for me, in his presence, to think of anybody or anything else but him. During the 10 days he spent in Stockholm we were constantly together, generally *téte-à-téte*, and spoke of scarcely anything but ourselves, and that with a frankness that would have amazed you. Still, I cannot, in spite of all this, analyze my feeling for him. I think I could best give my impressions of him in music set to De Musset's incomparable words:

> He is very joyful, and at the same time very gloomy—
> Disagreeable neighbor, excellent comrade—
> Extremely light-minded, and yet very affected—
> Indignantly naive, nevertheless very blasé—
> Terribly sincere, and at the same time very sly.

A real Russian he is into the bargain."

She went on to say: "I have never been so tempted to write romance as when with fat Maksim. Despite his vast proportions—which, by the way, are quite in keeping with the character of a Russian *boyar*—he is still the most perfect hero for a novel (a realistic novel, of course) that I have ever met with. I believe that he also is a good critic, with a touch of the sacred fire."

During Maksim's absence Sophia did finish the first draft of her mathematical work. It contained the final solution of the problem, which actually she had achieved somewhat earlier by extending the ideas of Weierstrass on ultraelliptic integrals. Considering time as a complex variable, she had applied the theory of functions to the problem, which included the motion of a pendulum and to some extent of a top and a gyroscope. She realized, however, that she could not polish the paper in time to meet the deadline. She therefore wrote to Hermite of her success but requested to be permitted to submit a first draft and later to have the final version substituted.

Presumably preserving her anonymity, Hermite consulted the judges, who agreed to the proposal, because they had decided anyway to delay the judging until October. In his reply to Sophia, Hermite stated: "It will be pleasant for me to pick up the corn from the field reaped by you." He further said he was dreaming of studying the way in which her hyperelliptic integrals were used in the problem.

Sophia also wrote to Weierstrass, but he, despite his high opinion of her, expressed doubt that she had really solved the problem and urged her to examine it diligently for error. She well knew, however, that she had indeed found the fourth algebraic integral that snared the elusive mermaid. But would some other contestant be equally or more successful? Her presentation must be as understandably clear and graceful as possible.

Upon Maksim's return to Stockholm he found Sophia pale, thin, and utterly weary from working at her desk long into the night. They discussed going with Mittag-Leffler and his sister to Caucasia via Constantinople or to the Italian lake country. This trip could follow attendance at the 800th anniversary of the University of Bologna, to which scholars from all over the world had been invited. Because of the expense of such a trip and her need for quiet to polish her treatise, Sophia declined to go. Therefore this plan was abandoned, and Maksim departed for Paris. They agreed to meet, just the two of them, in London in June. It would appear that Maksim misread Sophia's unconventionality. A wary bachelor, he expected an affair, whereas she aimed at marriage.

From the Grand Hotel in Paris on 8 March and again on 23 March, Maksim wrote such letters as might, with the exception of one sentence in the second, have gone to any masculine friend. He discussed the Franco-Russian *rapprochement* and the consequent popularity of Russians in Paris, foresaw the eventual involvement of Russia in a war with Germany, and referred derisively to Russian socialists in Paris whose lives were "filled with storms in a glass of water." But he also added a strong personal note: "I thank you that you do not oppose giving me a place in your life, and I only remind you that of necessity this place must be large," which could be taken also as a reference to his size.

Nobody, following their subsequent extended and intimate relationship, could have had a better appraisal of Sophia's political views at this time and later. He was himself very liberal. In fact, over a period of two years while writing his doctoral thesis in London, he had been a regular guest at Sunday dinners with Karl Marx and had spent many Sunday evenings with Friedrich Engels. His attention having been directed to the subject by Marx, he had written *An Outline of the Origins of the Family and Common Lands*, research which Engels expanded into *The Origin of the Family, Private Property, and Government*. He wrote after Sophia's death that although she enjoyed meeting persons holding extreme views, she was herself independent in thought, favored neither monarchy nor republic, and acknowledged no aristocracy other than that of the mind. She had no inherited religious or social prejudices and only hoped for a society in which each individual could live by his labor, could freely express his thoughts, and could freely actualize them in life. "To call her a socialist or communist," he declared, "would be to sin against truth." It may be said further, one must suppose, that she was an elitist and believed that a worthwhile society needs an elite intellectual class—not necessarily the ruling class—to represent the superiority to which society as a whole can aspire.

[283]

Such were Sophia's views in her full maturity. How much she had been influenced by Maksim it is impossible to say. It would seem that her political beliefs tended to take on some of the coloration of persons close to her at various periods in life. First there was Aniuta, who introduced her into Petersburg nihilist circles of the non-violent stripe. The good nihilist renounced the traditional role of a woman so that the human characteristics she held in common with males could emerge. Some nihilists believed only revolution could accomplish what Sophia thought education and persuasion could effect. In this limited sense Sophia remained a nihilist all her life. When she married another nihilist, he had already put aside many of Herzen's views, together with his own activism, believing instead that science offered the best future for mankind; and Sophia to a considerable extent added this notion to her beliefs. Then, without at all holding socialist or revolutionary views herself, she became a minor participant in the French Commune, but only out of deep concern for Aniuta's safety and then out of humanitarian sympathy for the wounded. It was only when emotionally adrift after Vladimir's suicide that she turned finally to socialism. This conversion was strongly influenced by her lifelong sympathy for Poland's plight under Russian rule. The socialists in Paris with whom she associated were almost exclusively Poles, such as Lavrov and the woman she so greatly admired, Marie Mendelson. But Sophia really remained a passive socialist, much talk and little action. Possibly she did, however, pass along occasional subversive messages in her letters to Aniuta in Russia. Also she indicated to her Parisian socialists that since the proximity of Sweden to Russia offered a favorable escape route for militant Russian socialists, she would attempt to create in Stockholm a favorable climate to receive such persons. Probably there never were such escapees, but Sophia during her early years in Sweden did in a cautious way discuss socialist ideas with friends there, including those already holding similar views to a greater or lesser extent, such as Karl Branting and Baron Nordenskiöld, and it became generally known that she was at least sympathetic to socialism. At this time she wrote to Lavrov requesting him, for the benefit of the Baron, to recommend books explaining the aims, unclear to her, of the various Russian revolutionary parties. After her death Lavrov would state that she had never expressed to him her own convictions regarding socialism, although she had attended lectures at the Paris Socialistic Congress, but that he knew her as a loyal ally of young Russia and a person sympathetic to the conditions of the contemporary Russian woman. Following Aniuta's death, and as Sophia became immersed in her mathematical and literary work, what remained of her socialistic commitment weakened until—as Maksim attested—she could not be considered a socialist at all. In such a way, then, did Sophia's views evolve, without further change to the end of her life. She was only entirely constant in her attachment to Mother Russia.

ii

IN REPLYING to the doubts of Weierstrass about the accuracy of her mathematical work, Sophia assured him that she had made no error. "To my joy," he responded on 22 May, "you have succeeded very well without my help." He sent her pages of his own newest equations, along with a mild complaint about the errors, pretentions, and intrigues of his Berlin colleague, Kronecker.

The latter, apart from his usual jealousy, felt slighted in connection with the mathematical prize that Oscar II of Sweden would award the following year in observance of his sixtieth jubilee. Carl J. Malmsen, the elderly Swedish mathematician turned politician, had proposed to the King that the jury consist of one German or Austrian (Weierstrass), one Frenchman or Belgian (Hermite), and one Italian or Russian (Briosk, Chebyshev, or Kovalevsky). Kronecker could not object to his colleague, but he could strike indirectly, fearing the choice might go to Sophia, and so he objected to any Russian judge. He was also miffed that Weierstrass had been asked to propose four questions, the prize to be awarded for the best development of any one of these. Kronecker's intrigue resulted in a jury consisting of himself, Weierstrass, and Mittag-Leffler. But he could not alter the four questions.

iii

INSTEAD OF waiting until June as planned, Sophia rushed off to London in late April. Maksim was occupying furnished rooms with a male friend and for her reserved an opposite apartment. He knew London well from his student days and had many friends there, friends dating from the time he had been taken into the circle of George Eliot and George Lewes and through them had become a member of the Athenaeum Club. For over a month Sophia and Maxim dined together, visited museums, and walked in the countryside. Although they grew closer they also quarreled. Maksim valued his independence as a bachelor, had doubtless expected something more than friendship, and when at times Sophia's intensity in conversation became tiresome, he occasionally withdrew to see other persons, some probably feminine, whereas Sophia in friendship as in love demanded absolute concentration upon herself and reacted with jealous resentment.

And so, instead of proceeding to the Italian lakes, as Sophia had hoped, she departed alone to see her Paris friends. First among those friends, of course, was Marie Mendelson, whose primary attraction for Sophia lay not in her socialism, not in her bravery, not even in her Polish patriotism, but rather in her charm and good taste. She was a most attractive woman and dressed beautifully. She was mentioned in French newspapers as one who set an example in Parisian fashion. Sophia would get this friend to choose dresses for her, although she could never wear dresses as becomingly as the charming Pole.

When Marie wrote her recollections of Sophia, she observed that each of Sophia's many friends retained a different estimate of her nature. Her nature was so rich that she could give to the person interesting her at a particular time exactly what she thought most suited him. She preferred one-to-one relationships, one at a time, and even in a group concentrated on one person. "Somehow," Marie wrote, "she was never able to achieve a balanced and constant and varied intercourse with different persons simultaneously. On the contrary, with one person and then another she was always living through a process of attraction and disappointment, enthusiasm and depression, effusion and stubborn silence. In devoting herself attentively at a given time to one person, man or woman, she would pass over everybody else." Then when she had satisfied temporarily her interest or curiosity, had settled some question in her mind, she would turn away, like a child discarding a toy, and in this way offended many persons who did not comprehend her nature. Marie observed further that Sophia had one other trait that confused many and offended a few—that of irony, or a sudden apprehension of the absurd, which produced peals of golden laughter, either over the errors of others or over her own mistakes. She even laughed, sometimes through tears, when her dream castles and ice palaces collapsed in ruins. How very different could be the impressions created by Sophia is indicated by the fact that Marie, while recognizing her genius, was misled by her changeability, and in consequence denied her a logical mind, the very characteristic that mathematicians found central to her nature.

Sophia herself once admitted that like a chameleon she tended to take on the coloration of the person she was with. In concentrating on one person at a time, as had just happened and would happen again and again with Maksim, Sophia expected a similar concentration by that person upon herself, and when the other person's attention wandered off to other persons or other interests, before her own attention had been sated, she felt rejected and unhappy. This trait of hers, therefore, while it yielded excellent results when focused upon some abstract subject, some goal of achievement, only caused her sooner or later, and sometimes repeatedly, to experience emotional tension in every interpersonal relationship. If the other party complained of neglect, on the other hand, she would ask for indulgence—as she did in a letter to Marie, who had rebuked her for not writing—maintaining that her character was that of "all reasonably passionate people," and that only one short-term interest, whether mathematics, literature, or a person, could "engulf" her at one time.

iv

ON 22 JUNE Sophia received word from Weierstrass that he and his sisters would spend July and August in the Harz mountains at Salzburg. She accepted his invitation to join him there, where he promised to keep under "stern observation" his favorite pupil, so that she would labor daily in making her prize entry as precise and well-written as possible. He well knew how Sophia, having once solved a problem, lost interest in its final presentation. On the more mundane side, he advised her that the Müller Hotel would cost her eight to ten francs a day; that she should bring her own tea, because that at the hotel was revolting; and that when registering she should prefix her surname with "von," as this would effect a significant improvement in service.

Upon arriving in Salzburg she found Weierstrass surrounded by younger mathematicians—Mittag-Leffler, Adolf Hervitz, George Hettner, and perhaps Paul DuBois-Reymond. She soon complained that she had to sit alone over her work while the others gathered around their beloved master to engage in much interesting conversation and to benefit from his ideas and inspiration. She was also distracted by her thoughts of Maksim. After hours she found relief in the social activities, however, and for exercise walked with the Weierstrass sisters, with Hettner's young new wife, and occasionally with one of the mathematicians.

When her work was complete, in the style approved by Weierstrass, she forwarded the result to Paris and herself returned to Stockholm. There she felt so weary from work and so over-excited by her uncertainties concerning Maksim that late one night (apparently at this time) she suffered a heart seizure and fell ill. She recovered barely in time to resume her lectures. Her spare time until Christmas she spent in literary work.

V

A FRENCH notary named Charles Bordin, about fifteen years before the first Nobel prize, had left 15,000 francs to be divided as premiums among five scholars over a period of years. According to the rules, per-

sons winning had to add in a perfected way, or at least in a very substantial manner, to the state of knowledge on problems propounded
by the French Academy of Science. In order that a famous name would
not influence the judging, entries had to be labeled anonymously with
a motto keyed to a sealed envelope containing the name. On three
previous occasions the mermaid problem had been considered by such
persons as Euler, Lagrange, and Poisson who achieved partial success
without being able to master the final and most difficult part of the
solution.

From the fifteen entries submitted in 1888 the jury selected Sophia's.
The winning entry was announced at a general meeting of the academy
as that bearing the motto: "[In French] Say what you know, do what
you must, then be what will." The jury declared it to be a remarkable
work in mathematical physics and proclaimed that "the author was
not satisfied with merely adding to the results . . . that have come to
us on this subject from Euler and Lagrange" but had "formed out of
his discovery a deeper research by using all the possibilities of modern
theory," and that "the author's method of solving the problem by
using the theta functions with two independent variables allows him
to give a complete solution in the most precise and elegant form." In
view of this the jury proposed that the author be awarded the full premium of 3,000 francs plus an additional 2,000 francs in recognition of
the elegance of the presentation. Members having agreed to this, the
envelope was opened to disclose the winner, not some renowned male
scientist but a small Russian woman. Weierstrass' insistence on the importance of style had nearly doubled the award.

Notified in Stockholm of her triumph, Sophia requested a leave of
absence for the next semester and with Anna Charlotte hastened to
Paris to attend a formal Christmas Eve meeting of the academy. Seated
beside the president, and following a series of acclaiming speeches by
various academicians, she received the highest scientific recognition
ever accorded a woman to that day, and for long after.

During the days that followed Sophia became the toast of Paris at
receptions and dinners in her honor. She was entertained by, among
others, her friend Bertrand, by Count Luigi Menabrea, the Italian ambassador and one-time professor of mechanics, by Count Löwenhaupt
from Russia, and by a prince, probably Louis Lucien Bonaparte. She
was feted not only as a rarity among women but doubtless to some
extent as a Russian. Because of the Franco-Russian alliance in the of-
fing, Russians had gained in favor what the Poles had lost in French
society.

Of those activists for Polish independence that Sophia had known earlier in Paris, few except Marie Mendelson and her husband remained, and the latter's ideas were changing. Peter Lavrov and Varvara Nikitina were both dead. Ludwig Varansky had been condemned to hard labor. Red-headed Simon Dikshtein had escaped from a Russian prison but committed suicide in Switzerland. The young naval officer, Vladimir Lutsky—one possibility as the unidentified admirer in Paris with whom Sophia's soul had once ventured so close—had surrendered at the Russian embassy in Constantinople and lived in comfortable banishment in southeastern Russia.

Sophia's new admirer was present, however, to observe her triumph; but Maksim was not included in invitations, and having no understanding of mathematics, was not much impressed by her victory. They occupied adjoining rooms in a hotel near the Pasteur Institute, on the square where the statue of Lavoisier soon would be placed. I. I. Menchikov, who was then working at the institute, called on them. He had resigned his university post in anticipation of being dismissed, for which Sophia rebuked him, saying that by resigning he only made things easier for those opposing him. Later on, while at the Russian zoological station on the Riviera, having already announced to the world his theory of phagocytes involving red and white blood cells, Menchikov was not amused by Sophia's idea of a dramatic scene to be written into a play, a scene in which ballerinas dressed in red or white costumes would represent the battle between red and white blood cells. After Sophia's death Menchikov told Maksim he had once been Sophia's suitor.

Seemingly Sophia and Maksim while still in Paris remained on the same Platonic terms that had characterized the early years of her marriage to Vladimir. Nothing is clear. But taking into account Sophia's desire for marriage and Maksim's for freedom, it is even possible that they did not become intimate for a long time, despite appearances. At any rate, Maksim became alarmed by Sophia's expectations and, just before the new year, left unexpectedly for Monte Carlo.

On 2 January 1889, in replying to her letter addressed to him at the Hotel Splendid, he wrote:

"You have written me many stupid things, unjust and undeserved reproaches, and generally have disclosed yourself to be, in the fullest sense of the word, a woman. Needless to say, none of the things you mentioned did take place, nothing unusual, except the following— upon hearing that you had requested a leave of absence from Stockholm University and had signed a certificate of illness, I became frightened by your lack of consideration of this step. It seems to me that the result will be the loss of your chair, and since French promises are written in sand, you would have to teach in the provinces or give up professorial activity. In view of this, thinking that the expectation of a mutual life was the deciding factor for you, I preferred to disappear temporarily.

"My advice to you now—return to Stockholm where your little daughter lives and where your friends are waiting.

"If I loved you, I would have written otherwise."

The effect of such a letter on a proud nature can be imagined. Her mathematical glory meant little. She had been rejected as a person. She who had expected devotion, while holding much of herself in her own keeping, had been abandoned. Had she been an actress enjoying a public triumph, her desirability would have been enhanced in his eyes, but not as a woman with weakened eyes and furrowed forehead devoted to science.

Maksim's letters to Sophia were provided by his nephew's son, Professor P. E. Kovalevsky, to the author of an article published in New York in 1954 in *Novyi zhurnal* (*The New Review*). What letters may have been lost or destroyed is unknown, but those preserved considerably altered the previous understanding of Sophia's relationship with Maksim. In the foregoing letter he denied loving her, and in no other did he state otherwise. He always addressed her formally as "Sophia Vasilevna"—never as "Sonya" or "Sofa" or in any endearing manner. All except two unimportant letters from her to him were lost in the Russian Revolution, so that the correspondence must remain one-sided, as obviously was their love.

Having received the brutally frank letter from Maksim, Sophia in early January addressed Mittag-Leffler, expressing her resolve to begin a new mathematical work and to interest herself in practical things. She expressed gratitude for his friendship. "Yes," she declared, "I think it is the only good thing that life has really given me! How ashamed I am to have done so little to prove to you how much I value it. But forgive me. I am not at this moment in control of myself. I receive so many letters of congratulation, and, by a strange irony of fate, have never felt so miserable in my life—unhappy as a dog! I think, however, that dogs are more fortunate and can never be as unhappy as people and in particular as women. At the present time the thing that I can do—is to keep this sorrow to myself, to hide it within the depths of my soul, to try to behave myself as prudently as possible in public and not give occasion for gossip." Anna Charlotte, of course, kept her brother informed regarding Sophia.

It was a little late to be concerned about gossip. It had already been spread among Russians in Paris and through them to the motherland. And Mme. Hermite? Probably there was no second invitation from her.

vi

THE EXPOSITION of 1889 brought many visitors to Paris, including Edvard Grieg, who was enjoying much popularity. Possibly Sophia heard his compositions, but it is noteworthy that despite her early music lessons (or perhaps because of the tearful scenes with her governess in connection with them), Sophia remained somewhat indifferent to music. Ellen Key concluded that Sophia loved music from observing her at a performance of Beethoven's Ninth Symphony in Stockholm, but what Sophia probably enjoyed was being present alongside Maksim. There is no hint that she cared in the least that Tchaikovsky and the "mighty five" had been establishing Russia in the forefront of European music. Unlike so many mathematicians who find in music almost a branch of their specialty, and find it relaxing, she to some extent resembled Weierstrass who simply could not tolerate music. Sophia did have interest in such dramatic forms of music as the opera and ballet. Despite the efforts of her old tutor, Malevich, she was largely indifferent to art and architecture and sculpture. In all her years in Paris she probably never once visited the Louvre.

Sophia did, however, have dinner with Grieg. She and Anna Charlotte were guests of the Norwegian literary man, Jonas Lie, who lived in Paris and whose works fill fifteen volumes. Sophia had first met him four years earlier. Anna Charlotte maintained he was the only person who fully understood Sophia. Lie's guests at a festive dinner also included the composer's wife, as well as Knut Vikzel, Ida Erikson, and the Swedish poet whose work Sophia admired, Johan Runeberg.

At the dinner there occurred a sentimental incident. Champagne having flowed freely, Lie was in high spirits. "He made one speech after another, bright and sparkling and full of imagination, and yet withal—as was his wont—somewhat involved and obscure," Anna Charlotte recollected. "The spontaneity and poetic fervor inherent in all his utterances gave to his cordiality a special charm. He spoke of Sonya, not as a great mathematician, nor even as a successful author, but as little 'Tanya Raevsky,' whom he said he had learned to love so truly and for whom he felt so great a sympathy. He said he was sorry for the poor little misunderstood child who so longed for tenderness. He doubted, he said, whether she had ever been understood. Life, he had heard, had lavished on her every gift upon which she set no value; had given her honors, distinction, success. But it had denied her what she most wanted. She still remained standing there with great wide-open eyes, yearning for a touch of tenderness. There she stood with her empty outstretched hands. What did she want? Only an orange."

Oranges being rather scarce, a loving parent might give one to a child or put one in a Christmas stocking.

Rising in turn to thank Lie, Sophia with tearful eyes and moving voice responded briefly: "I have had many speeches made about me in my life, but never one so beautiful."

Later she told Anna Charlotte that this casual friend who, apart from her book, knew nothing of her inner life, had penetrated farther into her inmost soul than even her most intimate friends.

vii

WEIERSTRASS ON 1 February, while vacationing at Wernigerode, wrote Sophia in Paris to know "at once" and "exactly" where future letters should be sent. His annoyance rather suggests that he had already heard about the adjoining rooms.

"I didn't congratulate you," he continued, "on the victory you had at Christmastime, first because I thought that you, surrounded by the adoration of all Paris, as Hermite wrote to me, were not in need, and second because I was ill and in bad spirits. Needless to say we, my sisters and I and all your friends that are here, Fuchs, Hettner, Knoblauch, Hensel, P. DuBois, and the recently returned Hansemann, are all very much pleased by your success. I felt a particular satisfaction, since according to competent judges my 'faithful pupil'—'my weakness'— was not just empty boasting."

Knowing of her fast pace in Paris, he urged her to consider her health and to return to Stockholm. He mentioned talk of her receiving a permanent professorship and hoped that on her return journey she would stop in Berlin to rejoice with friends. He also reminded her of her daughter, remarking that his stepson, having heard of Sophia's premium, had remarked: "Now Aunt Sonya will bring Fufu beautiful toys from Paris."

Having been rejected by Maksim, Sophia's thoughts not surprisingly turned back to Mr. H. in Berlin. She informed him that she was remaining in Paris on leave to do research in the area of mechanics, mentioned her daughter in Stockholm, and sent warm regards to his children. If actually she thought of giving up her career for marriage, perhaps she wondered whether life with a German mathematician would not be better, anyway, than with a Russian sociologist, even assuming she could get the latter to propose.

Correspondence with Mr. H. continued during the following

months. In December of 1890, in fact, she would address him from the Riviera as follows: "If you could have seen how terribly overjoyed I was yesterday when your letter was given to me! How good of you that you love me with all my faults; I am very happy to possess such a friend. The major reason for my silence was that I put off writing from day to day so that I could give you the exact time of my arrival in Berlin. I shall see you very soon. I ask you to write me, my dear friend. Would it be convenient for you to receive me at the end of January?" Their meeting did not occur, however. By twice stressing friendship Sophia was perhaps signaling her lack of romantic intentions, and yet she seemed to be sustaining his interest, just in case, while meanwhile her expectations see-sawed with Maksim.

· · · viii

RETURNING TO the chronology of events, by late February of 1889, having brooded over her relationship with Maksim, Sophia resolved to submerge her pride. Her excuse for going to the Riviera was to regain her health, which was indeed precarious. Probably she asked to be received. At any rate it took little if any encouragement from Maksim for her to join him on the Riviera, where he had purchased Villa Batavia at Beaulieu near Nice. Russian acquaintances were staying in the vicinity, writers and professors, including the rector of the university at Geneva, Karl Fogt, several of whose books Vladimir had published.

Apparently Maksim's greeting was correct but cool, so that instead of comforting words she was thrown back on her own misery. The situation between them remained as touchy as before. A gulf lay between her love and his gentlemanly bearing. She whose brain had been independent of gender was now being tormented by sex. Maksim had no wish to take a wife, especially not one to share with the world, and therefore in mid-March, perhaps to effect her departure, he left to spend six months on his Kharkov estate. He promised to correspond.

Several weeks before Easter that year Sophia was therefore back once again in Paris, as indicated by a letter to her daughter, who was living with the Mittag-Lefflers: "My dear Fufulia. How are you? Why do you write me so infrequently? I thought a great deal about you two weeks ago. During Shrovetide I was in Nice (this is in the south of France, and it is very beautiful there). With Maksim Maksimovich we looked out of a window as masses of people in carriages of strange appearance passed by. We had baskets of flowers and threw bouquets like bombs to those driving by. They answered with the same."

Word of Sophia's visit with Maksim quickly reached Moscow and the ears of her friends, for on 18 March Sophia addressed Julia: "You write some kind of mysterious hints. Naturally I can answer nothing until you write me something definite. If you have heard some gossip about me, then please tell me. Be assured that this will not disappoint or offend or even surprise me. Rumors reach me from other sources that the good Moscow people are busy sorting my poor bones, but nevertheless it would be interesting to know what exactly is said about me."

At about this time Anna Charlotte who had gone on to Italy informed Sophia of her engagement to the mathematician she had met the previous year, the Duke of Cajanello. "What a happy 'child of the sun' you are to have found so great, so deep a love at your age!" Sophia responded. "That is really a fate worthy of such a lucky soul as yours. But it has always been so. You were *happiness*, and I am, and most likely shall always be *struggle*." She made reference to themes in their play, *Struggle for Happiness*.

At this time Sophia was engaged in translating from the Swedish version and rewriting in Russian, chapters from the story of her early life. Two of these chapters she sent to Maksim for criticism—and, it would seem, to stir his interest in her. In his letter of 20 April 1889 he was not complimentary. The first of the chapters he advised destroying (it may have been one of several that she did not use). The second chapter he marked with numerous notes and, having reread Tolstoy's *Childhood and Youth* and Rousseau's *Confessions*, as some basis for judgement, suggested that her viewpoint was too adult for the child of twelve that she was recreating. Whether she followed his advice is not known.

Also at this time another honor came to Sophia. She further refined and broadened her solution to the mermaid problem. This paper she entitled *"Sur une propriété du système d'équations différentielles qui définit la rotation d'un corps solide autour d'une point fixe."* It was presented to the Swedish Academy of Science, which awarded her a premium of 1,500 *kronor*. It seems not unreasonable to suspect that the Swedish premium, although doubtless merited, came partly as an effort by the Swedes to retain the bright star of their young university. It would appear in *Acta Mathematica* the following year, 1890, the same year in which—to anticipate events momentarily—*Acta* published her *"Sur un théorème de M Bruns,"* a paper she presented at a conference of mathematicians in Stockholm. In that she advanced a more simple proof of a theorem of Bruns which concerned the property of the potential function of a homogeneous body. After Sophia numerous mathematicians examined in different ways the problem of a rotating solid body, and several developed special variations, but her general solution, using hyperelliptic integrals to solve the differential equations of motion for an asymmetrical body (covering also a symmetrical one) remains for rotary motion about a fixed point.

Maksim expressed happiness in June over Sophia's success in winning the Swedish premium. He urged her not to rest on her laurels but to continue to produce new mathematical work, while he, with no hope for prizes, led his "idyllic existence in the bosom of nature far from city temptations and vice." He pointedly added that late night conversations about feelings were now replaced for him by early sleep. He was really saying he was quite happy without her. "Conversations" was the term they had come to use for arguments.

Apparently Sophia wrote back something flippant about his not having to go to the city to find female companionship, for he quieted her transparent jealousy by assuring her that in the vicinity of his estate there were not forty maidens but only two or three widows with broken nerves. Again he seemed to be saying he had no romantic interest in an overwrought widow such as Sophia.

ix

IN REPLY to a letter from Chebyshev, Sophia sent him a copy of her prize Paris work (probably proof sheets from *Acta Mathematica* of the work which ran for about fifty printed pages, roughly half text and half equations). The academy had given permission for publication in *Acta* prior to that in the academy's own journal, *Savante éstrangers (Foreign Scholars)*. In the latter journal the article appeared under a title assigned by the academy [in French]: *About one particular part of the problem of the revolution of a rigid body about a fixed point when the integration occurs with the help of the ultraelliptic functions of time*. Sophia also informed Chebyshev that Hermite and Beltran were very pleased that the French in the person of Poincaré had won the King Oscar II of Sweden prize and that Appell had been runner-up.

At a later date, incidentally, Weierstrass would write Sophia that as a judge he had been unable to correct some possible errors in Poincaré's work but had at the time submitted annotations to the King. He asked that *Acta Mathematica* print those annotations in the same issue as Poincaré's work. In his view: "The value of Poincaré's research lies more in its negative than its positive values."

In her rooms near the Pasteur Institute Sophia saw many Russian and Polish individuals, including of course Marie Mendelson. She toured the institute and probably met Louis Pasteur. One friend was P. I. Iakobi, who worked at a psychiatric hospital, and who apparently advised Sophia regarding her nervous condition. With him and several other friends Sophia soon rented a country house at Sèvres. Fufu arrived there with the Mittag-Lefflers, who had come like so many others to ascend the amazing Eiffel Tower and see other wonders of the international exposition.

Fufu's Russian was rusty, as she had not been back to Russia for two years; and Iakobi's son, Vania, just Fufu's age, having been born in France, needed Russian training even more. This training Julia supplied when she arrived with children's books in her luggage and began informal lessons. This was the only summer in Fufu's memory that she spent entirely with her mother.

Sergei Petrovich Botkin, prominent in Russia as a surgeon, with his wife and their daughter, Katia, also spent time in the country household of Russians. One day Fufu and Vania pledged Katia to secrecy and introduced her to their source of wild grapes, with the result that she became very ill during the night, but would not betray the secret, so that her father became alarmed. Next morning Fufu in fear and trembling had to disclose what Katia had eaten.

Another juvenile summer visitor was Urey Jaclar, then about fifteen but only about as tall as a 10-year-old. Lack of maternal care showed in his dress. He disliked France, hated school, and not long before had run away from his father to become an omnibus boy calling out stations. He was devoted to Sophia, who wanted to raise him, but Jaclar refused. Fufu corresponded with this cousin for several years; he wrote her poetry in French; but after Jaclar sent him off to the south of France to study rural economy, Fufu never heard from him again, and her later efforts to trace him were unsuccessful.

In mid-June Sophia attended the *Congrés international de bibliographe des sciences* held in Paris in conjunction with the exposition. There was also a women's congress to which she was a delegate. With so much going on that year in the French capital she could not bear the thought of returning to Sweden. Yet how else could she live? Thinking perhaps with her new fame she could obtain a professorship in France, she had, several months earlier, consulted Hermite. He had pointed out that she would need a French doctorate for that.

X

HAVING HEARD from Mittag-Leffler that Sophia definitely hoped to leave Stockholm, Weierstrass on 12 June 1889 wrote her frankly: "You have no desire stronger than to work in Paris. But where would that desire get you? You once sought a position in the highest women's school or something similar. But that could have been only a temporary wish. Such a position would be a degradation for you (it would have been said that you felt yourself insufficiently prepared for a university professorship, and by this you would have shown that women are unsuitable as professors of precise science).

"And yet at one time (and I think this is still true) your ideal was to prove in action the injustice of estranging women from taking part in the highest aims of men.

"I learn from Mittag-Leffler that you want to obtain a doctorate in Paris in order to gain access to a French faculty. I must in this connection point out one condition you have not considered. . . . I assume that this advice was given to you there only to frighten you away. I am confident also that if you place your work for defense, then some forgotten paragraph will be found according to which women are not permitted to defend. Ask Hermite what he thinks. Another circumstance arouses my doubts: a person to whom the title of doctor has been given by any faculty cannot cause that faculty greater affront than by receiving this same degree from another faculty of the same category. In a public defense [from which she had been excused] one even vows not to do this. Therefore, if you should defend in Paris, then you would be deprived of the Göttingen diploma. It might be possible to avoid this, but for all those interested in you at Göttingen this would be very unpleasant. In any case, in Germany as in Sweden, it would cause a terrible scandal, and even those that treat you well would turn away from you."

Even if she could actually obtain a French doctorate, Weierstrass doubted that she could obtain a worthy position but rather would have to teach in some provincial town. He advised her not to indicate to anybody that she wished to leave Sweden, at least not until her appointment as a permanent professor was clarified.

And so this escape gate for Sophia closed against her, and she reluctantly once more returned to Stockholm for the autumn semester.

CHAPTER 23

The Flame Flickers
and Flares

i

THAT HER position in Stockholm soon was declared permanent did
not make Sophia any happier in her isolation there. If she could not
work in Paris, she reasoned, then perhaps there was a place for her in
Russia, either as a professor or with a subsidy as member of the Imperial Academy of Science, or both. She therefore wrote to Chebyshev
about the possibility of obtaining a university appointment; and she
asked her relation, Lieutenant-General A. I. Kosich, governor of
Saratov Province, to petition Grand Duke Konstantin Konstantinovich to have her accepted as an academician. It was Kosich who as a
young colonel interested in Aniuta had aroused Dostoevsky's jealousy.

Kosich in his petition quoted Napoleon: "Every government must
value the return of its outstanding people more than the capture of a
wealthy city."

Inasmuch as no law prohibited women academicians, the Grand
Duke appointed a commission headed by Chebyshev to consider the
question.

The secretary of the academy on 23 October sent Kosich an answer,
couched in oblique language, praising Sophia's European accomplishment and fame, but concluding that Russia offered no position as
honorable as she occupied in Stockholm, because in Russia she could
teach only in the elementary grades or tutor in the Women's School for
Higher Courses.

So much for Sophia's hopes! If she could not be a Russian professor
it followed in the implied logic that she could not be an academician.
A reason had been found for rejecting her.

But she still had in Chebyshev a friend. On 8 November she received
a surprise telegram in French from him, conveying the decision of the

academy, made on his recommendation and that of two other mathematicians: "Our academy of science has just chosen you a member-correspondent, allowing this innovation for which heretofore there has been no precedent. I was happy to see the fulfillment of my most ardent and just desires."

This perhaps was a moral victory and later would be pronounced by Weierstrass to be a distinct honor, but it carried no privileges and yielded no subsidy.

Sophia did not admit defeat, however, as indicated when she thanked General Kosich for his efforts. "I am nevertheless happy that they decided to give me this now," she stated, "because if there is a vacancy for a real academician among them, then there will be no excuse not to choose me simply because I am a woman."

Many deserving Russian men were also denied, including her friends I. M. Sechenov (brain authority), D. I. Mendeleev (authority on gasses), I. I. Mechnikov (biologist), and the widely-known zoologist, Vladimir's brother Alexander, who did not become a member for several years. In congratulating Sophia, Alexander referred deprecatingly to the Imperial Academy as the German Academy, because dominated by men of German ancestry who could influence men of similar ancestry in positions close to the Tsar. The rank and German name of Kosich perhaps helped Sophia in being recognized at all.

ii

MAKSIM STILL held his important place in Sophia's thinking. Having rented out his Kharkov estate, in October of 1889 he returned to Beaulieu; but to forestall a visit by Sophia he informed her that he would shortly leave for Italy and then might proceed to Egypt. Not to be put off, she nevertheless asked if she could not come to him in Beaulieu, because in January she would have leave for a month. Could they not travel together in Italy?

His answer seemed needlessly cruel. "It is impossible for me to fulfill your request," he wrote on 4 December, "and the best reason for this is that I am not alone. With me lives a certain person whose past does not permit me to bring her into your company. Since she is a foreigner, not speaking a word of French, it is also impossible for me to leave her alone. In this way, circumstances make our meeting unthinkable. Yes, and I suppose for the best. I am very sad that I cannot thank you for your friendship [by having her as a guest], but you are too wise not to understand my helpless position. With a feeling of deepest respect, I remain obligated to you."

What could be more final? This seemed the ultimate blow. But still

Sophia would not give up. The once proud woman lowered herself to beg for a continuation of his friendship and correspondence. As a gentleman he could not refuse a generous response to so piteous an appeal. Therefore on 12 December, feeling that he had made himself sufficiently clear, he compromised:

"Your last letter touched me very much. My feeling of friendship for you remains strong and unchangeable. I would be very sad to stop corresponding with you and always receive with pleasure your news about successes and recognition which lately your own country does not deny you.

"No one could write about my agitated lady [his visitor], because no one has the slightest idea about this. The agitation arises independently of me: she arrived and sat down.

"If you spend all of January in Italy, then it is not impossible to see you. [In French]: 'Keep me in touch with your movements.' Your K."

No enthusiasm. No invitation to stay at Villa Batavia.

But Sophia would not be rebuffed. The General's daughter had an objective, as she had so many times before in her life, and she attacked directly. She went to Villa Batavia.

If there had been another woman there, she had departed by the time of Sophia's arrival. On the whole this visit brought Sophia more happiness than otherwise. Quite possibly they became lovers at this time. They again participated in the battle of the flowers in Nice. They walked daily on the steep paths along the seaside. When she could not be merry Sophia held herself in check and, pleading the necessity to work, sought the seclusion of her room. Indeed, at this time she probably wrote the "Fragment from a Novel Laid on the Riviera." In this, the character called M. M. Zvantsev precisely and unflatteringly fits Maksim:

"His figure is not one easily forgotten. For this reason even casual acquaintances always recognised him after many years of separation. A massive head very handsomely placed on his shoulders appeared quite unique and would have been excellent for a sculptor. The eyes were most striking of all, very large even for his large face, and blue, with dark lashes and eyebrows. His forehead was also handsome, despite its yearly increase of brow; and the nose, for a Russian nose, was wonderfully straight and of noble formation.

"Lower down things did not appear so favorably. His cheeks were too large and the lower jaw overly developed, but this was to a significant degree covered by a French beard, black with gray; and only in a moment of anger did the lower lip—yes, even the whole jaw—suddenly move forward, conveying something ferocious in the face. In ordinary times, however, the friends of Zvantsev agreed, his dominant expression was always kindly. Despite the enlarged jowl, his face was still very youthful and fresh."

Actually he was an impressive individual, but to tease him Sophia would call him "a Cossack from the wild country, who conquered the Turks and was in turn vanquished by fat."

It was probably during this visit that Sophia, while climbing along a picturesque mountain road near Nice, suffered a heart attack. "I was afraid," Maksim wrote much later, "that I wouldn't bring her back alive."

Following Sophia's return to her podium, Maksim in March sent her letters mentioning individuals arrested in Russia, students rounded up, and professors servile to the regime. Then when he suffered an attack of gout he imprudently mentioned sitting up all night in a chair while groaning in pain. At once she was ready to abandon all and go to him. That he did not want, not so soon again. He hastened to dissuade her from becoming a Sister of Mercy, assuring her that he was well cared for. Immediately she envisioned some other woman in attendance and insisted on coming during her Easter vacation. "You have just two weeks at your disposal," he then pointed out, "three days for the journey here, three days for the return, leaving nine days for Beaulieu. And all this for what? In order to be convinced that I am really alone, walking in slippers about the garden, reading and writing in the evening, and rubbing my feet with all kinds of trash." He warned, moreover, that if she came he would be exceptionally impolite from shattered nerves and the necessity of having to leave soon for England to pronounce "th" in the proper manner.

Sophia nevertheless would not be warned and soon arrived again at Villa Batavia, which for a general's daughter was a strategic mistake. Maksim indeed was in no mood for a difficult feminine guest. Her visit began and ended with recriminating "conversations," so that upon Sophia's return to Stockholm her friends noticed in her a distinct change. She bottled up her distress. She tended to avoid society. She lost weight and appeared aged. Obviously she could neither live with Maksim nor without him.

iii

AT THE close of her spring lectures Sophia, without disclosing reason or future plans, departed with Fufu for Russia, arriving in Petersburg on 21 May. Julia must have come to Petersburg for Fufu, unless the 12-year-old girl was entrusted to somebody else for the overnight trip to Moscow, where she would remain until the end of summer.

On the evening of Sophia's arrival Lamansky called and related the latest gossip about her. Next day she visited Vasily Grigorevich Imshevsky, an academician and founder of the Petersburg mathematical society; also she called upon Alexander Nikolaevich Pypin, a historian of Russian literature. The following day, after attending a final examination at the Women's School for Higher Courses, which she had helped found, and at which they presented her with a photograph of the school building signed by all students, she called upon Chebyshev.

Her intention thus becomes clear. She was, firstly, seeking a periodical to publish her *Recollections of Childhood*, and very likely Pypin suggested *Vestnik Evropy* (*The European Messenger*) edited by his cousin, N. G. Cherbykovsky, which did serialize the work. And secondly, this time in person, instead of through the petition of others, she was angling for full membership in the Imperial Academy of Science. Membership would yield her a salary on which to live while only requiring her presence in Petersburg for two months of every year.

Also, late at night on the day of her Petersburg arrival, Sophia had written a letter, filled with nostalgic images of the past, to M. I. Semevsky, Aniuta's rejected suitor, who had become a force in Russia's literary world. She expanded at great length about his visit so many years earlier to Palibino, about her father who was "in reality a kind and loving man who on principle surrounded himself, in the eyes of his family, with an aura of severity and inaccessibility," about her beautiful and talented sister and the secret talks they shared about Semevsky whenever she herself could escape her eagle-eyed governess, about life becoming a wicked stepmother for Aniuta, and how she herself, now fast becoming an elderly woman, had looked forward to a life in which her expectations did not resemble the reality. Altogether, the letter was a sad remembrance of former times, calculated to influence Semevsky; and within a few days he did indeed call upon her and asked her to indite something in his bulging autograph album.

It was Semevsky who some days later arranged to have a stenographic record of Sophia's address at her public appearance as the first woman corresponding member of the academy. The setting was probably the hall of the *duma*. Reports of the number present vary from over 1,000 to nearly 5,000. Those in attendance, besides friends and prominent individuals, included a great many young women eager to see and hear their champion of feminine education. Sophia expressed her happiness that the worldwide spread of popular education was being felt in Russia. Her address was in the nature of an inspirational account, with herself as the example, of what a woman could accomplish in the intellectual world. Apart from her deep interest in women's education, it is obvious that this well-publicized occasion came fortuitously, and probably by design, as part of her campaign to become a full academician. Her remarks appeared posthumously, edited by her brother, as "An Autobiographical Story" in Semevsky's *Russian Antiquity.*

She had also hoped to attend a meeting of the academy, in order to make herself known personally to members, but found that corresponding members could not attend meetings. She did not give up. She had intended in any event to call upon the academy president, the elderly and somewhat liberal uncle of the Tsar, Grand Duke Konstantin Konstantinovich, former Great Russian Admiral and former Viceroy of Poland. He was affable when she saw him at his palace but pointed out that there could be no change in the previous decision denying her full membership. Promising to consider her decision to attend meetings, he invited her to return another day. Full of hope she did return to dine with him and his wife, only to learn the worst. He declared how good it would be if she returned to live in Russia but firmly maintained it was outside the traditions of the academy to have a woman attend meetings in any capacity.

Doubtless at her request, Hermite as dean of the French mathematicians, had already written Chebyshev to ask, in view of his previous interest in Sophia, whether he might support her in her desire to become a full member of the Russian academy. He mentioned her reputation among world mathematicians, her feeling of exile in Stockholm, and her love for her native land. Of course nothing could come of this, as Hermite must have known.

In Hermite's own country, after all, no woman—not even years later in the case of France's own Mme. Curie (who after winning two Nobel prizes could only attain corresponding membership)—had ever been accepted by the French Academy of Science, and not until 1979 would a woman be chosen to full membership in that body. In fact, considering all this, it is surprising that Sophia had been so highly honored in France. Apart from her real accomplishment, it would appear that her known origins in the Russian aristocracy and more especially her persistence in friendship with French mathematicians, together with her personal charm, all had an effect.

Although unable to bend official Russia to her will, Sophia nevertheless had succeeded in arranging for several periodicals to publish her literary work. The *European Messenger* and *Russian Antiquity* have been mentioned. Another, *Russkaia mysl (Russian Thought)*, soon listed her with Anton Chekhov and others among future contributors, although she did not live to see this. In Petersburg she had been invited to dinners and suppers with old friends and new acquaintances. Thus, while disappointed regarding the academy, she could proceed on to see Weierstrass in Berlin with a feeling of time well spent. She resolved to produce such a flow of literary works and to solve such scientific problems that her popularity would grow to the point where her native land could no longer deny her the honor of being its first woman academician.

In Berlin she unexpectedly met Anna Charlotte, still on her honeymoon and en route to Sweden, who had paused to introduce her mathematician husband to the master. Anna found Sophia to be unnaturally excited, a sign, she thought, that her friend's apparent light-heartedness only masked deep uncertainties. Sophia avoided being alone with Anna for fear of being deeply questioned about Maksim.

"The only thing that she said to me about her personal concerns," Anna Charlotte recalled, "was that she never intended to marry again; that she would not be so commonplace; she would not do as other women did—forsake her work and mission in order to marry as soon as she had a chance." Sophia also stated that she would remain in Stockholm until she could support herself as an author.

It is apparent that Sophia had decided that only two acceptable, and mutually exclusive, choices remained—to marry or to remain a Stockholm professor. She chose the latter. She was too independent even to consider seeking the bounty of well-to-do Korvin-Krukovsky relatives. From her impecunious brother she could of course expect nothing, and probably little from the Shubert side. There was also her wealthy cousin "Michel" with whom she had studied for a time, long ago at Palibino. The previous year she had encountered him and his wife in Paris. The former idealist who had expressed such ideas of accomplishment had found quiet happiness as a staid and wealthy landowner, while his little Palibino confidant had been the one to achieve fame, from which she tasted only bitter ashes. Of course she with Fufu would at any time have been welcomed by Julia.

iv

WHEN SOPHIA parted from Anna Charlotte in Berlin she did disclose, without going into details, that she intended to meet Maksim, who during May had been a guest lecturer in Russian history at Oxford University. This new reticence with Anna in regard to Maksim suggests she had decided to put her relationship with him on a new basis; that she had decided, in fact, to lower all barriers between them. About this and other aspects of her life she had come to certain resolutions that she expected to follow firmly. In this connection she would be more regular in her habits, and as a beginning she resumed her diary, with entries while in Petersburg and then almost daily for a considerable time while with Maksim.

When she and Maksim met in Amsterdam on 21 June they were at first somewhat diffident. It was perhaps that both felt uncertain of this new phase in their relationship. Now they were to travel together as man and wife, from hotel to hotel, over a period of months, and for each this future held worrisome possibilities. Next day Sophia wrote in her diary: "Beware of conversations [i.e. arguments]. His nerves are taut, and with my nervousness I add to this, and in the end I'll succeed in making him tired of me. It is bad in my soul."

Although Sophia had crisscrossed Europe many times she had never before visited Amsterdam and found its buildings and canals and people charming. But the weather was cold, and to smooth over their uneasiness she suggested that they move on. This they did on 23 June, pausing for several hours at Köln, bathing in the Rhine, sleeping at Bonn. There Maksim audited a philosophy lecture, while Sophia wrote to Julia and Mittag-Leffler.

"At the present moment," she informed Julia, "as you can imagine, I am very happy. What will come later only God knows; with the frivolity native to me I do not think of the future. So far, thank God, we haven't met any Russians. I shall try in every possible way to preserve my incognito."

Next day they visited a castle and then proceeded by ship up the Rhine to Mainz. The following day, 26 June, they proceeded by carriage to Wiesbaden, the whole day marked by "conversations" that ended in an open quarrel and tears.

On 27 June their personal storm had blown over, and after a natural rain storm ended, the weather became amazingly beautiful. Next day they visited several professors at Heidelberg and spent the evening in a philosophical discussion. The following evening they saw *The Flying Dutchman* at a Mannheim theater. The succeeding day Maksim audited lectures in Heidelberg, but on the day following a professor expelled him from the lecture hall. Sophia indicated no reason; this suggests that probably the professor had learned of their open affair. So the pair departed for Baden Baden, where they had pleasant walks and visited Sophia's Aunt Charlotte. One evening they attended a theater and had another "conversation."

Next they entrained on 3 July for Switzerland, where they remained until the first week in September. For a time they stayed in Zurich, or at nearby towns such as Rapperswil, traveling by boat, carriage, or post stage. Sophia mentioned picturesque walks, visits to castles, lectures, a concert, and being confined indoors in rainy weather. She felt deserted when Maksim went alone one day to meet a Russian friend in Bern. It rained and according to her diary she wandered angrily in her room from corner to corner. She decided that it "wasn't entirely amusing" to be with Maksim. Upon his return she remained angry and went to sleep early. Next day, however, they became friendly again and traveled among snow-covered mountains to an Alpine resort in high Davos valley. Maksim, who was overweight and had twinges of gout, began to drink the waters there and weighed in at 285 pounds. He did not manage to lose more than two or three pounds.

On the evening of 10 July Maksim was "nervous and quite unbearable." So Sophia wrote letters to Anna Charlotte, to Lamansky, and to her Berlin friend, Mr. H. One sentence to Mr. H. read: "Here everything is so astonishingly beautiful that, contrary to the poet, one always thinks—happiness is where we are." She also sent Fufu ten roubles to have her picture taken and mailed. "However," she added, "if you have some other great desire, then you may use the money for that." She also wrote Fufu: "I am very glad to hear that you are doing your lessons. It is time for me to start studying, also, but I have turned out to be much lazier than you. I only talk of how I must start to work but every day find some excuse to be lazy."

In a July letter to Marie Mendelson she mentioned Anna Charlotte's marriage to a very pleasant person. "Happiness, madness, ecstasy!"

During these days of July she worked occasionally on her article on the peasant university, read Maksim's new book called *Law and Custom in Caucasia*, had "pseudo-philosophical conversations ending in gloom," quarreled over a charming Englishwoman they met, endured Maksim's sometimes morose disposition, and worked at translating her novel from Swedish into Russian.

She wrote Mittag-Leffler's mother a playful letter to say she was healthy and felt satisfied with her companion; that they had quarreled only three times in two and one-half weeks.

As the waters didn't reduce Maksim's weight or improve his disposition, they left on 6 August for St. Moritz, where Sophia was frightened by a cow and where they climbed a glacier. At this point Sophia ceased her diary entries for a month. From an undated letter written to Lamansky during this period, it is seen that the couple had to be cautious because of Russians at St. Moritz. For that reason and because the weather was cold and because they had rooms like cubbyholes, inasmuch as all the hotels were overflowing, they remained only three days before moving on to an apartment in Bellagio, Italy.

Lamansky had sent the July issue of *The European Messenger* in which Sophia's *Recollections* was being serialized. She asked for the succeeding August issue and also for any reviews. A critic in *Severnii vestnik* (*The Northern Messenger*) wrote: "By the strength of her literary talent our famous compatriot, without doubt, must occupy one of the foremost places among Russian writers."

On 5 September the two travelers arrived in Venice. One day they spent at a glass factory on the island of Murano. They attended an opera and at the cathedral a mass. Maksim's birthday, the eighth day of the month, "started out well but then became worse and worse," culminating in a scene in the evening. He was thirty-nine years old.

Following the pattern of moving on after a quarrel, they departed next morning, at which point the diary entries cease with the brief entry of 9 September: "We went away." Probably Beauleiu was the destination.

V

"Here I am again in Stockholm!" she wrote Julia on 23 September 1890. "I found Fufu taller, gained in weight, and not too spoiled. I myself am up to my ears in work. I must make up for lost time. The Countess is drowning in delight with her Count. She has put her new novel into the world, a novel describing [in French] 'in words sufficiently frank' her own life [including her first marriage], and the novel is now creating a real scandal in Stockholm. Many persons, however, are very enthusiastic about it, and she herself is so happy that what others think is entirely of no concern to her now."

Awaiting Sophia were letters forwarded by the magazine, some complimenting her on *Recollections*, some urging her to continue the work through her adult years. This was a new kind of popularity, not from scientific works that the general public could not understand but acclaim by unknown Russian readers whose hearts and not merely their minds she had touched by her efforts. While she could not be indifferent to such quick recognition, she also felt a superstitious fear that success in the literary world had come too easily and that she would have to pay for it.

Maksim wrote that he was happy that her success gladdened her. "Even the books I write are beginning to be attributed to you," he remarked in a letter of 20 October. "Only a week ago I received a letter from a literary agent in Paris concerning my Stockholm lectures with "Madame" as the opening salutation!"

Anna observed that Sophia's forced gaiety had vanished. Instead she appeared troubled and restless and only counted the days until the

Christmas holidays. But she hid her feelings and avoided intimate conversations. Her life had lost its balance. Mittag-Leffler was building a house in the Djursholm area of the city, and since Sophia liked to live in his neighborhood, he urged her to move. She would not make up her mind about moving nor would she examine his house while under construction. Curiously enough, when several friends with whom she was out riding paused there to inspect the house, she stubbornly remained alone in the carriage. Perhaps the only explanation for such strange behavior is to be found in her childhood dread of seeing a house under construction with empty, dark, gaping doorways lacking doors and eye-like window openings lacking glass. Apparently she was too nervous to be able to ignore submerged fears rising from the past.

Despite her previous resolution to continue teaching in Stockholm, now she simply did not want to consider any future for herself there. She began cutting ties, neglecting friends, withdrawing from society, while concentrating on her own rather desperate condition resulting from not knowing what she wanted to come next with Maksim. They had parted under strained circumstances, apparently, and with no definite plans for a future meeting. She lived only in expectation of an invitation. Finally she queried him.

Exactly one month after his previous letter, Maksim on 20 November extended a cold invitation to Villa Batavia. "In answer to your question, I will tell you that now, as always, I am very glad to see you, but it would be worthwhile for you to weigh *le pour* and *le contre*. *Le pour*: beautiful area, mild climate, and so forth. *Le contre*: Boborykim, Korotnev [professor of zoology], a gentleman whose recent meeting with us occasioned a scene memorable to us both.

"Since you have become very sensitive to [in French] 'what will be said about you,' I warn you that [in French] 'persons will not say anything flattering about you.' To keep you incognito would be unthinkable. To estrange one's self for two whole months—impossible. To gypsy about Italy after six months [actually, four] of gypsying—I haven't the strength. Moreover, I have to write, to have books at hand. Think it all through and act as you think best."

She had no need to think anything through. For several months she had been thinking through her entire situation. By this time she had reconsidered her decision of the previous summer. For a time literature had seemed to offer some hope of escape but, as she soon discovered, not a financially rewarding one. Besides that, her primary interest, her abiding genius, lay in the fields of pure and applied mathematics, which could only be pursued by persons with an income from some other source. By this time she must have had to admit to herself that nothing she could ever do would bring her a professorship in France or Russia and that it was probably impossible to become a Russian academician. In Sweden she was at a dead end. She longed for the cosmopolitan life of Paris or Petersburg and could no longer endure Stockholm where the streets, the houses, the people were orderly and as though washed clean; where life was thrifty, calm, hygienic, and, oh, so boring; where she felt herself always to be under a microscope and forced to live in a manner foreign to her nature. She was a disorderly Russian, thriving in an atmosphere of late hours, frequent tea-drinking, cigarette-smoking, and conversation in her own language with persons of her own sort. Sadly, moreover, her mirror told her what her calendar positively confirmed—that in a few short weeks she, who had already experienced several heart episodes and who often felt tired and nervous, would be forty-one years old.

Her available alternatives thus were clear, either to remain for years, unhappily, as a Stockholm professor, or by abandoning teaching to marry on the best terms possible. If such a marriage did not fulfill her longing for somebody who would say he could not live without her, at least she could live with an intelligent man of her own class whom she loved and who would be sympathetic and supportive.

On 30 November in a letter to her "Aunt" Julia, Fufu announced her mother's imminent departure for Beaulieu. To this letter Sophia added a postscript: "Dear Juliusha! Today I am going to the south of France, but whether to happiness or sorrow I don't know myself, more probably the latter. Farewell, my little friend, your Sofa." That "farewell" rather sounds as though she had also considered a third alternative, suicide, which more than once she had discussed in a theoretical way with Anna Charlotte.

For the trip to Beaulieu Sophia took five days, stopping en route in Berlin, which she found to be colder with much more snow than in Sweden. If she really did envision the possibility of resorting to the third alternative—which seems less than likely—perhaps she wanted to see Weierstrass for the last time. Regardless of that, she probably wanted to discuss her new mathematical problem and may even have discussed giving up her professorship. Long ago Weierstrass had declared that her real talent was for scientific inquiry rather than for teaching. This she could continue as the wife of a wealthy man. After leaving Berlin, once through the Alps she enjoyed the warmth of the south, prophetic of roses, camellias, and violets in Maksim's garden at Villa Batavia.

One may wonder whether Maksim was dismayed by Sophia's capitulation in giving up teaching for marriage. Whatever he may have felt, since apparently she had agreed to his terms, he was committed as a gentleman. Apparently their relations during this entire visit were pleasant. While sitting on the balcony of her room Sophia wrote Fufu a happy letter mentioning her view of flowers and orange trees.

Upon learning that Anna Charlotte and her husband would be returning shortly after Christmas to Naples, Sophia conceived the idea of meeting them in Genoa to introduce Maksim to the Count and probably also for a *tête-à-tête* with Anna. Unfortunately, because of a misdirected telegram, the couple passed right through Genoa while Sophia and Maksim waited in vain. They went sightseeing there, however, and on New Year's day walked among the monuments of the old cemetery, which were of interest to Maksim in his study of customs. While there Sophia half-whispered to him, superstitiously but not entirely seriously: "One of us will not survive this year, because we have spent the first day in a burial ground."

Upon returning to Villa Batavia and wishing to remain there to marry, Sophia applied to Mittag-Leffler for leave during the next semester. Such leave was denied, however, because another podium would be vacant and she would have to lecture on two subjects. She could not, of course, let Mittag-Leffler down. Her departure followed shortly.

CHAPTER 24

Too Much Happiness

i

As Sophia walked with Maksim to the station at Nice, a black cat crossed their path. Having from childhood experienced an unreasonable fear of cats, and having already been tormented by the premonition in the cemetery, she commented on this ominous new portent. Loathe to part, she persuaded him at the last to accompany her as far as Cannes.

From there, suffering the beginning of a cold, she proceeded to Paris, where she asked Jaclar why he had delayed in having published a story in French from her pen. She also told him of her planned marriage. Probably she was not introduced to the Frenchwoman, a former Moscow governess, with whom he had formed an attachment, a woman who disliked Aniuta's son, and who eventually got a wedding band from Jaclar.

Sophia also called upon several mathematicians, including Poincaré, who later declared that she had intended to expand on her two previous prize works, hoping to solve the more difficult problem involving the movement of a rigid body with the center of gravity lying on the equatorial plane of the ellipsoid of inertia.

In Berlin she again visited Weierstrass, because he was ill. The next morning she elected to return to Stockholm indirectly by way of the Danish islands. Very likely bad weather on the Baltic dictated that route, which involved changes of trains and several water crossings.

Because smallpox raged in Copenhagen she would not stay the night in a hotel there but pushed on, despite her cold and fatigue. At one point, unable to hire a porter late at night, she carried her own luggage through a rainstorm and became thoroughly chilled. Arriving in Stockholm on the morning of 4 February 1891, she felt ill but nevertheless the next day worked at her desk and the following day gave her scheduled lecture.

In her last conversation alone with Mittag-Leffler, who had become rector, she told him of her plan for a new mathematical work, which she thought would be the most important she had ever undertaken and would open a new path in the field of thought. She also told him she must have a leave of absence during April on whatever terms it could be obtained. Her intention was to marry Maksim, as later affirmed by Jaclar and her Stockholm friends. Whether she had come to an agreement with him that she could, after all, continue teaching for a time seems unlikely. It is also unlikely that the marriage could have been very happy. Both had personalities too independent for either to be submerged. Sophia's nature, moreover, was such that once she had achieved a goal she lost interest in that and began looking for a new challenge. Marriage might have been such a goal.

The evening of her last lecture she attended a party at the Gulden's, where she shared with friends her Italian and French impressions. But feeling unwell after a time, she slipped away alone. Having tried unsuccessfully to obtain a cab, she took the wrong omnibus and had a roundabout ride in the cold. When finally she reached home that Friday night, feverish and shivering, she took to her bed and never left it. Ellen Key, Teresa Gulden, and the latter's daughter, Elsa, took turns as nurses for the next three days.

On Saturday morning Sophia discussed with Ellen her plans for finishing her novel, and it was Ellen who later completed the last chapter according to Sophia's intention. Sophia grew worse in the afternoon, and having no physician of her own, she sent a note to Mittag-Leffler asking him to send his physician. The doctor mistakenly treated her for kidney trouble. Mittag-Leffler also visited her but was insufficiently alarmed by her condition to send for Maksim until the following day.

On that day, Sunday, Sophia voiced fears that her illness might be a long one. She could not bear to be left alone and expressed gratitude for every small service rendered by her faithful friends. In the evening she told Ellen: "If you hear me moan in my sleep, awaken me and help me change my position; otherwise I fear it may go ill with me. My mother died in such an excess of pain." She knew she had heart trouble, as had both her parents, but her pains actually were from severe pleurisy complicated by asthma.

By Monday morning Sophia fully realized the gravity of her illness and that she might succumb as had her sister. "I shall never get over this illness," she sadly told Ellen. Her thoughts then turned to her surrogate father and his illness when they had recently parted. Fearing that the shock of her death might harm him, she dictated a note to Gustave Hansemann, requesting him to prepare Weierstrass for the possibility. Her major worry concerned Fufu, who would be left an orphan. She asked that Teresa care for the child until suitable arrangements could be made for her in Russia. If she left a message for Maksim it was never made public.

Despite her own condition, Sophia wanted Fufu to enjoy a children's party scheduled for Tuesday and therefore asked one of her friends to assist in buying a gift. When preparing for bed on Monday evening Fufu donned the gypsy costume she intended to wear and pirouetted for her smiling mother. So that Sophia's friends could get some rest a St. Elizabeth's sister took their place that night. Sophia imagined a change for the better, and the doctor did not anticipate any immediate danger.

But at two o'clock Sophia awoke from a drugged sleep. During the next two hours she could not move or swallow and spoke with great difficulty. Teresa and Ellen were summoned, and they awakened Fufu to be with her mother at the end. Sophia died of pneumonia at approximately four o'clock in the morning of 10 February 1891. Teresa remembered her last words as: "Too much happiness." The news that he was too late reached Maksim in Kil, Norway.

ii

AN AUTOPSY disclosed that Sophia's lungs were completely affected, but her heart was so damaged, also, that, apart from its possible contribution to her death, she could not have expected a long life. Naturally there was great curiosity about her brain, found to be unusually large; this was supposed to be the reason for her exceptional mental capacity.

When informed in Naples of Sophia's last hours, Anna Charlotte at first conjectured that Sophia had committed suicide over unrequited love, and this not unreasonable but hasty guess was the source of that erroneous rumor. Anna regretted that her friend had not been able to have the calming consolations of a Russian priest and could not clasp the cross which to her was a much-loved symbol of the sufferings of mankind. Anna had recently become a Roman Catholic, as Weierstrass had always been, but over the years, during the period of her own religious uncertainties, Anna had engaged with Sophia in various discussions of life and the hereafter. While Sophia had rejected dogma, she believed in the eternal survival of the human soul. She feared death and what the unknown beyond might hold for her. On more than one occasion she told Anna that only fear of punishment in the next world had on several occasions held her back from voluntarily leaving this one. She feared, also, being buried before being actually dead and for that reason wished to be cremated, but in Anna's absence this desire was unknown to those in Stockholm, and in any event because of the autopsy was unimportant.

iii

IN THE drawing room of Sophia's apartment a coffin banked with flowers afforded Stockholm a last view of "Our Professor." Wreaths and flowers had begun to arrive soon after word of her death flashed to newspapers around the world. Floral tributes came from the School for Women's Higher Courses in Petersburg, the Women's Union of Frederica Bremer, the Women Writers Union in Copenhagen, the Northern Museum, Danish Women Students, several universities, and of course from friends. A branch of lilac inscribed to "Tanya Raevsky" came from a woman in the Swedish provinces. One tribute consisted of a wreath of laurel leaves with white camellias and a white ribbon reading: "To Sonya from Weierstrass."

When Weierstrass received word of Sophia's death, his sisters feared that his reaction would claim his life. His own last wish six years later was that the priest say nothing in his praise at the grave.

As Stockholm had no Russian church, the funeral procession, in which were friends, professors, students, and curious citizens, went directly to the hillside grave site at the New Cemetery. There at about the hour of three o'clock in the afternoon all gathered in a dense ring around the small cleared area in the snow. Breath vapors accompanied their words as a number of individuals spoke briefly or prayed aloud. Telegrams of condolence were read from the Imperial Academy of Science, from universities, from the new schools in several Russian cities, and from several organizations. The remarks of Maksim and Mittlag-Leffler were reported by the press.

Maksim spoke in French, expressing Sophia's gratitude, and that of Russians in general, to Sweden and to Stockholm University for giving her the opportunity to use her knowledge in a worthy manner, although to the end of her life she remained a Russian loving her motherland.

Mittag-Leffler in his commemoration spoke as university rector, recounting how as a pupil of the great Berlin master Sophia had come from the center of modern science to share her knowledge eagerly with every student having the will and ability to receive her riches, and that she had ever sought to comprehend the thoughts, doubts, sorrows, hopes, and dreams of each individual in a close scholarly relationship. In conclusion he addressed Sophia as though still alive: "I turn to you with a last farewell. I thank you for the depth and clarity with which you directed the mental lives of our students . . . who will ever honor your name. Thank you for the treasure of friendship with which you enveloped all those close to your heart."

During the days that followed letters continued to arrive at the university from every direction. The Moscow Mathematical Society called a meeting dedicated to its deceased member. A requiem liturgy or mass was said at the School for Women's Higher Courses which Sophia had helped found and support. Litvinova was there. She recorded that similar services were also held in Moscow and elsewhere.

Over the next several years Sophia's death brought forth psychological articles discussing whether a woman is able to combine scientific studies with a personal life and family duties, whether fame is obtained at too high a price, and whether in general the feminine mind can ever excel in mathematics. On that last point, it seemed to most persons that Sophia simply exemplified the exception to the rule that masculine minds are superior in abstract thought, but others then and especially since have held that sociological factors explain the difference in achievement. Most recently in the United States a Ford Foundation report on "The Problem of Women and Mathematics" concluded that both biological and sociological factors are involved and that the problem cannot be resolved. At any rate, in Sophia's case, she had a father who was mathematically inclined and a maternal grandfather and a great-grandfather who were outstanding in science. She had, moreover, inspirational encouragement from her old uncle and in Strannoliubsky and Weierstrass the very best in mathematical teachers.

In Petersburg on 9 April the Society for Obtaining Funds for Women's Higher Courses and the Russian Women's Mutual Charity Society jointly began collecting for a suitable grave monument. A monument was erected the following summer, when green grass covered the slope of the hillock in New Cemetery. It was dedicated as coming from the women of Russia and consists of an imposing Byzantine cross of black marble surmounting a wave of gray Finnish granite rising from a granite base.

A Petersburg reporter present was impressed less by the large wreaths from Russia leaning against the base of the monument, than by, higher up at the foot of the cross, a simple clay pot with a small shrub of Ivan and Maria. That perhaps was from Fufu. The reporter further noted that the view from the grave included clumps of linden trees and young birch in the foreground, in the distance green squares of waving grain, and on the horizon the blue line of a pine forest—altogether much like a scene in Sophia's native land.

Epilogue

i

SOPHIA NEED not have been quite so disturbed over her daughter's future. General Kosich promptly invited Fufu to consider his house her own and repeated his offer to Julia. Maria Sechenova (*nee* Bokova) asked Julia to be permitted to take as active a role as possible in Fufu's future. The Petersburg committee to support the School for Higher Women's Courses stood ready to be responsible for Fufu. Sophia's longtime admirer, Lamansky, also offered to raise and educate Fufu, and at this time wrote of Sophia to a friend: "It is hard to reconcile one's self to such a loss. It would be difficult to find another woman in whom there would be such a happy blend of intellect, talent, merriment, and liveliness." Maksim, Alexander, and especially Julia were also concerned about Fufu. The record is only silent with regard to Sophia's brother, who apparently wished to avoid any responsibility.

At first Teresa Gulden cared for Fufu as for one of her own, keeping her until summer in order not to interrupt her schooling and to give time for her future to be decided. Teresa wrote both Alexander and Julia suggesting that Maksim be permitted to adopt the child. As Sophia's perceived fiancé, he had agreed to Teresa's adoption suggestion. In great distress Julia wrote to Alexander, who telegraphed to calm her. In his following letter he stated he did not want to offend Maksim with a blunt refusal, having in mind all he had done and would do for Fufu, but indicated that Maksim would doubtless accept a different arrangement. He further assured Julia he would not agree to any adoption without her consent.

Then a week later he forwarded to Julia a letter from Maksim, pointing out how honorable were Maksim's intentions, and that the foreign adoption that frightened her so had not taken place. He indicated further that from both Teresa Gulden and Jaclar he had been informed that Sophia and Maksim were engaged and that a spring wedding had been planned.

Alexander became legally responsible for Fufu, but her real home was with her godmother Julia. She entered a Moscow gymnasium, completing the course in 1897. In that year her Uncle Fedor, Sophia's brother, married a Polish woman; he had a daughter, inherited the House of Shubert, and died in 1919. Years earlier his Palibino had passed to a cousin, Nicholas Korvin-Krukovsky. Fufu (Sophia Vladimirovna Kovalevsky) attended the Women's Medical Institute in Petersburg until 1907. In 1950 she spoke at the one hundredth anniversary observance of Sophia's birth and died two years later.

For about fifteen years Maksim was a visiting lecturer at Paris, Brussels, and Chicago while not living at Villa Batavia or at his estate. Then, at about the time he founded the constitutional-monarchist Party for Democratic Reform in Russia, he became for ten years a professor at the University of St. Petersburg and an academician. Tsarists considered him dangerously liberal; Lenin would brand him reactionary. He never married.

In the year of Sophia's death Maksim began his efforts to have published her literary work and proposed that she be the subject of a biography, which he declined to write himself because of the known nature of his relationship with her. Anna Charlotte, remembering the advice of Ibsen that Sophia could only be portrayed in a poetic memoir, attempted to supply this in an over-written book. The original edition in Swedish was called *Sonya Kovalevsky: Our Mutual Experiences, and Things She Told Me About Herself.* Although it did not please Marie Mendelson and was very short on facts, it was fairly successful in picturing one person's view of Sophia as an individual. Fortunately she did not delay in the writing, because while correcting the proofs, she died six months after the birth of a son, following less than eighteen months of joyous married life.

Mittag-Leffler continued to teach and to edit *Acta Mathematica.* In 1892 he wrote a memorial article about Sophia and in 1923 wrote an entire issue of some 200 printed pages of mixed French and German about the interlinked lives and works of Weierstrass, Sophia, and Poincaré.

ii

ABOUT DEPARTED individuals various questions may be asked regarding their lives. In Sophia's case three questions seem pertinent.

Was she happy? Did she contribute to knowledge? Did her life benefit others?

As to the first question, Sophia experienced less than a reasonably happy life. When at the end she exclaimed, "Too much happiness," seemingly she meant that the happiness she believed she had found at last was being snatched away, as though she did not really deserve it. Always in adult life she had swung from brief periods of delight to longer periods of depression, with gray flat spots in between. Happiness never lasted long. In that sense her life was not a personal success. Very likely her mother's denial of love, her father's withdrawn nature, and the tyranny of her principal governess had warped her early life, limiting her ability to achieve later an emotional balance to support her intellectual genius and yield gladness as well as fame.

The second question regarding a legacy of knowledge can in a secondary way be answered by pointing to her *Recollections*, which preserve for posterity what it was like for one aristocratic Russian girl to grow up in an urban-rural setting in the second half of the nineteenth century. What is of primary importance is to answer the question by assessing Sophia's place in mathematics and mathematical-physics, the fields of her principal effort. If her mathematical reputation in the late nineteenth century was due in part to the fact that she was truly unique in a field traditionally occupied only by men, this situation cannot affect her later position in mathematical history, because the novelty of her position as a professor of higher mathematics has vanished in a world where many women now work in mathematics. As the first of her sex she would only in the longer view be worth a footnote. Has the passage, then, of about 100 years dimmed her importance? Yes, inevitably to some extent, but this has also happened to a lesser degree to greater nineteenth century male mathematicians who were her friends and coworkers—such as Hermite and Schwartz and Weierstrass and Poincaré. As time moves on, new advances and reputations are made. But on her merit alone, and not as a woman, Sophia Kovalevsky will be found to have a secure niche in mathematical history. In the field of differential equations she was in a progressing line of development that included Euler, Lagrange, Monge, Laplace, Cauchy, Briot, Bouquet, Picard, Jacobi, Clebsch, DuBois-Reymond, Darboux, Lie, Kovalevsky, and so on. She made contributions to Abelian functions in the line after Abel that included Weierstrass, Picard, and following her, Poincaré. She helped advance theoretical mechanics, bearing on the integration and alteration in the form of dynamical equations, along with Lagrange, Poisson, Hamilton, Jacobi, and others. This last she did with her two works which won the

EPILOGUE

Bordin and the Swedish prizes. In her time these brought her world renown—and doubtless this snaring of the "mathematical mermaid" was the most difficult of all for her to accomplish—but time has shown that this discovery of a new case in which the differential equations of motion can be integrated did not lead to anything significant. Oddly enough it was the doctoral thesis written when a young woman that chiefly gives her a remembered place in science. In this she gave final form to a problem on which Augustin Cauchy had worked before her birth. Her approach combined with his became the Cauchy-Kovalevsky theorem to which, for example, Professor Fritz John in his current text, *Partial Differential Equations*, devotes six pages. And so, with regard to the increase of knowledge, Sophia's life was certainly successful. She set for herself most difficult goals, mastering what she considered an essentially lazy character, exercising her inflexible will to sustain her resolve to add to the body of scientific truth.

The third question to be asked at the end of her life is whether she beneficially affected the lives of others, directly or indirectly. In this also she must be considered a success, apart from the direct value of her work. Always sympathetic to orderly change for the improvement of social and economic conditions, she believed, as has been mentioned earlier, that education was the force by which such change could be effected. She felt she personally could best further education for women by herself opening for them a new field. In a more direct manner she aided a number of young women, such as one who earned a doctorate in chemistry and another a doctorate in law; she took the considerable risk of loaning her passport to one who disappointed her, and opened a place in a Finnish university for another who was unworthy. She functioned on the organizing and governing body for the Higher School for Women in St. Petersburg. Her principal influence, however, was by serving as a role model. Her inspiring example was much more successful in advancing the cause of women than if she had been a crusading activist, and she was thus a definite threat to the educational establishment of her own country. Without her example, without her fame, countless young women in many countries would not have been motivated to overcome barriers of inequality, including one woman who became outstanding in Sophia's field and has long served as a professor of higher mathematics in one of America's foremost technical institutions.

That Sophia is well remembered in the scientific world is shown by the fact that recently her name was assigned to a crater on the moon. She is thus one of less than a dozen women from all of history to be so honored.

[319]

S.V.K.'s Mathematical Works

1. Zur Theorie der partiellen Differentialgleichungen.
    (*Inaugural-Dissertation*, 1874; *Journal für die reine und angewandte Mathematik*, t. 80, p. 1—32, Berlin 1875.)
2. Über die Reduction einer bestimmten Klasse Abel'scher Integrale 3ten Ranges auf elliptische Integrale.
    (*Acta Mathematica*, t. 4, p. 393—414, Stockholm 1884.)
3. Om ljusets fortplantning uti ett kristalliniskt medium.
    (*Öfversigt af Kongl. Vetenshaps-Akademiens Förhandlingar*, t. 41, p. 119—121, Stockholm 1884.)
4. Sur la propagation de la lumière dans un milieu cristallisé.
    (*Comptes rendus des séances de l'académie des sciences*, t. 98, p. 356—357, Paris 1884.)
5. Über die Brechung des Lichtes in cristallinischen Mitteln.
    (*Acta mathematica*, t. 6, p. 249—304, Stockholm 1883.)
6. Zusätze und Bemerkungen zu Laplace's Untersuchung über die Gestalt der Saturnsringe.
    (*Astronomische Nachrichten*, t. 111, p. 37—48, Kiel 1885.)
7. Sur le problème de la rotation d'un corps solide autour d'un point fixe.
    (*Acta mathematica*, t. 12, p. 177—232, Stockholm 1889.)
8. Sur une propriété du système d'équations différentielles qui définit la rotation d'un corps solide autour d'un point fixe.
    (*Acta mathematica*, t. 14, p. 81—93, Stockholm 1890.)
9. Mémoire sur un cas particulier du problème de la rotation d'un corps pesant autour d'un point fixe, où l'intégration s'effectue à l'aide de fonctions ultraelliptiques du temps.

APPENDIX A

(Mémoires présentés par divers savants à l'académie des sciences de l'institut national de France, t. 31, p. 1—62, Paris 1890.)

10. Sur un théorème de M. Bruns.

  (Acta mathematica, t. 15, p. 45—52, Stockholm 1891.)

Courses Taught by S.V.K. at Stockholm

1. Theory of partial differential equations. (Fall of 1884 and spring of 1890.)
2. Theory of algebraic functions according to Weierstrass; also, elementary algebra. (Spring of 1885.)
3. Theory of Abelian functions according to Weierstrass. (Five semesters, autumn of 1885 through spring of 1887.)
4. Theory of potential functions. (Spring of 1886.)
5. Theory of the motion of a rigid body. (Autumn of 1886 and spring of 1887.)
6. On curves defined by differential equations according to Poincaré. (Autumn of 1887 and spring of 1888.)
7. Theory of the theta function according to Weierstrass. (Spring of 1888.)
8. Applications of the theory of elliptic-functions. (Autumn of 1888 and spring of 1889.)
9. Theory of elliptic functions according to Weierstrass. (Autumn of 1889.)
10. Application of analysis to the theory of whole numbers. (Autumn of 1890.)
11. Onward from the autumn of 1885 S.V.K. also taught a regular course in mechanics.

APPENDIX C

Letter: Karl Weierstrass to Lazarus Fuchs Concerning S.V.K.

Berlin, Potsdam Street 40
June 27, 1874

My deeply respected friend and colleague!

First of all I must express to you my deepest gratitude for the readiness with which you, upon arriving at Göttingen, took upon yourself the trouble of sending the information I wanted about the requirements for seeking a degree there for my pupil, Frau von Kovalevsky. What you wrote me in your letter of April 18 was fully corroborated by Professor Weber with whom, to my great happiness, it happened that I again spoke in Berlin. I heard from him, moreover, the very interesting statement that when the granting of diplomas was discussed at the jubilee of Göttingen University, Gauss [1777-1855] expressed regret that Sophia Germain [1776-1831] was not alive, because she had demonstrated to the world that a woman is just as capable as a man of doing something important in the most precise and abstract world of science and therefore has the right to receive a diploma.

Having heard this, without hesitation I encouraged Frau von Kovalevsky to seek a degree *in absentia* in your faculty and advised her to finish several works with which she has been occupied during the last several years, partly on her own initiative, partly at my suggestion. On my advice she will present three works to the faculty demonstrating that she has mastered different branches of mathematics to engage independently in useful research for science. [Only one was finally submitted.]

One of these dissertations concerns the problem of whether it is possible to extend, and if so how far, the theorems about the integration of

[324]

APPENDIX C

a system of ordinary differential equations with the use of power series, which I had first laid down in my dissertation concerning analytical factorials (Crelle's Journal, 51,S.[43,44]) and which soon after this were also proved by Messieurs Briot and Bouquet to the case where, for the determination of functions of several variables, the appropriate number of partial differential equations is given. Unquestionably this problem must sometime be fully examined. Frankly I myself was afraid to start this research and therefore was pleased even more that Frau von Kovalevsky undertook this work in the most thorough manner, but which in her last version has only moderate size.

The difficulties that first presented themselves—for example the unexpected and justified consideration of the observation that even such a simple differential equation as the many times examined

$$\frac{\varrho\varphi}{\varrho t} = \frac{\varrho^2\varphi}{\varrho\chi^2},$$

if one requires that φ for $t = o$, must coincide with a given function $\varphi(\chi)$, representable by a converging power series in χ, in general, unless $\varphi_0(\chi)$ satisfies the very special conditions, the function is always leading to a diverging expansion of $\varphi(\chi, t)$ in power of t—were overcome by the researcher's skill in the simplest and most satisfactory way. I am convinced that this work will arouse the same interest in you.

Her second work picks up and further extends the studies that Laplace made about the shape of Saturn's rings. The result of Laplace's study turned out to be valid only in the first approximation; a ring that satisfies the requirements of the problem, as formulated by Laplace, can not be generated by the rotation of an ellipse around a straight line parallel to its minor axis. Instead of the ellipse one must contemplate a figure which about both axes is curved differently; and which, under the assumptions made by Laplace, apart from the difficulties of calculation, can be determined to any degree of approximation. For the second approximation the calculations are carried out fully.

In the third dissertation my pupil is concerned with a problem I formulated. As you, esteemed colleague, know, several years ago I made a written communication to Herr Königsberger about the condition that an algebraic function $\varphi(\chi)$ must satisfy if among the integrals

$$\int F(\chi, \varphi\chi)d\chi,$$

where F represents a rational function of χ and $\varphi(\chi)$, there exist some that can be transformed into elliptic integrals. (Königsberger mentioned this communication in one of his works about the transformation of Abelian functions.)

Stated more completely, this theorem reads:

Suppose $\psi_1(\chi)...\psi_\varrho(\chi)$ is the complete system of Abelian integrals of the first kind, whose derivatives are expressed rationally through χ and $\varphi(\chi)$. Then, as is known, there are infinitely many primitive period systems of these integrals

$$2\omega_{11},\ 2\omega_{12}...2\omega_{1\varrho},\ 2\omega'_{11}...2\omega'_{1\varrho}$$
$$2\omega_{21},\ 2\omega_{22}...2\omega_{2\varrho},\ 2\omega'_{21}...2\omega'_{2\varrho}$$
$$\cdot \quad \cdot \quad \cdot \quad \cdot \quad \cdot \quad \cdot \quad \cdot \quad \cdot \quad \cdot$$
$$2\omega_{\varrho1},\ 2\omega_{\varrho2}...2\omega_{\varrho\varrho},\ 2\omega'_{\varrho1}...2\omega'_{\varrho\varrho},$$

for which the equations

$$\sum_1^\varrho \gamma(\omega_{\alpha\gamma}\omega'_{\beta\gamma} - \omega_{\beta\gamma}\omega'_{\alpha\gamma}) = 0$$

hold.

If (one assumes $\varrho > 1$) there is only one among the integrals $\int F(\chi,\varphi\chi)d\chi$ that can be transformed into an elliptic one, then there is also one of the form

$$c_1\psi_1(\chi) + c_2\psi_2(\chi)\cdots + c\varrho\psi_\varrho(\chi),$$

and in order that the latter exists it is necessary and sufficient that among the indicated period-systems there should be found one for which among the corresponding quantities denoted by me $\tau_{\alpha\beta}$ satisfy

$$\tau_{12} = \tfrac{\mu}{\nu}, \quad \tau_{13} = \cdots = \tau_{1\varrho} = 0$$

where μ,ν are positive integers (without common divisor).

Forming with these $\tau_{\alpha\beta}$ the function

$$\vartheta(\nu_1 \cdots \nu_\varrho | \tau_{\alpha\beta}),$$

one sees immediately that among the ϑ-functions obtained through a transformation of degree ν, one has the property to break up into a product of a ϑ-function of $(\varrho-1)$ arguments and an elliptic one. Hence one is able to obtain the algebraic relations, which hold among the constants of the functions of $\varphi\chi$.

Königsberger at another place examined the case where $\varrho = 2$ and $\nu = 2$ completely. I wanted the same to be worked out for $\varrho = 3$ and $\nu = 3$, and my pupil performed this work to my complete satisfaction. Although less originality was required in this assignment, still as you will agree considerable knowledge of the theory of Abelian functions was needed, with which Frau von Kovalevsky had indeed familiarized herself completely.

APPENDIX C

After all that has been said, I think you will be able to decide whether you consider it possible to support before your faculty the petition of my pupil in connection with the demands of the faculty for persons wishing to receive a diploma *in absentia*. Personally, without any hesitation, I would have accepted each of the named works as a doctoral dissertation. But in view of the fact that this is the first instance of a woman wanting to receive a degree for mathematical work, the faculty not only has good reason for imposing strict demands but also it is of great consequence in the interests of the candidate herself, as well as in mine. Therefore I firmly request that during the decision in this matter no notice be given to the fact that I also am interested.

Regarding the state of mathematical education of Frau von Kovalevsky in general I can assure you that I have had very few pupils who bear comparison with her intellectual grasp, judgment, eagerness, and enthusiasm for science.

I am ready to give such guarantees as may be demanded. But I would like to underline in particular that she never had any connections with Russian women students whose actions in Zurich and other places were not very commendable.

Apart from her, another is seeking a degree, a chemist, Fräulein von Lermontova, who has been with her constantly. Hofmann (who is going to write about her to Wöhler) reports that the latter produced superior chemical work.

In conclusion, I beg you, dear colleague, as soon as possible and convenient, to inform me of the last date for presentation of papers, after you have ascertained that these will not be refused. The works are basically prepared but require final polish, because the German language greatly impedes the author. I think they can be delivered by 15 July.

I ask you also to please inform me of the sum payable upon seeking a degree and generally what else must be done. For instance, would it be advisable for me to write to the dean of the faculty, to whom you could submit my letter for his preliminary orientation?

Everything else that I can still relate to you I shall save for my next letter, and I conclude the present overly lengthy one with the sincere desire that your activities in that university, with which in regard to its mathematical fame acquired long ago no other university can compare, will prove in every respect satisfying.

With friendly regards,
Weierstrass

Bibliography:
Principal Sources

1. *Acta Mathematica*, Vol. 16, pp. 385-392; Vol. 39, pp. 133-198, 246-256.
2. Adelung, Sophia von, "Childhood Memories of Sophia Kovalevsky" ("Jugenderinnerungen au Sophie Kowalewsky"), *Deutsche rundschau*, Dec., 1896, pp. 394-425.
3. Anonymous, *Kovalevsky Family Over 300 Years* (*Rod Kovalevskikh za trista let*), Paris, 1951.
4. Ball, W. W. Rouse, *A Short Account of the History of Mathematics*, London, 1908.
5. Bell, E. T., *Men of Mathematics*, New York, 1937.
6. Bell, E. T., *The Development of Mathematics*, New York, 1945.
7. Bobrinsky, Alexander A., *Noble Families Entered into the General Heraldry of the Russian Empire* (*Dvorianskie rody vnesenye v Obshchiĭ gerbovnik Vserossiĭskoy Imperiĭ*) 2 vol., St. Petersburg, 1890.
8. Cajori, Florian, *A History of Mathematics*, New York, 1980.
9. Cross, J. W., ed., *George Eliot's Life: as Related in her Letters and Journals*, 3 vol., New York, 1885.
10. *Dictionary of Scientific Biography*, ed. Charles C. Gillespie, New York, 1973, vol. 7, pp. 474-480.
11. Dostoevsky, Anna, *Dostoevsky Reminiscences*, ed. & tr. Beatrice Stillman, New York, 1975.
12. Efros, N. E., "S. V. Kovalevsky, Dramatist," ("S. V. Kovalevskaia, Dramaturg"), *Russkie vedomosti*, 2 Feb. 1916.
13. Encyclopedic Dictionary (*Entsiklopedichiĭ slovar*), ed. Borokvavz & Efron. St. Petersburg, 1895, Vol. 16 pp. 212 & 372.

BIBLIOGRAPHY OF PRINCIPAL SOURCES

14. Florinsky, Michael T., *Russia: A History and an Interpretation*, 2 vol. New York, 1953.
15. *Great Encyclopedia (Bolshaia Entsiklopediia)*, St. Petersburg, 1900, vol. 1, p. 138.
16. *Great Soviet Encyclopedia*, New York, 1975, Vol. 7, p. 5; vol. 12, pp. 619-621.
17. Hansson, Laura Marholm, *Modern Women*, tr. from German by Ramsden, Boston, 1896.
18. Ikonnikov, Nicholas F., *La Noblesse de Russie*, Paris, 1902-10-14-41.
19. *In Memory of S. V. Kovalevsky: Collection of Articles (Pamiati S. V. Kovalevskoĭ: sbornik stateĭ)*, *Akademiia nauk S.S.S.R*, Moscow, 1951.
20. Kannak, E., "S. V. Kovalevskaia and M. M. Kovalevsky," *Novyĭ Zhurnal*, New York, Dec. 1954.
21. Kennedy, Don H., *Kennedy Kith and Kin*, Ms., 1962.
22. Key, Ellen, extracts from biography of Anna Carlotta Leffler, section in reference no. 28.
23. Korvin-Krukovsky, F. V., letter to M. I. Semevsky: "Sofia Vasilevna Korvin-Krukovskaia," *Russkaia starina*, Sept., 1891.
24. Koteliansky, S. S., tr. & ed., *Dostoevsky Portrayed by His Wife*, London, 1926.
25. Kovalevskiĭ, Maksim M., *Russian Political Institutions*, etc. Chicago, 1902.
26. Kovalevsky, S. V., "Mathematical and Literary Works, 1874-1890," (*"Matematicheskie i literaturnye trudy S. V. Kovalevskoĭ"*), *Russkaia starina*, Nov. 1890.
27. Kovalevsky, Sophia, *The Nihilist (Nigilstka)*, Carouge-Geneva, 1895.
28. Kovalevsky, Sonya, *Recollections of Childhood*, tr. by Isabel F. Hapgood, with added sections by Anna Carlotta Leffler, Ellen Key, Lily Wolffsohn, and appendices, New York, 1895.
29. Kovalevsky, S. V., *Recollections of Childhood and Autobiographical Sketches (Vospominaniia detstva avtobiograficheskie ocherki)*, Akademii Nauk S.S.S.R, 1945.
30. Kovalevsky, Sophia, *Recollections (Vospominaniia o Sofia Kovalevskoĭ)*, tr. from Polish of Marie Mendelson, *Sovremennyĭ mir*, Feb. 1912.
31. Kovalevsky, S. V., *Scientific Works (Nauchnye raboty)*, ed. Pelageia Ia Polubarinova-Kochina, Moscow, 1974.
32. Kovalevsky, Sophia, *Vera Vorontzoff*, tr. Anna von Rydingsvärd, New York, 1895.

BIBLIOGRAPHY OF PRINCIPAL SOURCES

33. Kovalevsky, S. V., *Literary Recollections*, on the 125th anniversary of her birth (*Vospominaniia povesti*), Moscow, 1974.

34. Kovalevsky, S. V., *Recollections and Letters* (*Vospominaniia i pisma*), recollections by her mother, brother, Lermontova, Kovalevsky, diaries, letters, & miscl., *Akademiia nauk S.S.S.R.*, Moscow, 1961.

35. Kovalevskaia, S. Vl., daughter, "Recollections of Mother" (*"Vospominaniia o materi"*), section in reference no. 18.

36. Kuskova, E. D., "Sophia Vasilevna Kovalevsky," *Russkiĭ vedomosti*, 29 Jan 1916.

37. *Large Soviet Encyclopedia* (*Bolshaia sovetskaia entsiklopediia*), S.S.S.R., 1953, vol. 22 p. 565 & vol. 48 p. 216; 1951 vol. 6 p. 185.

38. Lavrov, P. L., *The Progressive Russian Woman* (*Russkaia razvitaia zhenshchina*), Geneva, 1891.

39. Leffler, Anna Carlotta, "Sonya Kovalevsky," tr. from Swedish by A. M. Clive Bayley, section in reference no. 28.

40. Letters, miscl., S. V. & Vladimir Kovalevsky, S. F. Shubert, *Golos minuvshego*, Feb. pp. 215-240; Mar. pp. 213-231; Apr. pp. 77-94, 1916.

41. Litvinova, E. F., *S. V. Kovalevsky: Woman Mathematician* (*S. V. Kovalevskaia: zhenshchina-matematik*), St. Petersburg, 1894.

42. Malevich, I. I., "Sophia Vasilevna Kovalevsky, Doctor of Philosophy and Professor of Higher Mathematics—In 'Recollections' for years 1858-1869" (*"Sofia Vasilevna Kovalevskaia, doktor filosofii i professor vyssheĭ matematiki—v vospominaniiakh pervago po vremeni eia uchitelia I. I. Malevicha, 1858-1868"*), *Russkaia starina*, Dec. 1890, pp. 615-654.

43. Nechkina, M. V., "Public and Literary Life of Sophia Kovalevsky" (*"Obshchestvennaia i literaturnaia deiatelnost S. V. Kovalevskoĭ"*), section in reference no. 19.

44. Pares, Bernard, *A History of Russia*, New York, 1953.

45. Poggendorff, J. C., *Biographische-Literarisches Handwörterbuch*, Leipzig, 1898.

46. Polubarinova-Kochina, Pelageia IA., "Life and Scientific Activity of S. V. Kovalevsky" (*"ZHizn i nauchnaia deiatelnost S. V. Kovalevskoĭ"*), section in reference no. 19.

47. Polubarinova-Kochina, Pelageia IAkovlevna, *Life and Work of S. V. Kovalevsky* (*Zhizn i deiatelnost S. V. Kovalevskoĭ*), *Akademiia nauk S.S.S.R*, Moscow, 1950.

48. Porter, Cathy, *Fathers and Daughters: Russian Women in Revolution*, London, 1976.

BIBLIOGRAPHY OF PRINCIPAL SOURCES

49. Prasad, Ganesh, *Some Great Mathematicians of the Nineteenth Century*, Vol. II, Benares, 1934.

50. Prudnikov, V. E., "A. N. Strannoliubsky, Pedagog and Mathematician" ("*A. N. Strannoliubsii, pedagog i matematik*"), section in reference no. 18.

51. Prudnikov, V. E., "S. V. Kovalevsky and P. L. Chebyshev" ("*S. V. Kovalevskaia i P. L. Chebyshev*"), section in reference no. 18.

52. *Russian Biographical Dictionary* (*Russkiĭ biograficheskiĭ slovar*) St. Petersburg, 1905, pp. 460-464.

53. Semevsky, M. I., "A Journey through Russia in 1890" ("*Poezdka po Rossii v 1890 G*"), *Russkaia starina*, Dec. 1890, pp. 713-716.

54. Shchepkina-Kupernik, T. L., "About the Premiere of the Drama by S. V. Kovalevsky and Anna Ch. Leffler, *Struggle for Happiness*" ("*O pervom predstavlenii dramy S. Kovalevskoĭ i A. Sh Leffler, 'Borba za cchaste' *"), section in reference no. 19.

55. SHtraĭkh, S. IA, *The Korvin-Krukovsky Sisters* (*Sestry Korvin-Krukovskie*), Moscow, 1934.

56. SHtraĭkh, S. IA., *The Kovalevsky Family* (*Semia Kovalevskikh*), *Sovetskii pisatel*, 1948.

57. Smith, David E., *A History of Modern Mathematics*, London, 1906.

58. Stites, Richard, *The Women's Liberation Movement in Russia*, Princeton, N.J., 1978.

59. Vavilov, S. I., "Sophia Vasilevna Kovalevsky, 100 Years Since the Day of Her Birth" ("*Sofia Vasilevna Kovalevskaia, k 100-letiiu so dnai rozhdeniia*"), section in reference no. 19.

60. Vorontsova, Liubov Andreevna, *Sophia Kovalevsky* (*Sofia Kovalevskaia*), *Molodaia gvardiia*, 1957.

61. Weierstrass, Karl, *Letters of Karl Weierstrass to Sophia Kovalevsky* (in German: *Briefe von Karl Weierstrass an Sofie Kowalewskaja*, and in Russian: *Pisma Karla Veierstrassa k S.V. Kovalevskoĭ*), ed. Polubarinova-Kochina, P. IA., Moscow, 1973.

62. Wolffsohn, Lily, biographical note, in reference no. 28.

INDEX

[333]

INDEX

INDEX

K

INDEX

Poincaré, Jules H., 205, 208, 219, 226, 235, 244, 248, 249, 260, 295, 311, 318
Poisson, S. D., 178, 288, 318
Polish problems and uprising, 59 et seq., 88
Polubarinova-Kochina, ix
"Posthumous Poetry," 275
Praskovia, nurse, 1, 8
Prévost, L'Abbé, 264
Principles of Psychology, 123
Prix Bordin, 249
prize paper, 295
"Problem of Women and Mathematics," 315
Proletary, The, 276
Public Lectures for Men and Women, 84
Pushkin, Alexander, 276
Pypin, A. N., 302

R

Raevsky, Tanya, 274, 314
Ragozin brothers, Victor and Leonid, 195, 196, 200, 205, 206, 213, 214-216, 218-220, 228
Rall, Baron A. A., 39
Rall, Sophia A., 39
Ralston, British Museum, 120
Ranthorp, 121
Rebellious Marriage, 97
Recollections of Childhood (Recollections of Sophia Kovalevsky, A Russian Childhood), vii, ix, 4, 8, 27, 31, 39, 57, 72, 80, 124, 263, 274, 275, 302, 307, 318
"Recollections of George Eliot," 120, 264
"Recollections of the Polish Uprising," 65
Resurrection, 277
Revue des Deux Mondes, 16, 60
Revue de Paris, La, 275
Richelot, F. J., 156
Rigoletto, 281
Rousseau, J. B., 294
Rozhdestvensky, Ivan G., 91
Runeberg, Walter, 260, 291

Russian Antiquity, 275, 303
Russian Thought, 265
Russian Women's Mutual Charity Society, 315
Russkaia mysl, 264, 303
Russkaia starina, 25, 54
Russkii vedomosti, 273
Russkii vestnik, 60
Russkoe slovo, 60
Rydingsvard, Anna von, 276
Ryzhakov, estate, 16

S

Saltykov-Shchedrin, M. E., 111, 265
Saint-Venant, 178
Sand, George, 51, 70, 97, 239, 263
Savante estrangers, 295
Scherer, Wilhelm, 178
School of Anna Vitlok, 272
Schwarz, Herman A, 153, 154, 178, 240
Sechenov, Ivan M., 85, 98, 106, 107, 108, 111, 187, 191, 216, 299
Semenkov, estate, 238, 253
Semenova, Tatiana, 109
Semevsky, M. I., 25-27, 49, 54, 63, 64, 136, 275, 302
Senkovsky, O. I. ("Baron Brambeus"), 6, 39, 119, 120
Serakov, 212, 213
Serfs, 30-35
Severny vestnik, 134, 239, 274, 307
Shabelskaia, A. S. (Montvid), 263
Shtakenshneider, E. A., 129
Shubert family, 181, 182, 255
Shubert, Fedor F. (Sophia's grandfather), 7, 37, 38, 39, 100
Shubert, Fedor F. (Sophia's uncle), 39
Shubert, Fedor I (Sophia's great-grandfather), 36
Shubert, Frederika, 37
Shubert, Sophia, 39
Shubert, Wilhelmina, 37
Shustianka, estate, 95
Siberia, 86, 245
Siemens, Sir Karl W., 199
Sikorsky, physician, 195

INDEX